Company Law

Company Law

Douglas Smith

OXFORD AUCKLAND BOSTON JOHANNESBURG MELBOURNE NEW DELHI

Butterworth-Heinemann
Linacre House, Jordan Hill, Oxford OX2 8DP
225 Wildwood Avenue, Woburn, MA 01801-2041

℞ A division of Reed Educational and Professional Publishing Ltd

First published 1999

British Library Cataloguing in Publication Data
A catalogue record for this book is available from the British Library

ISBN 0 7506 3702 1

Library of Congress Cataloguing in Publication Data
A catalogue record for this book is available from the Library of Congress

Typeset by Avocet Typeset, Brill, Aylesbury, Bucks
Printed and bound in Great Britain by by Martins the Printers Ltd,
Berwick Upon Tweed

PLANT A TREE

British Trust for Conservation Volunteers

FOR EVERY TITLE THAT WE PUBLISH, BUTTERWORTH-HEINEMANN
WILL PAY FOR BTCV TO PLANT AND CARE FOR A TREE.

Contents

Contents

Introductory comments

General comments

While this book may be read by those with an intrinsic interest in company law, it is anticipated that most readers will use it for assistance with assignment and examination assess-
ments that are set by professional bodies or academic institutions. With this in mind the
following observations are made.

This book as a learning aid

Both common and statute law are developing sources of law. Largely driven by the leviathan
growth of European law, British domestic statute law continues to increase. This means that
there is a considerable amount of law; this is particularly true of company law, which is
already highly developed. Students taking company law on either a degree programme or
professional course should not feel intimidated by the volume or complexity of law they will
be expected to cover. A student of average ability who is prepared to work reasonably dili-
gently, by adopting a systematic approach to study ought to be capable of achieving a very
good standard in assignment and examination work.

   To facilitate learning, the format of this book is that each topic is given a short introduction, designed to place what is going to be dealt with in a contextual background, followed by
a list of key concepts which indicate the crucial aspect of the topic. Relevant common law
principles or statutory provisions are fully explained, with illustrative case law liberally used
to show how the law has been applied to actual company problem situations. Incorporated
into the text are periodic review questions, and students should attempt these as they appear
before starting the next sub-topic. To consolidate learning, at the end of each topic is a full
summary of what has been discussed, and a student who is not confident that they have fully
understood the material ought to re-read the appropriate part of the text before proceeding to
tackle the questions set at the end. Where a fuller understanding is required, such as for
assignment work, recommendations for further reading are given towards the end of the book.

Specific advice

A text book is a learning tool that, used correctly, will considerably assist with whatever
subject has to be mastered. Any temptation that the reader has to try to memorize the contents of this publication ought to be resisted. Instead the reader is advised to follow this
sequence:

- firstly, recognize and appreciate the pertinent issues that are raised in each chapter;
- secondly, recognize and appreciate how the law attempts to deal with the issue under
  examination, i.e. *what* is the law trying to achieve? and *how* is it carrying it out?
- thirdly, learn the main points of the relevant chapter.

As far as recognizing issues is concerned, these ought to be readily discernible from the introduction to each chapter. In relation to the second and third points, careful reading of the text with the two questions repeatedly being applied should result in a good level of understanding. Indeed, it has been said that the learning approach to adopt in law is not to search for answers but to look for appropriate questions to direct at the issue or problem in hand. Once the correct question has been applied then the answer ought to fall into place.

To assist learning, each chapter ends with a summary of what has been covered. Summaries will highlight all of the essential features of a topic. Once these essential features have been learnt then 'in-filling' in the form of more detail can be carried out later. The precise nature and degree of any additional detail that is required may be determined by the form of assessment that is being used. If, for example, candidates are allowed to have access to a statute book in their examinations or if the examination is 'open book' then there is less of a need to attempt to memorize parts of sections or case facts. On the other hand, professional bodies tend to require demonstrations of factual recall without the benefit of material that can be taken into the examination. However, what is particularly prized by all examiners is deeper understanding of whatever is being tested. Here, not just the ability to reproduce information is called for but also the ability and confidence to evaluate this information and place it within a logical framework.

Assignment and examination technique

Examiners can only award marks for what is correctly provided, not for what is wrongly stated or omitted. Unfortunately, all too often, failure in an examination or assignment is the result of poor response technique. The following comments are intended to help candidates to improve in this important area.

Before you start

Read the instructions on the examination paper or assignment carefully, and make sure that you follow them. It is also essential, in an examination, to allocate appropriate time for each question to be answered and to discipline yourself to keep to this plan. For example, in a three-hour paper where four questions are required to be answered, you should leave 10 minutes for reading the paper and 10 minutes for revision and correction at the end. Consequently, you will have 40 minutes per question. Despite the temptation to write at length on one or more questions, you are urged not to exceed the 40-minute time allowance per question, otherwise you may later run out of time. Therefore, give time management the importance it deserves!

Read the questions carefully and decide exactly what they call for, and which of them you will attempt to answer. Make full use of your recommended reading time to select the set of questions best fitted to your own level of knowledge. Avoid any question whose meaning you are uncertain of, and do not tackle a multiple-part question if you feel confident in some parts, but not in others. Once you have chosen which questions to answer, then answer those specific questions and not others which you wish had been set.

Be aware of the types of questions you will encounter. They will be of two types:

- the essay;
- the problem format.

The essay

This will attempt to test your knowledge and recall in a certain area of law, e.g. 'Discuss the rule in *Trevor v Whitworth* and say how it is both supported and weakened in the Companies Act 1985.' The expected style is: an introduction followed by a discussion or argument followed by a conclusion. Students who have completed a good revision programme may prefer this type of question, which is intended to test factual knowledge as well as critical and analytical abilities in relation to a general area of law.

Pay special attention to the key word given in the essay you are asked to do:

1 *Examine*

   You need to explain the relevant legal principles or provisions. Where the examination related to a broad concept, such as 'Examine the contractual nature of the articles of association in company law', then in an examination there will be time to provide little more than an outline of the sub-principles involved.

   If the subject matter of the question is narrower, such as 'Examine to what extent a shareholder is bound by the articles of association', then more detailed treatment, derived from an investigation into appropriate case law, will be required.

2 *Critically examine*

   You need to be more judgemental and much less descriptive in the explanation given. What is required is a detailed exposition of the principle(s) being examined, which incorporates a discussion of respective strengths and weakness.

3 *Evaluate*

   You need to provide an informative commentary on the law. The approach to follow is to use selective judicial statements to construct a sound persuasive argument for or against whatever proposition is being questioned.

4 *Discuss*

   You need to provide a detailed critical statement of law with illustrations of its application. An exhaustive, but solely descriptive, account is insufficient.

5 *Advise*

   You need to present recommendations based upon an examination and application of legal principles or statutory provisions.

The problem format

This will consist of a situation within which one or more legal principles will operate. Students will be required to analyse the situation and say whether or not liability will apply. At degree level, problems are likely to consist of subtly altered facts taken from decided cases, intended to get students to examine a range of possible outcomes. Not only are knowledge and recall needed, but these must be applied to the problem situation. Always try to be systematic in the treatment of such problems. You are advised to adopt this approach:

1 State the legal principle(s), or rule(s) of law (common law or statutory), which you believe apply.
2 Provide legal authority to support what you have stated.
3 Relate 1 and 2 to the problem situation, referring to any exceptions or defences which may operate, together with legal authority for them.
4 Provide a reasoned conclusion in which you say whether or not someone is liable and justify it by briefly recapitulating the main reasons for your finding.

Generally, the essay question is a closed one while the problem question will frequently be open in that more than one outcome can be identified. There will always be a most appropriate outcome, but candidates putting forward a reasonable alternative, justified by legal authority, may well be able to obtain a reasonable or better mark.

On beginning to write

Follow the 'ABC Rule':
- *Accuracy*
  Make sure that what you say is correct and as precise as the level of your knowledge will permit.
- *Brevity*
  Do not use unnecessary words, still less unnecessary sentences or paragraphs. However, avoid the opposite extreme, such as saying 'X is liable' without saying why. Always provide a full but concise explanation.
- *Clarity*
  Use short sentences and, wherever possible, simple words. Keep your language simple and write legibly. Consider what you want to say before commencing to write. If you do this then vague statements ought to be avoided.

Also remember to be:
- *Orderly*
  Plan the structure of your answer. Make an essay plan before you start each question.
- *Relevant*
  Do not include material which has no valid bearing on the question. Avoid the temptation to display your knowledge by wandering from the question set.
- *Thorough*
  Do not omit essential points. Space should be left at the end of each examination response for any later correction or addition.

Things to avoid

Writing in the first person. Even though the question requires you to offer advice to X, it is always expected that advice will be tendered in the third, not the first person.

Use of semi-slang expressions, jargon or unclear abbreviations, and any attempt to be flippant. A law assignment or examination is not, admittedly, an English test, but remember that you are most probably sitting an examination at a university or for a professional body, and a good standard of English is expected.

Lengthy introductions. Introductions should be kept short; long ones are wasteful of time and gain no extra marks. It is sensible to have an introduction in the form of a definition. If answering a question on the fiduciary duties of directors, for example, say, 'A fiduciary duty is one imposed in certain relationships whereby one person is required to act in good faith for the benefit of another. In the question it appears that...' You may then proceed to give your substantive answer comments. Regrettably, many students prefer to begin by writing at length on what does not directly apply, e.g. 'First of all, before dealing with directors it is important to say that a company is not managed by shareholders but by directors...' There then follows up to two sides or more of material which, while correct, is irrelevant to the answer and earns no marks.

Providing facts to cases. You should always attempt to support legal principle by citing legal authority. This should consist of referring to cases by name only, e.g. *Salomon v Salomon & Co Ltd*, to support the principle that once the approved incorporation procedure has been completed the resulting company is given corporate personality independent of those who promoted the company. If unable to recall the names of the parties, then write the minimum necessary to show which case you refer to, e.g. 'in the case of the aunt who had the company issue more shares to stop her niece having a say in the management of the company' (*Clemens v Clemens*). It may be reassuring to fill up paper with a recitation of case facts but be warned – this is a sign of a weak student desperate to fill up paper rather than getting to grips with the legal principles themselves.

Reasonable reference to case facts is justified where it is used to distinguish between an apparent similarity with the facts of a decided case and facts given in the problem to be solved. This use of case facts should show that while at first sight the citation is attractive, it may, because of a crucial minor dissimilarity, not be followed. In respect to extensive reference (or quotations) to judgements, these should only be made if a point of law is contentious. When used it ought to be pointed out that the judgement (opinion) referred to is not regarded by all as being a definitive statement of the law.

Volunteering information. Unless directly required, other comments or observations should not be provided. Similarly, do not cite legal principles or refer to cases and statute aimlessly. First, you are wasting time; second, if what you volunteer is wrong then it will detract from what you have already correctly said.

Table of Cases

Table of Statutes

Table of Regulations, Rules, Orders and Directives

BIRTH OF A COMPANY

1 Nature and classification of companies

Introduction

Put simply, a company is a body of persons associated together for the purpose of trade or business. They may be incorporated or unincorporated. Most commonly a commercial *unincorporated* company is a partnership which is 'the relationship which exists between persons carrying on business in common with a view to profit' (Partnership Act 1890, s. 1(1)). With unincorporated bodies the law treats those engaged in business together no differently than if they were in business individually as sole traders. This is because an unincorporated body has no separate personality in law. By contrast, an *incorporated* company is an entity separate from its members. Incorporation may be derived from: Royal Charter, Special Act of Parliament or General Act of Parliament.

The common term for incorporated bodies is companies (for partnerships it is firms) and they come in a variety of forms: *limited* and *unlimited* depending on the liability of their shareholders; *private* and *public* depending on whether or not they are prohibited from inviting the public to subscribe for any of their securities; and *joint stock* having capital which is divided into transferable shares or stock.

Objectives

The purpose of this chapter is, firstly, to make students fully aware of the set of characteristics that attach to incorporated bodies. Secondly, it will allow students to become familiar with the procedures that need to be followed for incorporated status to be achieved. Thirdly, a system of classification will be put forward for incorporated bodies.

Key concepts

- Nature of incorporated bodies
- The statutory procedure for incorporation
- Classification of companies.

Origins of companies

Companies, under various guises, have been around ever since people have come together to form trading associations. They precede the modern world by being found in Rome, Greece and earlier under the Egyptian pharaohs. In medieval Britain there were Merchant Guilds which consisted of groups of merchants banding together to secure a local monopoly for a specific trade or supply of a staple commodity. The successful ones gained Royal Charters but while the Guild provided a framework for the control of the trade each guild member remained a sole trader.

As trade, especially overseas, expanded the rigid guild system proved too restrictive. Therefore, other more flexible associations began to emerge. For example wealthy individuals, nobility or merchants, would contribute money in order to buy and fit out a ship which would carry out a trading voyage. Each contributor would receive a share based on the amount invested in the enterprise. On the vessel's return (if it did return) once expenses had been covered any resulting profit would be distributed in accordance with the shares held by the members in the scheme. Merchant venturers was an early term for these members but an alternative became more common – joint stock holders – in that a joint stock or common fund of capital would be made available. This flexibility allowed for a calculated balance between risk and profit to be carried out. With some voyages being 'long and dangerous' the risk would be too great for one individual, even one with considerable wealth, to carry alone. Therefore, a body of individuals would act in concert with a mutual expectation that greater profits would be forthcoming from the increased risk being incurred.

Gradually, the joint stock arrangement spread from maritime trading to the establishment of trading posts, to founding overseas plantations, funding mining enterprises, and eventually becoming the means whereby large-scale manufacture could take place:

> Parallel with the growth in size of the industrial unit had come a dispersion in its ownership such that an important part of the wealth of individuals consists of interests in great enterprises in which no one individual owns a major part. (Berle and Means, *Ownership, Control and Success in Large Companies*, 1961; given in Hadden, *Company Law and Capitalism*)

Almost at the new millennium the joint stock company has developed, at one extreme, into a huge undertaking putting massive amounts of capital to work across nearly all continents where tens of thousands are employed to make profits for hundreds of thousands of shareholders; while at the other extreme it may be a one-person business where incorporation conceals a sole trader.

Nature of a limited company

Incorporated bodies

A corporate body is treated as being a person in its own right entirely separate from the individuals who comprise it. Corporate bodies fall into two broad categories. They are:

1 *A corporation sole*

Here the corporation is based on an office so that only a single person, the office holder, can be its human representative. However, the artificial person is the office, not the office holder. Examples of a corporation sole are the Crown, a Bishop of the Church of England, the Treasury Solicitor and the Public Trustee.

2 *A corporation aggregate*

These occur where a number of persons associate together for a common purpose with the 'product' of their association being recognized at law as an artificial person distinct from the individuals involved in its creation. Corporations aggregates may be created by Royal Charter or Act of Parliament – Special or General. For convenience these are dealt with in Table 1.1.

Table 1.1   Creation of corporations aggegates

Method	Liability of members	Contractual capacity
Royal Charter e.g. the BBC; professional bodies (ACA, CIMA, etc.); a University or Borough; the Stock Exchange. As a commercial trading venture this method is now of no importance; there are in fact only a handful of trading ones left	At common law the members are not liable for the companies' debts. However, the Charter may impose a liability on the members restricted to their shares	The same as a natural person (unlimited) and these cannot be modified by the creating charter. However, the Crown may annul the charter if the powers are exceeded
Special Act of Parliament (statutory company) e.g. British Gas plc, British Telecom plc, etc. They were commonly set up to provide essential services such as power, water and railways. More recently they were used to privatize national industries	Limited to the amount of capital contributed or guaranteed	Limited to the powers contained in the creating Act
General Act of Parliament These are registered companies in that they are registered under a general creating act, e.g. Companies Act 1985	Limited to the amount of capital contributed or guaranteed	Limited to the object clause in the memorandum of association *Ashbury Railway Carriage Co. v Riche* (1875) but now amended by Companies Act 1985, s. 35

The differences between a partnership and a limited company are shown in Table 1.2.

Large-scale partnership

While most partnerships are relatively modest in size, a small number are extremely large in respect to the number of partners and financial turnover. The accounting partnerships of

5

Table 1.2 Differences between a partnership and a limited company

Partnership	Feature	Company
Quick and cheap, e.g. oral or simple written contract; or even based upon the conduct of the partners	Creation	Registration with Registrar of Companies – more time consuming but an off-the-shelf company can be bought for less than £200
Can end with *Co.*	Name	Must end with *Limited* (Ltd) or *Public Limited Company* (plc) or their Welsh equivalents
Not separate from its members	Legal personality	An artificial person distinct from the shareholders. This still applies even with one-shareholder companies (*Salomon v Salomon & Co Ltd* (1897))
The partnership agreement is a private document	Disclosure	The company constitution, e.g. memorandum and articles of association – these are public documents that may be inspected as a right
Modest – partners pay income tax – affairs remain private	Continuing legal obligations	Registers to be kept; annual filing with public disclosure; annual general meeting; periodic election (or re-election) of directors and auditors
Unlimited unless a limited partner (Unlimited Partnership Act 1907). Therefore, judgement creditors can seize the business and personal assets of general partners (Partnership Act 1890, s. 9)	Legal liability of members	Limited either by shares or guarantee. Therefore, a shareholder's personal assets cannot be seized to pay company debts
Belongs to the partners	Property holding	Belongs to the company, shareholders have no direct claim on it (*Macaura v Northern Assurance* (1925))
Partners cannot contract with their firm	Contracts with members	A company can contract with its own shareholder and be sued by them and vice versa

Partnership	Feature	Company
New partners cannot be introduced unless all partners agree (unless agreement expressly allows). Indeed, a partner cannot transfer his share without the consent of the others	Transferability of Interest	Very marketable for a plc; may be a narrow market for a private company especially if articles place restrictions on the transfer of shares
Minimum of 2 with a maximum of 20 for a *trading* partnership; no upper limit for a non-trading firm	Number of members	Minimum of 1, no maximum
All general partners have the right of management	Managerial role of members	None unless also directors (a different capacity)
All general partners are agents of their firm (PA 1890, s. 5), e.g. they have implied authority to act in accordance with the scope of the firm's business	Agency aspects of members	Not agents unless also directors (a different capacity)
Modest	Opportunity for capital attraction	For public companies considerable
Uncontrolled as long as the partnership is solvent, e.g. withdrawal of profits and capital only subject to the agreement of the partners	Capital maintenance	Acquisition and withdrawal controlled especially in regard to a public company
Inflexible	Flexibility of capital structure	Flexible, e.g. various classes of share and loan capital can meet individual investment preferences
To sue partners who have joint and several liability for the firms debts, e.g. individual and collective liability	Creditors' action	Normally no right of action against shareholders
Cannot use a floating charge	Security for debts	Can use a floating charge
Any the partners like to make	Arrangements with creditors	Only if the Companies and Insolvency Acts allow
Death of a partner will dissolve the firm	Succession	Perpetual until the company is wound up

KPMG, Price WaterhouseCooper and Arthur Anderson each have hundreds of partners worldwide, providing financial, taxation and managerial consultancy that brings in an annual fee income of hundreds of millions of pounds. These 'super-partnerships' are really akin to medium-sized public companies.

Advantages of incorporated status

The following are the main reasons why the company format will be chosen as opposed to trading as a partnership:

1 The company as a separate entity is not dependent upon the continued existence of the persons who are from time to time its members (shareholders). This means that the death of a controlling shareholder will not terminate the company as it enjoys perpetual succession until it is wound up.
2 The company may, as is overwhelmingly the case, be incorporated with limited liability for its members or shareholders. This advantage is readily discernible from its name – ltd for a private company and plc for a public company.
3 A capital structure of differing classes of share (and loan) capital may be created to match the investment preferences of potential investors, e.g. ordinary shares, preferences shares and debentures.
4 As the number of members are not, as with many partnerships, limited to 20, a company has greater opportunities to obtain investment capital from a larger section of the public – especially if it is a public limited company.

Disadvantages of incorporated status

1 A shareholder cannot withdraw capital in the manner that a partner is able to do. Capital reduction of a company usually requires the consent of the court. Obviously, to realize his investment a shareholder may sell his shares but with some private limited companies selling shares may be restricted.
2 Annual returns and accounts (apart from certain exceptions) must be placed on file and open to public inspection.
3 Internal proceedings and administrative procedures generally are subject to heavier and more detailed statutory requirement than in the case of a partnership. The law is also more strict for a public company since here irregularities are likely to have greater consequences.
4 A company is subject to corporation tax as a going concern as well as to various costs on incorporation and dissolution.

Review question

The four advantages of incorporated status put forward in the text are those that are most commonly cited. Identify other factors that in recent years have made incorporation more attractive than remaining as a partnership.

Incorporation procedure

Once a decision has been made to incorporate a business the procedure that needs to be followed is simple and relatively quick, especially for a private company. Indeed, it is possible for a non-British subject on arrival at Heathrow airport to go into London or Reading and buy a ready-formed company off the shelf for around £200 including service charge. If there is no hold-up over payment (with cash or travellers' cheques being used) then our company purchaser could expect to be back at Heathrow later the same morning or afternoon with evidence of 'his' creation in his briefcase!

Off-the-shelf companies

These are also known as shelf companies or shell companies and exist only in name. They are set up for resale to people who are either unfamiliar with the procedure for creating a company or to those who are pressed for time. Those who set it up will be the subscribers for two shares and its first director and secretary. The purchaser will have the two shares transferred to two individuals he nominates and the founding director and secretary will resign, reporting their withdrawal to the Registrar. If the existing name is unsatisfactory then this may be altered in the normal way. Formerly, an off-the-shelf company would usually face a problem between the company's stated objects and those that the purchaser would wish to pursue. Now, however, such companies can be formed with a 'broad brush' object clause, e.g. as a general commercial company (s. 3A).

However, if a bespoke company is to be formed then the following decisions need to be taken:

- the name by which the company will be known;
- the object for which it is to be created to pursue;
- the place where business is to be carried on;
- the extent of the liability each member or shareholder wishes to incur;
- the amount of capital that the prospective shareholders wish to put up.

The responses to the above five considerations will form the basis of the memorandum of association.

Once the memorandum and articles have been drafted, the founding shareholders will become the *subscribers* to the company's constitution by signing their names beneath these documents. For a private company at least one subscriber is required, whereas with a public company it is at least two. By subscribing to these documents the first shareholders are entering into an implied contract with the company.

As a company is an artificial person then while there is evidence of its legal existence, such as a certificate of incorporation, its corporal existence is little more than a brass name plate outside its registered office. Therefore, to carry out the numerous tasks that are required, human hands are clearly needed. These natural persons who will act for the company as its agents will not be the shareholders but its officers, most notably the *director* and *company secretary*. Indeed, company law demands that there be at all times at least one director for a private company and at least two directors for a public company. Those who are to be the first officers must be identified at the time that incorporation is sought. Similarly, there must always be a company secretary with the first one being identified at the time incorporation is applied for. The company secretary may also be a director provided that there is at the same time at least one other director in office. While most directors are natural persons it is possible for another company to be a director – but of course in practice the company which is the director will delegate the directorship to one of its own officers. Similarly, another company (or partnership) may become a company secretary.

The Companies Act 1985 usually makes reference to members but the term shareholder is preferred by the author. However, if a company has not issued shares then members is the correct expression.

By law a limited company must have a *registered office*. This is frequently the company's principal place of business, but it may be situated elsewhere. The reason for an official address is so that it is known where official notices and legal documents may be validly served and delivered.

Documents to be delivered to the Registrar of Companies

The promoters of the company must deliver the following documents to the Registrar of Companies (s. 10):

A company with a registered office in Wales may use 'cyfengedig' or 'cwmni cyfengedig cyhoeddus', or their abbreviations, instead of 'limited or 'public' limited company'. The incorporation documents may also be submitted in Welsh with a certified English translation.

1 *A memorandum of association*
This has to be drafted in the prescribed manner. It must give the name of the company and say whether its intended registered office is to be situated in England and Wales, or in Scotland. The proposed objects of the company must also be given. Other requirements will depend on the type of company to be incorporated.

2 *The articles of association*
A company may provide either its own set of articles or, alternatively, say that the specimen set of articles under Table A will be adopted.

3 *Details of those who will become the first directors and secretary (Form 10)*
The details are to include the: name and address, nationality, business occupation, particulars of other directorships held or previously held within the last five years, and age. Each person referred to must give their signed consent to the appointment. Once incorporated they will assume automatic appointment (s. 13).

4 *A statement of the address of the registered office (Form 19)*
This will enable creditors, etc. to know where claims are to be served as well as being the place where statutory registers must be kept.

5 *The statutory declaration (Form 12)*
This is confirmation that all the legal requirements for incorporation have been met. The declaration of compliance is usually made by a solicitor engaged to assist with the incorporation, but failing this a person named as a director or secretary can make it. The declaration has to be witnessed by an authorized person. To be valid it must not be dated any earlier than the other documents.

6 *A statement relating to share capital*
This provides details of the share capital and is stamped to show that the necessary duty has been paid.

7 *The registration fee.*

The certificate of incorporation

Once the Registrar is satisfied that the memorandum and articles are valid, that the company's objectives are legal and that all other requirements have been met then a certificate of incorporation will be issued and advertised in the *London Gazette* (s. 13). The company obtains a separate legal existence from this moment even if later it is discovered that formation formalities were irregular.

The trading certificate

Only private companies may start trading and borrowing on the receipt of the incorporation certificate. The reason for the trading certificate is to give the promoters of public limited companies enough time to raise the minimum amount of authorized capital which is £50,000 (at least a quarter of which must be paid together with any premium). As there is no minimum amount for private companies they are subject to no delay – indeed, one share is enough (*Salomon v Salomon & Co.* (1897)). To obtain the trading certificate a further declaration is required by a director or solicitor saying:

i)   that the allotted share capital is at least £50,000;
ii) how much of the allotted share capital is actually paid at this time;
iii) what the preliminary expenses of the company were as well as identifying who paid them or agreed to do so;
iv) whether any promoter has received any benefit and what service was provided in return.

Review question

The incorporation procedure is too superficial. It ought to be made more demanding. Discuss.

Re-registration of companies

A private limited company to a public limited company

A private limited company with a share capital may by passing a special resolution at a general meeting change its status to that of a public limited company (s.43). Almost invariably the change will be motivated by a desire to gain access to greater capital. The resolution must authorize the alteration of its memorandum and articles so that they confirm to the requirement of a public limited company (ss. 43–48).

This will of course include the addition of the suffix public limited company (plc) to its name and any existing transfer restrictions on its shares will probably be removed.

An application, signed by a director or the company secretary, is then sent to the Registrar together with a statutory declaration that they also sign and a statement made by the company's auditor. Copies of the new memorandum and articles will also have to be forwarded.

The statutory declaration

This will confirm that the special resolution was duly passed and that the requirements in respect to share capital have been satisfied. If applicable the declaration will also confirm compliance with the valuation of non-cash consideration requirement. Finally the declaration must say that between the balance sheet date (see auditor's statement) and the date of the application net assets have not fallen to less than the aggregate of called-up share capital and undistributable reserves.

The share capital requirement

The new public company must have an allotted capital with a nominal value of at least £50,000 paid up to at least 25 per cent together with the whole of any premium on them. If a person undertakes to pay fully or partly, for any share or any premium, by doing work or performing services then this work or services must have been carried out before the re-registration will be sanctioned. And if any shares were allotted, fully or partly paid, on the basis that payment would consist of the transfer of an asset to the company, then this transfer must have taken place or, alternatively, there must be a contractual obligation to transfer the asset within five years of the share allotment.

Non-cash consideration requirement

If, during the period between the balance sheet date and the date of the special resolution, shares are allotted for payment other than cash the company is not allowed to be re-registered as a public one until what has been offered as payment has been independently valued (s. 103). The valuation report has to be made to the company during the six months before the shares were allotted. A copy of this report must accompany the application. Once satisfied that all is in order the Registrar will issue a certificate of incorporation confirming the company's new status.

Public limited company to a private limited company

There are several possible reasons why a public company may wish to change its status to that of a private one. They are: where only one director remains in office (s. 282); to avoid disclosure of share interests (s. 211); to allow on over-age director to remain in office (s. 293); or to allow an unqualified secretary to remain in office (s. 286). In addition, the decision could be made merely to take advantage of the less regulatory company framework in respect of private companies.

The new private company may be limited either by shares or by guarantee. The re-registration is achieved by means of a special resolution passed at a general meeting. The resolution needs to include instructions for the alteration of the memorandum and articles. The application when made needs to be signed by a director or by the company secretary and copies of the new memorandum and articles must accompany the re-registration application.

Clearly plc after its name will have to be deleted and probably the inclusion of a restriction on the right to transfer shares.

Minority protection for dissenting shareholders

The move to re-register as a private company may be opposed by:

holders of 5 per cent or more in nominal value of the company's issued share capital, or any class therefore; or

50 per cent or more of the company's members.

They have 28 days from the resolution being passed to apply to the court to cancel the resolution. The court's decision will be either confirmation or cancellation of the resolution, though a court does have discretion to make whatever orders it thinks appropriate, e.g. an order compelling the company to purchase the shares of the dissenting members (s. 54 (5)).

Classification of companies

Private company limited by shares

This is the commonest type of company and is frequently a family company in that it would be founded, owned and managed almost exclusively by members of one family. Indeed, in certain circumstances a court may find that the true relationship between shareholders is that of quasi-partners with each owing the other obligations of mutual trust and confidence (*Ebrahimi v Westbourne Galleries* (1973)). Currently approximately 98 per cent of all registered companies in the United Kingdom are private ones with many being one-person businesses.

In respect to share capital this will be given in the memorandum and it may have from one to an unlimited number of shareholders. There must be at least one director. However, the articles may give the directors powers to restrict the transfer of shares and these may be used to keep ownership within a family circle. As a private company it must not either solicit the public for capital or allow its securities to be publicly traded (Financial Services Act 1986, ss. 170, 143 (3)). Apart from a restricted exception the word *Limited* or *Ltd* must appear after its name.

Private company limited by guarantee

Guarantee companies are uncommon. As they may not distribute their profit surpluses to their members they are normally created to discharge charitable or professional purposes. In a limited by guarantee company members do not subscribe for shares but agree, if called upon, to make available a sum up to the stipulated amount (s. 1(2)(6)). This will be the guaranteed sum which often is a token amount of, say, £1 or £10. The total of the guaranteed sums will give the guaranteed fund. If shares are not issued then the term shareholder is inappropriate so that the guarantors will be called members with usually one vote each. The articles will say how many members can be admitted to membership with liability lasting for the duration of membership and, perhaps, if the company goes into liquidation, for up to one year after membership ceases (s. 2 (4) and s. 74 (2), Insolvency Act 1986).

In addition to being limited by guarantee it is possible to be limited by share capital. Here the members (or shareholders) will have dual liability; firstly in respect to their guarantee, and secondly in respect to any unpaid amount on their shares. On winding up once all liabilities have been discharged any remaining surplus must be applied to the objects for which the company was created for or, if those objects are fully satisfied, then used in the closest charitable or professional purpose that can be identified. Surpluses, therefore, must not be distributed to members.

This is application of the cy pres doctrine.

Because it is felt to be incompatible with their charitable or professional status, guarantee companies, subject to certain conditions being met, may be allowed to dispense with Limited or Ltd from their name (s. 30).

Public limited companies

This is the choice of company for capital intensive business enterprises. It may be limited by guarantee (rare) or by shares and having an authorized share capital of at least £50,000 of which at least £25,000 (25 per cent) must be paid up. As its nomenclature indicates, its securities may be both offered to the general public as well as being publicly traded. There must be at all times at least two shareholders (there is no upper limit) and two directors.

Unlimited companies

These are uncommon. The attraction of most companies is that they afford shareholders limited liability but here the shareholders or members (they may or may not have share capital) have *unlimited liability* (s.1 (2) (C)). This results in unlimited companies being similar to a partnership but for creditors to be able to sue members for the company's debts they need to petition for the company to be wound up, with members being then liable to contribute under the terms given in the memorandum or articles. If no statement of contribution is given in these documents then a member, as with a partner, has joint and several (individual and shared) liability. However, more privacy can be obtained with this type of company in that they do not have to file copies of their accounts with the Registrar (s. 254 (1)). This is provided that it is not currently or previously in the relevant accounting period a subsidiary of a limited company, or has been a parent of a limited company (s. 254 (4)).

Table 1.3 Company constitutions under the Companies (Table A to F) Regulations 1985

Form of company	Governing table	
	Memorandum	Articles
Private company limited by shares	B	A
Private company limited by guarantee and with a share capital	C	C
	D	D
Public limited company	F	A
Unlimited company with a share capital	E	E

The *memorandum of association* and the *articles of association* have their own separate chapters but briefly the memorandum consists of a series of statements which outline the company's powers and objects so as to fix the relationship of the company and the outside world. The much larger articles consist of regulatory matters for the management and organization of the company. Hence there will be provisions for: the *admission of shareholders*; the division of capital contributed into *shares*; how shares are to be *allotted* amongst the shareholders; *directors* to be appointed for day-to-day management but as ultimate control remains with shareholders provision will be given for *meetings* to be called; how *resolutions* may be tabled and how *votes* will be allocated; etc.

Private and public companies: differences

As mentioned earlier, the two most important forms of companies are *private*, because of their sheer number, and *public*, because of the huge sums of capital that they employ. While they are identical in concept they do have a number of differences many of which are very minor. The main differences are given in Table 1.4.

Group of companies

So far, references to companies have seen them as being free-standing entities. However, in business it is now common to find companies operating within a group. Perhaps, for example, a large commercial undertaking with, say, five product divisions may for convenience run each division as a separate legal entity by means of having five limited companies each reporting to a parent or holding company which will provide the necessary central direction. However, the group as a whole can be commercially integrated so that economies of scale can be obtained. But it must be remembered that as each company in the group is an artificial entity then any indebtedness of one company would only relate to that company with all other companies in the group, as well as the holding company itself, being unaffected with no obligation to support the stricken group member:

Table 1.4

Private	Feature	Public
Constitutional		
Minimum of 1	No of shareholders (s 1)	Minimum of 2
Must end with limited (Ltd) but possible exemption if limited by guarantee or under s 30)	Name	Must end with public limited company (plc) No exceptions possible.
Possible (s 49) Possible S 91)	Re-registration as an unlimited company	Not possible
Possible	Exclusion of statutory pre-emption rights	Not possible
	Restrictions on share transfers	Not possible
Share capital		
Not possible (s 143 FSA 1986)	Public listing of securities	Possible
Impossible (s 170 FSA 1986)	Advertising of its securities	Possible
No mimimum	Minimum capital required	£50,000 nominal
No statutory requirement to act	Serious loss of capital	Directors must contravene and EGM if the company's net assets fall to 50% or less of its called up share capital (2 142)
Semi-strictly controlled (s 155)	Prohibition or redemption of its own shares out of capital	Strictly controlled (s 151)
Possible – subject to conditions (s 171–177)	Purchase or redemption of its own shares out of capital	Not possible
Payment of shares		
Possible	Acceptance of work or services in exchange for shares	
None	Minimum payment on shares	Not possible (s 99) 25% of nominal value + if applicable the whole of any premium
No statutory requirement	Payment of shares by means of a non-cash asset	Possible if a) independent valuation and report (s 103); b) asset to be transferred to company within 5 years of allotment (s 102)
No statutory requirement	Acquisition of non-cash assets from subscribers shares within 2 years of incorporation	Possible only if asset independently valued and reported upon
No statutory requirement	Payment for subscribers' shares	Must be in cash
No disclosure need be made	Interest in shares	Need to comply with disclosure provisions under Part VI, CA 1985

Private	Feature	Public
	Trading	
Start trading immediately after incorporation	Commencement	Start trading only after incorporation and receipt of a trading certificate (s 117)
	Dividends	
No statutory requirement	Interim dividends	Must file interim accounts with Registrar for any proposed interim dividend (s 272)
No equivalent provision	Distribution restriction	No declaration of a dividend if company's net assets are less than the aggregate of its called-up share capital and undistributable reserves or if the result of the distribution would cause this to occur
	Accounts	
3 years	Retention of records	6 years
10 months	Period for delivery of annual accounts after end of accounting period (s 244)	7 months
Possible for 'small format companies' if special resolution passes (s 250)	Exemption from audited accounts	None
Possible if not in same groups as a public company (s 247)	Exemptions from accounting obligations for small or medium sized companies	None
	Resolutions	
Several possible e.g. dispense: with AGM; auditors; laying accounts and reports in a general meeting etc	Elective resolutions	None
May replace a resolution made in a general meeting	Written resolution of all shareholders	No equivalent provision
	Directors	
1	Minimum	2
No statutory restriction	Appointment resolution	A separate resolution for each director
No statutory age limit (unless company is a subsidiary of a public company – then same as for public company)	Age limit	Must retire at 70 unless exempted (s 293)

English company law possesses some curious features, which may generate curious results. A parent company may spawn a number of subsidiary companies, all controlled directly or indirectly by the shareholders of the parent company. If one of the subsidiary companies, to change the metaphor, turns out to be the runt of the litter and declines into insolvency to the dismay of its creditors, the parent company and the other subsidiary companies may prosper to the joy of the shareholders without any liability for the debts of the insolvent subsidiary. (Templeman LJ, Re Southard & Co Ltd (1979))

To be classified a subsidiary of another company it is sufficient if one of four criteria is satisfied. They are (s. 736 (1)):

a) that the holding company has a majority of the voting rights at general meetings of the company; or
b) that the holding company is a member of the company and has the right to appoint or remove a majority of the company's board of directors (the reference to a right to appoint or remove directors relates to directors holding a majority of the voting rights at board meetings on all, or nearly all, matters. Also here the right to appoint is where a person's appointment necessarily follows from his appointment as a director of the holding company, or the directorship is held by the company itself); or
c) that the holding company is a member of the company and controls it alone, or in agreement with other shareholders or members; or
d) where the company is a subsidiary of another company which is itself a subsidiary of a holding company.

Subsidiaries can be partly or wholly owned by a holding company. A *wholly owned subsidiary* is one which has no shareholders or members apart from the holding company and/or its other subsidiaries; or, alternatively, its shareholder or members all act on behalf of the holding company and/or its subsidiaries (s. 736 (2)).

Chapter summary

- Incorporated bodies may be incorporated in three ways: Royal Charter; Special Act of Parliament and General Act of Parliament. The body created can be based on an office (corporation sole) or it may consist of a group of persons associating together (corporation aggregate).
- When compared with a partnership (its nearest unincorporated commercial rival) it has a number of advantages: separate legal existence; limited liability for its shareholders; a flexible capital structure that is capable of raising for public companies large sums of investment monies. Major disadvantages are: possible restrictions on transfer of shares in private companies; public disclosure of financial information; the burden, especially for public companies, in meeting regulatory requirements.
- When registering under the Companies Act 1985 a stipulated procedure must be followed. Documents to be delivered to the Registrar are: the company's

constitution (memorandum and articles); details of the first directors and company secretary; the address of the registered office; the statutory declaration; a share capital statement; and the registration fee. If all is in order the Registrar will issue a certificate of incorporation but a public company must wait for a trading certificate before it can commence in business.

- Companies may be categorized: *private with share capital* where its securities are not available to the general public; *private by guarantee* with again no public offering of its securities but the members agree to pay up to a stipulated amount if called upon to do so; *public* (either by share capital or guarantee) where its securities if share capital is used may be offered to the public; *unlimited* where the members or shareholders have full legal liability in respect to the company's debts; *holding* company that exists primarily to own shares in other companies that are its subsidiaries; a *subsidiary* which is owned wholly, or partly, by another company called the holding or parent company.

- There are many differences between a private and public company. These are too numerous to list but the most obvious is that the private company must not offer its securities to the public or allow them to be publicly listed; whereas a public company may do both of these.

Discussion questions

1 Why have companies?
Discuss.
2 Discuss the nature of shareholders, and identify other parties who have relationships with a limited company.

Case study exercise

Laurel, a retired chartered engineer, teams up with Hardy, a computer wizard, and between them they develop a revolutionary lawn mower. Powered by solar energy it can still work at half-speed on bright overcast days. The in-built computer allows the mower to work without an operator so that it may be left to mow a lawn while householders do other things.

Laurel and Hardy would like to patent this mower and then put it into commercial production. One thing they are uncertain of is what form of business unit to adopt.

Offer advice to Laurel and Hardy on the respective choices they have and then make a definate recommendation.

Further reading

Company Law and Capitalism, T. Haddon, Butterworth (any edition).
Test of possession, J. Kay *Financial Times*, 28.2.1997 p. 17.

2 Corporate personality and lifting the veil

Introduction

In addition to recognizing natural (or human) personality the law will also recognize artificial personality in that a corporation (company), sole or aggregate, is treated by the law as a person in its own right entirely separate from the individuals who brought it into being. The company, as with natural personality, can contract and litigate in its own name as well as buying and selling property. Other forms of association may also have these attributes, but there it is the partners or sole trader who, in effect, are the principal parties to the action. Here it is the company itself.

As mentioned in the Introduction chapter, a company once incorporated is distinct and separate from its shareholders and directors. Often shareholders will also be directors so that with the advantage of limited liability a shareholder-director may have full involvement in running the company; but in the event of company failure they will be liable for only what they have committed themselves to invest in the company, e.g. the value of these shares, or if a company by guarantee then they will be liable only to meet that guarantee but no more.

Such separation of company and shareholder is clearly beneficial to shareholders and makes companies very attractive propositions. But like all benefits there is a price to be paid. Here it takes two forms. Firstly, the company and its officers are made subject to a demanding regulatory regime with sanctions imposed for non-compliance. Secondly, a court always reserves the right to examine a company's incorporated status and if it is discovered that incorporation is merely being used as a front behind which wrongdoing takes place then figuratively the *veil of incorporation* will be lifted so that the true relationship between the company and its manipulators can be identified. If the wrongdoing is sufficiently serious then the benefit of incorporation will be removed so that the corporators will bear full legal liability and be made to make amends for their injurious conduct.

Objectives

The purpose of this chapter is, firstly, to draw attention to the consequences of incorporation; and, secondly, for students to identify the circumstances that may arise whereby corporate status will be forfeited.

Key concepts

- The veil of corporate personality
- Lifting the veil.

Corporate personality

The significance of corporate personality may be readily appreciated from what probably continues to be the most important case in company law:

Salomon v Salomon & Co. Ltd (1897)

S, who had been in business as a sole trader, formed a limited company – S Ltd – and sold his business to it for £39,000. At this time there had to be at least 7 shareholders so S has S Ltd issue 20,006 shares giving 1 share each to 6 close members of his family while keeping 20,000 shares himself. S Ltd also issued to S a £10,000 secured debenture loan that entitled S, on the liquidation of S Ltd, to priority repayment. While S Ltd operated, S made all the decisions so that it was effectively a one-person company. However, after trading for one year strikes in the trade caused S Ltd to collapse with assets of £6,000. Unsecured creditors standing to lose £7,000 argued that they should have priority because S and S Ltd were in reality the same person. S disputed this, claiming that the priority on his debenture loans should be paid off before unsecured debts.

Held (House of Lords): As S Ltd had been properly formed it was an artificial person entirely separate from those who had created it and this included S. As no fraud was found to have been perpetuated on the creditors, S would be allowed to claim the £6,000 part-payment of his debenture loan.

Both the trial judge and the Court of Appeal unanimously agreed that on the facts corporate personality could not be sustained by S Ltd. However, a bare majority in the House of Lords disagreed.

Salomon v Salomon & Co Ltd is an example of a one-person company where one shareholder holds all, or virtually all, of the shares and in consequence can dominate company meetings as well as taking, if the company is profitable, all, or virtually all, of the profits (dividends). Approximately 97 per cent of all companies in Britain are 'one-person' private companies.

Review question

To what extent did the Court of Appeal and the House of Lords use different rules of statutory interpretation when deciding *Salomon v Salomon & Co Ltd*?

Consequences of corporate personality

The following are examples of the company being treated as a separate legal entity both from those who created it and from those who operate it.

1 Ownership of company property, even with companies where all the shares are held by only a few shareholders, belongs to the company and not to the shareholders:

Macaura v Northern Assurance Co. Ltd (1925)

M owned an estate and insured its timber. Later he transferred the estate and timber to a company in exchange for shares in that company but the insurance policy was not put into the company's name. The timber was subsequently destroyed by fire. M made a claim on the insurance policy for the value of the timber destroyed.

Held (House of Lords): His appeal must fail. The timber was legally owned not by M but by the company. As a shareholder M had no insurable interest in the timber and so could not benefit from the policy.

Shareholders in private companies are commonly inclined to think that 'their' company is synonymous with themselves. They may act on this mistaken belief at their peril:

R v Philippou (1989)

A husband and wife were the only shareholders and directors in a company registered in England. In order to buy property in Spain they had taken money from the company's bank account with the property going into the name of a Spanish company of which they were also its only shareholders and directors.

Held (Court of Appeal): The husband and wife were both guilty of theft of the company's assets. As the company was in law a separate person they had appropriated property belonging to another with the intention of permanently depriving the other of it (Theft Act 1968, s. 1).

---

2 Employment

While to a third party it may seem that a controlling shareholder-director, being so intimately bound up with the affairs of the company, cannot at the same time be an employee, this is in fact an erroneous opinion:

Lee v Lee's Air Farming Ltd (1961)

A husband and wife were the only shareholders of a small private company. The husband, the only beneficial shareholder and sole director, was killed while crop spraying. [mn2]His widow claimed under the workman's compensation acts but she would only be entitled to state compensation if the deceased was an employee.

Held (Privy Council): The deceased had in his private capacity an employment contract with the company. It made no difference that he was a controlling shareholder and governing director. Therefore, the widow was entitled to state compensation.

The Privy Council gave a strict application to the **Salomon** principle. The New Zealand Court of Appeal, which the Privy Council refused to follow, had found that there was an insufficient separation between Lee individual and Lee Air Farming Ltd. See also *Secretary of State for Trade and Industry v Bottrill* (1999)

However, in a later case a court was not so accommodating:

Goodwin v Birmingham City Football Club (1980)

G, a football club manager, formed a 'one-person' club – Freddie Goodwin Limited (FGL) – and contracted to provide his services to it. FGL then entered into a five-year contract with BCFC to supply G's services to it. After a series of poor results BCFC terminated the contract with FGL but was later sued by them for breach of contract. However, G had soon found a similar job at a higher salary.

Held: BCFC had broken the contract with FGL but only nominal damages of £10 would be awarded. This was because FGL had no separate existence from G, so that as G had mitigated his loss and as FGL's sole asset was its contract with G then it had to be taken that FGL had also mitigated its loss.

---

3   *Landlord and tenant*

Can a shareholder or member of a company, as its de facto sole owner, claim rights as a landlord or tenant?

Tunstall v Steigmann (1962)

S owned two adjoining business properties. In one she carried on business as a butcher while the other property was let to T. Subsequently, T's lease expired and he applied to the court under the Landlord and Tenant Act 1954 for a new tenancy. S gave notice that she opposed a new tenancy being granted claiming that she intended, as a landlord, to occupy T's premises herself by reason of having her butcher's business extended. At the same time as the lease renewal issue was being dealt with, S had transferred her business to a new company which she had set up and in which she owned all but two of the shares – these being held by her nominees.

Held: Under the Act S had not established an intention to occupy the premises for the purpose of a business to be carried on by *herself*. The business was in law to be carried on by the company that she had set up, which while virtually wholly owned and controlled by her, was legally a separate entity. Her opposition to a new tenancy being granted to T failed.

Lifting the corporate veil

On incorporation the company is taken to be a separate person in its own right. Therefore, as in *Salomon*, creditors are not able to take action against the members – only against the company. For this reason it has been said that incorporation acts as a veil behind which the members stand immune, apart from their contribution to capital, from liability. However, the concept of separate legal personality may lead to injustice and hardship so that public policy or statute will demand that a court pierces the veil in order to examine the true nature of the relationship between the company and its controlling members. Where the veil is lifted the effect is that the members will lose their limited liability and become fully liable. The veil is the commonest term for the barrier of incorporation that prevents a third party suffering a wrong done to him, in the name of the company, from taking direct action against those who actually run the company. Alternatives are a *cloak* or *sham* (by Lindley LJ in *Smith v Hancock* (1894) and a *mask* (Russell J in *Jones v Lipman* (1962)). However, Diplock LJ in *Snook v London & West Riding Investments Ltd* (1967) gave the term 'sham' a restrictive meaning:

> ... it means acts done or documents executed by the parties to the 'sham' which are intended by them to give to third parties or to the court the appearance of creating between the parties legal rights and obligations (if any) which the parties intend to create...

Where a 'sham' is alleged to exist a court, wishing to ignore the concept of corporate personality, must find that the function and or operation of the company amounted to 'an abuse of the corporate form' (a phrase coined by Professor Schmitthoff). Whatever label is applied there are several grounds (which often overlap) for the judicial lifting of the veil, the most notable ones being statutory provision related to companies and judicial interference.

Statutory provision related to companies

This is where Parliament will not allow the 'fiction' of legal liability to be used to commit fraud. As will be seen, the provisions are aimed at errant directors:

i)   *Where the number of members is less than two (s. 24)*
     Should the membership fall below two for more than six months then the member who knew that the company was carrying on business with less than two members, will be jointly and severally liable with the company for company debts incurred during the contravention period (Nisbet v Shepherd (1994)).

Section 24 CA 1985 has now been amended by the Companies (Single Member Private Limited Companies) Regulations.

ii) *Trading without a trading certificate (s. 117)*
     A public company is prohibited from trading or borrowing until it has been issued with a trading certificate confirming that the nominal value of the company's allotted share capital is not less than the authorized minimum. Again this provision is seldom invoked but when it is the veil of incorporation will be lifted so as to leave the director jointly and severally liable with the company for any transaction entered into by the company but which it is unable to meet within 21 days of being called upon to do so.

iii) *Use of an incorrect company name (s. 349)*
     An officer of a company or someone else the company authorizes to act will incur personal liability on signing or authorizing the signing of any bill of exchange, order for money, or goods, in which the company's name is not given correctly and in full. Liability will be to the holder of the document and will extend to the value specified. However, the company may step in and pay the amount itself. In addition the person at fault may be fined (s. 349 (4)). At one time it was felt that a court would be willing to avoid applying section 349 (4) where it was satisfied that a genuine oversight in signing the company's name had been made, preferring to apply some other rule of law. For example in Durham Fancy Goods Ltd v Michael Jackson (Fancy Goods) Ltd (1968) a director of the defendant company signed the

acceptance of a bill of exchange, drawn up by the plaintiff, without correcting the name that appeared on the bill – 'M Jackson (Fancy Goods) Ltd'. The company was then in liquidation but instead of the court applying the full rigour of section 349 (4) Donaldson J dealt with the matter under the equitable grounds of promissory estoppel and rectification. However, in a later case Donaldson J was not so accommodating:

Lindholst & Co A/S v Fowler (1988)

The plaintiffs prepared four bills of exchange in the name of 'Corby Chicken Co.'. The aptly named defendant signed the acceptance of the bills without adding the suffix 'Ltd'.

Held (Court of Appeal): The defendant would be held personally liable to the plaintiffs.

In Lindholst & Co. A/S v Fowler (1988) Sir John Donaldson took the opportunity of explaining his decision in Durham Fancy Goods Ltd v Michael Jackson (Fancy Goods) Ltd (1968):

> Mr Fowler accepts that, as a consequence of that section, he is prima facie personally liable to the plaintiffs. But, he says, this is an exceptional case in which he should not be held liable because of the principles of estoppel, which I applied as a trial judge in *Durham Fancy Goods Ltd v Michael Jackson (Fancy Goods) Ltd (1968)*. For my part I am quite unable to accept that. Once it is admitted that the contract was with Corby Chicken Co. Ltd, the obligation under the contract was to accept in a proper form for Corby Chicken Co. Ltd as prescribed by the statute. What occurred was not a compliance. Furthermore, I am quite unable to apply the doctrine of estoppel which I applied in Durham Fancy Goods to this case because, whereas in Durham Fancy Goods the form of words for acceptance was prescribed by the plaintiffs and they were estopped by what they had prescribed, in this case the form of words for acceptance was not prescribed by the plaintiffs or by the contract. The plaintiffs simply put forward bills of exchange addressed by the Corby Chicken Co., which both they and the defendant knew meant Corby Chicken Co. Ltd, and it was for the defendant to accept that bill in the proper form, as required by the statute.

With particular reference to rectification another Court of Appeal case also decided in 1988 dealt with the matter quite succinctly:

Blum v OCP Repartition SA (1988)

Bomore Medical Supplies Ltd (BMS), of which B was a director, ordered goods from the defendants. As part payment, cheques were drawn in the name 'Bomore Medical Supplies' which B signed. BMS went into liquidation before the cheques were paid.

Held (Court of Appeal): B was personally liable on the cheques he had signed. May LJ said of B's plea for rectification:

This case was decided under Companies Act 1948, s. 108 – now CA 1985, s. 349

> One may have sympathy for Blum in the predicament in which he finds himself, but the statutory provision is clear. The facts of this case are not in dispute and as a matter of law ... I do not think that the claim to rectification can afford him any defence.

However, a defendant facing a section 349 (4) action may 'strike lucky' as in *Jenice Ltd v Dan* (1993) where five cheques had been signed by Dan, a director of Primeken Ltd, in which the company had been given as PRIMKEEN Ltd. The trial judge (Titheridge QC) adopted a 'common sense approach' finding that as the omission of the letter 'E' caused no confusion in identifying the company in question the defendant ought to be excused liability.

iv) *Abuse of a statutory power (s. 429)*

Under section 429 a person attempting to take over a company has a legal right, when he acquires or contracts to acquire at least 90 per cent in value of the shares to which his offer relates, to give notice to holders of the remaining 10 per cent that he intends to purchase their shares. This power to buy out minority shareholders is to be exercised in a legitimate manner. If it is not then it may be interpreted as an abuse:

Re Bugle Press Ltd (1961)

B P had issued 10,000 £1 shares. T held 1,000 shares with S and J holding 4,500 each. S and J wishing to oust T from the company formed Jackson & Shaw Ltd which made a 'takeover' bid for B P at £10 per share. S and J both accepted the offer but when T refused they served him with a section 429 notice for the compulsory purchase of his minority shareholding. T petitioned the court claiming injustice.

Held: The compulsory purchase would not be allowed to go through. Jackson & Shaw Ltd was a mere sham designed to compulsory purchase a minority shareholder; it was an abuse of the s. 429 provision.

---

v) *Delinquent director (Insolvency Act 1986, s. 212)*

If in the course of the winding up of a company it appears that an officer of the company (either present or past) has misapplied or retained, or become accountable for any money or other property of the company, or been guilty of any misfeasance or breach of any fiduciary or other duty owed to the company; then the court may compel him to pay, restore or account for the money or property and make him pay interest on it. In respect to misfeasance or breach of duties the court can order him to contribute such sums to the company's assets as the court thinks fit.

Section 212 imposes identical liability on liquidators, administrative receivers or promoters of the company.

vi) *Fraudulent trading (Insolvency Act 1986, s. 213)*

On liquidation if it is discovered that there was an intention to defraud creditors, or any other fraudulent conduct, then those responsible will have unlimited liability, whole or part, for the company's debts. For fuller treatment see Chapter 18, 'Winding up'.

vii) *Wrongful trading (Insolvency Act 1986, s. 214)*

A liquidator can ask a court to declare a director to be personally liable to contribute to the company's assets if the director is found to have known of the possibility of insolvency but did not do enough to mitigate the creditors' losses. For fuller treatment see Chapter 18, 'Winding up'.

viii) *Breach of restriction in re-use of a company name (Insolvency Act 1986, ss. 216–217)*
Liability is imposed on directors and shadow directors of a company that has gone into liquidation who re-use any name by which the company was known by in the 12 month period before it went into liquidation. Similarly, liability is imposed where the re-used name while not identical is so similar as to suggest an association with the company (s. 216 (1) (2)).

A director in contravention of section 216 is liable to imprisonment, fine, or both (s. 216 (4)). In addition a person is jointly and severally liable with the company for debts of the company if at any time he was involved in the management of the company when section 216 was contravened. Liability will also attach if, while involved in management of the company, he acts or is willing to act on instructions given by a person whom he knows at that time to be in contravention of section 216 (s. 217 (1) (2)).

Thorne v Silverleaf (1994)

T had been a director of three companies all of which had gone into insolvent liquidation. Each of the companies had included 'Mark Spence' as part of their name. S, a creditor, claimed that T was jointly and severally liable with the company under ss. 216–217 for debts the company had incurred. S was successful at first instance but T appealed.

Held (Court of Appeal): T's appeal would be dismissed. The accusation that S had by aiding and abetting T to commit breach of s216 would not be sustained:

The monies claimed by S are not something to which but for a crime he would have no right or title. (Peter Gibson LJ)

---

ix) *Actions of a disqualified director (Company Directors Disqualification Act 1986, s. 15)*
A person is personally responsible for all the debts incurred by a company in any period that he was involved in the management of the company whilst serving a disqualification order. He will be similarly liable if he acts, or is willing to act, on the instructions of a person whom he knows at the time to be subject to a disqualification order (or to be an undischarged bankrupt) (s. 15 (1)). Liability is joint and several (s. 15 (2)).
Phoenix companies
This was the practice of forming a company for a fraudulent purpose such as to defraud creditors. Usually such a company would have been formed by dishonest directors. Typically they would allow the company to incur large trading debts by simply not paying the creditors. Finally when pressed for payment the directors will put the company into voluntary liquidation but will then shortly afterwards restart the business under the same or similar trading name, from the same premises, using stock as likely as not bought cheaply from the liquidator they appointed, employing the same staff as before and again going on to incur debts followed by liquidation, etc. This cycle would be repeated over and over.

To combat this type of fraud section 216 of the Insolvency Act 1986 prohibits a director of a company that has gone into insolvent liquidation from taking part (unless sanctioned by the court) in the management of any business using the same or similar trading name of the liquidated company As previously mentioned a director breaching section 216 will become personally liable for all debts and other liabilities of the company concerned while he was involved in its management (IA 1986, s. 217). In addition directors of *phoenix companies* are clearly liable for disqualification as directors under section 4 of the Company Directors Disqualification Act 1986 with the disqualification period likely to be at or near the maximum 15 years (CDDA 1986, s. 4 (3)). Should a disqualified director breach a disqualification order then as referred to earlier section 15 of the Company Directors Disqualification Act 1986 will come into operation.

A line of judgements seemingly establish that the courts regard as particularly important the position of taxation debts (see Re Lo-Line Electric Motors Ltd (1988)).

Review problem

In 1995 Edgar Beaver formed Vitality Limited of which he is the controlling shareholder and sole director. The business markets a range of 'pick-me-up' tablets. Initially the business prospers and Beaver is able to take generous director's fees as well as inflated expenses. However, after losing a supply contract to a health food chain of shops Vitality Limited collapses in 1997 with debts of £75,000.

In 1997 Beaver sets up another venture, Vitalife Limited, again marketing health improvement products. Several supply contracts are obtained but constant cash-flow problems mean that Vitalife Limited often buy in goods without having the means to pay, merely relying on anticipated future sales to 'bail them out'. Also in this period on a few occasions Beaver signs company cheques drawn in the name of Vital Life Limited.

In 1998 Vitalife Limited goes into insolvent liquidation. In 1999 Beaver starts up a third venture, Lifevite Limited, marketing skin care products.

In relation to corporate personality discuss the implications of the above.

Judicial interference

On the occurrence of certain circumstances a court may itself be willing to lift the veil of incorporation. However, it is not always possible with any degree of confidence to anticipate when the veil is likely to be lifted or when a court will insist that the *Salomon* principle is adhered to. The catechism that the veil will be lifted where equity demands that justice be dispensed begs the question how unjust must the circumstances be before equity will intervene? On occasions a court may say that justice may be served by the exercise of discretion, 'the eye of equity', such as in *Jones v Lipman* (1962) where the court found that a company in a group could be regarded as a facade if it had no independent existence and was used as a pretext for some dubious purpose. However, in a later Court of Appeal case, *Adams v Cape Industries* (1990), Slade LJ stated that it is not 'open to this court to disregard the principle of *Salomon v Salomon & Co Ltd*, merely because it considers it just to do so.' For convenience the examples provided have been placed under the following headings:

As an alternative to judicial interference, section 459, may be used to lift the veil. This section comparing unfairly prejudicial conduct is dealt with in Chapter 14, Minority Protection.

i) *Avoidance of a legal or equitable obligation*
   A court has wide discretion in this area:

Gilford Motors Ltd v Horne (1933)

H was subject to a valid restraint of trade covenant by G M his employer. To get around the restraint H got his wife to form J. M. Horne & Co Ltd which H began working for – competing with G M.

Held (Court of Appeal): Although H was not a shareholder or director in J M Horne & Co Ltd it was clearly a sham company formed to avoid an equitable obligation. The restraint was consequently enforced:

... I am quite satisfied that this company was formed as a device, a stratagem, in order to mask the effective carrying on of a business of Mr E B Horne. The purpose of it was to try to enable him, under what is a cloak or sham, to engage in business which, on contemplation of the agreement which had been sent to him about seven days before the company was incorporated, was a business in respect of which he had a fear that the plaintiffs might intervene or object ... (Lord Hanworth MR)

See also Yu Kong Line of Korea v Rendesburg Investments Corp. of Liberia and others (No. 2) [1998].

A more recent decision has affirmed that on the facts of a case a court is prepared to withdraw the protection afforded by corporate personality so as to make personally liable those directly responsible for committing a wrong:

Williams v Natural Life Health Food Ltd (1998)

W had been induced to take out a franchise of a health food shop on the basis of information supplied by NLHF. This information was later found to be negligent and W lost substantial sums through relying on it. As NLHF went into liquidation it was pointless claiming against it so W sued M the managing director and principal director of NLHF.

Held (Court of Appeal): The special circumstances were sufficiently abnormal for M to be made liable for W's losses. Here M had assumed personal responsibility for his company's affairs.

In *Williams v Natural Life Health Food Ltd* (1998), Hirst LJ said:

In my judgement, having regard to the importance of the status of limited liability, a company director is only to be held personally liable for the company's negligent misstatements if the plaintiff can establish some special circumstances setting the case apart from the ordinary; and in the case of a director of a one-man company, particular vigilance is needed lest the protection of incorporation should be virtually nullified. But once such circumstances are established, the fact of incorporation, even in the case of a one-man company, does not preclude the establishment of personal liability. In each case the decision is one of fact and degree.

ii)   *Abuse of judicial process*

Barakot Ltd v Epiette Ltd (1997)

In 1992 Bell, the controlling shareholder of B Ltd, sued E Ltd for repayment of a loan but his claim was rejected on the ground that at the time the debt had been incurred E Ltd had not been incorporated. However, in 1993 B Ltd sued E Ltd under the same loan but on this occasion reliance was placed on a written loan agreement which was dated after the incorporation of E Ltd. E Ltd countered by seeking to strike out the action on the ground that *res judicata* ought to be applied to B Ltd's action. B Ltd put forward the argument that it was a different party from that which had started the 1992 action since B Ltd was a different legal entity from Bell.

Held: At the relevant times Bell controlled B Ltd being its principal shareholder and sole director. Also on a successful action any resulting proceeds would go to Bell. Therefore, privity of interest between Bell and B Ltd was established so as to justify a finding of *res judicata* or, alternatively, to allow the 1993 litigation to proceed would amount to an abuse of the process of the court.

> *Res judicata is a rule that once a matter has been litigated and decided, it cannot be raised again between the same parties, though different parties are able to do so.*

---

iii) *Group enterprises*

The veil may be lifted in order to discover the true relationship between a holding and subsidiary company. Frequently land is owned by one company in a group with the business conducted on that land being done by another company in the group (a landlord and tenant relationship). If there is no long-term lease then the tenant can be legally evicted at short notice without payment of a business disturbance allowance.

DHN Food Distributors v Tower Hamlets LBC (1976)

DHN was a holding company for a group of companies. One wholly owned company, Bronze Investments Co., owned freehold property which was used by the other two companies in the group but it did not itself carry on any business. The land owned by Bronze Investments was compulsorily purchased by the local authority who paid the market value. As the two companies using the land could not obtain suitable alternative premises they were liquidated. DHN then tried to obtain business disruption compensation for the other two companies in the group.

Held (Court of Appeal): After lifting the veil and examining the relationship between the companies it was best to consider all three companies to be a single undertaking which was effectively the holding company. Additional compensation was therefore obtained.

In *DHN Food Distributors v Tower Hamlets LBC* (1976), Lord Denning with his usual vivid clarity declared:

> ... We all know that in many respects a group of companies are treated together for the purpose of general accounts, balance sheet and profit and loss account. They are treated as one concern ... This is especially the case when a parent

company owns all the shares of the subsidiaries, so much so that it can control every movement of the subsidiaries. These subsidiaries are bound hand and foot to parent company and must do just what the parent company says. This group is virtually the same as a partnership in which all three companies are partners. They should not be deprived of the compensation which should justly be payable for disturbance. Three companies should for present purposes, be treated as one, and the parent company, DHN, should be treated as that one ...

However, Lord Denning's fellow judges were not willing to fully support his observations and his judgement was later disagreed with in *Adams v Cape Industries plc* (1990). Therefore, in relation to a group of companies a court may refuse the invitation to lift the veil and decline to say that one company is the *alter ego* of another.

Dimbleby & Sons Ltd v National Union of Journalists (1984)

Two subsidiary companies had the same directors and management. One company became engaged in a trade dispute with the NUJ. The Union took industrial action against the other subsidiary hoping to put pressure on the company in dispute.

Held (House of Lords): Under the Employment Act 1980 no immunity could be given to the union when taking industrial action against the company not in dispute. The House refused to pierce the veil so as to examine the true relationship between the two companies.

In his judgement Lord Diplock said that for a statute to be able to pierce the 'corporate veil' it normally needs to be expressed in clear and unequivocal language that the veil may be lifted.

At present the most important case on lifting the veil of a company within a group is:

Adams v Cape Industries plc (1990)

A and 204 others had received judgement in a Texan court for injuries caused by exposure to asbestos dust in a factory to which the defendants had supplied asbestos. The defendants had not contested the action because they had no assets in the USA. However, the plaintiffs sought to enforce the judgement in Britain against CI (the parent company) and its wholly owned subsidiary Capsco Ltd – both incorporated in Britain. For an English court to enforce the foreign award of damages it had to be established that at the time of the proceedings CI had a presence in the USA. It was found that CI did have at the relevant time a US subsidiary as well as an independent marketing agent – did this constitute a presence?

Held (Court of Appeal): The corporate veil would not be lifted so that the presence of the subsidiary and independent agent could equal the presence of the defendants.

In *Adams v Cape Industries plc* (1990) the Court of Appeal could have followed the reasoning in *DHN Food Distributors v Tower Hamlets LBC* (1976) and found that the parent company (Cape Industries plc) and its US subsidiary were in fact a single economic entity. If it had done so then Cape Industries plc would have had the necessary presence in the USA so as to allow an English court to enforce the Texan judgement.

The unwillingness to support DHN may mean that it no longer represents the current thinking of the courts. In *Adams* the court adopted a legalistic approach:

> ... we do not accept as a matter of law that the court is entitled to lift the corporate veil as against a defendant company which is a member of a corporate group merely because the corporate structure has been used to ensure that the legal liability (if any) in respect of particular future activities of the group (and correspondingly the risk of enforcement of that liability) will fall on another member of the group rather than the defendant company. Whether or not this is desirable the right to use a corporate structure in this manner is inherent in our corporate law ...

iv) *Defence of the realm*
In times of war the veil may be lifted in order to discover the nationality of the shareholders or members having de facto control of the company. Should the controllers be enemy aliens then the incorporated status will be removed:

Daimler Co Ltd v Continental Tyre and Rubber Co (GB) Ltd (1916)
CTR was incorporated in England with its members being four German citizens, one German company and one British citizen.

Held (House of Lords): Effective control of the company was in enemy hands. For this reason the company would not be recognized as an entity separate from its membership. In consequence CTR was unable to sue D for a debt that they were owed.

---

v) *Agency*
Where the company is found to be a puppet of the controlling shareholders or members of another company, then the true relationship between them may be interpreted as one of principal and agent:

Re FG (Films) Ltd (1953)
FG was an English company for the purpose of making a film which could claim 'British' status. (At the time a certain proportion of films screened in Britain had to be classed as being British.) The company was 90 per cent controlled by an American company which provided the finance and staff for film production.

Held: The true relationship between the companies was that the English company acted as the agent of the American one for the purpose of trying to pass off an American film as being British. The film, therefore, did not qualify as being British.

There is a natural temptation when looking at parent (holding) and subsidiary companies to automatically regard the subsidiary as the agent of the parent. In actual fact even a wholly owned subsidiary may not be a true legal agent of its controller. (*Gramophone & Typewriter Ltd v Stanley* (1908)). In *Adams v Cape Industries plc* (1990) the Court of Appeal was at pains to apply agency principles in their strictest sense in that a subsidiary company had to have the authority to alter their principal's (e.g. parent company) legal relations with third parties. In *Adams* the subsidiary never had this authority; also, while being primarily concerned with marketing the parent company's products in the United States, it did show some independence by carrying on business in its own right.

vi)   *Quasi-partnership companies*

These occur where once the veil has been lifted it is found that the shareholders or members owe each other a duty of mutual confidence and support whereby their true relationship is one of partners:

Re Westbourne Galleries Ltd (1970)

E and N had been in partnership for many years trading in Persian carpets. They were equal partners. Later they formed a private company and became its first directors. Shortly afterwards G, N's son, became a director. G and N used their combined voting strength to remove E from his directorship and he (E) sought an order for the company to be wound up.

Held: On lifting the veil the true status of the company was that of a partnership. Therefore, E was really a partner and as such had a right to management but as the relationship of mutual confidence had broken down a winding-up order would be granted.

---

vii)   *Trusts*

Here the veil is pierced in order to find out who really controls the trust:

Abbey Malvern Wells Ltd v Ministry of Local Government and Planning (1951)

A school was operated as a company with shares being held by trustees of various educational trusts. The court was willing to lift the veil in order to examine the terms in which the trustees held the shares.

Concluding comments

From the above review of case law while individual 'post-mortems' allow the logic or justice of lifting the veil to be seen, in practice it is often extremely difficult to say, when faced with a particular set of circumstances, whether a court would be likely to uphold the sanctity of the *Salomon* principle or be prepared to depart from it. At extremes, such as a company being controlled by enemy aliens in time of war, or a blatant sham case where the company was created to avoid a legal obligation, there is little difficulty; a court seemingly can, when faced with such compelling considerations as national security or fairness, be relied upon to set *Salomon* aside. But other circumstances are more problematic. With single entity (group enterprises) or agency issues the considerations must apparently be rather exceptional for a court to lift the veil.

Clearly, if the courts were over-willing to lift the veil, as perhaps they were in *Goodwin v Birmingham Football Club* (1980), then their flexibility would undermine *Salomon* and make incorporation (unless Parliament shored it up by statute) less attractive. But if the courts adopted an over-strict adherence to *Salomon*, as perhaps they may have done in *Adams v Cape Industries* (1990), then this could lead to more abuses going unchecked.

Chapter *summary*

- Incorporated status means that a company is treated as being a legal person in its own right entirely separate from those who promote it (*Salomon v Salomon Ltd* (1897)).
- Major consequences of incorporation are: shareholders may own the company as an entity but the assets themselves are owned by the company; in a 'one-person' company the single shareholder may still be an employee; and a company, as a landlord, may be a different person from the controller of the company.
- Parliament has recognized that the Salomon principle may be unfairly exploited so statutory provisions have been provided to curb abuses. The most significant provisions are: use of an incorrect company name (s. 349); re-use of a company name (IA 1986, s. 216); delinquent directors (IA 1986, s. 212); fraudulent trading (IA 1986, s. 213); wrongful trading (IA 1986, s. 214); and a director in breach of a disqualification order (CDDA 1986, s. 15).
- Whilst the Salomon principle is long established, and one a court will usually uphold, circumstances may occur which, while not breaching a statutory provision, are such that a court will be willing to lift the veil in order to find out exactly how the company is internally controlled or what exact relationships it has with outside persons or bodies. Examples of judicial intervention are: abuses of court process; avoidance of an obligation; group enterprises, quasi-partnerships; and trusts.
- In any particular case, whether it is likely that the veil will be lifted or not is often difficult to determine. The courts need to strive for a middle position between strict adherence to Salomon and being too included to act as a law giver in dispensing justice in an *ad hoc* flexible manner.

Discussion questions

1 To what extent is the Salomon decision an iron-cast principle of modern company law?
2 Discuss the extent that the courts have been willing to recognize the substance rather than the form of corporate personality.

Case study exercise

Blackadder owns several town houses in Hallamfield, an English northern provincial city. The houses, let to students, provide only a modest return on capital and Blackadder contracts to sell them to Darling Developments for £160,000. The contract is signed in January with completion to be within six months (this period will ensure that all the tenants' unprotected leases will expire so that vacant possession can be given).

In February, Blackadder had an unexpected visit from Baldrick Properties, a London-based property company, who tell him of two future events that are yet to be made publicly known. Firstly, that Hallamfield has just been chosen by the Government for the transfer to it of a large government department with around 3,000 people expected to relocate. Secondly, that the European Commission will shortly announce a £3,000,000 grant to Hallamfield for city centre regeneration including improvement payments for its private housing stock.

Blackadder, realizing that property prices in Hallamfield are set to soar, tells Baldrick Properties of his contract with Darling Developments but is relieved when Baldrick Properties say that they have a cunning plan. What Baldrick Properties propose is that Blackadder forms a private limited company, George Limited, with the shares being owned 90 per cent by Blackadder and 10 per cent by Baldrick Properties. Blackadder is to transfer ownership in his houses to George Limited for a nominal payment and then Baldrick Properties will buy them from George Limited for £450,000. Blackadder agrees with this proposal and it is put into operation with Blackadder placing his shares in George Limited into a trust based in the Cayman Islands. On later being sued by Darling Developments for breach of contract Blackadder pleads poverty and says that he can afford only a small amount of compensation.

Under company law advise Darling Developments of their legal position.

Further reading

The Concept of Sham: A Fiction Or Reality?, N. Lee (1996), NILQ 377.
From Peeping Behind the Corporate Veil, to Ignoring it Completely, S. Ottolenghi (1990), MLR 338.
Lifting the Veil Between Holding and Subsidiary Companies, F.G. Rixon (1986), LQR 415.
Salomon in the Shadow, C.M. Schmittoff (1976), JBL 305.

3 Corporate criminal liability

Introduction

In recent years there has been a growing call to make companies criminally liable for the harm or injury suffered by third parties. The call is particularly vocal where death has been allegedly caused by a corporate failure to discharge its responsibilities. What seemingly ignites public anger is a perception, often false, that even when criminal charges are brought it is not against the company, as the true perpetrator, but against a lowly employee who is himself frequently felt to be little more than a hopeless victim of circumstances. Irresponsible companies have been too willing to use employees as a front for senior management to hide behind. Employees may, by a cynical management, be sacrificed to appease a public demand that a wrongdoer be produced to stand in the criminal dock and be publicly seen to be punished – employees as foot soldiers are expendable!

Objectives

The purpose of this chapter is to make students aware of the difficulties that currently apply in making companies criminally liable. In addition, students are expected to realize that the present legal position is accepted by most commentators as being unsatisfactory but that a change in social and judicial attitudes may well eventually mean that prosecutions against companies become more easy to obtain.

Key concepts

- A corporate directing mind or will
- Vicarious liability
- Corporate manslaughter.

Criminal liability of companies

Criminal offences range from corporate manslaughter to breach of regulation such as those relating to food safety or environmental protection. Offences may require the establishing of:

a) both *mens rea* (a guilty corporate mind) as well as an *actus reus* (the occurrence of the prohibited act); or

b) the criminal intention of *mens rea* is replaced by showing a sufficient degree of *guilty knowledge* together with the *actus reus*; or

c) with strict liability offences only the *actus reus* need to be shown.

The due diligence defence

Where the actus reus relates to a physical act, such as bigamy or rape, then no conviction is possible because the company, as an artificial entity, is deemed incapable of carrying out the act which only a natural person can commit.

Statutes imposing criminal liability on companies may contain a statutory defence whereby if the defendant company can show that it had taken *all reasonable precautions* and exercised sufficient *due diligence* to avoid the occurrence of the offence then the company will not be convicted. Where a company attempts to rely on such a defence the prosecution, to obtain conviction, will have to establish that senior management had failed to take all reasonable precautions or had failed to discharge due diligence.

Attachment of criminal liability

In order for a company to be found criminally liable, unless the offence is one of strict liability, it is necessary to show, dependent on the offence in question, either a guilty intent or guilty knowledge. To assist a court when determining whether or not such an intent or knowledge was present the following tests may be applied:

Was there a corporate directing mind or will?

Here only the acts and knowledge of the company's mind and will as given in its constitution, e.g. the directors or managing director, is attributed to it. An early case on directing mind and will was *H.L. Bolton (Engineering) Co Ltd v T.J. Graham & Sons Ltd* (1957) where Denning LJ said:

> A company may in many ways be likened to a human body, it has a brain and nerve centre which controls what it does. It also has hands which hold the tools and act in accordance with directions from the centre. Some of the people in the company are mere servants and agents who are nothing more than hands to do the work and cannot be said to represent the mind or will. Others are directors and managers who represent the directing mind and will of the company, and control what it does. The state of mind of these managers is the state of mind of the company and is treated by the law as such.

Review question

How helpful is Lord Denning's analogy to a company being like a human body?

The most authoritative expression of the directing mind and will test is the House of Lords decision in:

Tesco Supermarkets Ltd v Nattrass (1972)

The defendants, operators of a chain of supermarkets, had established what the court accepted was a reasonable and efficient system for ensuring that employees met the requirements of the Trade Description Act 1968. However, one supermarket broke the pricing provisions when the manager failed to supervise the work of an assistant.

Held: The manager was 'another person' in that he could not be classed as a director or other superior officer of the company; if he had been so classed then clearly he could not be 'another person' as he would effectively be the company itself.

In Tesco v Nattrass the company, in the form of personnel at the highest level, was found to have done all they should have done to avoid the trade description offence being committed. It was in the opinion of the House of Lords committed not by the company but by an employee. Lord Reid's judgement on a company's directing mind or will is particularly informative:

> A living person has a mind which can have knowledge or intention or be negligent and he has hands to carry out his intentions. A corporation has none of these: it must act through living persons, though not always one or the same person. Then the person who acts is not speaking or acting for the company. He is acting as the company and his mind which directs his acts is the mind of the company. There is no question of the company being vicariously liable. He is not acting as a servant, representative, agent or delegate. He is an embodiment of the company or, one could say, he hears and speaks through the persons of the company, within his appropriate sphere, and he is the mind of the company. If it is a guilty mind then that guilt is the guilt of the company. It must be a question of law whether, once the facts have been ascertained, a person in doing particular things is to be regarded as the company or merely as the company's servant or agent.

In relation to distinguishing between a person who is to be regarded as *being the company* and one who is taken to be one who is *working for the company*, e.g. an employee, Lord Reid continued to say:

> Normally the board of directors, the managing director and perhaps senior officers of a company carry out the functions of management and speak and act as the company. Their subordinates do not. They carry out orders from above and it can make no difference that they are given some measure of discretion. But the board of directors may delegate some part of their functions of management giving to their delegate full discretion. To act independently of instructions from them I see no difficulty in holding that they have thereby put such a delegate in their place so that within the scope of the delegation he can act as the company.

The doctrine will include self-employed managers (see *Worthy v Gordon Plant (Services) Ltd* (1989)).

However, case law is unsatisfactory in that the degree of delegation required to attach liability to the company varies considerably. In *NCB v Gamble* (1959) an employee who operated a weighbridge was found to have received sufficient delegation so that his knowledge and intent could be interpreted as being that of the company. This led to the conviction of the National Coal Board for a weight restriction breach. But in *J. Henshall Ltd v Harvy* (1965) a similar weighbridge operator was said not to be a company officer but only an employee with no corporate responsibility.

In his judgement Lord Reid provided the most limited attribution test, i.e. the directing mind and will must be given in the company's constitution. Here the employee was merely a pair of hands to do the work and being separate from the directing mind and will, as given in Tesco's constitution, it meant that the criminal offence had been committed by another person. Also it was said that a store manager who acted against a declared company policy could not be said to have been acting for the company and while certain tasks had been delegated to him there had been no delegation in respect to the ultimate authority or discretion of the company.

The judgement also illustrates how a court on locating the directing mind and will seeks to interpret the statutory provision under consideration so as to achieve Parliament's intention.

However, the 1972 *Tesco v Nettrass* decision may be contrasted with a decision made a generation later by the House of Lords in:

Re Supply of Ready Mixed Concrete (No 2) (1995)

An employee of the company acting against express instructions and without the knowledge of the company entered into an unlawful agreement in contravention of section 35 (1), Restrictive Practices Act 1976:

... (a company has) to be judged by its actions not by its language. An employee who acts for the company within the scope of his employment is the company. Directors may give instructions, top management may exhort, middle management may question and workers may listen attentively. But if a worker makes a defective product or a lower manager accepts or rejects an order, he is the company. (Lord Templeman)

In practice to say whether an employee is part of a company's directing mind and will, it may be necessary to closely examine a company's official and unofficial management structures and identify who reports to whom and what discretion has been delegated[mn5]. With a very hierarchical company an employee may be far removed from the governing centre of the company and no real delegation would have been given. On the other hand, in a company with a flat managerial structure (that is with only a few levels of management) an employee will be much nearer to central decision making. However, to avoid liability for an employee's acts the burden is to be a heavy one:

In Redfern (1993) the Court of Appeal said that what was looked for was delegation of the true power of management, not of mere administrative or executive functions; even if these functions were important it would not be enough.

Liability can only be escaped by completely effective preventative measures. How great a burden the devising of such measures will cast upon individual employers will depend upon the size and nature of the particular organizations. (Lord Nolan, *Re Supply of Ready Mixed Concrete* (No 2) (1995))

Another case, also decided in 1995, is of significance for its contribution to the directing mind and will analysis. This was the Privy Council's unanimous decision in *Meridian Global Funds Management Asia Ltd v Securities Commission* (1995) in which Lord Hoffman, on examining the directing mind and will test, said that such attribution of mind and will could be primary or general. *Primary attribution* was derived from the company's constitution and by implication from company law (e.g. the giving of powers to the board of directors to manage and represent the company); whereas, *general attribution* would take the form of agency or vicarious liability principles. If either form of attribution was not possible then to attach corporate liability recourse may be made to the language and interpretation of the obligation or rule which the company's employee had allegedly broken. For example, in *Tesco Supermarkets Ltd v Nattrass* the obligation imposed under the Trade Description Act 1968 was that proper precautions had to be taken to avoid the false pricing of goods. Lord Hoffman was of the opinion that in interpreting the obligation imposed, Tesco's board of directors had taken sufficient precautions for the company to avoid liability.

On examination of Lord Hoffman's decision it would seem that the true position of the seminal case of *Tesco Supermarkets Ltd v Nattrass* is that it relates to statutory interpretation.

Alternative terms for the directing mind and will test

The following have been used:

i)   the *alter ego* theory which originated with Viscount Haldene in *Lennard's Carry Co. Ltd v Asiatic Petroleum Co. Ltd* (1915) where he said that the directing mind and will of a corporation was its very ego and centre of the personality of the corporation:

... a corporation is an abstraction. It has no mind of its own any more than it has a body of its own: its active and directing will must consequently be sought in the person of somebody who for some purpose may be called an agent, but who is really the directing mind and will of the corporation, the very ego and centre of the personality of the corporation.

ii) the *identification* principle which attempts to identify those who actually control the company. Once identified, for criminal liability purposes, they are taken to be the embodiment of the company so that their knowledge and acts are to be ascribed as being those of the company – see the quotation of Lord Denning, taken from *H.L. Bolton (Engineering) Co. Ltd v T.J. Graham & Sons Ltd* (1957) earlier.

The anology to a company being comprised of organs, most notably its board of directors, has led to references to the organic theory. In El Ajou v Dollar Land Holdings plc (1994)

Vicarious liability

This is where a company may be liable for the criminal acts done in its name by an employee. Normally in English law a person is only legally responsible for his own acts and/or omissions but public policy had established that within certain relationships one party may bear liability for the actions or inactivity of others. One such relationship is employer and employee. Therefore, in order to more easily secure a prosecution instead of requiring that *mens rea* be shown to have existed on the company's part, statute may say that the company is liable if an employee himself had the requisite *mens rea*:

If the offence requires a natural person to commit the actus reus, such as a road traffic offence which requires a human driver, then vicarious liability will not operate so as to make the company liable per **Richmond-upon-Thames LBC v Pinn & Wheeler Ltd**

> ### Tesco Stores Ltd v Brent LBC (1993)
> Tesco were convicted of supplying an adult video to an under-age child in contravention of The Video Recording Act 1984 when the shop assistant who sold it was held to have reasonable grounds for believing that the purchaser was under age. Her *mens rea* was inputted to her employers and it was no defence for them to say that they neither knew nor had reasonable grounds for believing that the purchaser was under age. Here the court found that Parliament had intended that this defence only related to the mind of the employee and not to the controlling mind of the company.

Corporate criminal liability for contractors

While vicarious liability most commonly operates in the employer–employee relationship it is also possible that a company may be liable for the acts or omissions of contractors they have engaged. While vicarious liability may arise at common law it increasing arises through a statute that imposes criminal liability on a company for the actions, or inactivity, of independent contractors even though due diligence in their selection of the contractor took place. In *R v British Steel* (1995) the company was convicted under section 3, Health and Safety at Work Act 1974 when a subcontractor's actions caused the deaths of two workers. Here the operation of public policy was particularly prominent:

> It would drive a juggernaut through the legislative scheme if corporate employers could avoid criminal liability where the potential harmful event is committed by someone who is not the directing mind of the company. (Steyn LJ)

An authoritative case that well illustrates the principle is:

Re Supply of Ready Mixed Concrete (No 2) (1995)

In 1979 the Restrictive Trade Practices Court had ordered Pioneer Concrete and Ready Mixed Concrete not to make anti-competitive agreements. Subsequently, over a pub lunch employees of the two companies made a price fixing and job allocation agreement. In consequence of the RTPC Order being broken were the companies in contempt of court? The crucial question was whether they were parties to the agreement made in the pub. If they were then they would be in contempt; if not then they would not be. They argued that they were not on the basis that the agreement had been entered into without their knowledge and against their express prohibition.

Held (House of Lords): The companies were parties to the agreement and as a result were in contempt of court. Ignoring the directing mind and will doctrine the employees were found, notwithstanding their breach of the employers' prohibition, to have acted within the course of their employment so that liability attached through the operation of vicarious liability.

Overwhelmingly, vicarious liability will be imposed by statute that will say an employer is to be strictly liable for his agents (employees) per Gardner v Akeroyd (1952).

In his judgement in *Re Supply of Ready Mixed Concrete* (No 2) (1995) Lord Nolan said:

A limited company, as such, cannot carry on business. It can only do so by employing human beings to act on its behalf. The actions of its employees, acting in the course of their employment, are what constitutes the carrying on of business by the company ... When the roll was called at the public house meeting the employees attending did not respond as individuals: they did so as representatives of their respective companies, fully competent as a practical matter of fact to make the agreement on behalf of their companies, and to see that it was carried out. A consensus element was required because it takes at least two parties to make a restrictive practice agreement, but the consent required ... was not that of senior management or the board: all that was needed was the consent of the employees who could and did make the agreement effective.

Here an employee is an agent authorized, expressly or implicitly, to act for his employer, who has delegated authority to him and who will be liable for the acts or omissions that occur within the scope of the agent's authority.

and:

... I am unable to accept that a prohibition at some senior level against the making of an agreement or arrangement which is ignored by the employees concerned is nonetheless sufficient to prevent the employing company from being a party to the agreement or arrangement when made ...

followed by:

... if such an agreement is found to have been made without the knowledge of the employer, any steps which the employer has taken to prevent it from being made will rank only as mitigation. Liability can only be escaped completely by effective preventative measures. How great a burden the devising of such measures will cast upon individual employers will depend upon the size and nature of the particular organization ...

Review question

What is the justification for the adoption of vicarious liability to make a company criminally liable?

The distinction between vicarious liability and criminal liability through the directing mind and will doctrine

With *vicarious liability* operation of law will say that certain acts are criminal and that vicarious liability is to apply. It then becomes necessary to establish whether or not the employee in question (the company's agent) was really in law an employee and if he is, was he acting within the scope of his authority? With *directing mind and will* the company's agent must have a sufficiently senior position vis-à-vis the company so that it can be said that his guilty act and guilty mind were the act and mind of someone who was the directing mind and will of the company. If this is established then the company becomes directly liable.

The distinction was succinctly put by Bingham LJ in the corporate manslaughter case of *R v H M Coroner for East Kent ex parte Spooner* (1989):

A company may be vicariously liable for the negligent acts and omissions of its servants and agents, but for a company to be criminally liable for manslaughter ... it is required that the *mens rea* and *actus reus* of manslaughter should be established not against those who acted in the name of the company but against those who were to be identified as the embodiment of the company itself.

Therefore, with directing mind and will, liability attaches to the company only through its senior personnel, whereas with vicarious liability it covers the activities of all employees of the company including very junior ones per *Re Supply of Ready Mixed Concrete (No 2)* (1995).

While the important case of Tesco Supermarket Ltd v Natrass (1972) turned on the directing mind and will doctrine the case could (and, perhaps, should) have been solely decided upon vicarious liability.

Corporate manslaughter

For many years it was uncertain whether a company could be criminally liable for manslaughter. However, fortified by an opinion made by Bingham LJ in *R v H M Coroner for East Kent ex parte Spooner* (1989) that in principle it could, Turner J in *R v P & O European Ferries (Dover) Ltd* (1990) held that corporate manslaughter was a recognized offence in English law. In doing so he rejected arguments that there was no such offence and that manslaughter could only arise where one natural person killed another natural person. The acceptance of the existence of corporate manslaughter was a direct consequence of the development in the 1980s of the directing mind and will doctrine. By linking the company to the mind of its controlling officers it meant that their *mens rea* could be transferred to the company:

Manslaughter is the unlawful killing of another without malice. It may be either voluntarily or involuntarily and arises where death is caused: (a) by an unlawful and dangerous act; (b) by gross negligence; (c) or by recognized provocation or diminished responsibility which reduces murder to manslaughter.

> ### R v P & O European Ferries (Dover) Ltd (1990)
> A car ferry, owned and operated by the defendants, capsized while leaving Zeebrugge harbour with its bow doors open. Nearly 200 people were killed. The company and seven senior employees were charged with manslaughter.
>
> Held: The charge against the company, and six employees, had to be dismissed for lack of evidence to show that the controlling officers had been reckless. The system in operation had worked without problem on over 60,000 sailings and the ship's officers testified that the possibility of mishap had never occurred to them. On the several occasions when a vessel had left port with bow doors open no difficulties had been encountered.

In respect to the company the reason for the dismissal of the manslaughter charge was that as no natural defendant could be found guilty of manslaughter it must mean that there was no one who could be identified as having the required directing mind and will to attach the necessary *mens rea* to the company. In his judgement Turner J refused to take into English criminal law the proposition that the criminal actions of a number of individual defendants, none of whom could be held individually liable, could be aggregated together in order to attach criminal liability to their employer.

The principle of aggregation cannot be used to create from a number of individuals a resulting directing mind and will. An individual must be found to be liable before imputation to the company can take place.

There is for many people a suspicion that the authorities, when investigating the role played by a company in fatal circumstances, do not do so with the full rigour necessary to satisfy a court of law. However, it must be appreciated that the allegation of corporate manslaughter inevitably arises from disaster circumstances and the subsequent questions: what actually happened? what went wrong? who was to blame? may be extremely difficult to answer.

Whilst the charge of corporate manslaughter is difficult to sustain the first successful prosecution in England occurred in:

> ### R v Kite and OLL Ltd (1996)
> The company operated an activity centre on the Dorset coast. In consequence of canoeing fatalities the company was fined £60,000 for manslaughter caused by gross negligence. The *mens rea* imputed to the company was that of its managing director who was found to have known that safety standards were too low.

Corporate manslaughter: proposed law reform

The Law Commission in its report on involuntary manslaughter published in 1996 accepted that there were problems in obtaining corporate convictions where manslaughter had been caused by a failure to act. The major difficulty was identified as knowing when a duty to act for the safety of others is recognized in law. This very much related to the provision of a safe system of work and possible management failures when it does not materialize. The Commission did accept that in the modern law manslaughter could be created through subjective recklessness. This is where the defendant recognized that his conduct involved the risk of causing death or serious harm but notwithstanding this continued with his conduct and was found to be unreasonable in taking that risk.

What is innovative in the report is the recommendation for the creation of a new special offence of corporate killing which will be broadly similar to a new offence of killing by gross carelessness that will relate to individuals. A company will be convicted under the proposed new special offence where its conduct in causing death fell far below that which could reasonably be expected. In respect to death this ought to be taken to have been caused by the company if it is due to a failure in the manner in which the company's activities are managed or supervised so as to ensure the health and safety of those employed in, or affected by, those activities.

Reform of corporate manslaughter is widely felt to be needed for in the Zeebrugge case the narrowness of the directing mind and will doctrine meant that carelessness could not be imputed to the company. Yet the failure of two lowly but key employees (the assistant bosun and the chief officer) really showed that the company had failed to discharge its duty not to kill or injure people. Surely allowing a vessel to proceed to sea with its bow doors open was, notwithstanding no previous mishaps, gross negligence!

Legislating the Criminal Code, Involuntary Manslaughter, Law Commission Report 237, 1996.

Chapter summary

- To attach criminal liability a corporate directing mind (or will) needs to be identified. Case law indicates that this mind needs to be found in the upper echelons of management with early cases basing the degree of knowledge held by this mind as being the same as contained in the company's constitution.
- More recent cases have been prepared to broaden the degree of knowledge imputed to a directing mind whereby action of company officers and employees need to be examined – not just the language found in the company's constitution. Also, formal and informal management structures (e.g. reporting networks) may help identify who is the company as opposed to those who merely work for it irrespective of job title.
- Lord Hoffman's division of attributing facts or knowledge to the company (*Meridian Global Funds Management Asia Ltd v Securities Commission* (1995)) into two categories may become influential. *Primary attribution* is obtained from studying the company's constitution together with company law expectations and *general attribution* is based upon agency or vicarious liability principles. If both of these prove unsatisfactory then the rule of law allegedly broken may be examined.
- The use of vicarious liability may be an easier way to attach corporate criminal liability in that the company is made legally responsible for their employees' *actus*

reus with the *mens rea* being dispensed with. As long as the employee is working within the scope of his duties – even if he is working negligently – then the company becomes liable in law. Vicarious liability covers all employees, not just high status company officers. It also applies, in certain circumstances, to contractors.

- Corporate manslaughter is a recently recognized criminal offence founded on the directing mind and will doctrine. However, in practice it will be difficult to establish in that a single individual with the necessary guilty mind must be located – not a collection of individuals, each bearing some guilt, for aggregation is not permitted.
- The Law Commission in 1996 recommended the creation of a new criminal offence of corporate killing. This is apparently to be similar to a new offence of killing by gross carelessness that is to apply to individuals.

Discussion questions

1 To base corporate criminal liability on locating a directing mind and will is too favourable towards companies.
Discuss.
2 Individuals not companies need to be held criminally liable.
Discuss.

Case study exercise

An expensive advertising campaign promoting the Happy Valley Theme Park (HVTP) gave the grand-opening day as 1st May. HVTP is owned by Pleasure Developments Limited who became aware in late April that certain safety work may not be completed until after the opening. The managing director, Cecil Hardman, is away for a week but leaves a note for the acting operations manager, Heather Keen, telling her to 'sort this out but not to go over budget'. Ms Keen is already hard pressed and in order to obtain an operator's licence for several park rides she forges a safety certificate falsely saying that certain safety work has been carried out. A few days after the opening one of the rides collapses causing three fatalities.

Advise Pleasure Developments Limited of their legal position.

Further reading

Corporations and Criminal Responsibility, C. Wells (1993), Clarendon.
Legislating the Criminal Code: Involuntary Manslaughter, Law Commission (Law Com. No. 237) (1996).
Corporate And Vicarious Liability And Consumer Protection, P. Cartwright (1993), Consumer LJ, 63.
Corporate Liability and Manslaughter: Should We Be Going Dutch?, S. Field & N. Jorg (1991), Crim. LR, 156.

Corporate Criminality: Four Models of Fault, J. Gobert (1994), LS, 393.

Corporate Punishment, G. Slapper (1994), NLJ, 29.

The Attribution of Culpability To Limited Companies, G.R. Sullivan (1996), CLJ, 515.

Corporate Liability and Consumer Protection: Tesco v Natrass Revisited, C. Wells (1994), MLR, 817.

4 Company promotions

Introduction

Company promoters have had a colourful chequered history. Their precursors were the merchant venturers in Elizabethan England who would organize the funding through a syndicate of high risk ventures such as establishing trading posts in the new world or in financing vessels fitted out as privateers (legalized piracy). For his efforts the promoter would be allowed to have more shares than other syndicate members. With a few exceptions ventures remained relatively modest in size and promoters continued to rely on a small number of wealthy but largely cautious people who provided investment capital for enterprises at home or of empire.

Increasingly, however, the need for start-up capital to finance a growing number of projects was too great for the wealthy élite to provide. Therefore, investment opportunities began to be offered more widely. These would range from the modest well-thought-out to the hare-brained grandiose. The individuals who promoted them were entrepreneurs who, finding that existing sources of capital were either not forthcoming or too expensive, began to offer shares in their venture to a public consisting of anyone willing or foolhardy enough to invest in them. While many promoters were honest, if rather over-imaginative in their promotions, the opportunity to attract sums of money from the public proved irresistible to others. These were the chancers or speculators who did little more than gamble with the monies they received. Worse, some promoters were outright dishonest and would exploit the public's appetite for get-rich schemes, take advantage of their willingness to subscribe for worthless shares and then disappear with the proceeds.

It must also be noted that down to the late Victorian period the dominant political economic theory was *laissez-faire* (a policy of non-interference) so that it was generally believed that markets worked best without too much regulation. For this reason Parliament was unwilling to intervene to introduce protective legislation. Private law remedies of breach of contract were available but mistake or fraudulent misrepresentation were difficult to establish (negligent misrepresentation is comparatively recent). The parties made their own bargain and had to bear the consequences with the courts being reluctant to innovate over remedies. Gradually, however, the courts started to offer limited assistance to investors who had been dumped by seductive sweet-talking promoters. Also the public slowly learned from the mistakes of others (the establishment of a national press and improved literacy assisted this) in thinking that there were foolproof guaranteed paths to riches. Indeed the money public (middle classes) became better educated and more inclined to look long term so that Government Stock with an assured fixed rate had attractions and was preferred by many to the vicissitudes of the financial market.

The merchant venturers were early venture capitalists.

The public's clamour for shares in infrastructure projects led to the canal and railway mania of the eighteenth and nineteenth centuries with many routes being destined never to be profitable.

As a consequence of an increasingly wary public and a growing willingness of the courts to apply remedies more robustly, the promoter peddling shares in a sham company began to disappear. What also caused his demise was that an application to the London Stock Exchange for a listing (large company promotions had to have a listing for investor creditability) would be refused unless the company was able to produce audited accounts to confirm that it had traded solvently for a stipulated period (currently the Listing Rules require three years).

Objectives

The purpose of this chapter is to make students aware of the role that promoters have played in company formation. Also students need to appreciate that because of the intimate position promoters hold, the law has always viewed them somewhat ambivalently with the result that they are placed, vis-à-vis the company they promote, under a duty of good faith.

Key concepts

- Company promoters
- Promotions as fiduciaries of the company
- Contractual rescission
- Pre-incorporation contracts.

Definition of a promoter

No statutory definition is given in the Companies Act 1985 nor is one to be found in the Financial Services Act 1986. Therefore, case law needs to be trawled for assistance with the following being well accepted judicial definitions:

> ... one who undertakes to form a company with reference to a given project, and to set it going, and who takes the necessary steps to accomplish that purpose. (*Cockburn J, Twycross v Grant* (1877))

> ... the term promoter is not a legal term, it is a term of business, useful for the summing up in a single word of a number of business operations familiar to the commercial world by which a company is brought into existence. (*Bowen J, Whaley Bridge Calico Printing v Green & Smith* (1879))

A paid professional who assists with the company creation, such as a solicitor or accountant, is not a promoter (Re Great Wheal Polgooth Co. (1883)).

> ... the term 'promoter' involves the idea of exertion for the purposes of getting up and starting a company. (*Lindley J, Emma Silver Mining Co. v Lewis & Son* (1879))

These definitions focus on the work a person does before he may be called a promoter. Therefore, apparently a promoter will be a person responsible in whole or part for: the organizing prior to incorporation; the actual registration of the company; and the operation of the company immediately after incorporation has taken place. However, while the above definitions conjure up an active person beavering away to bring a company into existence a modern court would also include within the team a person who, while outwardly passive, was in reality the motive force for the company creation.

The promoter's duties

These are derived from case law not statute. They establish that while a promoter is not a trustee or agent he does have a *fiduciary relationship* with the company being formed. This requires him to act in good faith, deal fairly with and to make full disclosure of any profit or advantage that he gains on the promotion. Where there is a conflict of interest to avoid a breach of fiduciary duty, such as selling his own property to the company, disclosure should be made on the same basis as directors. Provided satisfactory disclosure is made the promoter is able to make a profit; however, a secret one is prohibited (*Salomon v Salomon & Co Ltd* (1897)). In respect to discharging the disclosure obligation the following comments may be made:

a) Disclosure may be validly made to a board of directors who can exercise an independent and intelligent judgement on the transaction in question. Therefore, disclosure to a non-independent board composed, for example, of the promoters who are to become the first directors (or their nominees) is invalid. This was succinctly expressed by Lord Cairns LC in *Erlanger v New Sombrero Phosphate & Co.* (1878):

I do not say that the owner of property may not promote and form a joint stock company, and then sell his property to it, but I do say that if he does so he is bound to take care that he sells it to the company through the medium of a board of directors who can and do exercise an independent and intelligent judgement on the transaction, and who are not left under the belief that the property belongs, not to the promoter, but to some other person.

or alternatively:

b) Disclosure may be validly made to shareholders of the company (these may include potential shareholders) with the disclosure being contained in the offer prospectus so that those who acquire shares know precisely what the promoter's interests are (*Gluckstein v Barnes* (1900)).

Where a promoter acquires property after the promotion has commenced then a court may regard him as holding that property as a trustee for the company. However, if this presumption is rebutted then the promoter may sell it to the company at a profit provided that he makes a proper disclosure (*Omnium Electric Palaces Ltd v Baines* (1914)).

Prospectuses have now given way to listing particulars which must be issued whenever shares are to be listed on the London Stock Exchange. (See Chapter 7, Public offer of shares.)

Erlanger v New Sombrero Phosphate Co. (1878) may be contrasted with *Lagunas Nitrate v Lagunas Syndicate* (1899) where the court decided not to follow the letter of the earlier case.

Valuation of non-cash consideration in return for shares – public companies

A promoter may agree to sell his own assets to the company in return for shares once it has been incorporated. A potential danger is that the assets may be overvalued. Therefore, in respect to *public companies* no allotment of shares to subscribers to the memorandum can be made (s. 104) unless the assets used as payment have been independently valued and a report made to the company (s. 108–111). The general prohibition relating to non-cash assets being sold to the company by a subscriber to the memorandum lasts for two years from the date of issue of its trading certificate and covers a consideration of 10 per cent or more of the nominal value of its issued share capital (s. 104 (1) (2)).

The prohibition may be overcome by having the consideration valued with a report on the matter, made during the six months immediately proceeding the agreement, being given to the company. Also the agreement must have been approved by an ordinary resolution of the company with copies of the resolution and report being circulated to shareholders (and to the subscriber if he is not himself a shareholder) not later than the provision of notice for the 'approval meeting' (s.104 (4)). After a resolution has been passed, a copy of it, accompanied by a copy of the report, must be delivered within 15 days to the Registrar (s. 111 (2)).

A promoter is liable for criminal fraud if he has made any untrue statements whether made in the prospectus or listing particulars or not. In addition a person convicted of an offence relating to the promotion of a company may be disqualified from direct or indirect management of a company for up to 15 years (Company Directors Disqualification Act 1986, ss.1–5).

Review question

Are the promoter's disclosure obligations satisfactory? If not, what improvements would you propose?

Remedies available to the company for a promoter's breach of fiduciary duty

The following four remedies apply:
   a) rescission;
   b) recovery of the undisclosed profit;
   c) retention of the property;
   d) damages.

Rescission

In respect to public companies the provisions relating to valuation of non-cash consideration in return for shares referred to earlier has reduced the value of the remedies given here.

With rescission the company, as the innocent party, may withdraw from the contract made with the promoter. That is, because of the promoter's failure to disclose the contract becomes *voidable* at the option of the company. The usual rules of rescission must be satisfied. These are: that the company has not expressly or by conduct ratified the non-disclosure; that there was no unreasonable delay in seeking rescission; that restitution is possible in that whatever was acquired from the promoter can be restored to him in substantially the same physical condition as it was obtained (any depreciation in value of property will in itself not be a barrier to rescission), and then the promoter returns whatever he received from the company (money or shares); and finally that there must be no innocent third parties who will suffer hardship if restitution is ordered.

Recovery of the undisclosed profit

Where rescission is possible then an undisclosed profit is recoverable from the promoter concerned. However, if the remedy of rescission is lost then recovery of an undisclosed profit is only possible if the promoter obtained his interest after he became a promoter. This is on the basis that the promoter breached his fiduciary duty and therefore the company is allowed to recover the profit made:

It must be remembered that a promoter called to account for a profit that he has made will be allowed to deduct his promotion expenses – it is only the undisclosed profit that is clawed back.

Gluckstein v Barnes (1900)

G and three others formed a syndicate to buy the Olympia exhibition hall in London and to sell it to a company which they were going to promote. The hall was bought for £140,000 together with debts associated with it which effectively reduced the price to £120,000. The hall was then sold to the promoted company for £180,000 with subscribers being led to believe that the promoters had paid £140,000 for it, i.e. a disclosed profit of £40,000 but an undisclosed one of £20,000.

Held (House of Lords): G had to pay the company his share of the secret profit.

The scenario in *Gluckstein v Barnes* (1900) was stridently put by Lord Macnaghton in an often quoted passage:

These gentlemen set about forming a company to pay them a handsome sum for taking off their hands a property which they had contracted to buy with that end in view. They bring the company into existence by means of the usual machinery. They appoint themselves sole guardians and protectors of this creature of theirs, half-fledged and just struggling into life, bound hand and foot while yet unborn by contracts tending to their private advantage, and so fashioned by its makers that it could only act by their hands and only see through their eyes. They issue a prospectus representing that they had agreed to purchase the property for a sum largely in excess of the amount which they had, in fact, to pay. On the faith of this prospectus they collect subscriptions from a confiding and credulous public. And then comes the last act. Secretly, and therefore dishonestly, they put into their own pockets the difference between the real and the pretended price.

Retain the property

Although able to rescind the contract here the company will elect to keep the property but only pay the same price as that paid by the promoter with any over-payment being refunded. In consequence the promoter will forfeit his profit. Clearly the outcome here is the same as in recovery of the undisclosed profit above.

Damages

Damages may be claimed for negligent or fraudulent misrepresentation (Misrepresentation Act 1967, s.2), with the measure of damage being the amount of the undisclosed profit (*Re Leeds & Hanley Theatre of Varieties* (1902). This remedy may be taken if rescission is not possible.

Review question

The remedies available to a company to use against a promoter are not as good as they appear.

Discuss.

Pre-incorporation contracts

There are two types of these. They are:

a) *Contracts on behalf of the company*
A contract made on behalf of the company before its incorporation cannot bind the company (Re Northumberland Avenue Hotel Co. (1886)). Even if after incorporation it attempts to ratify the contract it will still be unenforceable (*Kelner v Baxter* (1866)). Normally, therefore, it is the promoters who will bear liability.

b) *Those allegedly contracting for the company under s. 36C:*

> A contract which purports to be made by or on behalf of the company at a time when the company has not been formed has effect, subject to any agreement to the contrary, as one made with the person purporting to act for the company or as agent for it, and he is personally liable on the contract accordingly.

Although Kelner v Baxter established a 'cast iron' rule it is not an absolute one. In Newbourne v Sensolid (Great Britain) Ltd (1954) the contract was said not to have been made with the person acting for the company (as in Kelner) but with the non-existent company itself and therefore it was not an enforceable contract against anyone.

Phonogram Ltd v Lane (1982)

Before incorporating a company, Fragile Management Ltd, L signed a contract 'for and on behalf of Fragile Management Ltd'. Under the contract L received an advance of £6,000 which was to be repaid if P did not enter into a recording contract within one month. It turned out that Fragile Management Ltd was never incorporated nor was a recording contract entered into. P sued for the return of the £6,000 advance.

Held (Court of Appeal): Although at common law L would not be liable on his signature as he was only authenticating a company signature, he would, however, be liable under statute.

The decision in *Phonogram Ltd v Lane* (1982) means that a promoter will be personally liable for pre-incorporation contracts made on behalf of the company they are seeking to form and this liability will still apply even if the promoter claims to be only an agent for the company. To avoid liability will, despite the wording of section 36C, be extremely difficult. However, if promoters, acting as agents, make contracts and then purchase an existing ready-made company off the shelf then section 36C will not apply so that the company may ratify the contracts (*Oshkosh B'Gosh Inc. v Dan Marbel Inc. Ltd* (1989)).

A promoter may be advised to include in pre-incorporation contracts a term that he is to be released from liability when the company is incorporated and it enters into a contract with the third party on the same terms as with the promoter. To guard against the company after incorporation not entering into such a contract another term in the promoter's contract can say that if the second contract is not entered into within a stipulated period then the promoter (or in fact both parties) may rescind.

Chapter summary

- A promoter is exclusively defined by the common law as one who carries out a variety of tasks relating to getting a company up-and-running. However, while usually a promoter is very active the term includes someone who is inactive but is nevertheless identified as being the individual behind the move to incorporation.
- The promoter stands as a fiduciary in relation to the company he is endeavouring to create. As such the promoter owes a duty of loyalty not to abuse his position by making an undisclosed profit from the promotion. Therefore, all material circumstances must be disclosed, especially where the promoter sells his own property to the company. Disclosure must be to an independent board of directors or to shareholders (current or prospective).
- If a promoter obtains property after the promotion process has started then it is likely that he will be taken to hold it as a constructive trustee for the company pending its incorporation. Such a presumption may be rebutted.
- Stringent provisions exist to cover the situation of a promoter selling non-cash property to a *new public company* in return for shares. This requires that to avoid over-payment the property must be independently valued not more than six months before the transfer agreement is made with the report being sent to the company. The protective period is two years from receipt of the certificate to trade and applies where consideration (payment) is 10 per cent or more of its nominal value of issued shares. The company has to approve the agreement by an ordinary resolution with relevant copies (resolution and valuation report) being sent to shareholders. If the resolution is passed then the Registrar must have copies within 15 days.
- Should a promoter breach his fiduciary duty then several remedies become available to the company: rescission – subject to the normal rules being satisfied (no delay, *restitutio in integrum*, no prejudice to innocent third parties); recovery of the undisclosed profit; retention of the promoter's property at its true value; and damages.
- A promoter making a pre-incorporation contract on behalf of the company will not bind the company nor can a company ratify the contract. However, under both agency principles (*Kelner v Baxter* and statute (CA 1985, s. 36C) the promoter will be personally liable on it.

Discussion questions

1 How may someone intending to form a company avoid personal liability on contracts they make on behalf of the proposed company?

2 A promoter must not place himself in a position in which his personal interest conflicts with those of the proposed company.
Discuss.

Case study exercise

Dick Turpin is a talented but impoverished artist. What particularly annoys him is that while he is convinced that his own work is of the highest quality it sells poorly, while work of artists that are *collectable* sell for comparatively high sums even though in his opinion they are inferior to his. After complaining in this vein his friend Ivan Naughtie persuades him to open an art gallery in York. It is decided that a company, Ebor Art Galleries Limited, will be formed.

Naughtie provides much of the brainwork, aiming the venture at rich art followers who are told that a provincial gallery would do very well. In order to acquire prestigious premises and opening stock Turpin solicits subscriptions for shares ranging from £25,000 to £50,000. In total £1.7 million is subscribed. In setting up the company Turpin enters into the following transactions on behalf of Ebor Art Galleries Limited:

a) a three-year lease on premises in central York. The lessor accepts as payment of the deposit and the first six months rent shares in the company;
b) the acquisition from Naughtie of several paintings that he owns. These are bought for £170,000;
c) the acquisition at a public auction of: a highland scene by Louis Bosworth Hunt; two male figures by Henry Scott Tuke; and a portrait by Angelica Kauffman. In total £145,000 was paid for these paintings.

Shortly after the company was incorporated the subscribers were alerted to the following:

i) that Naughtie's paintings had been offered for sale last year at a third less than the price the company paid for them;
ii) that the police wish to interview Turpin over his alleged forgery of works by second ranking (but still valuable) Victorian and Edwardian painters (these include Bosworth Hunt and Scott Tuke).

Advise the subscribers of the legal position under company law.

Further reading

Security Of Transactions After Phonogram, N.N. Green (1984), MLR, 671.
Agents Without Principals : Pre-incorporation Contracts and Section 36C of the Companies Act 1985, A. Griffiths (1993) LS, 241.
Who Is A Company Promoter?, J.H. Gross (1970), LQR, 493.

THE COMPANY
CONSTITUTION

5 The memorandum of association

Introduction

This is the document that regulates the affairs of the company in respect to outsiders. As the company is a legal person but one without a physical existence (the certificate of incorporation is merely evidence of its non-physical existence) it has to be described and the memorandum will do this largely for the benefit of outsiders.

Objectives

The purpose of this chapter is, firstly, for students to realize that a company's external legal relations are determined by the memorandum, and also that this document requires minimum disclosures in relation to capital, objects and the country of registration. Secondly, students must fully understand the contractual capacity of companies and the consequences that follow from the memorandum.

Key concepts

- The memorandum must contain certain information given in the form of clauses.
- The name chosen by the company must satisfy common and statute law before it will be accepted for registration.
- Modern statute law has made the object clause far less significant than formerly.

Content of the memorandum

The following are mandatory clauses and must be provided or else registration will be refused. Other clauses may be included if it is so wished:

1 the *name* of the company;
2 the situation of the *registered office*;
3 the *object* for which the company was formed;
4 whether or not the liability of members is *limited*;
5 the *authorized share capital* of the company;

Should a provision in the memorandum conflict with one appearing in the articles then the memorandum is paramount (Welton v Saffery (1897) and see also Ashbury Railway Carriage Co. v Riche (1875) given later). If a provision in the memorandum is unclear then clarification can be sought by referring to the articles.

6 the *association* clause; and if it is a public limited company

7 a statement that the company is to be a *public company* (s. 1 (3)).

The memorandum must be signed by at least two members (those will be subscribers to the memorandum) and it must end with a declaration of association, i.e. a statement that they wish to form a company. It is common for the subscribers to the memorandum to agree to take one share only with additional shares being allotted at a later date.

Obviously one subscriber for a single-member company.

1 The name clause

A company may be registered with any name as long as it is not a prohibited name. The registrar controls the use of company names and any that are judged prohibited or misleading will be rejected. On receipt of the memorandum the chosen name will be entered on a computer which has a programme to reject prohibited names and to refer to the registrar's staff names which include words controlled by law.

a) *Statutory requirement*:

   i) If the members of the company have limited liability, the last word of the name of a private limited company must be 'Limited' or 'Ltd' (or the Welsh equivalent for Welsh companies) (s. 25 (2)).

   ii) The last words of the name of a public limited company must be 'Public Limited Company' or 'plc' (or the Welsh equivalent) (s25 (I)).

      In a limited number of circumstances it may be possible for a company to dispense with the word Limited at the end of the name (s. 30). In response to new companies this can only be for a private company limited by guarantee whose objects are the promotion of commerce, art, science, education, religion, charity or any profession or anything incidental or conducive to these objects.

      To gain the exemption it is also a condition that all profits must be directed to meeting its objects, that no dividends be paid and that on winding up any surplus be transferred to another body with similar objects to those which it had.

      Normally the registrar will only grant an exemption under s. 30 if a statutory declaration is delivered to him which states that the company does conform to the exemption. The declaration must be signed by a director or the secretary or a solicitor responsible for the company formation. If an exempt company breaches s. 30, then it can be ordered to use the word 'limited' in the normal manner. An exempt company will not have to publish its name outside all its business premises (s. 348) or on its cheques or receipts (s. 349); however, it must give notice that it is limited on its letters and orders (s. 351).

For old companies the limitation relates to private companies in existence on the 25th February 1982 who held a licence under section 19, CA 1948 whereby they were excused the use of the word Limited.

b) *Prohibition of certain names from registration (s. 26)*
These are:

   i) limited, unlimited or plc other than of its end;

   ii) a name which is the same as or very similar to that of an existing company. The registrar keeps an index of the names of: registered companies, overseas companies established in Great Britain, limited partnerships and industrial and provident societies. Should a chosen name be the same, or too similar to one already in the index, then it will either be refused registration or, if the similarity is spotted too late, the offending company will have 12 months to alter it;

iii) where the Secretary of State believes that a criminal offence would be committed. Statute law, in protecting certain names, will make it a criminal offence for them to be mis-used. Examples being the Red Cross, ANZAC, the NSPCC. Also the Banking Act 1987 makes it a criminal offence for an undertaking to use in its name 'bank' unless it is recognized by the Bank of England;

iv) when the Secretary of State considers a named to be offensive. This occurs where a company may attempt to gain a connection through the use of a name to a central government department or to local government. Here the prior permission of the Secretary of State is required.

Words and expressions also requiring the permission of the Secretary of State are given in the Company and Business Names Regulations 1981 (as amended).

Further powers are given to the Secretary of State whereby he is able to demand at any time that a company with a name that gives the public a misleading impression to the extent that it causes public harm change its name (s. 32). This power applies even when the registrar has himself accepted a name as being appropriate:

Association of Certified Public Accounts of Britain v Secretary of State for Trade and Industry (1997)

The Secretary of State, using his powers under s. 32, directed that the ACPAB change their name as he found the word 'certified' misleading and potentially harmful to the public. The ACPAB challenged the validity of his direction.

Held: Firstly, the word 'certified' in the name was likely to mislead members of the public into believing that there was something special about the qualification, training and experience of the members of the association when, at present, there was not. Secondly, this misleading name was likely to cause harm. In consequence the s. 32 direction was confirmed.

Under section 32 the Secretary of State has the burden of proof and must make out that a name, in full or part, is both *misleading* and that it is likely to result in *harm* to the public. A misleading name, without any likely harmful consequence in its use, will not come within section 32. However, it is not necessary that actual evidence of the public being misled or that the company intended to mislead anyone is produced – although these matters may help to determine whether section 32 was being correctly exercised.

c) *The tort of passing off*

This is where one trader will present its goods, or services, as being those of another trader. In the context here it is the business name that is being passed off. In essence, passing off is the theft of another trader's reputation, e.g. their goodwill.

Exxon Corporation v Exxon Insurance Consultants International Ltd (1982)

EC had invested heavily in creating and promoting a new corporate name and trade mark. EI, a small insurance business unconnected to EC, later began using the word 'Exxon' as part of their trading name.

Held: El had tried to pass themselves off as being associated with EC's business. El were consequently ordered to use another trading name.

Review question

What restrictions are imposed on the choice of name by a limited company?

Publication of the company's name

Unless exempt under s. 30, a company must publish its name:

a) outside all its places of business (s. 348);
b) on all business documents (s. 349);
c) on, if it has one, its seal (s. 350).

Should these provisions be disregarded then criminal liability will mean that the company may be fined £200 and company officers who knew of the omission will be personally liable to creditors when signing documentation without the full name of the company being given. If the signatory puts Ltd for Limited or Co. for Company he will not incur any personal liability. But if he uses an ambiguous abbreviation or omits Ltd then he may be liable.

In relation to the use of an incorrect company's name, see Chapter 2, Corporate Personality and Lifting the Veil.

Durham Fancy Goods Ltd v Michael Jackson (Fancy Goods) Ltd (1968)
'Michael Jackson' was abbreviated to 'M. Jackson'. The signatory was personally liable. also:

Blum v OCP Repatriation SA (1988)
The printed account title on a cheque omitted 'Ltd'. The director who drew the cheque was held to be personally liable.

In addition a company must on its business letters and order forms publish its country of registration, e.g. England & Wales or Scotland, the address of its registered office and its company registration number (s. 351).

The Business Names Act 1985

A company who carries on business under a different name from their registered name is required to:

a)   give their registered name on all business documents, e.g. letters, invoices, receipts, orders and demands for payment; and
b)   display the registered name and address in a prominent position in any business premises to which suppliers or customers have access; and
c)   at the request of any person with whom it does business to supply in writing details of its name and address.

Change of name

This may be achieved by the passing of a special resolution to alter the memorandum and articles. The application signed by a director or company secretary must be on the official form accompanied by copies of the new memorandum and articles. If the Registrar agrees to the change then a new certificate of incorporation will be issued. The change of name will be effective from the issue of the new certificate (s. 28).

2 The registered office

This clause will state whether the company is registered in England and Wales or in Scotland. The actual address is usually given in the articles of association but commonly the registered office is not where the business will actually operate from. As a company is not able under the Companies Act 1985 to change its domicile, registration will fix its nationality for all time. However, a company can change its address within the domicile by means of an ordinary resolution or a resolution of its board of directors if they are allowed to do so by the articles (s. 287)

Domicile is the country in which a person is permanently resident. Technically, a change of nationality could be obtained with the consent of Parliament but in practice such a notion for a company would be absurd.

The purpose of the registered office clause is to able outsiders to know where writs and other legal documents are to be served and where various registers are kept. Should there be no registered office then a writ may be served on the secretary and directors at an office that is unregistered.

Re Fortune Copper Mining Co. (1870)

The registered office of the company had been demolished without another office being nominated. A writ was served on the secretary and director at an unregistered office.

Held: The writ had been validly served.

Conveniently, a prospective litigant may under the County Court (Amendment) Rules 1989 serve a writ against a company at their local place of business as opposed to having to do so at their registered office.

Registers that must be kept at the registered office

These are:

1 *The register of members*
   The contents should include: the full name and address of each member: how many shares they hold and the amount paid on them; if applicable what class of share is held; the share certificate number; the date of entry on the register and, if applicable, the date membership ceased. (s. 352)
   The company is allowed to close this register for a maximum of 30 days each year to enable dividend warrants to be prepared (s. 358). During the closure period share transfers cannot be entered nor can anyone inspect the register.

2 *The register of directors and secretary*
   The contents should include the names, addresses, nationality and their business occupation. Additionally, details must be given of other directorships currently held by the directors as well as others held within the previous five years. (s. 288)

The register must also provide the same information on shadow directors.

3 *The register of the director's interest in shares or debentures*
Directors must notify their company within five days of carrying out any transaction in their own or a related company's securities. To guard against securities being bought by a proxy, notification covers securities in a spouse, child or nominee of a director. (s. 325)

4 *The register of debenture holders*
On issuing debentures a company is not obligated to keep a register but if they do then provisions exist to cover this (ss. 190, 191). The register will record their names and the serial number of the debenture.

5 *The register of charges*
The contents should include a brief description of the property charged, the amount of the loan and those entitled to the security. All floating charges on non-land property need to be recorded. (s. 407)

6 *The register of interests in shares of a public company*
The shareholding notification threshold figure is 3 per cent with any change also being notifiable (s. 211). Shares held in the name of a spouse, child or any company in which a person is interested are also notifiable. Notification also applies to concert parties where two or more investors acting together with a common purpose acquire shares in a public limited company. Here each would have to notify the extent of his holding even if below the 3 per cent figure. (ss. 204–6; see also the City's Panels *Code on Takeovers and Merges*)

Registers have to be open for inspection by every member free of charge and to others on payment of a token fee (s. 356). On changing their registered office a company is given 14 days grace to move its registers to the new location (s. 287).

Other documents that are normally kept at the registered office are:

1 copies of instruments creating charges;
2 minute book of general meetings;
3 copies of any contract for an off-market purchase, market purchase or contingent purchase by the company of its own shares – such copies are to be kept for 10 years from completion of the purchase;
4 directors' service contracts;
5 minute book of directors' meetings;
6 accounting records.

As an alternative to retention at the registered office, 4 may be kept at the principal place of business, and 5 and 6 may be kept at any convenient place.

Any change to the registered address must be notified to the Registrar within 14 days and published in the London Gazette.

3 The object clause

The object clause states the purpose for which the company was formed. Prior to the Companies Act 1989 a company could only perform such activities as were stated (or which could reasonably be implied) in the object clause. Subject to certain exceptions, neither the company, nor those dealing with it, could enforce an *ultra vires* contract, i.e. a contract that was beyond the power stated in the object clause, even if every member of the company assented to it:

Ashbury Railway Carriage Co. v Riche (1875)

The memorandum gave the company power to make and sell railway carriages. The directors subsequently bought a railway concession in Belgium. The articles gave express power to the company to extend its business beyond the memorandum by special resolution. The company passed a special resolution to ratify the purchase.

Held: The purchase was ultra vires and hence illegal:

If every shareholder had said, 'that is a contract which we authorize the directors to make,' it would be void. The shareholders would thereby by unanimous consent have been attempting to do the very thing which by the Act of Parliament (i.e. the Companies Act) they were prohibited from doing. (Lord Cairns LC)

The object clause would not be construed too strictly in that a certain leeway could be navigated by the company. This meant that anything which was reasonably incidental would come within the object clause and so be validly carried out:

See also Evans v Brunner Mond & Co (1921) referred to in Chapter 11, Directors.

Foster v London, Chatham and Dover Rail Co. (1895)

The company acquired land for its railway. The railway was built on arches which it let as workshops, etc. Neighbours objecting to noise and rubbish claimed that the lettings were ultra vires.

Held: The lettings, being fairly incidental to the object of the company, were valid.

In *Ashby Railway Carriage Co. v Riche* (1875) the House of Lords was unwilling to say that buying a concession to operate a railway was reasonably incidental to the main purpose (object) of the company, namely the manufacture of railway rolling stock.

Powers not expressly given in the object clause may also be implied if they are reasonably necessary to ensure that the stated object can be achieved. Therefore, a trading company has implied power to borrow and to buy land providing of course that borrowing and land purchase were both linked to trade (see *Re Kingsbury Collieries* (1907)). This broadening of the object clause by implication was extended to the grant of a pension, or other appropriate reward, to its directors or employees provided that the benefit conferred was done in good faith for the benefit of the company in promoting its legitimate interests and prosperity. (See *Cyclists' Touring Club v Hopkinson* (1910) and *Re Lee, Behrens & Co. Ltd.* (1932).)

The courts and the Department of Trade and Industry (DTI) much prefer a short object clause such as:

Table F of Table A–F Regulations 1985 provide a similar specimen, short clause for an imaginary company called 'Western Electronics'.

The object of the company is to carry on business as a general commercial company.

This will mean that the company will have the powers to carry on any trade or business with its agents, especially its directors, gaining almost unlimited authority to contract for it. Therefore, such objects would be ideal for small private companies whose shareholders are also directors. The judicial preference for short objects was a reaction to past attempts by companies to evade the ultra vires rule by drafting lengthy object clauses (*Re German Date Coffee* (1882)) or by using the ploy of splitting the objects into a number of separate clauses (*Cotman v Brougham* (1918))

Originally object clauses were provided to protect members and creditors in that by requiring companies to remain within their objects it would prevent capital subscribed by members being used for other than the stated objects of the company and also suppliers would know that goods provided on credit would be used for prior known purposes. Therefore, a company with an object related to transportation could not lawfully go into a new venture such as pearl finishing on the Caledonian Canal! However, it was felt by many that the object clause did not give the desired level of protection to either members or creditors. In 1985, the Prentice Report recommended the abolition of the ultra vires doctrine. In particular it was asked how the doctrine could effectively protect creditors if they could not enforce their ultra vires contracts against the company. The argument advanced was that members of a public company can simply sell their shares if they are not at ease with the activities of the company; while members of a private company may more readily invoke the wide range of laws relating to minority protection if they are dissatisfied with the company's activities. However, abolition was not possible as it is a requirement of the European Community that all companies have an object clause. The Government's response to the Prentice Report was to reform the doctrine and this was achieved through the introduction by sections 108–110, CA 1989 of additions to the Companies Act 1985. The effect of these additions is to considerably reduce the ultra vires doctrine.

The EC requirement is found in Article 9, EC First Company Law Directive. This was introduced into British law by means of s. 9, European Communities Act 1972.

A company's contractual capacity (CA 1985, s. 35)

1 *The validity of a company's acts*

The validity of an act done by a company shall not be called into question on the ground of lack of capacity by reason of anything in the company's memorandum.

Therefore, a company's capacity is not limited by its memorandum and a completed act will be totally protected and enforceable by both parties. However, the authority of an individual director to act may be restricted by the articles or by the board of directors. Where this occurs then the effect of the section is reduced.

2 *Proceedings by a member*

A member of a company may seek an injunction to prevent a company from entering into contracts which would be outside its stated object. But a member has no right to seek an injunction once the contract has been entered into. If a company is required to do an ultra vires act to fulfil a legal obligation which arises from a previous act of the company then a member will be unable to ask for an injunction. This restriction also applies to section 35A, CA 1985.

3 *The directors' duty*

The directors of a company are still bound to act within the limitations of the memorandum but should they go beyond it then the company can by special resolution ratify their acts. The directors concerned will remain liable for breaching the memorandum unless the company passes a second special resolution to excuse them liability. If the company, e.g. shareholders, ratifies then they cannot of course, unless ratification was a fraud on the minority, obtain an injunction to prevent the ultra vires transaction from going ahead.

The power of the directors to bind the company (CA 1985, s. 35A)

The directors' power is deemed to be free of any limitation. So that where a person deals with a company in good faith, the power of the board of directors to bind the company, or to authorize others to do so, shall be deemed to be free of any limitation under the company's constitution.

A person 'deals' with a company if he is a party to any transaction or other act which the company is a party to. The use of the word 'act' in both sections 35 and 35A indicates that it is not necessary for a contract to have been entered into, hence the choice of the word 'transaction'. It may well be, for example, that a charitable/political gift or donation is covered by these amendments. Knowledge that the act is beyond the powers of the directors is not in itself deemed to be bad faith. It is possible, in the absence of case law, that the lack of good faith now means the presence of fraud. However, good faith is presumed unless the contrary is proved. In respect to the word 'constitution', this includes not only the company's memorandum and articles but also limitations placed upon the directors by means of resolutions passed at meetings or agreements between members.

As with section 35, a member may seek an injunction to prevent an abuse of power by a director but cannot do so once a legal obligation on the part of the company has already arisen. Again, as with s. 35, the directors remain liable for abuse of their power, but their action may be ratified by the company through the passing of an ordinary resolution.

For section 35A to operate a plaintiff has the burden of establishing that:

a) he was unconnected with the company;
b) he acted in good faith;
c) he was dealing with the company;
d) he is not in business with the directors or with others authorized by the board;
e) the limitation was derived from the company's constitution.

A party to a transaction with a company is not bound to enquire as to whether it is permitted by the company's memorandum, or as to any limitation on the powers of the board of directors, to bind the company or authorize others to do so.

Section 35B has effectively abolished what was the doctrine of constructive notice which meant that persons dealing with a company could not claim ignorance of its constitution – as a company's memorandum and articles are public documents they are open for public inspection, i.e. a third party was deemed to have knowledge of their contents.

A broad statement of a company's objects (CA 1985, s. 3A)

A company's objects clause may now include an object that the company can carry on business as a 'general commercial company'. This means that the company can carry on any trade or business whatsoever and has the power to do anything which is incidental to the carrying on of any trade or business. However, lenders may still specify the purpose for which the loan is advanced. The company may then be liable for breach of contract if the loan money is used for other purposes.

The Department of Trade and Industry's wish for a short object clause is now fulfilled.

Section 3A appears to negate the European Community requirement that all companies must be registered with an object clause. However, members and persons dealing with a company really ought to be aware of the wide varying powers of companies with a 3A type object clause and to guard themselves accordingly. One unclear aspect is whether a company's ability to do anything incidental to the carrying on of any trade or business relates to the current business activity only, or whether it will also include any business activity in the future.

Alteration and extension of the objects clause (CA 1985, s. 4)

A company registered with a specific object may by special resolution alter its object clause to include a provision to enable it to carry on business as a general commercial company. It is possible for dissident members holding at least 15 per cent of the nominal value of the company's issued share capital (or any share class of it), or if the company is not limited by shares then at least 15 per cent of the company's members, to petition the court asking that the alteration be cancelled (s. 5). Such a petition must be made within 21 days after the date on which the alteration resolution was passed.

A petitioner must not have voted or otherwise consented to the resolution (s. 5).

Voidable transactions involving directors (CA 1985, s. 322A)

Transactions entered into by the company with its directors or connected persons which exceed the directors' power are voidable at the option of the company.

General comments on ultra vires

From the above sections it would appear that the ultra vires doctrine has been, in the absence of fraud, effectively abolished in relation to a company's acts involving outsiders. Shareholders are given some protection in so far as they may seek an injunction to restrain the company from performing on ultra vires act. However, this may have limited effect if the dissidents number fewer than 25 per cent and hence are unable to prevent a special resolution altering the object clause. In this case they may apply to the court within 21 days to have the resolution set aside if the dissidents hold at least 15 per cent of the shares. Shareholders still retain their rights (particularly under sections 459–461) to apply to the court for relief if the affairs of the company are being carried on in a manner unfairly prejudicial to some part of the shareholders. This may include relief where the company enters into transactions beyond its stated object.

Directors retain their liability for exceeding their powers. They may, however, be relieved from liability by special resolution if they act beyond the company's stated object, or by ordinary resolution if they exceed their own powers but act within the company's capacity.

Review question

Discuss how amendments to the Companies Act 1985 have overturned old case law on the contractual capacity of companies.

4 The liability clause

The liability clause does not relate to the company but to the shareholders (members) of it.

If the company is limited by shares or by guarantee then this clause will simply state, 'The liability of the members is limited'. Generally commercial companies are limited by shares so that the liability clause will fix the liability of shareholders to the amount, if any, still outstanding on their shares. If the company is limited by guarantee the clause will limit liability to the amount which the members (guarantors) have agreed to contribute to the assets in the event of liquidation. As a form of shareholder protection a shareholder's liability cannot be increased without his written consent (s. 16)

Companies limited by guarantee are normally formed for educational or charitable purposes obtaining their capital usually through endowments or subscriptions. Such companies may also be limited by shares so that dual liability applies in that on liquidation not only will the guarantee have to be honoured but also payment of any outstanding amount on unpaid shares. In practice, however, the amount guaranteed will be quite small.

Alteration of liability

It is possible for a limited company to use re-registration procedures to become an unlimited company and vice versa (ss. 49–52). However, once one re-registration has been given then a second one is forbidden (ss. 49, 51).

As the main advantage of incorporation is to obtain limited liability for its members, unlimited companies are rare. Where they occur the liability of their members is the same as general partners in a partnership in that they must, if assets are insufficient to cover liabilities, contribute without limit to pay off company debts. However, an advantage of unlimited companies is that they do not have to file annual returns with the registrar (unless the company is a subsidiary of, or the holding company of, a limited company) and so may gain a degree of privacy (s. 254). Also there is no restriction on the return of capital to members.

Re-registration

The following procedures may be utilized.

A private limited company to an unlimited company

The application to re-register must set out the alterations to the memorandum and articles that will be necessary. In addition the registrar must receive the following:

- the official form of assent to the re-registration signed by, or on behalf of, *all* the members;
- a statutory declaration by the directors that the signatories constitute the whole membership of the company;
- a copy of the new memorandum and articles.

Clearly members need to think carefully before agreeing to the resolution to re-register for if it takes place then they would become fully exposed if the company went into insolvency.

If the application is successful then the registrar will file all the above documents and issue the company with a new certificate of incorporation which signifies that from that moment on the company's status has been changed (s. 50).

An unlimited company to a private limited company

A special resolution needs to be passed at a general meeting (s. 51) that after re-registration the company is to be limited by shares (and what the capital will be), or by guarantee. The application itself needs to be on the official form signed by a director, or the company secretary, and sent with a copy of the new memorandum and articles to the registrar on or after the day on which a copy of the resolution is received by him.

If the registrar is minded to grant the application then all the documents submitted will be filed and a new certificate issued (s. 52). The new certificate confirms that the company is now changed to a private limited one and the alterations to the memorandum and articles approved by the special resolution take effect.

An unlimited company to a public limited company

The procedure is the same as for the re-registration of a private limited to an unlimited company but clearly the special resolution needs to include a statement that it is to be limited by shares and what the capital is to be (s. 48).

5 Capital clause

If shares are divided into classes, e.g. ordinary or preference, then this is usually done in the articles.

If the company has a share capital then this clause will state the authorized or nominal capital and its division into shares of a fixed value of any amount (s. 2). The fixed value chosen becomes the nominal or par value of the shares. For a public limited company it must not be less than the prescribed minimum (s. 11) currently set at £50,000 (s. 118). Each subscriber to the memorandum undertakes to take the number of shares set against their name and for both private and public companies this is at least one share.

Shares may be issued at the nominal value (called par) or at a higher than nominal value (called premium) but not below their nominal value. However, once allotted (or even before) the shares will find their own market value which may have little relation to the nominal value given by the promoters or the first directors. Indeed if the issue is spectacularly unsuccessful the market price could be a discount to their nominal value. This market discount is permitted but as mentioned such a discount is not permitted on issue.

Alteration of share capital

See Chapter 8, Capital, for the methods that may be used to alter a company's share capital.

6 The associate clause

A minor may subscribe (Re Laxon & Co. (1892). His contract to take shares is voidable but not void. Also all members may be non-British.

The subscribers to the memorandum declare that they desire to be formed into a company and agree to take the number of shares given opposite their full names. Each subscriber must sign the memorandum in the presence of least one witness old enough to understand what he is doing (s. 2). There must be at least two subscribers (unless it is a single-member company) and their obligations are to pay for the shares they have subscribed for, to sign the articles (if they do not then their constructive signature will bind them) and to appoint the first directors (if the articles say that the subscribers are to act as directors until such appointment is made then they must do so).

The role of the Registrar of Companies

The registrar must not register an applicant's memorandum until he is satisfied that all the statutory requirements have been complied with. Once satisfied that all is in order then the memorandum and articles will be registered and filed. At this point a certificate of incorporation will be granted. If the company is limited then this will be stated on the certificate and if public limited then this will also be stated. The certificate is conclusive evidence that all the requirements of the Act have been met so that a later discovery of an irregularity in the registration process will not invalidate the registration.

The date of incorporation is the date from which subscribers to the memorandum, or later members of the company, will be a body incorporated under the name given in the memorandum or any later alteration. The newly incorporated entity is now legally recognized in its own right and may exercise all the functions of an incorporated company (*Salomon v Salomon & Co.* (1897)). The persons named in the statement of directors and secretary will be taken to have been duly appointed as the first directors and secretary.

Chapter summary

- The memorandum fixes the powers and objects of the company and the outside world.
- Restrictions over the name of a company are meant to prevent: confusion (with an existing company's name); committing a criminal offence (certain names are protected); being offensive (a wide discretion is given to the Registrar and Secretary of State); or taking another trader's reputation (the passing off of a trade name).
- A company's name must have the suffix *limited* or *public limited company*. However, certain private limited companies may dispense with 'limited'. These are companies with charitable, religious or educational objects.
- The Companies Act 1985 and the Business Names Act 1985 both require publication or display of company names, e.g. on business documentation, at a company premise or when requested to do so by an interested party.
- The object clause formerly governed what a company could do, any act outside the object being termed ultra vires and hence illegal. While courts were willing to imply activity reasonably incidental to the stated object they, together with Parliament, were not prepared to go too far and hence companies began to have long object clauses.
- A company may alter the liability of its members by means of re-registration procedures. These require: a special resolution passed to alter the memorandum and articles; an application signed by a director or company secretary sent to the Registrar with copies of the new memorandum and articles. A new certificate of incorporation is later issued.
- The capital clause will state the amount of capital that a company is authorized to issue (for a public limited company there is a minimum of £50,000) and how it is divided into shares of a fixed amount. The shares can be issued at their authorized value (also termed nominal or par value), or at a higher than nominal value (known as a premium), but they cannot be issued at a discount – although on trading the market price may be below their nominal value.

Discussion questions

1 Explain in outline the compulsory content of a memorandum of association.
2 In what circumstances must a company disclose its name?
3 Under the Companies Act 1985 what protection is given to a person entering into a contract with a company that is ultra vires by that company's object clause given in its memorandum of association?

Case study exercise

A group of investors decide to form a company called Princess Diane (Mementos) Limited. Its object clause states that it will:

   1 carry on business as a manufacturer and supplier of souvenir ware;
   2 borrow money to enable 1 above to be achieved;
   3 take 1 and 2 to be main and independent objects.

(Assume that the company is incorporated.) Subsequently the company pass a special resolution that they will stop being involved in souvenir ware and switch to trout farming, requiring additional working capital. The Wessex Bank plc loan the company £250,0000 secured by a fixed charge on the company's freehold factory-shop.

   a) Comment on the likelihood of the name chosen for the company being registered.
   b) Advise Wessex Bank plc whether they will be able to recover their loan.

Further reading

Abolition of the Ultra Vires Doctrine and Agency Problems, J. Poole (1991), Co. Law, 43.
Ultra Vires in Modern Company Law, K.W. Wedderburn (1983), MLR, 204.
As the company's constitution (memorandum and articles) may be taken
collectively, see also Further Reading at the end of Chapter 6, Articles of Association.

6 The articles of association

Introduction

The articles of association is the document that internally regulates the company. It is similar in concept to the list of rules that regulate a club or society. With companies the articles deal with such managerial matters as: the admission of members; the issue and transfer of shares; the powers delegated to the directors; the procedure of meetings; the declaration of dividends; and the appointment of a company secretary.

Objectives

The purpose of this chapter is to enable students to appreciate fully the importance of the articles in acting as a contractual document, binding the company and its shareholders or members.

Key concepts

- The significance of Table A articles
- The legal relationships vis-à-vis the company and members that the articles create
- That alteration of the articles is possible but must be made for the benefit of the company as a whole.

Table A articles

Every company limited by shares must have a set of articles. These articles can be very long and the specimen given in the Table A–F Regulations 1985 is 118 paragraphs in length. If a company does not produce their own articles then they are deemed to be governed by Table A (s. 8).

Companies by guarantee or unlimited companies have Table C, D or E specimen articles.

Table A takes the stance that shareholders are remote from their board of directors and need formal elections at annual general meetings (AGM) where a third of directors will retire by annual rotation. Underlying Table A are restrictions to prevent power concentrations from developing, e.g. directors offering themselves periodically for re-election, and to assure properly constituted board meetings, AGMs, etc. If it is intended to form a small private company, especially one that is essentially a family one, then a structure as envisaged by

Table A will be unsuitable in that a simplified form of articles may be desirable, e.g. no periodic re-election of directors, informal company meetings. Therefore, while keeping some Table A provisions to meet legal requirements much can be jettisoned. In practice companies usually modify Table A to suit their own needs, and if a public company, to meet conditions imposed by the Stock Exchange Council. In particular, private companies follow Table A with only minor alteration and this results in a saving on costs.

The articles, whether individually drafted or the Table A specimen, must be signed by each subscriber to the memorandum in the presence of at least one witness who will attest the validity of the signature (s. 7 (3)). Clearly the articles must not contain anything illegal or this will ultra vires the memorandum. Indeed, as the articles are subordinate to the memorandum it means that the articles cannot give powers that are not given by the memorandum. However, matters that need not be placed in the memorandum can appear in the articles and for purposes of interpreting the former it is possible, as the two documents are to be read together, to seek guidance from the latter (*Anderson's Case* (1877)).

The consequences of the memorandum and articles

Also termed a statutory contract.

On registration the memorandum and articles bind the company and the members as if each member had individually given his seal (s. 14). Therefore, on subscribing to the memorandum and articles the first members enter into an implied contract between themselves and the company. This contractual construction of the articles is long established (*Welton v Saffery* (1897) and has been affirmed by the European Court of Justice in *Powell Duffryn plc v Petereit* (1992).

It is said that a member acquiring his interest in the company accepts the risk that this may happen.

The case dealt with whether a term could be implied into the articles. The decision was that the articles of association are different from a normal contract so that a term could not be implied for business efficiency.

Although creating a contractual relationship, the normal remedy on breach by the company is not a damage award against the company but an injunction served on it. This is because a court is anxious to keep the company's capital intact. However, if a member is owed any sum, such as an unpaid dividend, then he is allowed to sue to recover what is owed. Also the contract will be valid even though its terms may be altered in the future without the unanimous agreement of the members (s. 9) and when shares are transferred; provided that it is done in accordance with what the articles may say, the recipient will take them with the encumbrance that he will have to adhere to the memorandum and articles.

A difficulty with section 14 is that it is still unclear as to the true nature of the contract that it creates. Uncertainty has not been helped by conflicting judicial decisions. A concise summary of section 14 was given by Steyn LJ in *Bratton Seymour Service Co. Ltd v Oxenborough* (1992):

By virtue of s. 14 the articles of association become, upon registration, a contract between a company and its members. It is, however, a statutory contract of a special nature with its own distinctive features. It derives its binding force not from a bargain struck between parties but from the terms of the statute. It is binding only in so far as it affects the rights and obligations between the company and the members acting in their capacity as members. If it contains provisions conferring rights and obligations on outsiders, then those provisions do not bite as part of the contract between the company and the members, even if the outsider is coincidentally a member. Similarly, if the provisions are not truly referable to the rights and obligations of members as such it does not operate as a contract. Moreover, the contract can be altered by a special resolution without the consent of all the contracting parties. It is also, unlike an ordinary contract, not defeasible on the grounds of misrepresentation, common law mistake in equity, undue influence or duress. Moreover, as Dillon LJ has pointed out, it cannot be rectified on the grounds of mistake.

From the above it can be seen that under section 14 a number of binding relationships are created. These are discussed in the following sections.

The company is contractually bound to each individual member in his capacity as a member

Some commentators on company law have periodically raised the issue that section 14, in both the current Companies Act and in its antecedents, does not in fact bind the company so that in saying that it does is the use of a legal fiction. But the Law Commission when examining shareholders' remedies noted that while section 14 does not expressly state that the company is bound by its own articles it was, in their opinion, clear in the wording used in the section that the company was so bound. Accordingly, the Law Commission felt, on this point that there was no reason to amend section 14.

Therefore, by implication the company is contractually bound to each member:

The Law Commission's Report on Shareholder Remedies (Law Com. No. 246, October 1997; the prior Consultation Paper was No. 142).

Pender v Lushington (1877)
The articles said that members would have 1 vote for every 10 shares held but that no one member was to have more than 100 votes. One member had over 1,000 shares but was unable to use his full voting potential. He therefore transferred some shares to P who was his nominee. At a meeting the chairman, L, refused to accept P's votes on the ground that the transfer to P had been a ploy to avoid the provisions in the articles.

Held: P's votes had to be counted as not to do so would be a breach of his person rights as a member.

also:

Wood v Odessa Waterworks Co. (1889)
OW had applied its profits to the construction of works at the expense of paying its shareholders a dividend. To get over the problem its directors, who were allowed by the articles to declare a dividend, passed a resolution granting the shareholders interest bearing debenture bonds.

Held: What was proposed by the directors' resolution was not in accordance with the articles and therefore the directors were restrained by an injunction from acting on the resolution.

See also *Salmon v Quin & Axtens Ltd* (1908) which supported *Wood v Odessa Waterworks Co.* (1889). Both *Pender v Lushington* and *Wood v Odessa Waterworks Co.* are examples of minority protection.

Should a member wish to take action against the company for breach of contract then the limitation period is 6 years as s. 14, contracts are not, despite the notional signing by seal, speciality contracts (Limitation Act 1980; *Re Compania de Electicidad de la Provincia de Buenos Aires Ltd* (1980)).

However, it must be stressed that a company is not bound by a provision given in the articles to a member acting in another capacity:

> ### Eley v Positive Life Assurance Co. (1876)
>
> The articles of PLA contained a clause appointing E, who was a shareholder, as the company's solicitor for life. He was later dismissed from the appointment and brought an action for breach of contract.
>
> Held: The articles did not form a contract between E and PLA for although he was a shareholder the articles could not give him contractual rights in any other capacity including that of a company secretary.

Where a person takes a position with the articles setting the remuneration then while the articles are not themselves a contract, per *Eley v Positive Life Assurance Co.* (1876), the terms contained in the articles may be incorporated into the service contract:

> ### Swabey v Port Darwin Gold Mining Co. (1889)
>
> Directors had served PDGM without an express service contract but the articles did provide for remuneration at a fixed rate per year. PDGM tried to reduce this by a retrospective resolution and S, a director, sued for breach of contract.
>
> Held (Court of Appeal): Although the articles did not constitute a contract it was nevertheless possible to obtain from the articles terms under which the directors served.
>
> also:
>
> ### Re New British Iron Co. (1898)
>
> Article 62 provided that the remuneration of the directors should be an annual sum of £1,000. A director sued the company for his fees.
>
> Held: The articles are not in themselves a contract between the company and the directors:
>
> But where, on the footing of the articles, the directors are employed by the company and accept office, the terms of article 62 are embodied in and form part of the contract between the company and the directors. (Wright J)

Such terms may be changed by alteration of the articles but a change must not be retrospective.

Table A, article 84 appointment

If the company does not have its own articles then the specimen articles under Table A will apply. Those appointed to senior positions within the company would be advised to have a separate contract between the company and themselves or else they may be at risk:

> ### Read v Astoria Garage (Streatham) Ltd (1952)
>
> R was appointed managing director of AG for an unspecified period. Later R was dismissed by the board with one month's notice and this was confirmed by the company passing an ordinary resolution at a general meeting. R claimed damages for breach of contract as no reasonable period of notice had been given.

Held: R's claim would fail for as he had been appointed under Table A he could be dismissed without notice by a resolution at a general meeting.

also:

Re Richmond Gate Property Co. (1965)

A managing director had been appointed under Table A which provides that '... a managing director shall receive such remuneration ... as the directors may determine.' The company went into liquidation before his salary was set. He sued for breach of contract.

Held: His claim would fail as no salary had been fixed.

The managing director's claim for a quantum meruit (i.e. for as much as he has earned or deserved) also failed as the existence of an express contract excludes a quantum meruit claim.

Review question

A company's articles of association contain:

> Burns is appointed chief executive officer for as long as he wishes to hold that position with his salary being recommended by the company's remuneration committee and confirmed by the company in a general meeting.

Burns is later summarily dismissed from his position and seeks compensation. Advise him.

Each member of the company in their capacity as a member is contractually bound to the company

Therefore, provisions in the articles must be treated as being contractual terms:

Hickman v Kent Sheep Breeders Association (1915)

The articles of the association provided for disputes between the company and its members to be referred to arbitration. The association wished to expel H from his membership and he applied for an injunction to restrain them from starting a legal ction.

Held: H was entitled to succeed for the dispute concerned membership rights and the articles provided for initial reference to be made to arbitration rather than legal action. This provision had to be honoured.

But if the matter is not related to a membership issue then the articles will not apply:

Beattie v Beattie Ltd (1938)

The articles provided that any dispute between the company and a member be referred to arbitration. A director (B), who was also a member, fell out with the company and sought to use the articles to stop the company taking court action instead of arbitration.

> Held: As the dispute was between the company and B in his capacity as a director his claim must fail. It had nothing to do with membership.

A member being bound by the articles also applies in respect to an alteration of the articles in that any alteration, provided that it is made in the proper manner, will be binding as if the alteration had been originally in the articles (*Borland's Trustee v Steel Bros & Co. Ltd* (1901).

Members of the company are contractually bound to each other

Pre-emption rights obligate a company who wish to issue equity shares to first offer them to existing members on the same, or more favourable, terms and in proportion to their present holding (s. 89).

Where disputes arise commonly in small, private companies, they are normally over pre-emption rights, or where the articles will require members to buy the shares of a member who wishes to 'retire'. The company is not itself a party to these actions as the contract is directly enforceable member-to-member:

> ### Rayfield v Hands (1960)
> The company articles stated: 'Every member who intends to transfer his shares shall inform the directors who will take them at a fair price.' R told the directors that he wanted to transfer his shares but the directors declined to take them.
>
> Held: The use of the word 'will' gave them no option; it imposed on them a legal obligation to buy the shares offered.

With private companies, where the shareholding is often within a family circle, it would be distasteful for members to sue other members. Therefore, it is common to have in the articles a two-stage 'transfer' process in the following manner:

a) The transferor informs the company that he wishes to transfer shares (a transferor failing to do so may be sued by the company).
b) The company will then inform other members of this fact and enquire whether they want to buy them (if the company fails to do so then the members may sue it).

Review question

To what extent are the articles binding on:

a) the company;
b) the members?

Alteration of the articles

Alteration of the articles may be achieved in three ways:

1 Alteration by special resolution

2 Alteration through assent
3 Alteration by a written resolution made by a private company.

Alteration by special resolution

An alteration to the articles will require a special resolution to show that the corporate collective will is such that a change ought to be made (s. 9). Any clause in the articles which says that they are inalterable is invalid (*Southern Foundries v Shirlaw* (1940)).

See also *Russell v Northern Bank Development Corporation Ltd* (1992) referred to later.

Invalid alterations

Certain alterations, even if a special resolution is passed, are prohibited. These are:

a) an alteration against: the general law; the Companies Act; or the company's memorandum;
b) an alteration which increases a member's liability unless that member gives his written consent (s. 16). Therefore, a member cannot be forced to buy more shares;
c) an alteration to abolish the annual general meeting (s. 366);
d) an attempt to shorten the notice period of a general meeting to less than 21 days or 14 days (s. 369);
e) an alteration that deprives members of their minority protection rights (see later);
f) an alteration that is retrospective in its effect (see Swaby v Port Darwin Mining Co. (1889)).

Where an alteration results in a breach of contract with a third party

An alteration to the articles cannot be used to justify a breach of contract with a third party. This includes the situation of a shareholder having a separate contract with the company:

Southern Foundries Ltd v Shirlaw (1940)

Under a written agreement, not subject to the articles, S was appointed in December 1933 as managing director of SF. The articles of SF said that a managing director could be removed from office 'subject to the provisions of any contract between him and the company'. In 1936 SF was taken over by Federation Foundries Limited who altered the articles of SF giving a power to dismiss any director on provision of notice. In April 1937 SF attempted to remove S from being a director which meant that another article operated to remove him from the position of managing director. S claimed damages for breach of contract.

Held (House of Lords): S's dismissal under the altered articles equalled a breach of his service contract and he was therefore entitled to damages. Even if S's service contract had been subject to the articles there were no grounds, in the original articles, to dismiss him by reason of notice so dismissal would still have been wrong.

This was a Table A situation in that the articles stated that the board of directors may appoint one of their number to be the managing director. Consequently, a managing director so appointed will automatically lose that office if his directorship ceases.

In *Southern Foundries Ltd v Shirlaw* (1940) Lord Porter stated the general principle thus:

(i) A company cannot be precluded from altering its articles thereby giving itself power to act upon provisions of the altered articles, but so to act may nevertheless be a breach of contract if it is contrary to a stipulation in a contract validly made before the alteration.

(ii) Nor can an injunction be granted to prevent the adoption of the new articles. In that sense, they are binding on all and sundry, but for the company to act upon them will none the less render it liable in damages if such action is contrary to the previous engagements of the company.

From the judgement in this case it is accepted that any member voting for the alteration will also be liable to the plaintiff, provided that it was inevitable that the alteration would result in the contract being broken, on the basis that their vote induced the company to break its contract with the third party.

Voting on the alteration to the articles

Voting as a member is a personal property right but no member may use a veto to deprive others of the opportunity for alteration. Weighted voting rights are perfectly valid (*Bushell v Faith* (1970)) and are in fact not uncommon on a resolution to alter the articles. Also an agreement outside the articles between members as to how they will use their voting rights may be legal:

Russell v Northern Bank Development Corporation Ltd (1992)

Tyrone Brick Limited and its four shareholders entered into an agreement, that was said to take precedence over the articles, that:

> No further share capital shall be created or issued in the company or the rights attaching to the shares already in issue in any way altered ... without the written consent of each of the parties hereto.

The company, through its board, later tried to increase the nominal capital and R sought an injunction to prevent this on the basis that the increase would be a breach of the agreement.

Held (House of Lords): The principle that a company cannot forfeit its right to alter its articles was confirmed. However, an agreement outside the articles between shareholders as to how they will use their vote on an alteration of articles resolution is not automatically invalid. Here the company's undertaking was unenforceable but not that of its shareholders even though it effectively required all the members to support such a resolution for it to be successful.

The House of Lords also accepted that a requirement for the unanimous consent of shareholders to an alteration of articles was invalid whether it was given in the memorandum, articles or in a separate agreement.

Where the alteration amounts to fraud on the minority

Where the company has different classes of shares the articles usually provide that rights of each class may be altered with the consent of a certain majority of the shareholders of that class. What may lead to conflict between shareholders is where a general meeting will itself attempt to alter the rights of a class of shareholders without the consent of that class. While it can be argued that all shareholders know that their rights may be altered at any time by a special resolution there is a suspicion that a majority shareholder could alter the articles in order to deprive minority shareholders of their rights. To curb mis-use of the special resolution procedure minority protection has been developed. Therefore, the question to ask is whether or not the majority have exercised their powers for a valid corporate purpose that will benefit the company as a whole or, alternatively, will benefit holders of a share class generally; or, will the alteration unfairly discriminate against the minority? The following are two illustrations of the rule that an alteration must not be primarily designed to injure other members:

a) *An alteration that causes the minority a financial injury*

Menier v Hooper's Telegraphic Works (1874)

The majority of the shareholders of Company A were also shareholders of Company B. At a meeting of Company A the majority passed a resolution to compromise (e.g. to settle out of court) an action against Company B in a manner felt to be favourable to Company B but unfavourable to Company A.

Held (Court of Appeal): The minority shareholders of Company A were successful in their petition to have the compromise resolution set aside – the majority had put something into their own pockets at the expense of the minority.

---

b) *An alteration to expropriate a shareholder's interest*

Dafen Tinplate Co. Ltd v Llanelly Steel Co. (1920)

The shareholders of LS included steel companies who appointed the directors of LS. To avoid conflicts of interest the articles of LS were altered so that an existing shareholder could be bought out at a fair price set by the board. DT, a shareholder of LS, usually bought its steel from LS but later wanted to buy elsewhere. LS regarded DT's action as disloyal and attempted to exercise the right to buy them out at a fair price.

Held: The alteration to the articles was void. It went too far in that any shareholder could be forced out whatever his conduct.

This case can be contrasted with *Sidebottom v Kershaw, Leese & Co.* (1920) that immediately follows.

Apparently, for an alteration to be valid it, firstly, must be within the powers given in the memorandum; and secondly, there must be no injury to the legitimate interests of the minority without a reasonable prospect of advantage to the company as a whole. The following are two illustrations of this principle in operation:

a) *Where the majority may be allowed to exclude the minority*

Sidebottom v Kershaw (1920)

The directors of a private company were given by an alteration of the articles the power to demand of any shareholder who competed against the company that he transfer his shares at a fair price to nominees of the directors.

Held: The alteration was valid as it would be for the benefit of the company as a whole in that any competitor against the company would be ousted from the membership.

---

b) An alteration that while seriously affecting the interests of the minority was for the overall benefit of the company:

Allen v Gold Reefs of West Africa Ltd (1900)

The articles gave GRL a lien on all shares 'not fully paid up' in respect to calls due to the company. A owed money on unpaid calls but he also held other shares that were fully paid (and hence not subject to a lien). GRL later altered its articles deleting the words 'not fully paid' so that it would now have a lien over all of A's shares.

Held (Court of Appeal): The alteration, even though it affected only one shareholder (A), had been for the benefit of the company as a whole and was therefore valid.

What is benefit of the company as a whole?

There are in fact two questions that need to be asked. Firstly, *what* is meant by the phrase 'benefit of the company as a whole' when used as a test to determine the legality of an alteration to the articles; and, secondly, as a company is an artificial person unable to think for itself, and hence dependent on others for guidance, *who* exactly decides what is for its benefit as a whole? These questions, as they are so interrelated, cannot be separated.

Historically, the issue has proved problematic. In *Brown v British Abrasive Wheel* (1919), Astbury J is believed to have set out a two-part test. Firstly, the decision to alter the articles had to be 'within the ordinary principle of justice', e.g. made in good faith; and, secondly, the actual alteration had to be 'for the benefit of the company as a whole'. But in *Sidebottom v Kershaw, Leese & Co.* (1919), a Court of Appeal case decided later in the same year, a majority said that the test, for the benefit of the company as a whole, was an undivided one. However, judicial clarity came in:

Shuttleworth v Cox Brothers & Co. Ltd (Maidenhead) Ltd (1927)

Article 22 of the articles stated that CB was to have five directors and:

... each of them shall be entitled to hold office so long as he shall live unless he becomes disqualified from any of the causes specified in article 22.

Article 22 went on to provide several causes which would justify his disqualification. S, a director, was also appointed the works manager and on 22 occasions within 12 months he failed to account for monies he had received. After an inquiry he was dismissed from his position of works manager. The other directors wishing also to dismiss him from his directorship held an extraordinary general meeting and altered article 22 by adding to the specified dismissal causes '(or) if he shall be requested in writing by all the other directors to resign his office.'
Later all four directors requested in writing that S resign his directorship. S claimed wrongful dismissal.

Held: The alteration to the articles and the action taken under it were both valid. As Shuttleworth, over a period of a year, had persistently defrauded the company it was for the benefit of the company as a whole that he be dismissed.

The significance of *Shuttleworth* is in the Court of Appeal rejecting the proposition, given in earlier cases, that it is for the court to say what is for the benefit of the company in favour of letting the shareholders themselves determine this:

> It is not the court which manages the affairs of the company, it is the shareholders through the directors whom they appoint; and so long as the shareholders act honestly and endeavour to consider only the matters they should legitimately consider, namely, the interests of the company as a whole and such action as will promote those interests, it seems to me quite immaterial that the court would come to a different conclusion. The absence of any reasonable ground for a decision that a certain action is conducive to the benefit of the company may be, first of all, a ground for finding lack of good faith, because it may be said that there were no grounds on which honest people could have come to this decision and you may infer bad faith; but, secondly, given honesty, the fact that the company has come to a decision for which there are no reasonable grounds may show that they have not considered the matters that they ought to have considered. On both those grounds you may set a decision aside, but, in my view, if they act honestly, and if the decision is such that honest and reasonable people might come to, the fact that the court would have come to a different decision is no grounds whatever for the court interfering. (Scruton LJ)

Effectively, in *Shuttleworth* the court substituted a subjective approach for an objective one; but see later comments on the counter view.

The reason why the courts are unwilling to second guess the majority shareholders who pass an alteration resolution was succinctly put by Scruton LJ in *Shuttleworth* that:

> to adopt any view of that sort would be to make the court manager of the affairs of innumerable companies instead of the directors to whom the shareholders have entrusted that right of management.

Consequently, only in circumstances so exceptional that the allegation to be acting in the interests of the company as a whole seems clearly to be perverse will a court intervene. An example of this reluctance to become involved is illustrated by:

Greenhalgh v Aderne Cinemas (1951)

The articles included a pre-emption clause. Here a majority shareholder wanted to transfer shares directly to an outsider without first offering them to existing members. He used his greater voting strength to pass a resolution altering the articles so as to achieve his objective. The resolution meant that the majority shareholder could sell his shares to a non-member but G, a minority shareholder, had to offer his shares to the majority shareholder first.

Held: There was no fraud on the minority as the majority shareholder action would result in members having the benefit of more marketable shares.

It must be mentioned that the debate concerning whether there is a one- or two-part test for determining the question for the benefit of the company as a whole has yet to be resolved. Some commendations side with a two-part test still being present putting forward the view that courts, wary of becoming embroiled in internal company conflicts, prefer to concentrate on the subjective part of a two-part test at the expense of the objective part so that it merely appears that there is an undivided test *Shuttleworth v Cox Brothers & Co. Ltd* (1927) is cited for this proposition. This is yet another reason why apparently so simple a question – what is to be the benefit to the company as a whole? – is so difficult to answer satisfactorily. In practice, though, a court does seem to adopt a balance sheet approach in that the interests of minority shareholders are carefully compared to the perceived benefit that will occur to the company as a whole if the alteration is confirmed.

Unfair prejudicial act on members

Unfair prejudicial acts are dealt with in Chapter 14, Minority Protection.

There are provisions where a court may stop or (rarely) amend a proposed alteration to the articles on the ground that the alteration as it stands is unfairly prejudicial to a member(s) (s. 459). Where this alternative action is available, minority shareholders ought to consider it seriously as courts are prone to be more willing to exercise their discretion when dealing with a petition for unfair prejudicial conduct than when having to decide whether to quash a resolution to alter the articles.

Review question

For a public limited company how can the articles be altered and what restrictions apply?

Alteration through assent

When *all* the members agree to the alteration then no meeting or resolution is required:

Cane v Jones (1980)

All members signed an agreement which took away the chairman's casting vote. Later some members said the alteration was invalid as no special resolution had been tabled.

Held: Where all members are in unanimous agreement they can make a binding decision on any matter requiring a majority of votes at a general meeting. The alteration was therefore valid.

The decision in *Cane v Jones* (1980), that the unanimous consent of all members to an alteration negates the need to hold a general meeting at which a resolution is passed, is known as the *Duomatic principle*:

> ... where it can be shown that all shareholders who have a right to attend and vote at a general meeting of the company assent to some matter which a general meeting of the company could carry into effect, that assent is as binding as a resolution in general meeting would be ... (Buckley J, Re *Duomatic Ltd* (1969)).

Alteration by a written resolution made by a private company

This provision is intended to provide private companies with an efficient method of altering their articles without having to hold a general meeting. Simply any change to the articles that could have been made by a resolution in a general meeting (e.g. a s. 9) may also be made by means of a written resolution signed by all the members of the company who at the time of the resolution would be entitled to attend and vote at a general meeting (s. 381 (A)). This provision will still be available even though the articles may require a different method for alteration. This statutory method of alteration is the same as alteration through unanimous assent under the common law, i.e. the *Duomatic* principle is applied.

Notification and publicity of an alteration to the articles

Notification to the Registrar

An alteration of the articles whether by special resolution under s. 9, or by the unanimous consent of the members, must be notified to the Registrar of companies with 14 days of the alteration (s. 380). The alteration will then be registered. The Registrar must be provided not only with a copy of the resolution or agreement but must also receive a full set of the articles incorporating the necessary alterations. Failure to notify the Registrar of an alteration, or to provide him with a copy of the amended articles, is a summary offence for which the company, or any of its officers, may be fined if the omission was found to have been done, or authorized, knowingly or wilfully (s. 6 (3)).

Publicity in the London Gazette

After receipt of the alteration to the articles the Registrar will arrange for a notice to be published in the *London Gazette* saying that he has received an alteration to the articles. The significance of the notice in the *Gazette* is that until it is published a company cannot hold another party to the alteration unless the other knew and consented to the alteration. In addition, if a person can show that despite publication he was unavoidably prevented from knowing of the alteration then it will not be fully effective until 15 days after notice of it was published (s. 42).

Chapter summary

- For internal management every company must have a set of articles signed by subscribers to the memorandum. Table A articles are commonly adopted with appropriate modifications
- The articles establish a contractual relationship between the company and its members (s. 14), also between member and member, but it is a special contract that has yet to be fully defined.
- One consequence of s. 14 is that the company is contractually bound to members but only in their capacity as a member. Case law has featured recording of votes (per *Pender v Lushington*; *Wood v Odessa Waterworks Co.*), but no liability applies where a member is acting in another capacity (per *Eley v Positive Life Assurance Co.*), but the articles may contain terms that can be drawn down into another contract (per *Swabey v Port Darwin Gold Mining Co.*).
- Under the articles each member is contractually bound to the company so that provisions relating to membership matters in the articles equate to contractual terms (per *Hickman v Kent Sheep Breeders Association*), with non-membership matters not applying (per *Beattie v Beattie Ltd*).

- Under the articles members are contractually bound to each other (per *Rayfield v Hands*).
- The articles may be altered by means of a special resolution (s. 9) but a number of alteration resolutions are automatically invalid, most notably an alteration to overcome a breach of contract with a third party (per *Southern Foundries Ltd v Shirlaw*).
- Voting on an alteration resolution is a personal property right and a member may vote in their own interest. Agreements outside the articles on joint voting may be valid (per *Russell v Northern Bank Development Corp Ltd*): Weighted voting rights are also valid (*Bushell v Faith*) but the use of a veto to block the votes of others (interference with a personal property right) is not.
- An alteration must not be a fraud on the minority (per *Menier v Hooper's Telegraphic Works*; *Dafen Tinplate Co. Ltd v Llanelly Steel Co.*), but if justifiable the majority may exclude the minority from membership (per *Sidebottom v Kershaw, Leese & Co. Ltd*; *Allen v Gold Reefs of West Africa Ltd*).
- The concept of benefit of the company as a whole is problematic. Whether there is a two-part test (per *Brown v British Abrasive Wheels*), or a single test (per *Shuttleworth v Cox Brothers & Co. Ltd*) is still unclear. What is settled is that it is for the shareholders themselves to determine what is in the company's best interests. Consequently, only in exceptional circumstances will a court be willing to intervene and declare an alteration invalid (per *Greenhalgh v Aderne Cinemas Ltd*).
- To set aside an oppressive alteration, as an alternative to minority action, the plea of unfair prejudicial conduct on a minority may be made.
- An alteration where all the members agree is valid without a resolution or general meeting (per *Cane v Jones*), i.e. the Duomatic principle is in operation.
- A private company may use the simplified method of alteration by means of a written resolution which is based upon the Duomatic principle.
- Alterations must be notified to the Registrar within 14 days of their being made and subsequently published in the London Gazette.

Discussion questions

1 The s. 14 contract is a strange beast!
   Discuss.
2. The power to alter the articles '... must be exercised not only in the manner required by law, but also bone fide for the benefit of the company as a whole and it must not be exceeded' (Lindley MR, Allen v Gold Reefs of West Africa Ltd (1900)).
   Discuss.

Case study exercise

Alicia Young is the marketing director of HomeNest Limited, a Sheffield city centre department store. Her appointment under the articles is for ten years. She owns 5 per cent of the ordinary voting shares with members of her family owning a further 20 per cent. The board of HomeNest Limited have recently been informed that Ms Young, without their knowledge, has been advising a property company proposing to open an out-of-town shopping centre in the north of Sheffield. In consequence of this the board intend to alter the company's articles whereby while retaining her title of director Ms Young will be effectively demoted.

Advise the board of the legal implications of their intended course of action.

Further reading

The Relative Nature of a Shareholder's Right to Enforce the Company Contract, R.R. Drury (1986), CLJ, 219.

The Enforcement of 'Outsider' Rights, G.V. Prentice (1980), Co. Law, 179

Vetoes and Voting Agreements: Some Problems of Consent and Knowledge, C.A. Riley (1993), NILQ, 34.

Competing Interests and Conflicting Principles: An Examination of the Power of Alteration of Articles of Association, F.G. Rixon (1986), MLR, 446.

As the company's constitution (memorandum and articles) may be taken collectively, see also Further Reading at the end of Chapter 5, Memorandum of Association.

OBTAINING AND CONTROLLING CAPITAL

7 Public offer of shares

Introduction

The main reason why a public limited company is created is because the business venture to be pursued calls for more capital than is usually available to a private company. The source of large-scale capital is public subscription for shares or debentures offered by the company. Overwhelmingly, the majority of those who promote and manage a company are honest; but on occasions unscrupulous persons have set up sham companies and announced to the public a plausible and glittering business venture, afterwards proceeding to obtain investment sums from a credulous public who are financially fleeced when the spurious venture collapses. A blatant example of this practice would be termed a *bubble company* which had been formed with no real business to undertake, often as a means to defraud an unsophisticated public.

To protect a gullible public who are apt to invest in haste instead of after informed deliberation, considerable procedural regulation has to be followed by public companies who wish to offer their securities to the public or who wish to have their securities listed on the London Stock Exchange generally as a precursor to issuing securities to the public.

The most notorious bubble of all was the South Sea Bubble which burst in 1720. Many investors-cum-gamblers were ruined including Sir Isaac Newton who lost considerable sums, although Guy's Hospital in London was founded on the profits of one investor who perceptively took his money out in time.

Objectives

The purpose of this chapter is to make students recognize that there is a real probability that false claims could be made in documents issued in conjunction with public offers of company securities. Therefore, students are required to be aware that mechanisms exist to try to prevent the public being duped.

Key concepts

- Methodology of public share issues
- Disclosure obligations
- Listed and unlisted public securities
- Investor remedies.

The type of legislative regulation

The regulation of public issues of securities is contained in the Public Offer of Securities Regulations 1995 and Part IV, Financial Services Act 1986 as amended by the Regulations. To establish the specific regulations that operate it is necessary to determine the origin of the securities obtained. If from a company with an existing official listing on the London Stock Exchange (LSE) for its securities, or from a company with an application for an official listing, then the Financial Services Act 1986 will apply. Where securities are obtained without the company either having an official listing on the LSE, or not having applied for such a listing (i.e. unlisted securities) then the 1995 Regulations will operate.

In recent years the issuing of company securities has been considerably affected by EC Directives designed to ultimately achieve a uniform EC market for company securities.

Types of public share markets

The most well known public share market is the *London Stock Exchange* (LSE) for companies who have gained a listing for their securities. For public companies without such a listing their shares may be traded on the *Alternative Investment Market* (AIM). This market operates under the guidance of the LSE and caters for companies: which are rather too small for a listing on the main board (LSE); or those without a sufficiently long track record to be eligible for a LSE listing; or, alternatively, for companies which have only a small percentage of their securities in public hands and in consequence are ineligible for a LSE listing. It should be appreciated that the AIM is a regulated but fairly relaxed market.

Private companies

A private company limited by shares that offers any of its securities to the public commits a criminal offence (s. 81), although the subsequent allotment will be valid (s. 81 (3)). Notwithstanding section 81 a private company limited by shares can offer its securities to a *restricted public* (s. 60) which is:

All references in this chapter relate to the Financial Services Act 1986 unless otherwise stated.

- an existing shareholder (or their family), or debenture holder, of the offeror company; or
- an existing employee (or their family) of the offeror company.

Here no prospectus is necessary as the offer is deemed to be a 'domestic' one.

Also no private company must issue any advertisement offering its securities for sale (s. 170). However, an order by the Secretary of State for Trade and Industry may sanction an advertisement where:

- it is of a private character;
- it is directed at a specialist market; or
- the Secretary of State is prepared to use his discretion.

Methods of public issue for newly issued shares

1   *Direct invitation to the public*
    The public are invited to subscribe for shares through the publication of listing
    particulars. Those taking up the offer will be termed *subscribers* so that the shares
    will be acquired through *subscription*. If the issue is not taken up then the company
    bears the loss unless it was underwritten. This method is rarely used.

2   *An offer for sale*
    This may be divided into two categories:
    a) The company will transfer for an agreed price all of the shares to an issuing house
       (such as a merchant bank) which in turn will publish listing particulars seeking
       public offers at a slightly higher price which will give the issuing house its profit.
       As this is for the company a no risk method (the issue being fully underwritten), it
       is very common. The issuing house will receive from the company renounceable
       letters of allotment and they will later assign their rights over to the purchasers.
    b) An offer for sale may be by tender. Here the offer will state a minimum tender
       price (really a minimum purchase price) but the tender process will eventually
       indicate the actual sale price, termed the striking price. For example, if more
       shares are offered than applications received then the minimum tender price will
       become the striking price but if applications received exceed the shares offered,
       the striking price will be pitched higher at a price at which sufficient applications
       were received for all the shares offered to be sold. All shares will be sold at the
       strike price even though normally most applicants would have tendered higher or
       lower. The advantage of the tender process is that it prevents stagging, which is
       the speculative purchase of new shares for an immediate sale. The disadvantages
       of the process are that it is more complex than other methods of share issue and
       investors are less enthusiastic for it.

3   *A placement*
    An issuing house (such as a merchant bank or stockbroker) will subscribe for shares
    and then (once they have received an allotment from the company) invite their
    clients to buy them at a slightly higher price to give them their turn or profit. The
    clients are usually institutional investors but if the shares are to be listed on the Stock
    Exchange then a certain proportion must have been made available to the public. If
    the issue is not successfully placed then the intermediary will be left with those
    shares not taken up. While holding shares the issuing house will not be a shareholder
    of the company. Alternatively, the issuing house will place, as an intermediary,
    shares as an agent for the company receiving an agreed commission called
    brokerage.

    A placement is also known as selective marketing of shares. A certain proportion of any share issue to be quoted on the LSE must be made available to the public through the Exchange.

4   *A rights issue*
    This is the modern practice adopted by established companies who want to obtain
    more capital. New shares are issued and offered to existing members in proportion to
    their existing shareholding, e.g. the opportunity to acquire a new share for every five
    currently held. To make the issue attractive to investors a discount is given on the
    shares usually in the 10–20 per cent range. If the rights issue is made exclusively to
    existing shareholders in that only they may accept then this would be termed a

restricted rights issue. Otherwise with a rights issue existing shareholders not wanting to take up their right to acquire more shares will be able to renounce their right and others may be willing to buy shares at the full price so that the existing shareholder will be able to pocket the discount given.

The provisional letter of allotment sent to shareholders will tell them how many shares they are individually entitled to acquire. This letter may be renounceable in that a shareholder not wishing to take up any or only some of his allotment is able to sell his rights to others. However, a non-renounceable letter will not prevent transfer of the rights given.

Official listing of securities

Securities include shares, debentures, documents through which shares may be obtained and share certificates. No investment can be admitted to the Official List of the LSE unless the procedure given in Part IV, Financial Services Act 1986 is followed (s. 142 (1)).

Application for an official listing

An application must be made to the competent authority – the International Stock Exchange of the United Kingdom (s. 142 (6))   in the manner required by the 'listing rules' although other conditions may be attached (s. 144). Unless the issuer of the securities consent no listing can be considered (s. 143) and the decision whether to grant a listing has to be made within six months of the application or six months of the LSE receiving additional information that it requested (s. 144 (4)).

The listing rules (Admission of Securities to Listing) are commonly referred to as the Yellow Book.

Refusal to list

The LSE may refuse a listing application if it believes the admission of the securities would be detrimental to investors or the issuer has already failed to meet a listing in another European Union state (s. 144 (3)). A refused applicant can ask for judicial review of the decision.

Listing particulars

The content

The listing rules will give this but the basic information is to be:
i) the registered name of the public company; and brief details of the directors, auditors, solicitors and any other persons responsible for the listing. The directors must make a declaration that to the best of their knowledge and belief the information they have provided for the purpose of the listing issue is correct. If the company has been incorporated for less than five years then details must also be included;
ii) the capital to be subscribed – how much is payable in cash – and what type of security it will be put into (with shares the expected market value must be at least £700,000 – with other securities a lower sum is allowable provided that an adequate market in them can be expected);
iii) the voting and dividend rights for each class of share that has been issued. If anyone holds 3 per cent or more of the issued share capital then they must be identified (all securities are to be freely transferable);

iv) information on the company's audited trading history over at least the last 3 years; the accounts have to contain a directors' statement that in their opinion the company is a going concern.

Imposition of a general duty of disclosure

The listing particulars must give the information that potential investors and their advisers would reasonably require to make an informed decision whether to purchase the securities or not (s. 146). Therefore, the following ought to be included: information on assets and liabilities; profits and losses; current results and future prospects; rights given with securities (s. 146). The general duty of disclosure only applies to the information known to the persons responsible for the listing particulars or the information which they could discover on making reasonable enquiries.

When deciding what information is to be included so as to discharge the general duty of disclosure, regard ought to be had:

i) to the nature of the securities and of their issuer;
ii) to the nature of the persons likely to consider buying them, e.g. less information need be given to professionals in financial services than to ordinary members of the public;
iii) that certain matters may reasonably be expected to be within the knowledge of such professional advisors as may be found in (ii) who may reasonably be expected to be consulted by a potential purchaser;
iv) to any information advisable to investors or their professional advisors under the Financial Services Act 1986 or any other Act.

Once the listing is granted the company has to agree to meet a continuing duty to disclose to the LSE all information necessary to protect investors and to maintain an orderly market in the security listed (s. 153). Should this continuing duty of disclosure be broken then the LSE may temporarily suspend or permanently discontinue the listing (s. 145).

Exceptions from disclosure in the listing particulars

The LSE may grant an exemption from the general duty of disclosure where it would be:

- against public interest to disclose;
- seriously detrimental to the issuer – but an exemption will not be granted if the non-disclosure would be likely to mislead a potential purchaser; or
- if the information is of minor importance and would not influence the assessment of the investment opportunity.

Supplementary listing particulars

If after the preparation of listing particulars in respect to the application and before commencement of dealings in the securities listed there is:

a) a significant change affecting the original particulars, or
b) a significant new matter arises which would have been included in the listing particulars if it had arisen when the particulars were prepared,

then the issuer of the securities must submit to the LSE for approval and subsequent publication a supplementary which lists particulars of the change or new matter (s. 147 (1)).

Significant means anything affecting the making of an informed assessment, e.g. the matters that need to be disclosed under the general duty of disclosure.

Registration of the listing particulars

A copy of the listing particulars must be sent to the Registrar of companies before they are published. A statement saying that this copy has been sent to the Registrar must appear in the particulars (s. 149 (1)). Failure to provide the Registrar with an advance copy is a criminal offence punishable by a fine (s. 149 (3)).

Advertisements in connection with listing applications

The LSE must approve the contents of an advertisement, or if it is felt that a proposed advertisement is innocuous, authorize its publication without actually approving it (s. 154). The publication of an advertisement without official approval will mean, if the person responsible was unauthorized, that a criminal offence has been committed. If the company is charged then any of its officers who negligently allowed it to occur would also be found guilty (s. 154 (3)). More likely is that an authorized person is responsible, for which the civil remedies in Part I, Financial Services Act 1986 will apply.

A defence is available to non-investment business people who prove that they believed on reasonable grounds that the advertisement or information in it had been approved or its issue authorized by the Stock Exchange.

Review question

Explain how a limited company may raise considerably more share capital and the legal provisions that apply.

First public offer of listed securities

Where shares are offered to the public for the first time a draft prospectus must be submitted to the LSE for approval and subsequently it has to be published (s. 144 (2)). For securities other than shares, listing particulars must similarly be submitted, approved and published (s. 144 (2)) as is the case where any securities are not offered for the first time.

To all intents and purposes the listing rules impose similar obligations and liabilities in respect to disclosure and compensation as they do in respect to unlisted securities that came under the Public Offer of Securities Regulations 1995. Again the provisions as to who is responsible for the document and the defences to liability that are available are similar under both. Therefore, these provisions will be dealt with under first offering of unlisted securities (see below).

First public offer of unlisted securities

Any advertisement, notice, poster or document announcing the issue must say that a prospectus will be available from X address (Reg. 12).

To come under the Public Offer of Securities Regulations 1995 a public offer of securities must be substantial and the offeror has to publish a prospectus free of charge from a UK address (Reg. 4 (1)), with a copy being delivered to the Registrar of Companies (Reg. 4 (2)).

An offer of securities for the first time will include securities that are of the same class as securities that have previously been offered by the same offeror to the UK public. But if the number or value of the securities to be offered are less than 10 per cent of the number or value of the securities already made available and up-to-date detailed information about that class of securities (equivalent to that demanded by the 1995 Regulations) is available then there is no need to duplicate this information by having to issue a prospectus (Reg. 8 (5)).

Exemptions from the regulations

The following exemptions apply under Regulation 7 equally to the first public offering of listed securities as they do to the first public offering of unlisted securities:

a) where the total payable for the securities offered does not exceed ECU 40,000, or the minimum amount which an investor can invest is ECU 40,000 or more;

b) where the offer is made to persons whose business is to acquire, hold or manage investments;

c) where the offer is to be made to no more than 50 persons;

d) where the offer is to a restricted circle of persons whom the offeror reasonably believes to be sufficiently knowledgeable to understand the risks involved in accepting the offer;

e) where the securities are offered to bona fide members of a club or association and it can be reasonably ascertained that the members share a common interest in the purpose to which the proceeds of the offer will be put;

f) where the securities are offered by a *private company* to existing: members or their families; employees or their families; or are offered to holders of its debt securities (debenture holders);

g) where the issue is of bonus shares (Reg. 7 (2) (m);

h) where the securities are offered by an *incorporated company* to its employees, or former employees, or to their spouse or to their children under the age of 18;

i) where the securities are offered to the UK government, local authority or to a public authority;

j) where the securities are offered in connection with a takeover offer or a merger caused by the EC Merger Directive 78/855;

k) where the securities are offered with a genuine invitation to enter into an underwriting agreement;

l) where the shares are not transferable.

> Examples would be a bank or investment trust.
>
> Such as professional persons operating within the financial service sector.

Form and content of the prospectus (unlisted securities)

This is given in Schedule 1 to the 1995 Regulations and relates to details about the issuer and the securities being offered. In addition a prospectus must contain all such information which is within the knowledge of any person responsible for the prospectus, or which it would be reasonable for them to obtain through enquiries, that investors would reasonably require and reasonably expect to find. The objective of this provision (Reg. 9) is to enable investors to make an informed assessment of:

a) the assets and liabilities, financial position, profits and losses, and the prospects of the issuer of the securities; and

b) the rights attaching to the securities being offered.

> The prospectus wherever possible must be written in plain English (Reg. 8 (3)).
>
> Regulation 9 does not apply to pre-emptive share issues.

Supplementary prospectus

There is a need to publish a supplementary prospectus for unlisted securities (Reg. 10) when:

a) there is a significant change affecting any matter in the prospectus;
b) a significant new matter occurs which would have been given in the prospectus if it had arisen when the prospectus was prepared; or
c) there is a significant inaccuracy in the prospectus.

The Registrar must be given a copy of any supplementary prospectus that is published.

Review question

Fairwind Sailing Club operate through a limited company and wish to raise some money from their members to build a new slipway. The company secretary says that a notice ought to be put up in the clubhouse asking for members willing to put some money into the venture to contact the management committee.

Discuss the legality of the secretary's proposal.

Statutory damages for misrepresentation and omission

Statutory compensation for false or misleading statements or for omissions are provided on the following basis:

Legislation	Coverage	Application for LSE listing
ss 150–152	Listing and supplementary listing particulars	Listed securities
s. 154A (introduced) Sch.2(3), 1995 Regs	Prospectus and supplementary prospectus	Listed securities
Regs 14 15	Prospectus and supplementary prospectus	Unlisted securities

Liability is not dependent upon whether or not the claimant placed reliance upon the mis-statement or had knowledge or not of any omission.

Any person who has suffered damage or loss as a result of acquiring listed or unlisted securities where untrue or misleading statements were made in, or omissions from, listing particulars or prospectuses, may expect to be compensated by the person responsible for those untrue statements or omissions.

Method of statutory damage assessment

The amount claimable is to be assessed under the tort of deceit which attempts to restore the claimant to the position he was in before the untrue or misleading statement or omission had been made (*Smith New Court Securities Ltd v Scrimgeour Vickers (Asset Management) Ltd* (1994)). The damage or loss is that which was suffered at the time the securities were obtained (*Davidson v Tulloch* (1860)). In addition a claimant may also look to the common law in respect to rescission or damages (s. 150 (4) and Reg. 14 (4)).

Those liable to pay compensation

The 'persons responsible' may be:

i)   the company, provided that it authorized the issue or offer of securities;
ii) the offeror of the securities if they are not the company;
iii) all directors of the company who either held office when the listing particulars or prospectus were published or who agreed to take responsibility for them;
iv) any person who accepted responsibility for all or part of the listing particulars or prospectus with this acceptance being stated in these documents;
v)   any other person who authorized the contents of the listing particulars or prospectus, though this does not include professional advisors unless they expressly accepted responsibility.

Defences available to those found liable

Liability is not absolute, and the following defences or exceptions are available under s. 151 and Reg. 13:

a) a director who had no knowledge of the listing particulars or prospectus publication, or who did not consent to its publication, and on becoming aware of the publication immediately gave reasonable public notice that publications had been made without his knowledge or consent;

> This is a plea of innocence or reasonable belief.

b) i) a responsible person who reasonably believed after making reasonable enquiries when the listing particulars or prospectus was delivered for registration that the statement(s) made were true and not misleading, or that an omission was not significant;
   ii) he continued in that belief until the securities were acquired, and the securities had been acquired before it was reasonably practical to issue a correction to potential purchasers or, alternatively, he had taken reasonable steps to bring a correction to the attention of a purchaser;

c) a responsible person who relied on a statement made by an expert who consented to its inclusion, and it was reasonable to believe in the expert's competence. The person seeking to establish this defence then has to go on to satisfy (b) (ii) above;

> An expert is to include: engineer, valuer, accountant, or other person whose qualifications or experience give authority to statements that they make.

d) the loss resulted from a fair and accurate reproduction of a statement by an *official person* or was from an *official document*, and it was included in the securities document accurately and fairly.

Misrepresentation at common law

In relation to untrue statements contained in listing particulars or in a prospectus this may amount to misrepresentation which may be defined as a materially untrue statement that induces someone to enter into a contract. Here the plaintiff (claimant) will have to show that he relied fully or partially on the statement, i.e. that he had been induced to purchase the securities by means of the untrue statement. A *fraudulent* misrepresentation is one made with an absence of belief in its truth, or knowing it is false or made recklessly (*Derry v Peek* (1889)); *negligent* misrepresentation is one made with no reasonable grounds for believing it to be true (*Esso Petroleum Co. Ltd v Mardon* (1976)); *innocent* misrepresentation is one made with reasonable grounds for believing it to be true (*Leaf v International Galleries* (1950)).

Remedies for misrepresentation

There are two remedies for misrepresentation that may be claimed:

1 *Rescission*

This is an equitable remedy awarded at the court's discretion. A claim can only be made against the plaintiff's immediate contractual party, i.e. the company issuing the securities that were allotted to him or, alternatively, against the offeror of the securities. If granted, an order for rescission will enable a purchaser to return the securities and to receive back the purchase price together with any interest payable. Rescission is lost where:

a) the purchaser after discovering the misrepresentation retains the securities and so by his conduct affirms the contract; similar affirmation occurs where the purchaser attends a company meeting;

b) the purchaser fails to seek rescission within a reasonable time of discovering the true facts;

c) an innocent third party may be prejudiced;

d) the purchaser is unable to return the securities, i.e. restitution is impossible;

e) the issuing company goes into liquidation.

While rescission is available for all three types of misrepresentation courts frequently refuse to grant it for innocent misrepresentation, preferring instead to award damages. (Misrepresentation Act 1967, s. 2 (2)).

2 *Damages*

Damages may be awarded on a compensation basis under section 2, Misrepresentation Act 1967. However, if the maker of the statement shows that he had reasonable grounds for believing and did in fact believe, up to the time the contract was entered, that the facts represented were true then he has a statutory defence to a damage claim (Misrepresentation Act 1967, s. 2 (1)). For this reason the maker of an innocent misrepresentation may escape liability. If an action in fraudulent misrepresentation is taken then damages may be assessed under the tort of deceit.

Negligent mis-statements

Dependent on the circumstances it may be possible for a plaintiff to claim under the *Hedley Byrne* principle for the economic loss suffered. The plaintiff will need to show:

i) that there was a special relationship of proximity between the parties so that the defendant will owe the plaintiff a duty of care;

ii) that the defendant claimed a special skill or judgement;

With fraudulent misrepresentation time runs from when the fraud is discovered.

Again only the immediate other contractual party may be sued, directors and experts are excluded.

Hedley Byrne Ltd v Heller & Partners Ltd (1964). See also Caparo Industries Ltd v Dickman (1990).

iii) that the plaintiff relied on this skill or judgement and the defendant knew or ought to have known of this reliance in that it was likely to be acted upon.

Where a misleading statement, while inducing the plaintiff to acquire securities, will not come under the Financial Services Act 1986 or the 1995 Regulations then an action under *Hedley Byrne* has attractions. However, the principle was subject to a narrowing redefinement in *Al Nakib Investments (Jersey) Ltd v Longcroft* (1990) where the High Court said that although directors could owe a duty of care to direct purchasers of shares who had relied on a prospectus, there was no duty owed if shares had been purchased on the open market even if a prospectus had been relied upon. The rationale is that where a statement is made specifically for one purpose, e.g. to further a direct share issue by the company, then it was not to be used for another purpose even if they are somewhat associated.

The rationale in *Al Nakib Investments (Jersey) Ltd v Longcroft* (1990) was echoed in a later case:

Possfund Custodian Trustees Ltd and another v Diamond and others (1996)

Seeking to float on the USM the D's issued a prospectus for a company's shares which contained serious misrepresentations about its true financial position. Subscribers (including the plaintiffs) who had obtained shares on the basis of the false information attempted to recover their losses from the D's: directors, auditors, and their financial advisors. Before a full hearing took place the D's tried to have the case struck out alleging that there was no reasonable cause of action.

Held: Lightman J refused to strike out the claim, then reviewed the issuing of shares to the public by unlisted companies and went on to make a number of findings and observations. These were:

1 The simple issue of a prospectus did not in itself assume a special relationship towards those who bought the shares. This was so even though it is clearly foreseeable that unless the issue totally crashes then at least some shares will be bought.
2 However, circumstances could exist where it could be said that a defendant did assume a responsibility to the plaintiff and in consequence it would be fair, just and reasonable to create a special relationship between them.
3 The wording in Regulation 14: '... shall be liable to pay compensation to any person who has acquired the securities to which the prospectus relates ...' is designed only to protect subscribers of shares and not later purchasers of them.

The third part of Lightman J's decision has been criticized for seemingly being based upon his finding that Regulation 14 is to be interpreted differently from what is taken to be the equivalent compensatory provision in section 150, Financial Services Act 1986 which reads:

> Formerly the provision in Reg. 14, Public Offers of Security Regulations 1995 was contained in section 166, FSA 1986.

... shall be liable to pay compensation to any person who has acquired any of the securities in question ...

If Lightman J's interpretation of Regulation 14 is correct then it means that the class of person being able to gain compensation under the Financial Services Act 1986 will be wider, including for example subscribers and recent later purchasers, than those using the Regulations, i.e. only the subscriber. If this is the true position then it does seem unfair in that a later recent purchaser of shares in a listed company will be treated, in the event of a loss caused by false listing particulars, more favourably than a later recent share purchaser in an unlisted company suffering a similar loss but caused by a false prospectus.

Also it goes against what is now established share market practice in that a prospectus is not only intended to initially sell shares but is intended to assist in the creation of an active subsequent market in those shares.

If Possfund Custodian Trustees Ltd and another v Diamond and others (1996) is correct then subsequent recent purchasers of shares in unlisted public companies caused by reliance on a false prospectus must try particularly hard to come within the special relationship in order to mount a Hedley Byrne type action in negligence against whoever authorized the untrue prospectus.

Criminal liability

Financial Services Act 1986

Any person who makes a statement, promise or forecast which:

i)   he knows to be misleading, false or deceptive, or
ii) he makes recklessly, or
iii) dishonestly conceals any material fact,

is guilty of an offence if he does so for the purpose of inducing, or is reckless as to whether it may induce, another person to enter into a contract in the UK to buy or sell securities (s. 47).

It is also a criminal offence for any person to create a false or misleading impression as to the state of the market in respect to prices or values of securities if done for the purpose of inducing another person to acquire or dispose of securities (s. 47). A person so charged may escape conviction by proving that he reasonably believed that his act or conduct would not create a false or misleading impression (s. 47).

In addition where it is proved the offence was committed by a company with the consent or connivance of, or alternatively it was caused by any negligence on the part of:

a) any director, manager, secretary or other similar officer or of anyone purporting to act in that capacity, or
b) a controller of the company,

then they will along with the company be guilty of a criminal offence (s. 202 (1)).

Theft Act 1968

Should a person obtain by deception property from another person with the intention of permanently depriving him of it then he commits a criminal offence. In this instance property equals money paid for securities and deception can arise either through a deliberate act or by recklessness (Theft Act 1968, s. 15).

Chapter summary

- There are two authorized markets for trading in public shares. The largest is the *London Stock Exchange* with the *Alternative Investment Market* for smaller or more recently formed companies or for those where the public hold only a modest amount of its shares.
- Several methods of issuing shares to the public are available. These are: an *offer for sale* with the company selling its shares to an *issuing house* which then publishes listing particulars and sells them on to the public, or a *sale by tender* in which offers above a stated minimum price are invited; a *placement* where an intermediary will place shares with financial institutions and the public; or a *rights issue* where the company gives existing shareholders the opportunity to buy more shares.
- An application for listing on the London Stock Exchange must be supported by *listing particulars* of: the company, directors, auditors, capital to be subscribed; as well as information on shares already issued; together with details of assets versus liabilities, profits versus losses, current and future prospects. All of this information must be provided under a duty of disclosure which will last throughout the listing duration. Listing particulars must be registered with the Registrar before publication.
- If required by significant changes occurring after listing particulars have been issued then *supplementary listing particulars* must be issued.
- For a first public offering of listed securities a *prospectus* approved by the London Stock Exchange must be published to meet the provisions of the Financial Services Act 1986 (FSA 1986). Similarly, a prospectus must also be published for a first public offer of unlisted securities to meet the requirements of the Public Offers of Securities Regulations 1995 (POSR 1995). However, the Regulations permit exemptions that small numbers of investors may come within.
- Damages are available under the FSA 1986 and the POSR 1995 for misrepresentations contained in a prospectus or for omissions of information. Assessment of damages will be based on the tort of deceit.
- Those liable to pay compensation are: the company; the offeror of the securities (if different from the company); the directors of the company at the time of publishing the listing particulars or prospectus; and those who authorized the contents of the listing particulars prospectus.
- In addition to *statutory damages* remedies may also be claimable for *contractual misrepresentation* – these are rescission and damages at common law. A third possibility for damages is a claim for *negligent mis-statement* under *Hedley Byrne* but current case law indicates that only subscribers (purchasers of shares direct from the company) can claim, not subsequent purchasers.

Discussion questions

1 In respect to prospectuses the disclosure obligations defeat the whole object of disclosure.
Discuss

2 Discuss available remedies to an investor induced to take shares by false statements made in a prospectus.

Case study exercise

After prospecting in Indonesia for several years Anglo-Indonesian Mining Limited (AIM) announce that it has discovered a valuable gold deposit to be called the New Millennium Mine (NMM). Gabby Haynes, Head of Exploration for AIM, is reported in the financial press as saying that the mine will be one of the world's richest with recoverable gold estimated at 47 million ounces. To exploit the discovery additional capital is required to pay mining fees to the Indonesian government and put in a 27 km road so that heavy mining equipment can be brought in.

Subsequently, a share prospectus is published in which several statements are made concerning the NMM's expected earning potential based upon a South African mining consultant's report prepared after his inspection of thousands of mineral samples provided by AIM. In the prospectus it was claimed that 'the NMM could contain as much as 73 million ounces of gold, yielding a billion pounds in profit.' Illustrative projected profit and loss figures were also given together with a favourable supporting statement from Harlequin Associates (financial advisors to AIM).

During the validity of the prospectus the South African consultant notified AIM that testing equipment used to analyse the samples had been incorrectly calibrated and his amended forecast is for 45 million recoverable ounces of gold. The directors of AIM do nothing apart from reminding the consultant that there is a confidentiality clause in his contract of appointment.

A few months after the share invitation contained in the prospectus expired the financial press in Britain begin to repeat rumours that appeared in the Jakarta media that the NMM may have only 'insignificant' amounts of gold ore. Responding to shareholder demands AIM reluctantly agree to an independent investigation into NMM. The report produced is damning with findings that claims for the mine's prospects were based on data falsified to an 'unprecedented' scale. The ore samples were discovered to be taken not from drilling at the NMM but had been 'borrowed' from adjoining mines.

In a written statement Ivor Crook, chairman and chief executive of AIM, said:

We share the shock and dismay of our shareholders that the gold we thought we had at NMM now appears not to be there.

The statement went on to say that legal, accounting and investigative personnel had been retained to find out how the falsified data had been 'generated'. The effect of this saga on AIM's share price is shown in Figure 7.1 in an abbreviated form.

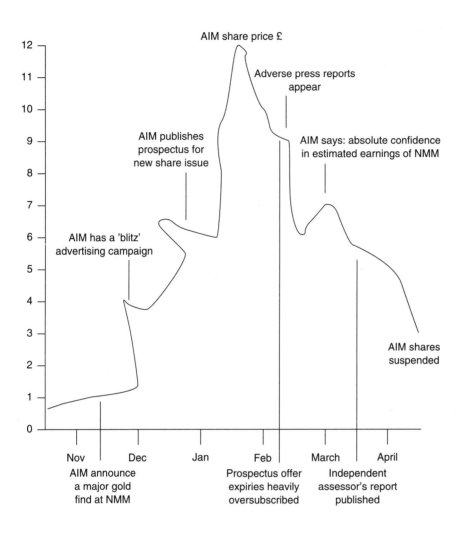

AIM share price £

Adverse press reports
appear

AIM publishes
prospectus for
new share issue

AIM says: absolute confidence
in estimated earnings of NMM

AIM has a 'blitz'
advertising campaign

AIM shares
suspended

Nov   Dec   Jan   Feb   March   April

AIM announce
a major gold
find at NMM

Prospectus offer
expiries heavily
oversubscribed

Independent
assessor's report
published

Task

Three acquaintances, Tom Dick and Harry, knowing that you are studying company law approach you for legal advice. Tom explains that he subscribed for 1,000 shares at £5 per share in AIM. This was after receiving a prospectus. On the last day of trading before the shares were suspended they were officially priced at £1 although no one seemingly was actually buying. Dick says that his application to buy shares in AIM was unsuccessful but he later bought 250 at £12 from someone who had been successful in the prospectus issue. Harry bought 500 shares in the prospectus issue but admitted that he had done so on the recommendation of a friend in the Indonesian government.

Offer advice to Tom, Dick and Harry as well as referring to other pertinent legal matters that may apply.

Further reading

Encyclopedia of Financial Services, Law, Sweet & Maxwell.
Damages for Mis-statements in Company Prospectuses, S. Griffin (1991), Co. Law, 209.

8 Capital: classification, maintenance and alteration

Introduction

While a company as a going concern will be primarily interested in capital as a financial resource, such as *working capital* that pays for the day-to-day running costs of the company (e.g. wages and trade purchases), or *venture (risk) capital* that will enable it to achieve its medium or long-term commercial objectives, the Companies Act is greatly concerned that capital subscribed by shareholders is properly maintained. Therefore, capital in company law has special meanings and directors are required to act as its custodians for essentially it is a fund of last resort for creditors. If directors were free of restriction they could 'water down' the capital by, for example, declaring generous dividends paid out of capital or by giving back capital to shareholders in other ways. Indeed with a small private company, where all the directors are shareholders, they could, if unrestricted, pay themselves enhanced directors' fees out of capital. Such actions if allowed would considerably prejudice the position of creditors in that if the company failed they would probably find that the corporate coffers were empty. For this reason capital must be maintained and only in approved circumstances may this provision be dispensed with.

Objectives

The purpose of this chapter is to enable students to, firstly, gain an understanding of the central importance of capital, and, secondly, acquire familiarity with various restrictions that surround it.

Key concepts

- Classification of capital
- Maintenance of capital

- Reduction of capital
- A company's acquisition of its own shares
- Share capital redemption.

Share capital

This is share or equity capital as opposed to debenture capital contributed by debenture holders – see the capital clause of the memorandum in Chapter 5, Memorandum of Association.

The sums held by a company, comprising amounts received from share issues with (if appropriate) the share premium and share redemption accounts, represent the funds contributed by its shareholders. They also normally indicate the percentage of the net assets of the company that each member owns.

As capital is of supreme importance, it features in both the memorandum and articles. In the memorandum the capital clause is there to reassure creditors that the capital sum represents a fund to meet, in the event of business failure, company liabilities such as debts owed to creditors:

> One of the main objects contemplated by the legislation, in restricting the power of limited companies to reduce the amount of their capital as set forth in the memorandum, is to protect the interests of the outside public who may become their creditors ... (who) are entitled to assume that no part of the capital which has been paid into the coffers of the company has been subsequently paid out, except in the legitimate course of its business. (Lord Watson, *Trevor v Whitworth* (1887))

Hence a company is not able to arbitrarily alter its capital without first going through a stipulated procedure including altering its memorandum by means of an ordinary resolution (s. 121), provided that such an authority is given in its articles (Table A, article 32) and informing the Registrar who in turn will publicize this in the London Gazette (s. 711).

In respect to the articles, the directors' authority to increase the capital of the company is only possible if the shareholders have previously given this power in the articles. This restriction on directors' powers acts as a safeguard to shareholders for without it directors would capriciously be able to issue more capital and so dilute the stake of existing shareholders which would importantly affect their voting rights. Alternatively, shareholders may have invested in the company believing that its capital assets would be sufficient to make a success of the business and an unauthorized capital reduction would be deceitful to such a belief.

The classification of capital

Capital, without qualification, is the amount by which a company's assets exceed its liabilities: whereas share capital is the amount raised by a company through an issue of shares.

The capital clause states the *authorized* or *nominal capital* of the company. This is the amount that the shareholders have authorized the directors to raise by issuing shares. The clause in the articles will describe how it is to be divided into shares of a fixed amount. Under the specimen provided in Table B, for a private company limited by shares, it is stated that, 'The share capital of the company is £50,000 divided into 50,000 shares of £1 each.' The company, in this example, may not need to raise £50,000 immediately so that it may issue only £30,000 £1 shares. It will then have an *issued* or *subscribed capital* of £30,000 which is the amount of capital that the directors have issued and which shareholders are liable to pay. This forms the fund from which, in the event of later insolvency, the creditors can expect to be paid.

The subscribers to the memorandum have the right to take up the shares personally allotted to them. If they decide not to exercise this right then they are able to transfer their right to others. However, it has to be appreciated that the directors have the right to call up any payment still due on the shares as the subscribers, when signing the memorandum, entered into a contract agreeing that they would ensure that the shares would be paid for and later holders of the shares will be similarly bound.

It is therefore possible for a company to delay payment of the full amount by asking members to, for example, subscribe only 50p per share on allotment. The company would then in our example have *paid-up capital* of £15,000 – hence shares may be issued *fully paid* or *partly paid*. The paid-up capital ought to be identical to the called-up capital but discrepancies may be caused by some shareholders refusing to meet a call.

The terms of the issue will determine when the company may call up the additional capital with a schedule of instalments or *calls* usually being provided. Should a call not be paid on time then this will equal a breach of contract and may lead to the shares being forfeited. The *uncalled capital* on partly paid shares is a debt owed to the company by the shareholders and this will be the limit of their future liability. This type of capital, the difference between the paid-up capital and the nominal value of the issued capital, acts as a reserve fund to be called upon at any time by the directors or at a predetermined occasion. Should shareholders wish to take control of uncalled capital away from the directors then they may do so by means of a special resolution to create a reserve capital fund whereby a call can only be made in the event of liquidation – such a resolution may reassure creditors who without it may press for the return of their money.

> Called-up capital is: (a) the total sum of the calls made on shares, whether or not they have been met; (b) any share capital paid up without actually being called; and (c) any share capital to be paid at a specified future date under the articles.

In practice most companies issue their shares fully paid as this guards against calls not being met (also shareholders tend not to like the uncertainty of an unexpected call being made) and in addition the Stock Exchange normally requires this of public limited companies.

Alteration of share capital

Provided the authority is given in the articles (Table A, article 32) a company may pass an ordinary resolution to alter its capital clause in order to:

> The directors will make a decision to alter the share capital and this will be put as an ordinary resolution to the members. If approved, a copy of the resolution must be sent to the Registrar within one month (s. 122) except for an increase when it is 15 days (s. 123).

a) *Increase the nominal share capital;*

b) *Consolidate shares*

For convenience where shares have been issued in small denominations, such as with a par value of 10p, they may be consolidated into a larger amount such as £1 shares. If this is carried out then each member will receive one-tenth of their existing shares but the new denomination will still represent on identical percentage of the total. Existing share certificates will be called in for either amendment or more probably for cancellation with new ones being issued;

c) *Split or sub-divide shares*

This is the opposite of share consolidation. It may be used where it is felt the denomination is too high for the shares to be 'psychologically' attractive to investors – e.g. owning 10,000 £1 shares may be felt to be more satisfying than owning 1,000 £10 shares even though they both represent the same amount;

d) *Cancel nominal share capital.*

Maintenance of share capital

The maintenance of capital restrictions does not generally apply to unlimited companies as creditors are not exposed to the same degree of risk as they are with limited ones.

As outlined above, capital is a fund held by a company to be available to meet creditors' claims. Capital is therefore strictly controlled. For example, dividends cannot be paid out of capital but must originate from profits. Indeed, a public company is unable to make a distribution unless the amount of its net assets is not less than the aggregate of its called-up share capital and undistributable reserves (s. 264). Also, in respect to a public company, if net assets fall to half or less of its called-up capital a director(s) must, on becoming aware of this, call within 28 days an extraordinary general meeting to take place within 56 days of knowing of the fall in net assets. The purpose of this extraordinary meeting is to decide on a course of action, such as reduction in capital. The maintenance of capital principle is the price shareholders pay for the benefit of limited liability in that creditors rank before members when claiming in liquidation against company assets and the asset of share capital has generally to be kept intact. A company, as a going concern, is only able to return capital to its members either through a reduction of capital scheme or by repurchase of its shares. Both of these, which are discussed later, are closely controlled.

Increasing authorized share capital

If the current articles do not permit an increase in share capital then they need to be altered. This will require a special resolution (s. 9) but an issue of new shares must not be designed to injure a minority (Clemens v Clemens Bros Ltd (1976)).

As this is a managerial matter the directors must firstly decide that the authorized capital be increased to a sum they feel is appropriate. Then, secondly, provided that the articles allow for it, an ordinary resolution to increase the authorized capital is put either before an extraordinary general meeting, or, alternatively, put to the next annual general meeting. The resolution has to be approved by a simple majority. Thirdly, if approval is given then a certified copy of the resolution has to be filed at Companies House within 15 days and if any special conditions are imposed on the new shares to be issued, such as voting rights, then they have to be given on Form 123 sent with the resolution copy. The increased figure will then be the official registered authorized capital with the memorandum and articles being revised accordingly.

The new capital may be in the form of ordinary, preference or deferred shares. While the nominal capital of a company may be increased even though not all of its authorized capital has been issued, it is normally the case that new capital is required because all the authorized capital has been exhausted.

Reduction of share capital

Reduction of capital may be either the cancellation or reduction in the liability on partly or fully paid shares, or the return of unwanted share capital.

In order to protect creditors and members a company is only able in limited circumstances to reduce its capital. To do so at will may be deceitful on creditors who gave credit believing that the company had sufficient capital assets to meet its liabilities in full, i.e. that capital is used as security. Therefore, reduction of capital is subject to greater control than the other types of alteration of capital under section 121.

For share capital to be reduced the procedure to be followed is that the power to do so has to be given in the articles (Table A, article 34). If the articles do not contain such a power (because, perhaps, it is only in the memorandum) then they need to be amended. Once this preliminary point is satisfied then a separate special resolution has to be passed by the shareholders followed by an application to the High Court for the resolution to be confirmed (s. 135 (1)). Retrospective confirmation is not possible. Once the court order is obtained a copy has to be sent for filing to Companies House and the company memorandum will of course be amended. When deciding to confirm a resolution a court will, it seems, be solely concerned with whether the correct procedure has been followed and only exceptionally will it refuse to grant confirmation where it believes the reduction to be unfair to any class of shareholder (*Re Holder's Investment Trust Ltd* (1971)).

After giving a general consent, section 135 (2) continues to give specific ways in which a reduction of capital may occur:

a) to extinguish or reduce liability on share capital not paid up. As an example this would be where a company decides that further calls on partly paid (or even on wholly unpaid) shares is unnecessary;

b) to cancel paid-up share capital which is lost or unrepresented by available assets. As an example this would occur where a company's assets have fallen relative to the share capital. For example, a company with share capital in the articles of £100,000 divided into 100,000 £1 fully paid shares; if its assets are now worth £50,000, it may reduce its capital to 100,000 shares of 50p nominal value;

c) to repay any paid-up share capital which is in excess of the company's needs. As an example this would occur where a company sells a valuable asset for cash and decides that it does not need this excess capital. Therefore, if it had 100,000 £1 fully paid shares it could reduce its nominal capital to 100,000 50p fully paid shares returning 50p per share to the members.

The loss of capital must be permanent and not temporary (Re Jupiter House Investments (Cambridge) Ltd (1985)). However, if the company gives the court an undertaking to safeguard creditors' interests then the court may confirm capital reduction in respect to a temporary loss (Re Grosvenor Press plc (1985)).

As a measure of creditor protection, where the reduction relates to unpaid share capital or repayment to a member of any share capital already paid, then the company, when applying to the court for a confrontation order, must list, together with details of their debts, every creditor entitled to object to the capital reduction (s. 136 (4)). The court can order a notice to be published so that unlisted creditors may have the opportunity to join the list within a set period (s. 136 (4)). It is a criminal offence to conceal creditors or misrepresent their claims (s. 141). Any creditor may object to the proposed reduction although a creditor's objection may be ignored by the court if the company discharges that debt or sets aside (in cash or by acceptable guarantee) a sum equal to the creditor's claim (s. 136 (5)).

The actual mechanics of the reduction will be for the company to decide. It may take the form of *all round reduction* where the capital is written off all the shares in proportion to the nominal value or it may be written off only one class of shares leaving others unaltered (*Re Quebrada Copper Co.* (1888)). However, no reduction scheme will be sanctioned by the court if it is felt to be unfair to any class of shareholder, or where creditors would be prejudiced (*Pool v National Bank of China Ltd* (1907)). A reduction not in breach of these two considerations will still receive the court's sanction even though there may be an ulterior motive for it such as where a company threatened with nationalization decides to reduce its capital (*Westburn Sugar Refineries Ltd ex parte* (1951)).

An issue of bonus shares

Bonus shares paid out of capital (a capitalization issue) represents a reduction of capital. The decision to make an issue is made by the directors authorized by an ordinary resolution of the shareholders. For a fuller treatment of an issue of bonus shares see Chapter 9, Shares.

Review question

How may capital be:

a) altered;
b) reduced; or
c) increased?

The acquisition by a company of its own shares

The general prohibition

Both at common law (*Trevor v Whitworth* (1887)) and statute (s. 143 (1)), a limited company is unable to acquire its own shares. If it did so then such an acquisition would be void. That this is not a cast-iron rule can be seen from the exceptions that shortly follow. A number of justifications for relaxing the general prohibition have been put forward. The main ones are:

i) It enables shareholdings in a private company to be retained more easily within a family circle. For example, a shareholder wishing to dispose of shares is able, should other shareholders not be in a position to purchase them, to sell them to the company.

ii) It enables all companies that have issued redeemable shares to have flexibility in being able to buy them back before their redemption date. For example, if the redeemable shares were currently priced at £3.50 per share but had to be redeemed a year hence at £5 per share then it may be a sensible use of a company's surplus cash to buy the shares back now rather than having to do so later at the higher price.

iii) It increases the marketability of company shares. For example, a venture capitalist, such as a merchant bank, will be more willing to provide capital for shares if it knew that at a future date it would be able to 'bale out' by selling the shares back to the company.

iv) It makes an employee share-purchase scheme more attractive in that employees will know that on leaving the company's employment they will be able to sell their shares back to the company.

Exceptions where a company is allowed to acquire its own shares

A surrender or forfeiture of shares may be carried out as part of a capital reduction programme under s. 135 and requires confirmation by the court.

As with most general prohibitions a number of exceptions apply. These are:

a) Where its own fully paid up shares are acquired without payment by it of valuable consideration (Re *Castiglione's Will Trusts* (1958)).

b) A forfeiture of shares
Holders of partly paid shares who fail to meet a call are in breach of contract and are liable under the articles to have their shares forfeited to the company. Directors have to give at least 14 days notice of a forfeiture demand (Table A, article18). If the

unpaid amount and the interest on it is still unpaid then the directors may by resolution forfeit the shares and this will include any dividends payable but not yet paid (Table A, article19). A power to forfeit shares must be exercised for the benefit of the company as a whole and not for some other purpose such as relieving a friend from liability (Re *Esparto Trading Co.* (1879)).

On forfeiture the former holder of the shares loses his membership of the company but still remains liable for the monies payable on the shares together with interest. The directors may waive payment (whole or part) or may seek to enforce the debt giving no allowance for the value of the forfeited shares (Table A, article 21). Under the articles the directors may have the authority to resell or re-allot forfeited shares (Table A, article 20). An exercise of such a power has to meet general sale and allotment requirement but any sum already paid on them may go towards the shares being treated as being partly paid. To avoid forfeiture a shareholder may voluntarily surrender the shares. (*Trevor v Whitworth* (1887)).

c) A surrender of shares

If the articles permit it, a member may voluntarily surrender shares. Failing such a provision (Table A is silent on the matter), then surrender is possible if done firstly to avoid forfeiture taking place and secondly where the shares are surrendered in exchange for new shares of the same nominal value but with different class rights. Strictly, a surrender will be void if it equals a purchase of the shares by the company – this is because of the rule that a company cannot be a shareholder of itself. Also a surrender will be void if it was agreed to by the company as a way of relieving a shareholder of his liabilities. On surrender the same points apply as for forfeited shares: right to resell or re-allot; right to sue a former holder or to waive legal action; loss of membership by the former holder; etc.

The following exceptions are dealt with separately elsewhere in this chapter:

d) a purchase of redeemable shares;
e) a purchase of its own shares;
f) as part of a capital reduction scheme.

Other exceptions are:

i)   under a court order relating to the alteration of the objects clause (s. 5);
ii) on the reregistration of a public company as a private one (s. 54);
iii) a court order relating to unfair prejudice; and
iv) a gift.

Financial assistance by a company for the purchase of its own shares

As with many company activities there are pluses and minuses in a company being able to give financial assistance to purchase its own shares. Many large companies in order to focus on core activities may wish to divest themselves of non-core subsidiary companies through management buy-outs. To achieve this the holding company may grant the directors of a subsidiary loans to buy up the subsidiary's share capital. Or a company may provide a loan to enable a director to buy company shares so as to satisfy a share-owning requirement.

Where acquisition of its own shares through forfeiture or surrender occurs then they should be held on a temporary basis (EC Second Directive). If forfeited or surrendered shares in a public company are not reissued within 3 years then they must be cancelled (s. 146).

Legislation adopts an ambiguous approach to the issue by imposing a general prohibition on financial assistance but then going on to provide a number of exceptions to the prohibition.

However, a real fear for creditors and shareholders is that financial assistance could be too freely available so that the share capital could be soon run down; or, in relation to private companies, financial assistance could result in ownership and control passing out of the hands of an existing family circle to outsiders.

The general prohibition

It is illegal for a company directly or indirectly to give any financial assistance for the acquisition of any of its shares or shares of a subsidiary (s. 151 (1)). Additionally, where a person has acquired shares in a company and in doing so has incurred a liability (e.g. having to pay for them) it is unlawful for the company or any of its subsidiaries to give financial assistance directly or indirectly for the purpose of reducing or discharging that person's liability (s. 151 (2)).

In Charterhouse Investments Trust Ltd v Tempest Diesels Ltd (1986), Hoffman J said of financial assistance that, 'The words have no technical meaning and their frame of reference is in my judgement the language of ordinary commerce.'

The term *financial assistance* is given a wide interpretation and includes a loan, gift, provision of a guarantee or indemnity etc. with a catch-all category of any other financial assistance by a company whose net assets are as a result reduced to a material extent or which has no net assets (s. 152 (1)). Put simply, there should not be financial assistance or help for the purpose of acquiring the shares (per Aldous LJ, *British & Commonwealth Holdings plc v Barclays Bank plc and others* (1996)). Any attempt to evade the general prohibition by means of an informal agreement to provide financial assistance will fail (s. 152 (3)) although an unrecorded undertaking would be difficult to establish:

Heald v O'Connor (1971)
The controlling shareholders in a company lent monies to the buyer of the company with the loan being secured by a floating charge on the company's assets. The buyer also guaranteed the loan.

Held: The loan amounted to financial assistance and as an illegal transaction was involved the seller would be unable to enforce the guarantee.

Where s. 151 is broken the following consequences operate: the financial assistance provided is declared void; the company and any of its officers found responsible are liable to an unlimited fine and a maximum of two years imprisonment or both (s. 151 (3)); every director party to the breach is guilty of a breach of his duties and must compensate the company for any losses which it had suffered.

Exceptions to the general prohibition on financial assistance

Financial assistance is permissible (s. 153 (1) (2)):

In both (a) and (b) financial assistance must be provided in good faith and in the interests of the company.

a) if the *principal purpose* in giving financial assistance is not to give it for the purpose of share acquisition. Therefore, if a company gave a normal cash bonus to its employees some of whom, recognizing a good investment opportunity, used their bonus to purchase shares in the company, then this would be a lawful purchase as the principal purpose of the financial assistance was not share purchase but performance of a contractual obligation;

b) where the financial assistance for the share acquisition is an *incidental part of some larger purpose* of the company. Therefore, if Company A wishing to cement a strategic alliance with Company B agrees to acquire 10 per cent of the shares in Company B, obtaining finance for the purchase from a bank with Company B acting as guarantor, then this share purchase was an incidental part of a larger company plan or purpose.

In *Brady v Brady* (1989) Lord Oliver in the House of Lords, when applying s. 153 (1) to a complex scheme designed to overcome a management deadlock between two shareholder brothers, said that the words *larger purpose* had to be given a narrow meaning or else s. 151 would lose its effectiveness.

Other exceptions are (s. 153 (3)):

a) a distribution of a company's assets by way of a dividend lawfully made or a distribution made in the course of the company's winding up;
b) the allotment of bonus shares;
c) a reduction of capital confirmed by order of the court under section 137;
d) a redemption or purchase of shares made in accordance with provisions in the Companies Act;
e) anything done in pursuance of an order of the court under section 425 (compromises and arrangements with creditors and members);
f) anything done under an arrangement made in pursuance of section 110 of the Insolvency Act 1986 (acceptance of shares by the liquidator in winding up as consideration for sale of property); or
g) anything done under an arrangement made between a company and its creditors which is binding on the creditors by virtue of Part 1 of the Insolvency Act 1986.

Further exceptions are (s. 153 (4)):

a) where the lending of money is part of the ordinary business of the company and a loan is granted in the normal manner. Therefore, a bank lending in the ordinary course of business to a customer who uses the loan to buy shares in the bank is valid;
b) where the loan is provided in good faith and in the interests of the company to support an employee share scheme (CA1989, s. 132). Therefore, a company may guarantee loans given by a bank funding share purchases in an official employee share scheme;
c) where the loan is to employees (not to include directors) to help them purchase fully paid shares to be held by them as beneficial owners. Therefore, a company wishing help to defeat a hostile takeover bid could provide loans to enable employees also against the takeover to acquire fully paid shares in the company.

Special restriction for public companies (s. 154)

In the case of a *public company* the exceptions given under s. 153 (4) apply only if the company has net assets which are not thereby reduced or to the extent that those assets are thereby reduced if the assistance is provided out of distributed profits. Net assets means the amount by which the aggregate of the company's assets exceeds the aggregate of its liabilities, the calculation being derived from the company's accounts taken immediately before the financial assistance is given.

Relaxation for private companies (s. 155)

A *private company* is allowed to give financial assistance for the acquisition of its shares, or shares in its holding company, if it to is a private company. The proviso is that, like the special restriction on public companies given above, the company's net assets are not thereby reduced, or to the extent that they are thereby reduced, the financial assistance is provided out of distributable profits.

The conditions which must be satisfied for the relaxation under s. 155 are similar to the requirements for a private company to use its capital to redeem or purchase its own shares (see the sections that follow). However, here the financial assistance must not be given more than 8 weeks after the statutory declaration (s. 156) with the special resolution being passed either on the date of or within the week following the statutory declaration. Creditors have no right of objection but members who have at least 10 per cent of an issued share class (if the company is not limited by shares, then 10 per cent of the members) may object.

> The scheme in Brady v Brady (1988) was held to have involved provision of financial assistance in reducing liability for the purchase of shares (s. 151 (2)) but was allowed under sections 155 and156.

Review question

Amanda, Brenda and Clare are equal shareholders in ABC Limited. Amanda is shortly to emigrate to Canada and wishes to dispose of her shares but neither Brenda nor Clare want to purchase them. After pondering the problem Brenda and Clare come up with the following:

a) As ABC Limited is profitable why can't it buy Amanda's shares?
b) Amanda's brother Tom is interested in buying his sister's shares but while his bank will lend him the money to do so it demands a guarantor in respect of the loan. Brenda and Clare propose that ABC Limited give the guarantee.

Discuss the legality of these proposals.

Redemption of share capital

A company may, under its articles (Table A, article 3), issue redeemable shares (s. 159). Such shares may be redeemable after the expiry of a set time period, or on the occurrence of a specified event, or at the option of the company or shareholder (s. 159 (1)). Most commonly the shares will be redeemable preference shares but redeemable ordinary shares may also be issued. However, since a company's share capital cannot consist entirely of redeemable shares it is necessary that when a redeemable share issue is made, and also when it is later redeemed, that there are non-redeemable shares in existence. As there is no provision to reclassify them a redeemable share issue has to be so described on its issue.

Redeemable shares must also be fully paid at the time of redemption (s. 159 (2) (3)) and the redemption must be for cash with the redeemed shares being cancelled although the company's authorized capital remains the same – but of course its issued and paid-up capital is diminished by the nominal value of the redeemed shares (s. 160 (4)).

To maintain capital, detailed rules relate to the redemption of redeemable shares. These are:

> If the reduction reduces the issued capital of a public company to under £50,000 then it must re-register as a private company.

a) *Payment for redemption* may only come from the proceeds of a new share issue (made for the purpose of the redemption, or from distributable profits (s. 160 (1)).

b) *Where distributable profits* are used to pay for the redemption, then a sum equal to the nominal value of the redeemed shares must be credited to a non-distributable capital redemption reserve (s. 170). Apart from a reduction of capital (s. 135), a redemption of shares, or a purchase of shares out of capital (s. 171), the capital redemption reserve may only be used for the allotment of fully paid bonus shares.

c) If the redemption includes *payment of a premium* then the premium must be provided only out of distributed profits. However, if the shares were originally issued at a premium then a share premium account can be issued provided that it does not exceed the smaller of:
   i) the premium received on the issue of the shares being redeemed; or
   ii) the balance on the share premium account.

d) If the redemption payment comes from a new share issue and the nominal value of the new issue is less than the nominal value of the redeemed shares then the difference has to be credited to the capital redemption reserve.

> A third possibility that only relates to private companies is that if these sources of payment are insufficient then a private company may tap its capital.

Redemption of share capital by private companies

This is dealt with under the section 'Use by a private company of its capital to redeem or purchase its own shares' that follows later in this chapter.

Purchase by a company of its own shares

Generally what has already been said in relation to redemption of shares also applies to a company wishing to purchase its own shares whether issued as redeemable or not (s. 162). The authority to purchase must be given in the articles at the time of purchase but need not have been present when the shares were issued. If the purchase is financed from distributable profits then an appropriate transfer to a capital redemption reserve is needed.

> A company cannot purchase its own shares if in consequence only redeemable shares are held.

Table A, article 35 allows a company to purchase its own shares, including redeemable ones, and further allows a private company to use capital to pay for them, whereas a public company is restricted to using distributable profits and/or the proceeds of a fresh issue of shares:

> In *Actos and Hutchinson plc v Watson* (1994), Lightman J pointed out that if a takeover of a target company was prohibited when the target held shares in the bidding company, it would probably result in target companies actively using this ploy to avoid being taken over.

Actos and Hutchinson plc v Watson (1995)

AH sought to take over Actos Ltd (A) whose only asset was a large shareholding in AH. The takeover had been carried out at arm's length with independent directors of AH receiving separate legal and financial advice that the takeover was in the best interests of AH and its shareholders. However, the issue was raised that AH were, by buying shares in A, indirectly acquiring its own shares hence the takeover could not be completed.

Held: The rule in *Trevor v Whitworth* and section 143, CA 1985 did not prevent AH from acquiring A's entire share capital especially as the independent directors of AH had acted correctly to safeguard the interests of shareholders and creditors. Also s. 23 (membership of a holding company) could be applied whereby A, after the takeover, could retain its shareholding in AH but A's voting rights would be suspended during AH's ownership.

Approval for a purchase of its own shares may be made in one of three ways. These are:

a) *Market purchase of its own shares (s. 166)*

Here as the shares are purchased on a recognized stock exchange this method relates solely to public companies as there are no recognized markets for shares in private companies.

Shareholders give their approval for such purchase by means of an *ordinary resolution* stipulating: the maximum number of shares to be purchased; the minimum and maximum price range; and the period in which the purchase can occur (which must not exceed 18 months from the resolution being passed). Holders of the shares that are proposed to be purchased are free to vote on the resolution. If wishing to make a market purchase the company must send a copy of the resolution to the Registrar within 15 days of it being passed. When a market purchase is actually made then within 28 days of obtaining the shares the company must inform the Registrar of the number and class of the shares (s. 169).

b) *Off-market purchase of its own shares (ss. 163–164)*

This covers the situation where the purchase is made other than by a standard market procedure, i.e. the purchase is other than from a recognized stock exchange or, alternatively, is purchased on such an exchange but the shares concerned are not publicly traded on it. Here a contract of purchase, stating the purchase price, is made available to shareholders for at least 15 days ending with the date of a general meeting where members have to approve by special resolution the purchase. Names of members holding shares covered by the contract have to be given but these prospective sellers of the shares are not entitled to vote. With a public company, approval for an off-market purchase must give a date not exceeding 18 months from when the resolution was passed on which the authority to purchase expires. A copy of the purchase contract has to be retained at the company's registered office for 10 years from the date of the purchase (s. 169). As with market purchase a share return is made to the Registrar.

c) *A contingent purchase of its own shares (s. 165)*

This method depends on circumstances such as where, in a private company, directors must have a certain shareholding but on their relinquishing their directorship the shares will be returned to the company. Contingent purchase is treated in the same way as off-market purchase and the company may be obligated to buy its own shares with the contract of purchase really being an option to buy. A contingent purchase must be authorized in advance by a *special resolution*.

Compare the prospective seller in a market purchase of shares where he is allowed to vote.

Use by a private company of its capital to redeem or purchase its own shares

As earlier mentioned such use of capital applies only to private companies, not to public companies, and as it goes against the principle of maintaining capital it is subject to close regulation. Capital cannot be the exclusive source of finance for the redemption or purchase of its own shares but has to be used as a supplementary source in addition to distributable profits. The *permissible capital payment* is the amount by which the price of the redemption or purchase exceeds the sum of distributable profits plus the proceeds of any fresh issue of shares made for the purpose of the redemption or purchase. Therefore, to be able to resort to capital a private company must firstly exhaust its distributable profits and reserves (s. 171).

If capital is so used then the procedure to be followed is similar to an off-market purchase of its own shares. The payment from capital will take place 5–7 weeks after the special resolution was passed. As such a use of capital potentially disadvantages the creditors it is necessary that the directors make a statutory *declaration of solvency* (s. 173) by stating the amount of the permissible capital payout as well as stating that having made a full enquiry into the affairs and prospects of the company, they are of the opinion that:

i)   there will be no reason why the company will be unable to pay its debts immediately after the payment out of capital is made; and
ii) the company is able to carry on business as a going concern throughout the following year.

To deter possible abuse an auditor's report must be attached to the declaration stating that after enquiring into the matter the permissible capital payment given in the declaration was correctly calculated and that the auditors are not aware of any circumstances to make the directors' opinion unreasonable.

In order that creditors are made aware of the intention to reduce capital the following publicity must take place:

a)   Within 1 week after the resolution is passed a detailed notice of it must be published in the *London Gazette* (s. 175 (1)).
b)   The company must publish a similar detailed notice in a national newspaper or, alternatively, send a copy of the notice to all of its creditors (s. 175 (2)).
c)   The statutory declaration and auditor's report must be made available at the company's registered office during business hours for inspection by members and creditors from at least the date of publication of the notice in the Gazette until 5 weeks after the date of the resolution (s. 175 (6)). The declaration and report also have to be available at the meeting at which the resolution is passed.

Shareholders and creditors have the right, within 5 weeks after the resolution, to petition the court for it to be cancelled (s. 176 (1)). The court can cancel or affirm the resolution (with or without imposing terms or conditions) (s. 176 (2)). If a member makes the application the court may well order the company to buy the shares of the objecting member (s. 176 (3)).

Should the company start liquidation proceedings within one year after payment out of capital then those who received it may be liable to contribute to the assets of the company whose shares were redeemed or purchased, as is any director who signed the statutory declaration of solvency unless he is able to show that he had reasonable grounds for believing that solvency existed. In addition a director who makes a declaration without having reasonable grounds for the opinion expressed in the declaration is liable to imprisonment, fine, or both (s. 173 (6)).

A contributor is only liable in respect of the extent to which payment out of capital relates to his shares; all directors are jointly and severally liable with contributing directors.

A final point

From the above it can readily be appreciated that maintenance of capital provisions are both numerous and complicated. Therefore, it is perhaps to be expected that capital maintenance was cited in the Department of Trade and Industry consultation paper *The Modernization of*

See Appendix 1. *Company Law* (March 1988) as being an area of company law that was considerably over-regulated. Should company law be subject to major overhaul then it can be expected that capital maintenance will feature prominently in the reform.

Chapter summary

- *Share capital* represents a fund available to creditors in the event of company failure and as such it must be maintained – this is the rule in *Trevor v Whitworth*.
- Capital can be categorized in several ways with *authorized* or *nominal* being the amount that a company is permitted by its articles to raise through the issue of shares. *Paid-up* capital is the fund obtained by a share issue in which the shares are fully paid with *uncalled* capital being the money owing on partly-paid shares – it is a reserve to be called upon at any time the directors think fit.
- Authorized or nominal capital may be *increased* on the directors' recommendation (and if the articles permit) with the company at an EGM or AGM passing an ordinary resolution – a copy of which is to be sent to the Registrar for filing.
- The importance of maintenance of share capital means that any *reduction* is subject to control, e.g. a special resolution exercising an existing power in the articles followed by High Court approval and notification to the Registrar (s. 135 (1)). Other more specific ways to reduce capital are given under s. 135 (2).
- *Acquisition* by a company of its own shares is subject to a general prohibition (*Trevor v Whitworth*; and s. 143). However, several exceptions are available: a bequest of shares to the company; forfeiture; surrender; share redemption; permitted purchase; as part of capital reduction scheme; alteration of memorandum; company re-registration; court order relating to unfairly prejudicial conduct.
- Similarly, with *financial assistance* for the purchase of its own shares there is a general prohibition (s. 151 (1)) followed by a number of exceptions. Financial assistance is widely interpreted – any form of finance is assistance!
- The main *exceptions* for financial assistance are (s. 153): if the principal purpose of financial assistance is not for share acquisition or where it is an incidental part of a larger purpose. Other exceptions are s. 153 (3): as a distribution by way of dividing or in winding up; allotment of bonus shares; approved capital reduction (s. 137); redemption of shares; a compromise or arrangement with creditors or shareholders. Yet more exceptions are s. 153 (4): where lending money is in ordinary business; supporting an employee share scheme; and helping employees to purchase fully paid shares (Note: all of the last three exceptions must be utilized in good faith and a public company may use them only if the company has net assets which are not thereby reduced or, if they are, then the assistance is provided out of distributed profits.) Private companies are allowed to give financial assistance if a procedure similar to share redemption or purchase is followed.
- The articles may allow a company to issue *redeemable shares* (ordinary or preference) provided that at all times there are ordinary shares in existence. With public companies payment for redemption can only come from proceeds of a new issue or distributable profits but a private company may also use its capital.

- In respect to a company *purchasing its own shares* the articles must allow this with approval being an ordinary resolution for a market purchase with notification to the Registrar within 15 days and a later share return; a special resolution for an off-market purchase with again a return to the Registrar; and a special resolution for a contingent purchase.
- A *private company* may use its capital to redeem or purchase its own shares once its distributable profits and reserves have been used up. A special resolution is needed but the directors must make a declaration of solvency supported by an auditor report and appropriate publicity. Shareholders and creditors have 5 weeks in which to petition for the resolution to be cancelled.

Discussion questions

1 The prohibition on financial assistance by a company for acquisition of its own shares is too restrictive.
Discuss.
2 Discuss the rule in *Trevor v Whitworth* and say how it is both supported and weakened in the Companies Act 1985.

Case study exercise

Anthony and Cleopatra are a married couple who each own 50 per cent of Bacchus Limited of which they are the only directors. Anthony is a former international rugby player who does occasional guest appearances on television. The company specializes in providing corporate hospitality at most big sporting events with Anthony bringing in the clients and ensuring that they have an enjoyable day while Cleopatra takes care of the catering.

As a consequence of divorcing, the former couple decide to split the business into two parts: Anthony will form his own public relations company (Inter-Public Limited) with Cleopatra becoming the sole director/shareholder of Bacchus Limited. As the remaining part of Bacchus Limited will be larger than the part that will become Inter-Public Limited, Cleopatra agrees to make Anthony a cash payment of £35,000 which will 'even out' the difference. However, as Cleopatra experiences difficulties in obtaining the £35,000 she decides to get Bacchus Limited to pay Anthony so that she becomes a debtor of Bacchus Limited.

Before their agreement is put into effect the parties fall out. Anthony demands more of a 'fair share' and refuses to hand his shares in Bacchus Limited over to Cleopatra. Cleopatra is adamant that the agreement is 'watertight' rejecting Anthony's contention that it breaches company law requirements.

Advise the two warring parties of the legal position.

Further reading

Financial Assistance by a Company for the Purchase of its Shares, M.J. Sterling (1987), Co. Law, 99

COMPANIES'
SECURITIES

9 Shares

Introduction

Generally, the courts will describe shares in a company as being a form of property (a chose in action) but in one early case a definition was offered:

> A share is the interest of a shareholder in the company measured by a sum of money, for the purpose of liability in the first place, and interest in the second, but also consisting of a series of mutual covenants entered into by all the shareholders.

The term *measured by a sum of money* alludes to the nominal value while the reference to *liability* is that the shareholder (or member) is under a legal obligation to the company to pay for his shares on application, allotment, or when called upon to do so. In respect to *interest* the shareholder has an interest in the company which confers certain legal rights, such as voting or an entitlement to a dividend. This interest is a personal property right but it must be stressed that as the company is a separate legal person the assets of the company are owned exclusively by the company itself. Finally, *mutual covenants* makes the point that a shareholder's rights are contractual and these are now to be found in section 14, CA 1985.

A shorter definition is: '(a) share is a certain amount of interest in a company' (Charles Wordsworth, The Law of General and Other Joint Stock Companies, 1854).

Objectives

The purpose of this chapter is to make students familiar with the type and characteristics of shares. Students are also required to understand that payment for shares and alteration of any rights attached to them are both subject to control.

Key concepts

- The share certificate
- Types and characteristics of shares
- Pre-emption rights
- Payment for shares
- Rights to dividend payments.

The share certificate

A share certificate issued in the correct manner is valid evidence of a member's legal title to the shares covered by the certificate (s. 186). As a document that evidences title a certificate may be deposited as security to support a loan granted to the shareholder. If the deposit is substantial the creditor will usually insist that their interest is registered as a charge – that is as a claim against the shares so that in the event of the debtor not repaying the sum advanced, the creditor will be entitled to receive payment out of the fund represented by the shares.

The content of the share certificate will normally follow Table A, article 6 providing: a certificate serial number is used (unless all the shares are fully paid, rank equally in all respects and are of the same class); it states the company registered number and address, the name of the registered holder, the number and description of the shares covered by the certificate, the degree to which they are paid up, and the date of the certificate; and it is sealed and witnessed.

In the event of a dispute over the lawful ownership of shares the name appearing in the Register of Members is to be taken as the true recording of ownership. However, if the company through its officers are shown to have been negligent in relation to either issuing shares or in maintaining the register then an action in negligence may be possible. Should someone have relied upon the certificate as giving evidence of title, or the amount paid on the shares, then on an inaccuracy in the certificate being discovered, the company may be estopped (i.e. prevented) from denying the accuracy of the certificate and in consequence have to compensate the party who relied on the certificate (*Re Bahia & San Francisco Railway Co. Ltd* (1868)). But the company may be able to reclaim the compensatory amount from the person it knowingly issued the share certificate to unless that person was innocent (*Dixon v Kennaway* (1900)). If a share certificate was issued indicating the shares to be fully paid when in fact they were only partly paid then a person relying on this incorrect statement cannot be asked to pay the uncalled part (*Bloomenthal v Ford* (1847)). But this will not apply to a person who knew that the shares were not paid for in full in cash (*Re African Gold Co.* (1899)).

Forged transfers carry no value even if the holder acts in good faith:

> ## Ruben v Great Fingall Consolidated (1906)
> R lent money to the company secretary on the security of a share certificate. The secretary signed his own name on it, forged the names of two directors and put the company's seal on it.
>
> Held (House of Lords): The certificate was a forgery and the company was not bound by it.

Once the forgery is established the legal title of the true holder should be reinstated and any later holders in good faith can pursue their own claims for compensation against any party held to be liable. The company may (dependent on circumstances) have to repay dividends to the true holder of the shares, but an insurance policy can cover such payments. Minor irregularities in the execution of a transfer will not equal a forged transfer such as the incorrect numbering of shares (*Re International Contract Co.* (1872)).

Bearer share warrants

Share certificates endorsed to *Bearer* are known as warrants. They are negotiable documents in a similar manner to uncrossed cheques with negotiation (transfer) being by simple delivery from one person to another. Normally share certificates are not negotiable because to transfer ownership an entry in the company's Register of Members is required. Warrants may

Estoppel will not apply to a forged share certificate, nor can it operate in favour of a person who lodged a forged transfer (Ruben v Great Fingall Consolidates (1906).

In a situation like Ruben v Great Fingall Consolidated (1906) the company may be liable in tort for the fraud of its officer – provided that it was committed in the course of his employment (Lloyd v Grace, Smith & Co. (1912).

be issued by any company entitled to do so by its article and subject to the share warrants being fully paid (s. 188). As invariably private companies restrict in their article the right to transfer shares, warrants are always issued by public companies unconcerned that their shares are easily transferable.

Dividend coupons are normally attached to bearer warrants and the holder of the warrant will tear off the appropriate coupon and present it to the company, or its agent, for payment. On issuing bearer warrants a company becomes subject to detailed rules about communication to warrant holders over dividend declarations and the calling of general and class meetings.

On issuing a share warrant the name of the former shareholder is removed from the Register of Members but a holder of a warrant can at any time hand in the warrant and have his name entered on the register. Technically as a warrant holder does not appear on the Register of Members he is not a member of the company, but the articles may say that he is to be treated as being one.

Types of share capital

A company is not bound to issue all its shares with the same class rights and most often the shares will be of different types with varying rights. The articles will provide the power to do this with the specimen being given in Table A, article 2. In fact a company may issue at any time different types of shares provided that in doing so it does not breach its memorandum (*Andrews v Gas Meter Co.* (1897)).

There are several different types of shares which may be issued:

1 Ordinary
2 Preference
3 Deferred
4 Bonus
5 Redeemable.

Ordinary shares

In financial terminology ordinary shares are called equities. Holders of ordinary shares have the residual rights of participation in income and capital after other obligations have been fully satisfied (s. 744) but there is no legal right to a dividend until one has been officially declared. As an investment, ordinary shareholders carry the most risk in a company but they stand to gain the most benefit if the company proves to be prosperous, for they will share in the remainder of a distributable surplus of profits after fixed dividends are paid to the preference shareholders (assuming that preference shares have been issued).

Normally ordinary shareholders will have one vote per share but non-voting ordinary shares may be issued. These are uncommon and are disliked by the Stock Exchange. It is always possible to keep control in the hands of a minority, which may be particularly useful in a private company, by means of weighted voting rights and this device will dispense with the need to issue unpopular non-voting shares.

Preference shares

The characteristic of this type of share is that it has a preferred fixed dividend that must be paid before the ordinary shareholders receive anything. Dividend entitlement is usually expressed as a percentage of the nominal value of the shares and they may be:

a) *cumulative*, which means that if the company is unable to pay a dividend in any year, it must accumulate the arrears of unpaid dividends from year to year until they are paid before the ordinary shareholders can receive any of the profits; or alternatively,

b) *non-cumulative*, which means that if the company is unable to pay a dividend in any particular year, the preference shareholder will not receive any dividend relating to that year – i.e. the 'lost dividend' will not be carried over to a more prosperous year. Unless the company's constitution expressly described their issued preference shares to be non-cumulative then they will be presumed to be cumulative (*Webb v Earle* (1875));

(c) *participating*, which means that these are preference shares which receive their fixed dividend in the normal manner, but which then participate further in the distributed profits along with the ordinary shareholders after a certain fixed percentage has been paid on the ordinary shares.

Preference shares occasionally have voting rights but these rights may be different from the ones given to ordinary shares – usually they will be limited to voting at meetings dealing with variation of their own rights. The fixed dividend payable on preference shares may not be paid out of capital and becomes payable only when it is declared with no dividend payable to ordinary shareholders before the preference shareholders have received their dividend.

A company that has already issued some preference shares may issue later preference shares which will rank in order of issue. Therefore, second preference shareholders will only receive a dividend after first preference shareholders have received their fixed dividend (but before any further participating dividend, if existing, is paid). Subsequent preference shares issues may be made.

Further points on preference shares are:

The articles will normally say that they have a priority right of return of capital – if not then preference shareholders will be treated equally with the ordinary shareholders.

The articles will normally provide that arrears of dividends previously declared are payable and then only if surplus assets are available (Re *Crichton's Oil Co.* (1902)).

The arrears will be paid out of the assets which remain after the payment of other obligations.

Review question

Ordinary shares are a more attractive investment than preference shares.
Discuss the merits of this statement.

Deferred shares

Deferred shares used to be fairly common but are now becoming rare. Previously promoters of a company would agree to take up a share issue of deferred shares (hence they are also known as *founders' shares*) in order to show their confidence in the enterprise. If the promoters became directors after the incorporation of the company then this type of share could be termed *management shares.*

Deferred shares may carry heavy voting rights when compared with ordinary shares and they may participate to a fairly high degree in the company's surplus assets on the company's liquidation. As far as dividends are concerned they normally attract a payment after a dividend of a certain percentage has been paid on other shares. Holders of other classes of share disliked deferred shares as promoters on occasions often took disproportionately high voting rights so as to stifle effective dissent from other shareholders. The Stock Exchange listing regulations have considerably reduced the number of deferred shares issued by public limited companies, many of whom have converted them into ordinary shares.

Bonus shares

Bonus shares are extra shares issued to existing members, usually in proportion to their current holding, without obtaining direct payment for them (Table A, article 110). However, they must be either fully or partly paid up with payment coming from:

a) distributable profits;
b) the share premium account or a capital redemption issue; or
c) any other reserve which is not available for redistribution.

The transfer of monies into the share account increases the company's capitalization but because the number of shares on the market will be increased the effect is to reduce the share price.

Authority to issue bonus shares has to be given in the articles with Table A, article 110 permitting such an issue provided that an ordinary resolution is passed. After the issue an allotment return has to be made (s. 88(2)).

A bonus issue may also be referred to as a script issue, or a capitalization issue or a free issue. However, if payment is derived from (b) or (c) then it is not strictly a capitalization since the funds used are already regarded as being capital. Should payment come from (a) then the issue is hardly a free bonus since the payment monies could have been distributed as dividends.

Redeemable shares

A limited company with share capital may, if authorized by its articles, allot shares which are redeemable, or liable to be redeemed at the option of the company or the shareholder (s. 159). To be redeemed, shares:

a) must have been issued as redeemable; and
b) must be fully paid; and
c) can be converted into redeemable shares.

For fuller treatment of redeemable shares see Chapter 8, Capital: Classification, Maintenance and Alteration.

Calls

Although it is now much less common a company may issue shares partly paid with the balance being paid when called by the company to make payment. A shareholder is contractually bound to meet a call as the monies outstanding on the shares represent a debt owed to the company. The procedure for making calls will normally be given in the articles and usually it will be for the directors to pass a resolution at a board meeting (Table A, article 16)

Calls may be used where it is felt that a particular issue will be too large for many prospective shareholders to pay in full on application.

instructing the secretary to give the relevant shareholders notice of the call (Table A, article 12 stipulates at least 14 days). Should a call not follow the formal procedure then it will be invalid (*Re Cawley & Co.* (1889)) so that a shareholder may ignore it and restrain the directors from any attempt to make him forfeit his shares. Similarly, a call will be invalid if the directors make it not for the benefit of the company as a whole but for their own advantage. Here either an injunction can be sought to prohibit the call or, alternatively, if it has proceeded before the directors' self interest was discovered then they may be compelled to hand over to the company any benefit they received.

For an example of directors making a call in their own interests see Alexander v Automatic Telephone Co. (1900) given in Chapter 11, Directors.

If the articles permit then the directors may allow shareholders to pay an amount outstanding on their shares before a call has been made. But the directors must authorize such payments only if they are for the benefit of the company as a whole:

Sykes Case (1872)

As a consequence of the company having no cash the directors had not been paid. However, they later paid into the company's bank amounts remaining due on their shares and a few hours later paid themselves this amount as directors' fees.

Held: The 'in advance of calls' payment was not for the benefit of the company so that the directors remained liable to pay the amount still due on their shares.

The authority of the company needed for the allotment of shares

The directors may issue more shares up to the maximum authorized in the memorandum but beyond this no new shares may be allotted without the authority of the company either by the articles or in a general meeting by an ordinary resolution giving directors the authority to issue more shares. The authority may be specific or general but it must state the maximum amount and the time period during which they can be issued which is not to exceed 5 years (s. 80).

Once an allotment has been made the shares must be issued within two months of allotment or entry in the Register of Members unless the articles state otherwise. For shares listed on The Stock Exchange an issue period of 14 days from allotment applies. However, members may by an ordinary resolution revoke an authority previously given. A breach of s. 80 will not invalidate the issue but any director who knowingly contravened it will be guilty of an offence under the Companies Act. All allotments once made have to be filed at Companies House on form 88(2).

Employees' shares or subscribers' shares (these are shares indicated in the memorandum to be taken up by these who subscribe to the memorandum) may be issued by the directors under their general power to manage.

The proper purpose rule

As with the exercise of all directors' powers, these powers in relation to share issue must be exercised in good faith for '*the proper purpose*'. *Prima facie*, this means that the company must be in need of finance – other purposes being questionable. Therefore, it is improper to issue shares to:

a) defeat a takeover bid (*Hogg v Cramphorn* (1967));
b) facilitate a takeover bid (*Howard Smith Ltd v Ampoll Ltd* (1974));
c) secure the passing of a resolution;
d) prevent the removal of directors;
e) deprive shareholders of special voting rights.

If the directors do make an issue for improper purposes then it is violable but may be ratified by the company provided that no votes are recorded by the members to whom the shares were improperly issued. However, in *Clemens v Clemens Bros Ltd* (1976) ratification was not allowed since it amounted to the director ratifying her own breach of duty.

Review question

Directors, as *de facto* managers of a company, may issue shares whenever they feel that it is appropriate to do so.
Discuss the validity of this statement.

Statutory pre-emption rights

If the company has already issued ordinary shares or participating shares carrying the right to participate in the surplus assets on winding up, the holders of them have a statutory right to be offered a proportion of any new ordinary shares that are issued. This proportion must be as nearly as practicable equal to the proportion in nominal value of shares already held by them of the total ordinary shares. For example, a shareholder holding 1 per cent of the ordinary shares must be given the first right to buy 1 per cent of the new ordinary shares (s. 89 (1)). The new shares must be offered on the same or more favourable terms as those made to any other person. Shareholders receiving a pre-emption offer must have at least 21 days to decide whether to take up the offer (s. 90 (6)).

Pre-emption rights are valuable in enabling a shareholder to retain his 'ownership proportion' in the company but a private company may exclude the right from operating by means of a suitable clause in the memorandum or articles (s. 91 (1)). A private company, it must be remembered, is restricted to offering new shares only to its own shareholders or employees and not to the public. In respect to public companies the directors may, by the articles or by a special resolution, be given a power to allot ordinary shares or full participating shares without having first to offer them to existing shareholders (s. 95 (1)).

The pre-emption provision does not apply in the following circumstances (s. 95):

a) in relation to bonus, employee or subscriber shares. Nor does it apply to shares issued wholly or partly for consideration other than cash, e.g. where a company issues shares in order to finance a share-for share takeover bid;
b) where directors are given a general authority under s. 80 to allot securities and are

also given the power by the articles, or by a special resolution, to allot shares without having to comply with the statutory pre-emption rule;

c) where the members have passed a special resolution to remove pre-emption rights in regard to a specific issue of shares following a written recommendation by directors. The directors have to recommend the resolution and state their reasons for wanting to suspend the pre-emption rule;

d) where a *private company* by its memorandum excludes or modifies the pre-emption rights (s. 91).

The pre-emption rights on the issue of shares must not be confused with pre-emption rights that a company may by its articles impose on a transfer of shares.

Should the pre-emption rule be broken then every officer of the company who knew of the breach will be liable to compensate any member entitled to receive the offer and as a consequence suffered a loss (CA 1985, s. 92).

Class rights

Each type or class of share issued by a company will have their own particular rights which are called class rights. Most commonly class rights are given in the articles and are attached solely to the shares. However, in exceptional circumstances it is possible for class rights to be attached to the shareholder as opposed to the shares (*Cumbrian Newspapers Group Ltd v Cumberland & Westmorland Herald Newspaper & Printing Co. Ltd* (1987)).

Variation of class rights

Class rights are not set in stone but may be varied over time. Where the company has different classes of shares then the procedure set out in s. 125 has to be followed. An overview of this procedure is:

a) *Where there is no variation clause*
   i)   If the class rights are in the memorandum then to vary them all members must agree to the variation resolution.
   ii) If the class rights are given in the articles then to vary them holders of three-quarters of the shares of the class must agree in writing to the variation, or alternatively at a class shareholder meeting an extraordinary resolution needs to be passed.
   iii) If the class rights are given in the terms of the share issue the procedure will be the same as for (ii).

b) *Where there is a variation clause*
   i)   If the class rights are in the memorandum and the variation clause in the articles then the variation must be made in accordance with the variation clause provided that the clause was in existence at the company's incorporation.
   ii) If both the class rights and the variation clause are in the articles then the variation must be made in accordance with the variation clause.
   iii) If both the class rights and the variation clause are in the terms of the share issue then the variation must be made in accordance with the variation clause.
   iv) If the variation relates to either the directors' power to allot shares (s. 80), or to a reduction of the company's share capital (s. 135) then the variation has to be made in accordance with the variation clause.

Meaning of 'variation'

In the absence of detailed statutory provision it has been left to case law to say when an alteration of class rights will equal a variation. Traditionally judges have been loath to be too generous in finding that variation has taken place:

White v Bristol Aeroplane Co. Ltd (1953)

It was argued that a new share issue would by 'watering down' the voting rights of existing members (in that their future votes would become a much smaller proportion of the total than previously) equal a variation.

Held: The Court of Appeal rejecting the argument found that there was no variation of class rights.

Similarly in *Greenhalgh v Arderne Cinemas Ltd* (1946) where voting rights were increased for one share class at the expense of another class there was no variation. Even a drastic reduction of a class right (*Re Mackenzie & Co. Ltd* (1916)) or, harshly, the reduction of a class right to zero value (*Dimbula Valley (Ceylon) Tea Co. Ltd v Laurie* (1961) will not constitute a variation.

Where courts are willing to say that alteration of a class right will be a variation that may be protected through a court action is where the nature or quality of the right is being altered, such as by changing a voting right of one vote per share to one vote per five shares. Similarly alteration of dividend rights would equal a variation.

Minority protection – a statutory right to object.

Holders of at least 15 per cent of the issued shares of the class subject to the intended variation may, provided that they did not vote in favour of the variation, apply to the court within 21 days to have the proposal cancelled. The application has to be made by a member of the class concerned who has to have been appointed to do so in writing by others of that class. (s. 127). This statutory right of objection is potentially valuable but in practice it is of modest benefit. Firstly, as discussed earlier courts give a very narrow meaning to variation so that aggrieved minority holders may not have their complaint recognized. Secondly, a court has considerable discretion when hearing an application and may decide to confirm the variation on the basis that the complaining minority may either use equity to secure a remedy, as in *British American Nickel Corp. Ltd v M. J. O'Brien Ltd* (1927) where at a class meeting a resolution to achieve a variation was held not to have been passed in good faith, or alternatively, challenge the variation as being unfairly prejudicial conduct under sections 459–461.

Review question

Hardwick Limited intend to use a share premium account to fund the issue to ordinary shareholders of preference shares with restricted voting rights. Existing preference shareholders will receive no new shares.

Under statute any alteration of a provision contained in a company's articles for the variation of the rights attached to a class of shares, or the insertion of any such provision into the articles, is itself a variation of those rights (s. 125). Also where class rights are repealed, as opposed to being altered, then such obligation will equal a variation (ss. 17, 125, 127).

Discuss the legality of this proposal.

Payment for shares

Share capital is a guarantee fund for creditors. Many of the rules relating to payment for shares are intended to ensure that the company has a right to receive such payment, i.e. at least the nominal value of the shares issued.

The requirements are more demanding for public companies where the payment rules are:

Section 101 does not apply to shares issued under an employee share scheme.

a) A public company may not allot shares unless they are paid up to at least 25 per cent of their nominal value together with the whole of any share premium – this is the excess over the nominal value of the shares and the issue price (s. 101). Should there be a share premium then it must be transferred to a share premium account and is only to be used in specified ways (s. 130).

b) In respect to payment other than by money (consideration other than cash) there are limited exceptions such as payment in the form of goods, patent rights or services. However, major restrictions apply, the main one being s. 103 which prohibits a public company from allotting shares for non-cash unless within 6 months prior to the allotment the consideration has been valued and reported on by an independent qualified person. A copy of the report has to be delivered to the registrar.

c) If s. 101 is broken then an allottee (or any later purchaser who was aware of the breach) will be required to pay the additional amount plus interest.

The meaning of 'payment for shares'

The following apply:

a) Shares must always be paid for. Therefore, a company is not allowed to make a gift of its shares.

b) Payment for shares must be in money or money's worth which may include business goodwill or know-how (s. 99 (2)), but see (c).

(c) In respect to a *public limited company*:
   i) as they may not accept payment in the form of a promise to perform work or provide a service for the company, it means that payment for their shares must be in cash or non-cash assets (s. 99(2));
   ii) shares issued to a subscriber to the memorandum in reliance of a promise in the memorandum must be paid in cash (s. 106).

Should a public limited company breach s. 99 (2) then any person to whom the shares were allotted becomes liable to pay their nominal value, plus premium, plus interest to the company. Subsequent purchasers who were aware of the breach will similarly be liable.

The issue of shares at a premium

Shares are seldom issued at their nominal value, usually being issued at a higher price. The difference between nominal value and issue value is the premium. The reason for a premium may be due to the net assets of the company being greater than the nominal value of the shares being issued; or, because an earlier issue of the same class of shares has achieved a market value exceeding their nominal value and the new issue will be pitched at this market value figure.

What is important is that any share premium is safeguarded. Therefore, a premium cannot be distributed as dividend but must be paid into a share premium account (s. 130 (2)) viz.:

a) in paying up unused shares to be issued to members as fully paid bonus shares; or
b) in writing off the company's preliminary expenses; or
c) in writing off expenses, commissions, discounts on an issue of shares or debentures; or
d) in providing the premium payable on the redemption of the company's debentures.

In addition the premium may be used to pay the premium on the redemption of redeemable shares that were issued at a premium.

Issuing shares at a discount

Clearly, if shares could be discounted, i.e. fully paid shares issued for less than their nominal value, then it would prejudice creditors. Therefore, shares may not be issued at a discount (s. 100) unless the discounted shares are issued:

i) when underwriting commission is paid; or
ii) where a private company exchanges issued shares for an over-valued payment.

Similar sanctions apply to contravention of s. 100 as to contravention of s. 99 (2).

Allotment for non-cash consideration

The perceived danger is that a company may allot shares for a non-cash payment that is less than what would be obtained for a cash payment. For this reason detailed provisions apply. They are:

a) *Public companies*
   Where the non-cash asset is to be transferred at a future date, then the transfer must take place within 5 years of the allotment (s. 102 (1)), the under-cash asset must be independently valued with a report on the valuation made to the company within 6 months prior to the allotment taking place (a copy of the report has also to be sent to the proposed allottee) (s. 103 (1)) and the valuation of the non-cash asset (with, if appropriate any cash adjustment) must not be less than the nominal value of the shares plus any premium (s. 103 (1)). If either sections 102–103 are broken then the allottee and any later holder of the shares who knew of the breach will be liable to pay cash for the shares together with interest.

b) *Private companies*
   With public companies there is a desire in law that shareholders get value for money when taking non-cash assets. However, in respect to private companies there is no similar desire or protective requirements. In exceptional circumstances a court will examine the adequacy of the consideration, for example:

The independent valuer must be qualified to be the auditor of the company and if the report is not his own then it has to be provided by another person he holds to be sufficiently knowledgeable and experienced.

– where the transaction is fraudulent
– where the consideration is past
– where the inadequacy appears on the face of the contract.

Issue of shares by public companies for non-cash assets

s. 104 does not apply to shares issued as subscriber shares which must be paid up in cash (s. 106).

Section 104 requires an independent valuation and report of non-cash consideration when shares are allotted. Clearly, s. 103 could be circumvented by not actually *allotting* shares but by later *issuing* them. Therefore, for two years following the issue of its trading certificate similar valuation requirements apply when a public company acquires non-cash assets (having an aggregate value equal to 10 per cent or more of the nominal value of the issued share capital) from a subscriber to the memorandum. In addition the acquisition has to be approved by an ordinary resolution a copy of which, with the valuation report, being delivered to the registrar within 15 days of its being passed. Contravention of s. 104 operates on the same basis as breach of ss. 102–103. However, a court may find it just and equitable to exempt a person from liability for breach of ss.102–104 (s. 113).

Review question

Discuss how a company is obligated to obtain at least the nominal value of its issued share capital from its members.

Share transfers

Every shareholder has the right to transfer their shares even if the transfer is intended to avoid liability. The procedure required for the transfer of shares will be given in the articles. Some private companies are somewhat restrictive over share transfers fearing that the company could pass from family control to outsiders. Hence the articles will probably shore up pre-emption rights giving the directors power only to sanction a share transfer if they actually approve of it. Alternatively, the directors may be given the power to compel a shareholder to transfer shares if an irreconcilable conflict of interest arises (*Sidebottom v Kershaw, Leese & Co. Ltd* (1920)) Also the directors are usually allowed to refuse a transfer if a share is not fully paid. If Table A articles are used then the transfer procedure is given in A23–28. For transfer of shares in a public limited company the transfer system used by the Stock Exchange will apply. Currently it is the CREST system that is in operation.

Dividends

A share is a right to receive a certain proportion of the profits of the company. With publicly quoted companies it is the practice to distribute profits in the form of dividends twice yearly – the first after the interim or half year figures have been announced with the second, final dividend being paid with the full year results. Shareholder dividends can only be paid out of profits. If the company has not earned sufficient profit then while a debenture holder may receive interest on their loan from capital, shareholders would receive nothing. Over the years a constant fear has been that companies will artificially inflate their level of profits in order to pay out unrealistic dividends. For this reason a company can only make a distribution out of its accumulated realized profits less its accumulated realized losses (s. 263). Additionally, a *public company* is required to write off its unrealized losses against realized and unrealized profits before it is able to make a distribution out of the remaining realized profits (s. 264).

Realized profits means profits either received or recognized to exist under current accounting practice, e.g. a sale validly entered in the books as a debt owed the company although payment has not been actually received (*Re Oxford Benefits Building and Investment Society* (1886). Profits which are merely expected are not sufficiently certain to be relied upon for the recommendation of a dividend. Similarly, an asset that has appreciated in value, such as property, will give an increased 'paper profit' but until the asset is sold there is no actual realized profit. Therefore, for dividend purposes the 'paper profit' has to be ignored. A realized loss exists when costs related to sales for a particular year exceed the income obtained from those sales. An unrealized loss arises where assets fall in value, such as commercial property during a recession, those assets not having yet been sold.

A particular problem for companies is the position of bad debt. This is unpaid debt that is not expected to be paid. While in any business such losses are practically unavoidable, proper allowance has to be made otherwise an optimistic underestimate of bad debt could result in artificially high dividends being declared. For this reason a company's bad debt provision, which is taken to be a realized loss (s. 275) (1)), must be a genuine estimate based on the company's recent trading experience. If the company is newly created then the estimate may be derived from whatever industry the company is in.

A future liability that cannot at present be properly valued is best dealt with by means of a provision (Schedule 4). This will consist of a fund equal to the 'guesstimate' of the likely future cost. If such a fund is set up then it has to be regarded as a realized loss even though no actual loss has yet been incurred (s. 275 (1)).

Shareholders, even where the company is profitable normally have no automatic right to a dividend but must wait until a resolution is presented at a company meeting to approve a dividend recommendation made by the directors. However, with some companies the articles may say that where the company achieves a certain profitability then the shareholders are to receive an automatic fixed dividend (*Evling v Israel and Oppenheimer* (1918). The directors when making a dividend recommendation are required to be guided by the latest set of audited accounts. Also the directors must, when recommending a dividend, act in good faith for the benefit of the company as a whole. A policy of always distributing all realized profits as dividends, without looking to future contingencies, may be a breach of the directors' duty of care. A dividend distribution that breaches the requirements of ss. 263–264 will mean that a shareholder who at the time of the distributions knew or who had reasonable grounds for believing it was made improperly will be liable to repay the dividend to the company (s. 277).

A prolonged failure to pay a dividend when profits are apparently available may be a ground for petitioning for the company to be wound up, for example for unfairly prejudicial conduct (s. 459) or possibly under the just and equitable ground.

Special or super dividend

Sometimes a company will give shareholders an extra dividend in addition to a normal payment. This extra dividend is known as a special or super dividend. Companies making such payments may be doing so to return surplus cash to shareholders and so make the shares more attractive to investors, or the payment may be promised in the course of a takeover battle to help ensure that shareholders stay loyal to the incumbent board or directors. For non-tax paying shareholders, such as institutional investors, this type of dividend is particularly attractive.

Script dividends

Here, shareholders are given the choice of receiving their dividend in cash or subscribing for an equivalent value in shares. This form of dividend is becoming more common.

Chapter summary

- A correctly issued share certificate is an evidential document of ownership but should this be disputed then the name found in the members' register will be taken to be the legal owner. A failure on the part of the company properly to maintain the register provides grounds for a negligence action. Also the company may be estopped (prevented) from denying the accuracy of a certificate it has issued. A forged share certificate, or a forged transfer, are both legally ineffective.
- Bearer share certificates are termed warrants and are negotiable instruments. As such transfer of ownership is achieved through simple delivery as opposed to the transfer of a normal share certificate whose transfer is dependent on the register of members being duly amended. Unless the articles say otherwise a warrant holder is not a member of the company.
- There are several types of shares: ordinary, preference (cumulative, non-cumulative, participating) and deferred. Each type has its own class rights relating to voting, dividends and priority in liquidation entitlement.
- Class rights are usually given in the articles and overwhelmingly relate to the shares as opposed to a shareholder. Class rights may be varied under the procedure set out in s. 125. Courts are extremely cautious in saying that a change to class rights will equal a variation that comes within s. 125. When variation applies then minority members (at least 15 per cent of the issued shares in the affected class) may within 21 days apply for cancellation of the proposed variation. However, a court in using its discretion may be unforthcoming, preferring complainants to use other avenues of redress.
- Provided they were issued as being redeemable then once fully paid the shares can be redeemed by the company.
- Directors may issue shares up to the maximum permitted by the memorandum but beyond this a new share issue requires the approval of the company either through an authority given in the articles or by means of an ordinary resolution passed at a company meeting.
- Authority to issue new shares lasts for up to 5 years and the maximum number of shares allowed to be issued has to be stated.
- Directors when sanctioning a share issue must do so in good faith for valid reasons. This is termed 'with proper purpose' rule. Case law has established what are improper purposes but the company is able, through ratification, to make good an improper purpose.

- If more shares are issued then existing members have legal right of first refusal. This is termed 'pre-emption rights' which must be available for at least 21 days (unless members have already accepted or rejected the offer). Several exceptions occur where pre-emption rights do not apply.
- In order to protect the interest of creditors, payments for shares, especially where a public limited company is involved, are subject to control notably in respect to payment by non-cash consideration. There are similar protective provisions that relate to the allotment of shares for non-cash consideration.
- Shares may be issued at a premium, i.e. at higher than their nominal value, or at a discount, i.e. at lower than their nominal value. A premium has to be paid into a share premium account which can only be used for limited purposes. Discounting on shares is restricted to when underwriting commission is paid or where a private company exchanged shares for an over-valued payment.
- Share dividends can only be paid out of profits when a dividend recommendation, made by the director, is approved at a company meeting unless uncommonly the articles automatically permit a dividend payment when a stipulated profitability has been achieved. When recommending a dividend directors must have done so in good faith for the benefit of the whole company after being guided by the latest company audited accounts. Future contingencies need to be fully considered.
- In recent years, special dividends which are an additional dividend to normal ones have become more common.

Discussion questions

1 Discuss each of the following:
   a) preference shares;
   b) the pre-emption rights of existing members;
   c) the circumstances in which shares may be issued at other than their nominal value.
2 When a company issues shares under the Companies Act 1985 it must receive proper payment for them.
   Discuss.
3 Discuss why the law is anxious to control the payment of dividends and say what form the control takes.

Case study exercise

Over many years the trading position of Sovereign plc, a manufacturer of traditional designed lawnmowers, has deteriorated so that for the last few years it has incurred losses. Currently the company's issued share capital of 25 million ordinary £1 shares (of which half are uncalled) is no longer represented by realizable assets. A new board of directors is aware that any future profits will be eaten up by having to cover earlier losses so that members would have to wait several years before receiving a dividend. Therefore, the action plan the board wish to implement is: firstly, to split the share capital into ordinary 50p shares and to remove the members' liability on the partly paid shares; secondly, once profitability is achieved as large a dividend as possible is to be paid. The finance for this is to come from profits augmented by revaluing the company's freehold land. The revaluation surplus will go into a specially created revaluation reserve fund.

(a) Advise the board how to proceed in implementing the first part of their action plan.

(b) Comment on the legality of the second part of the proposed action plan.

Further reading

Realized Profits: Unrealistic Conclusion, C. Noke (1989), JBL, 37.
Can Shares in Companies be Defined? R. Pennington (1989), Co. Law, 140.

10 Debentures

Introduction

A company requiring capital may in addition to issuing shares to members obtain loan capital from banks or other financial institutions through the issue of debentures. A debenture is a long-term loan, typically for between thirty to forty years, made at a fixed rate of interest. A person taking a debenture in exchange for a loan does not become a member of the company but a creditor and in the event of liquidation will have a preferential claim on the company's assets.

Objectives

The purpose of this chapter is for students to know that debenture borrowing by a company is common with creditors virtually always taking security (fixed or floating charges). But to be valid against other claimants for the security, it needs to be registered. In addition recognition is expected that even with registration there are a number of problematic areas that may mean the security taken is ineffective. Where a company issues a number of debentures then students must appreciate the technicalities that operate in respect to which debentures rank before others.

Key concepts

- A company's common law and statutory right to borrow with ultra vires borrowing condoned in respect to creditors
- Debentures may be of different types
- Fixed and floating charges used as security
- Crystallization of a floating charge but circumstances may mean the security is lost
- Registration formalities
- Priority of registration.

A company's power to borrow

Every trading company has an implied power to borrow money for the purpose of its trading and also to charge its property as security for payment of loans. This common law position is supported by the Companies Act 1985 which states that a company may in its memorandum of association say that its object is to carry on business as a general commercial company and this will allow it to do whatever is incidental or conducive to carry on any trade

Before a company can borrow it must be in business. Private companies can borrow as soon as they are incorporated; public limited companies must wait until they receive a trading certificate to confirm that the capital requirements have been satisfied (s. 117).

or business including borrowing (s. 3A). The borrowing powers of a trading company are generally exercised by the directors but this is a matter for the articles.

Non-trading companies have no power to borrow unless the memorandum gives them power to do so. If the memorandum is silent on this matter then it may be extended to allow borrowing to take place.

Ultra vires borrowing

The memorandum may limit the power to borrow, for example it could say that the company may not borrow more than two-thirds of its paid-up capital. Where a company borrows beyond its powers the borrowing is said to be ultra vires. The same applies where a company borrows within its authority but for an ultra vires purpose the borrowing is itself tainted with illegality. Although a company should not have gone against its memorandum or obtained loans to pursue unauthorized purposes an outsider, such as a creditor, will not be bound by the ulra vires rule so that they will be able to enforce the loan contract and any security against the company (s. 35 (1)).

A company's memorandum and s. 3A will give it the *capacity to* borrow but that power is normally exercised by the directors who have the borrowing *authority*. If directors while acting within the capacity of the company exceed their authority then provided the outsider dealt with the company in good faith then the directors' unauthorized actions will bind the company irrespective of what the memorandum contains (s. 35A).

Definitions and explanation of debenture terms

The term debenture has several meanings. However, under the Companies Act 1985 it is taken to mean any company document which acknowledges indebtedness (Lemon v Austin Friars Investment Trust Ltd (1925)).

A debenture is a document creating or evidencing a debt (*English & Scottish Mercantile Investment Trust v Brunon* (1892)). In commercial use a debenture is a secured loan on the company's present and future assets taking the form of a contract entered into with a creditor in which the company promises to repay a fixed sum with interest

Debentures can be issued to a specific creditor, such as a bank, or alternatively to represent a loan issued to the public which will be traded on the Stock Exchange in a manner similar to shares. This will be termed *debenture stock*, which may be irredeemable or perpetual so that the inconvenience of a fixed term is avoided. It can also usually be transferred in any amount which adds to its marketability. Therefore, an investor (creditor) can instruct his broker to buy £10,000 worth of, say, second series debentures in the XYZ plc. He may keep this debenture stock for many years or immediately re-sell them in full or in part. He can do this as they are tradable securities. Debenture stock is almost always secured by a trust deed. Consequently, the rights of the stockholders lie primarily against the trustees who administer the charge given by the company.

A *perpetual* debenture is one without a date fixed within which the company is obligated to buy them back – therefore, they are not payable on demand. However, the loan advanced will become payable if any of the events specified in the debenture contract occur, e.g. failure to pay interest, presentation of a winding-up petition, the appointment of a receiver etc. An *irredeemable* debenture does not mean that the company can never pay off the debenture but that the debenture holder can never demand payment (*Re Joseph Stocks Ltd* (1912)).

A reference in a debenture issue (series) to being *pari passu* means that all the debentures in the issue are equal in that they all have to be paid rateably. So if the company does not have sufficient funds to buy back all of them, they have all to be paid proportionally the same sum due to them for capital and interest (*Midland Express Ltd* (1913)). If pari passu was not used the debenture would be payable according to the date of issue, or, if many or all were issued on the same day, then according to the numerical order (*Gartside v Silkstone etc. Co.* (1882)).

Debenture at a discount

As debentures do not form part of the capital of the company, unlike shares, they may be issued at a discount (*Re Regent's Canal* (1876) and *Moseley v Koffyfontein Mines Ltd* (1904)), unless the debenture issue allows an immediate right to convert into shares in which case a discount cannot be given (*Campbell's case* (1876)). As debentures are not part of the capital it means that interest on them becomes a debt that can be paid out of capital (*Hinds v Beunos Ayres etc. Co.* (1906)).

The company cannot issue new debentures to rank pari passu with a previous issue unless it expressly reserves the right to do so (Gartside v Silkstone etc. Co. (1882)).

Redeemable debentures

A debenture issue may state that a certain proportion of the issue will be redeemed each year or that it reserves the right to do so. In respect to selecting debentures to be redeemed this may be achieved through drawing by lot or by buying back on the open market, e.g. the Stock Exchange. When a specific redemption date is given on an issue the company may set up a redemption fund for that purpose; alternatively a new issue of debentures may be used to pay for the buy back.

After redemption the company is able, unless it contracted in its articles or elsewhere not to reissue them or a resolution has been passed to cancel them, to reissue them or replace them with other debentures (s. 194). If reissued then the new holder will have the same priority rights as if they had never been redeemed (s. 194), but a redemption date for the reissue must not be later than the redemption date of the original issue (*Re Antofagasta (Chile) and Bolivia Railway Co. Trust Deed* (1939)).

With redeemable debentures, to make the issue a success the redemption price may be higher than the issue price so that a holder, in addition to interest, will eventually make a capital gain on his investment. If a debenture is bought back at a discount to its issue price the resulting 'profit' becomes one that can be realized for dividend purposes unless the articles prohibit this.

Bearer debentures

A bearer debenture is simply a debenture made payable to the holder or bearer. The significant characteristic of this type of debenture is that it is a negotiable instrument so that the following apply:

a) it is transferable by delivery;
b) a transferee in due course gets a good title independent of any defects in the title of the transferor;
c) no notice of transfer need be given to the company that issued the debenture.

Unless a debenture is a bearer one it has to be registered; hence all non-bearer debentures are registered debentures.

Of the above characteristics the second is of great importance as illustrated by:

> **Bechuanaland Exploration Co. v London Trading Bank (1898)**
> BE held bearer debentures of an English company that were kept in a safe to which their secretary had the key. Unknown to BE the secretary later used the debentures as security for a loan from LTB. The bank took them in good faith having recently received from BE an assurance that their secretary was absolutely trustworthy.
>
> Held: As bearer debentures they were negotiable which meant that the defendant bank gained a good title to them.

The debenture trust deed

The trustees will normally be a trust corporation, such as a subsidiary of a bank, specializing in this type of financial administration. Their fee will commonly be paid by the company issuing the debenture but the trustees will owe fiduciary duties to the debenture stock holders (the beneficiaries).

Where a series of debentures are to be held by many holders, such as under a public offer of debenture stock, then a trust deed is normally used. Indeed if the charge is a legal fixed charge and there are more than four debenture holders then a trust deed must be used. Should the company break the agreement then a term in the deed will entitle the trustees to appoint a receiver to protect the property used as security. This is possible because the charge is made out in favour of the trustees who hold it in trust for the debenture stockholders. For this reason it is the trustees who are creditors of the company (the same as straight debenture holders) and not the debenture stock holders (*Re Dunderland Iron Ore Co. Ltd* (1909)). What is convenient about a trust deed being used is that trustees can enforce the collective rights of the debenture stock holders whereas, with most probably a fluctuating body of individual holders, left to themselves it would be more difficult for them to look after their individual interests.

Registered debentures

As an alternative, the debenture issue may allow a holder to transfer the debenture free of equities, i.e. free of the claims of others.

A company is not obliged to keep a register of debenture holders but if it does then it is usually kept at the company's registered office (s. 191) and is open without charge to inspection by debenture holders and shareholders; others may inspect it on payment of a small fee. If a registered debenture is transferred a *proper instrument of transfer* must be used (s. 183) and this has to be received by the company before a transfer can be registered and a new debenture certificate issued (within two months of receipt of the transfer instrument). Unlike bearer debentures, registered debentures are not negotiable instruments so a transferee takes it subject to any claim that the company may have against earlier holders at the date of transfer (*Re Rhodesia Goldfields Ltd* (1910)). To overcome this problem and make debentures more marketable, a term in the debenture contract may say that all monies will be paid by the company to the registered holder irrespective of the interest of others:

Re Goy & Co. (1900)

The debentures contained a clause that the principal and interest would be paid to any transferee without regard to any remedy available to the company against the transferor. A resolution was passed to wind up the company. C, a director, then transferred his debentures to R. C has been in breach of his duties towards the company but R was unaware of this.

Held: R took the debentures free from the company's claim against C.

Therefore, provided that the transferee registers his holding he will be protected by such a term.

Charges

As will readily be appreciated, from a creditor's viewpoint an unsecured business loan, even where the debtor company is held in high regard by commercial rating agencies, is still a risk. During the period that the debenture will be held unforeseeable circumstances may arise that could cause what was felt to be a 'rock-solid' company to default on the debenture contract. For this reason *unsecured debentures* are rare. This is where a debenture holder has no legal redress if full repayment is not made on the specified repayment date. All that the holder can do is patiently wait until the company is liquidated (or petition for liquidation himself) then claim as an unpaid creditor. Should the liquidated company (as commonly happens) be unable to pay all its debts in full then the holder of an unsecured debenture, being towards the end of the queue for payment, may well end up with little or nothing. Therefore, as a safeguard, virtually all debentures are secured against the debtor company's property or other assets. The security taken will be in the form of a charge. In this context a charge will give the debenture holder, as creditor, a legal right to receive repayment of all sums he is owed out of a specified fund or, more commonly, out of the proceeds following the sale of specific property: A charge may be fixed, floating or a combination of both.

An unsecured debenture is also known as a simple or naked debenture. This is the opposite of a mortgage debenture which is secured by means of a legal charge on company property or other assets.

Fixed charge

A *fixed* or *specific* charge can be applied to valuable specific company assets such as land or buildings which are particularly attractive to creditors and will meet the requirements that the asset charged be identifiable (*Re Yorkshire Woolcombers Association Ltd* (1903)), although future *identifiable* assets may also be used (*Re Atlantic Medical Ltd* (1993)). However, provided that it is not too prone to technological obsolescence a creditor may wish to attach a fixed charge to machinery. Similarly, present and future book debts can be used (*Siebe Gorman & Co. Ltd v Barclays Bank Ltd* (1979)). These are debts owed to the company that arise out of normal trading and appear, or ought to appear, in a properly kept set of books (*Independent Automatic Sales Ltd v Knowles and Foster* (1962)).

The characteristics of a fixed charge are straightforward but on occasions care has to be taken to ensure that in the analysis of the circumstances a correct identification is made:

> ## Re New Bullas Trading Ltd (1994)
> NBT gave a debenture to 3i plc with what was stated to be a fixed charge over their book and other debts owing to the company. A condition said that all monies, as these debts were paid, had to be paid into a specified bank account and dealt with according to instructions given by 3i. If no instructions were given then the monies were to be realized from the fixed charge and used as security for a floating charge under the same debenture. 3i plc never gave any directions and on the later appointment of an administrative receiver the question raised was what type of charge covered the book debts – fixed or floating? If fixed the debenture holder would be paid *before* the preferential creditors; if floating then the debenture holder would be paid *after* the preferential creditors. (There were insufficient assets to satisfy both creditors.)
>
> Held: While the book debts were uncollected they were subject to a fixed charge, but on realization without any direction by the debenture holder on what was to happen to the proceeds, they became subject to a floating charge.

In his judgement in *Re New Bullas Trading Ltd* (1994) Nourse J said that a label attached by the parties to the charge being fixed or floating will be inconclusive if other terms of the debenture are inconsistent with it, i.e. a court must concentrate on the substance of the charge and not the description given by the parties to it (see also *Re G.E. Tunbridge Ltd* (1995) and *Re Climex Tissues Ltd* (1994)).

Fixed charges are not popular with companies as they are not allowed, without the written permission of the debenture holder, to deal in the asset charged (*Re Yorkshire Woolcombers Ltd* (1903)). Should a company breach this requirement and dispose of the charged asset then a buyer without notice of the charge will not be subject to it. However, a charge once given should be immediately registered and registration is constructive notice that a charge exists and so prevents a buyer of the charged assets from pleading lack of knowledge of the charge.

Floating charge

A floating charge covers all assets not already subject to a fixed change and relates to a general class of assets which due to their changing nature are not readily identifiable. This type of charge gives the creditor the right to be paid, after the sale of the asset charged, up to the value of the asset charged in priority to a number of other categories of creditors, but not before a fixed charge creditor. The characteristics of a floating charge were given by Romer LJ in the leading case of *Re Yorkshire Woolcombers Association Ltd* (1903). They are:

a) It attaches to a class of assets present and future.
b) The class of assets charged, in the ordinary course of business of the company, may change over time.
c) The company may continue to deal in the assets so charged without reference to the debenture holder until some step is taken by or on behalf of those interested in the charge.

Shortly after the Court of Appeal's decision in *Re Yorkshire Woolcombers Association* (1903) it was affirmed by the House of Lords in *Illingworth v Houldsworth* (1904) where Lord Macnaughton took the opportunity to contrast a floating charge with a specific one:

> A specific charge, I think, is one that without more fastens on ascertained and definite property or property capable of being ascertained and defined; a floating charge, on the other hand, is ambulatory and shifting in its nature, hovering over and so to speak float- ing with the property which it is intended to affect until some event occurs or some act is done which causes it to settle and fasten on the subject of the charge within its reach and grasp.

From a company's point of view a floating charge is particularly attractive in that it permits security to be given but assets charged can still be dealt in subject to a slight limitation that the charge document may contain a term requiring any dealing to be limited to the normal course of the company's business. Such an express term will strengthen the implied position under *Re Yorkshire Woolcombers Association* (1903). A company's ordinary course of dealing is that which is in any way authorized by its memorandum as long as it remains a going concern (*Governments Stock Co. v Manila Railway Co.* (1897). Indeed a company may sell its whole business if this is so authorized in the memorandum (*Re Borax Co.* (1901), although this may be deceitful on the debenture holders.

Review question

Distinguish between a fixed and floating charge.

Advantages and disadvantages of a floating charge to a debenture holder

For debenture holders there seem to be three advantages and three disadvantages of having security in the form of a floating charge.

Advantages

1 The holder gains security without which the loan would not have been granted.
2 The charge will cover not only present assets but also any future assets the company may acquire. Therefore, there is not a need to have the charge 'updated' to cover newly acquired assets.
3 Should the company get into financial difficulties the debenture holder can appoint an administrative receiver (Part III, Insolvency Rules (1986)) which will block other cred- itors from appointing an administrator.

Disadvantages

1 As the assets normally subject to a floating charge are less permanent than the assets subject to a fixed charge it may mean that a company getting into financial difficulties will not be able to resist the temptation to dispose of its more realizable assets and as there is no need to inform the debenture holder it may mean that when they come to claim their security most of the assets will have already been disposed of. With the security gone a debenture holder would become an unsecure creditor.
2 There is a danger that a fixed charge will be created after the floating charge is taken with the later fixed charge ranking ahead of the earlier floating one:

Governments Stock Co. v Manila Railway Co. (1897)

Debentures were taken with a floating charge. Three months' interest became due but the debenture holders took no steps to enforce their security. The company then gave a fixed charge over specific assets. Finally, the debenture holders acted.

Held: The fixed charge had priority over the floating charge. The debenture holders' floating charge merely 'floated' until they took some steps to enforce their security. Here they had acted too late and allowed a latter charge to gain priority.

To provide some protection against this danger a *negative pledge* clause may be inserted in the charge document whereby the company undertakes not to give a later charge over the assets covered by the floating charge that will rank in priority to, or pari passu with (i.e. ahead of, or equal to), the floating charge. Such pledges are now standard clauses in the large majority of floating charge contracts. Where a debenture holder believes that the company are going to breach the negative pledge clause then he may seek an injunction to prevent the loss of priority (or having to share it), or alternatively, apply for the appointment of a receiver (*Re London Pressed Hinge Ltd* (1905)).

However, the use of a negative pledge clause is, in practice, of modest benefit for a later chargee without actual notice of this provision in the debenture will not be subject to it, and knowledge that a debenture has been registered is not itself constructive knowledge as to what the contents are:

Part IV, CA 1989 contained a revised system for the registration of company charges which, inter alia, would replace section 399 of CA 1985 with a new provision allowing a negative pledge clause to be used with registration being deemed constructive knowledge of the clause's existence in respect to later chargees. At present Part IV has not been introduced so that s. 399 CA 1985 remains in force.

Re Valletort Steam Laundry Co. (1903)

Debentures were secured by a floating charge containing a provision that the company were not to create any charge that would have priority over the one already given. The company manager forgot this and later gave a bank a fixed charge. Coincidentally the bank held some of the earlier debentures on deposit for a customer.

Held: The bank's charge would have priority over the earlier floating charge that secured the debentures. Merely keeping debentures for safe custody was not enough for constructive knowledge of their contents to operate.

---

3 The security may be weakened by any of the following:
   i)   A reservation of title clause, whereby a seller retains title in goods until the buyer makes full payment. A floating charge on crystallization will not attach to these goods so raw materials or component parts (both are commonly subject to this type of clause) etc. will not be available to a debenture holder. Therefore, a receiver appointed by a debenture holder, after the creditor's failure to meet the terms of the debenture contract, may find that the floating charge is valueless in that a supplier with *Romalpa* clauses in the contract of supply will be legally able to recover his goods. This effectively means that the floating charge is valueless as the assets they were believed to cover do not in fact belong to the company.

Retention of title clauses are derived from *Aluminium Industries Vaassen BV v Romalpa Aluminium Ltd* (1976) (hence *Romalpa* clause for short) where the clause stipulated:

> The ownership of the material to be delivered by AIV will only be transferred to the purchaser when he has met all that is owing to AIV no matter on what grounds.

The attraction of a *Romalpa* clause to the seller is clear – it reserves a seller's right of title to unpaid goods and enables the seller to trace and recover them in priority to other creditors including those with a floating charge. Under *Romalpa* an unpaid seller's rights exist provided that the goods supplied remain identifiable and in the possession of the buyer. Incorporation of goods supplied into other goods may mean that identifiability is lost so that benefit of the *Romalpa* clause is forfeited:

Borden v Scottish Timber Products (1981)
Resin was supplied under a contract containing a reservation title term. It was known to the supplier that the resin would be processed to make chipboard.

Held: This resin ceased to exist when it was processed so that the seller's reserved title was lost.

Many *Romalpa* style clauses are relatively simple and do not require registration as a company charge as in *Clough Mills Ltd v Martin* (1985) where the seller, by retaining legal title in the goods, precluded the buyer from giving a charge on goods that he did not own. But increasingly *Romalpa* clauses have become more sophisticated so that now extended clauses (really a series of sub-clauses) to be valid need to be registered (*Re Bond Worth* (1980) and *Re Curtain Dream plc* (1990)). Registration is essential where the clause relates to the proceeds of a resale of goods. A *Romalpa* type clause not registered when it ought to have been will be void:

Reservation of title clauses are permitted under sections 17 & 19, Sale of Goods Act 1979 and are common in contracts of supply.

Re Weldtech Equipment Ltd (1991)
An English company went into liquidation after having received goods on credit from a German company. A reservation of title clause purported to assign book debts to the German company but this charge had not been registered under section 395 of CA 1985.

Held: The reservation of title clause was void for lack of registration.

In practice *Romalpa* clauses are seldom registered because, firstly, it is inconvenient to have to do so for each individual contract (presumably a rolling *Romalpa* is needed); and, secondly, if it was registered then it would rank behind any charge over a class of assets, which may well include the goods covered by the clause, already registered. As the majority of companies do have bank borrowing, and as banks always insist on taking a floating charge, registration by a supplier of his set of *Romalpa* clauses would merely mean that he formally accepts that the banker's security would have priority over his own.

Because of the growing plethora of case law what started as a simple concept is now highly complex, leading regrettably to some uncertainty as to what the law actually is in some areas. A floating chargee may be able to use this uncertainty to challenge an unpaid sellers right to recover goods – or at least to use the threat of litigation to negotiate a settlement between the parties.

ii) Statutory preferential debts owed by the company will have to be paid out of floating assets (unless there are other assets available). This means that a receiver appointed by a debenture holder will under s. 40, Insolvency Act 1986 have to stand aside while, perhaps, many other creditors obtain payment for their debts out of the assets that he has taken possession of.

iii) A creditor holding an execution order will have to be paid if need be from floating charged assets.

Preferential debts of a company are derived from Schedule 6, Insolvency Act 1986 and are set out in Chapter 18, Winding Up.

Review question

How effective to those who use them are:

a) a negative pledge clause; and
b) a *Romalpa* type clause?

Crystallization of a floating charge

A company is able to deal in assets covered by a floating charge up until crystallization occurs (*Re Borax* (1901)). Crystallization is where the floating charge converts into a fixed charge. It takes place when certain conditions make monies payable and the debenture holder takes steps to enforce his security. Merely asking for payment is insufficient to crystallize the charge (*Cox-Moore v Peruvian Corporation Ltd* (1908)). The conditions for crystallization are:

Occurrence (a) may be termed pre-crystallization; while (b) to (e) can be termed automatic crystallization in that they occur through the operation of law. Automatic crystallization is a loosely defined term so that some commentators will include (a) within it.

a) a breach of contractual condition in the charge contract (*Re Brightlife Ltd* (1986));
b) the commencement of winding the company up: voluntarily (*Re Roundwood Colliery Co.* (1897)), or compulsorily (*Re Colonial Trusts Corporation* (1879));
c) the non-court appointment of a receiver (*Evans v Rival Granite Quarries Ltd* (1910));
d) a creditor taking possession of assets that form part of the floating charge (*Re Hamiton's Windsor Ironworks* (1879));
e) the company stops trading (*Re Woodroffes (Musical Instruments) Ltd* (1986)).

The effect of crystallization is to make the assets subject to the floating charge become identifiable so that the floating charges figuratively fall to earth (crystallize) into an equitable fixed charge, i.e. a charge on the specific assets of the company identifiable at time of crystallization (*Re Griffin Hotel* (1941)).

Invalidity of a floating charge under the Insolvency Act 1986

Grounds for invalidity are derived from public policy considerations succinctly encapsulated by Hoffman J in *Re Brightlife Ltd* (1986):

> The floating charge was invented by Victorian lawyers to enable manufacturing and trading companies to raise loan capital on debentures. It could offer the security of a charge over the whole of the company's undertaking without inhibiting its ability to trade. But the mirror image of these advantages was the potential prejudice to the general body of creditors, who might know nothing of the floating charge but find that all the company's assets, including the very goods which they had just delivered on credit, had been swept up by the debenture-holder. The public interest requires a balancing of the advantages to the economy of facilitating the borrowing of money against the possibility of injustice to unsecured creditors. These arguments for and against the floating charge are matters for Parliament rather than the courts and have been the subject of public debate in and out of Parliament for more than a century.

Invalidity can occur in one of four ways. They are:

1 Avoidance of floating charges (Insolvency Act 1986, s. 245)
2 An invalid preference (Insolvency Act 1986, s. 239)
3 A transaction at an undervalue (Insolvency Act 1986, s. 238)
4 An extortionate transaction (Insolvency Act 1986, s. 244).

Avoidance of floating charges (Insolvency Act 1986, s. 245)

Where a company goes into liquidation within a certain period after giving a floating charge then the charge will be valid only in so far as the company received consideration at the same time as, or after, the charge was created. The aim of s. 245, which is directed solely at floating charges, is to stop an insolvent company from giving a floating charge to secure past debts and so prejudice their other unsecured creditors. A liquidator or administrator can claim that the change was invalid if created within the following periods before the liquidation commenced or an administration order was applied for:

a) two years – if the charge was in favour of a *connected person*;
b) one year – if in favour of anyone else provided in this instance the company was either insolvent when creating the charge or insolvency became a result of the transaction under which the charge was created;
c) at any time between the presentation of a petition for an administration order and the making of that order.

Under section 249, Insolvency Act 1986 a *connected person* is:

a) a director or shadow director of the company or an associate of theirs; or
b) an associate of the company.

A shadow director is simply a person in accordance with whose instructions the directors are accustomed to act (CA 1985, s. 741), whereas an associate is given in s. 345, Insolvency Act 1986 a wide meaning. It includes:

- a spouse, a relative (e.g. sibling, uncle, aunt, nephew, niece as well as lineal ancestor and descendant!) and the spouse of a relative;
- a business partner and their spouse or the relative of a partner;
- an employee or employer;
- a company if the person concerned controls it – personally or with the associates;
- a trustee if the person concerned is a beneficiary.

An example of section 245 in operation is:

Re Destone Fabrics Ltd (1941)

In 1940 the company was insolvent but still issued a debenture to Zimmerman secured by a floating charge over its assets and also to secure a loan of £900. The loan went into the company's bank account and on the same day two sums each of £350 were paid to two directors for fees due with £200 being paid to a guarantor of the company's overdraft. Six months after the issue of the debenture the company was wound up. The liquidator applied to have the debenture set aside, arguing that it had been invalidly issued to pay certain creditors and to give Zimmerman a charge so as to prevent other creditors from sharing in the company's assets.

Held: As the object of the charge was to obtain cash for other creditors it was not valid because section 322 of CA 1948 required that cash in good faith be paid to the company at the time of or subsequently to the creation of and in consideration of the charge!

Section 245, Insolvency Act 1986 has replaced s. 322, CA 1948. The provisions contained in the former are identical to those that were found in the latter.

In *Re Destone Fabrics Ltd* (1941) the charge given to Zimmerman would have been valid if given in good faith to enable the company to continue trading – hopefully to escape from insolvency. Simmonds J found that the motive in giving the charge was not to benefit the company but was a contrivance to benefit directors:

> ... I find it impossible to believe that the purpose of this transaction was anything else but, by the issue of this security, to procure the payment to certain directors of the sums due to them in preference to other creditors of the company ...

He went on to say:

> The ultimate test in such cases may well be whether the transaction is to be regarded as one intended bone fide for the benefit of the company, or whether it is intended merely

to provide certain monies for the benefit of certain creditors of the company to the prejudice of other creditors of the company.

An invalid preference (Insolvency Act 1986, s. 239)

Where the floating charge was created within two years for a connected person (or six months for anyone else) of a company going into liquidation or an administration order being made against it, the charge may be classed as an unlawful preference. The principle in operation here is that all creditors should be treated equally so where a floating charge is given to one creditor, then by obtaining security for his debt he is placed in a better position than other unsecured creditors.

Should a liquidator or administrator wish to challenge the validity of an alleged preference then they must establish that:

For an illustrative case of a liquidator challenge see Re MC Bacon (1990) given later.

a) the debtor was insolvent at the time the preference was made or, alternatively, became so as a result of the preference having been given;
b) the debtor was influenced by a desire to put the creditor in a more favourable position then they would have been in had the preference not been given. Should the creditor be a connected person then there is a presumption that the company was influenced by such a desire;
c) the preference was given within the statutory periods.

A transaction at an undervalue (Insolvency Act 1986, s. 238)

This provision relates to where a floating charge is effectively a gift (i.e. no consideration is provided) or more pertinently for a consideration worth much less than that provided by the debtor, i.e. the company. If any of those circumstances exist and an administrative order has been made against the company, or it has gone into liquidation, then the administrator or liquidator can apply to the court to have the floating charge set aside. The operable time limit is that the transaction at an undervalue took place within a two-year period ending with the making of an administrative order or commencement of a winding up. A court hearing the petition is able to make whatever order it thinks fit for restoring the position to what it would have been if the company had not given the floating charge. However, a court is not able to make any order in respect to an undervalue if it is satisfied that the company when it entered into the transaction related to the floating charge:

a) did so in good faith, for the purpose of carrying on its business; and
b) there were at this time reasonable grounds for believing that the transaction would benefit the company.

Re MC Bacon (1990)

On suddenly losing its main client and with two directors deciding to retire the company experienced a financial crisis. On learning of this their bankers sought to protect their unsecured lending by taking a debenture secured by a floating charge. This was given to keep the overdraft facility alive. Eight months after the crisis started and three months after the charge was given the company went into liquidation leaving unpaid debts split between unsecured creditors (£330,000) and the bank overdraft (£235,500). The liquidator applied to have the debenture (with its floating charge) set

---

aside as a voidable preference under s. 239 or as a transaction at an undervalue under s. 238.

Held: The decision to give the security had not been influenced by any desire of the directors to improve the bank's position should liquidation occur. It had been given to stop the bank demanding repayment of the overdraft and hence kept the company trading – accordingly no preference had been given. Also the secured debenture had not been a gift for valid consideration had been received in that it kept the business going. The company had acted in good faith and they had reasonable grounds for believing that the company could be turned around. There was, in consequence, no undervalue.

Subsequent purchases of property under a preference or undervalue: Insolvency (No. 2) Act 1994

When hearing a petition alleging individual preference or a transaction at an undervalue (IA 1986, ss. 239, 238), a court is given wide powers to dispense justice as it sees fit (IA 1986, s. 241). When doing so it will take into account the position of a later purchaser in good faith of property under a preference or undervalue. If the court is of the opinion that the later purchaser had acted in good faith then the floating charge may not be set aside. The Insolvency (No. 2) Act 1994 helps to clarify what good faith may amount to. A third party knowing that a preference or undervalue had been given at some time may still show that when he took the property he had acted in good faith. However, lack of good faith is presumed to exist where the third party is connected with, or is an associate of, the company. This presumption is rebuttal but clearly for someone particularly close to a company it will be very demanding to do so.

An extortionate transaction (Insolvency Act 1986, s. 244)

Section 244 is modelled on the extortionate consumer credit provisions found under sections 138, 139 and 171 of Consumer Credit Act 1974.

The transaction that created the debenture containing the floating charge may on an application made by an administrator or liquidator be set aside, or otherwise dealt with, by the court if it considers it is, or was, extortionate. The time limited for this provision is that the transaction must have been entered into at any time in a three-year period ending on the day on which the administration order is made or the company starts liquidation proceedings. Extortionate credit has to be examined in relation to the degree of risk accepted by the creditor but the following guidance is provided:

a) the terms of the credit are, or were, such as to require grossly exorbitant repayments; or

b) it otherwise grossly contravened ordinary principles of fair dealing.

When an application is made there is a presumption that it is extortionate and it is then left to the creditor to rebut it.

Review question

What is meant by transactions at an undervalue or a preference and what can an aggrieved person do about them?

Registration of charges

There are a wide range of charges, including fixed and floating ones over company assets, that must be registered by delivery of details to the Registrar of Companies within 21 days of their creation (s. 398). On receipt the Registrar will enter them in the Register of charges which is open to public inspection (s. 401) but the 21 days within which a charge needs to be registered may on occasions result in a search of the register not revealing that a charge had very recently been taken. To guard against this possibility the company's own register of charges, which a company is obligated to keep (s. 407), could be examined but non-registration in this register will have no effect on the validity of the charge.

CA 1989 contains provisions that are intended to replace the registration requirements under CA 1985. However, no date has ever been given for the introduction of the 1989 system. At present the CA 1985 regime on charges still applies and this is what will be dealt with here.

Charges that have to be registered are given under s. 396:

a) a charge for the purpose of securing any issue of debentures;
b) a charge on uncalled share capital of the company;
c) a charge on land (wherever situated);
d) a charge on book debts of the company;
e) a floating charge on the company's undertaking or property;
f) a charge on calls made but not paid;
g) a charge on goodwill, or on any intellectual property (e.g. copyright, patents, trade marks).

Essentially, what has to be registered is any transaction for value that gives a third party the benefit of a company asset, however it is described, without going so far as to give him actual entitlement to that asset (*Gorringe v Irwell India Rubber Works* (1886)).

The information that has to be included in the registration is set out in s. 401 (1) (a):

i)   the date of its creation;
ii)   the amount secured by the charge;
iii) brief details of the property charged;
iv)   the persons entitled to the charge.

The Registrar will file the above information in the charges register noting the date of its receipt. Copies of the filing will be sent to the company and the chargee who will then have proof that the registration has been completed. Should anyone require a certificate of registration then the Registrar will provide one. A certificate showing the date of delivery of the registration particulars to the Registrar is conclusive evidence that registration requirements are satisfied even if in fact they are not (see *Re Nye Ltd* (1971)), and that delivery was no later than the date stated on the certificate (see *Exeter Trust v Screenway* (1991)).

Failure to register a charge

Although the primary duty to register is with the company any interested party can themselves register. Therefore, a debenture holder can adopt a safety first stance and register the charge himself, recovering registration costs from the company (s. 399). Failure to register will leave the company and any officer in default liable to a fine (s. 399). However, the most serious consequence of a failure to register within the 21-day period is that the charge will be void against any claim an administrator, liquidator or creditor of the company may make in respect to corporate assets (s. 395, *Re Kent & Sussex Sawmills Ltd* (1947)). But the debt itself then becomes immediately repayable (*Parkes Garages (Swadlincote) Ltd* (1929)).

Late registration

There is a facility for late registration outside the 21-day period by means of a court order served on the Registrar. But it is essential that registration is applied for as soon as the failure is discovered (s. 404, *R v Registrar of Companies, ex parte Central Bank of India* (1985). Late registration is discretional and a court will only extend the time for registration if satisfied that it is in the circumstances just and equitable to do so without prejudice to the right of creditors before the date of actual registration (*Re Spiral Globe Ltd* (1902)). However, it must be remembered that strictly speaking an unsecured creditor does not acquire any rights against the assets of the company until the company starts winding up.

If a company was uncertain of the likely court response to an application to register late it could always cancel the debenture that has not been duly registered and issue fresh ones (The Defries & Co. Ltd)

The priority of charges

The priority of charges may well determine the actual value of the security held:

a) *Priority between fixed charges*

The general rule is that registered legal fixed charges rank in order of their creation. Also a registered fixed charge taken in good faith for value will gain priority over an earlier legal or equitable unregistered fixed charge. This is because as the earlier legal or equitable fixed charge was registered, then as registration is taken to be constructive notice of its creation, no priority can be taken.

Should a company, after giving a legal fixed charge on an asset, break the terms of the charge and sell the asset, the third party who bought it will still be subject to the charge even if they had no actual notice that the fixed charge existed. If the company gave an equitable fixed charge but broke the terms of the debenture contract by disposing of the asset to a third party, then the charge will remain valid if the new owner of the asset, at time of purchase, had notice that it was subject to a charge.

b) *Priority between fixed and floating charges*

A fixed charge, it will be remembered, covers specific assets while a floating charge hovers over a general class of assets but does not attach itself to any particular asset until crystallization takes place. This means that a later registered fixed charge will take priority over an earlier floating charge (*Re Hamiltons Windsor Ironworks Co. Ltd* (1879)).

To guard against the loss of priority a 'negative pledge' clause may be inserted into the floating charge whereby the company undertakes not to create a later charge which will deprive the floating charge of its priority or to rank pari passu (equal) with it. The floating charge, with its 'negative pledge', is then registered. The difficulty is that while registration is constructive notice that registration has taken place it does not give constructive notice that the 'negative pledge' was registered with it (*Earle (G&T) v Hemsworth RDC* (1928)). Therefore, a person taking a later fixed charge without knowledge of the 'negative pledge' can still gain priority over the earlier floating charge provided of course that they had no actual knowledge of it (*English & Scottish Mercantile Investment Trust v Brunton* (1892)).

c) *Priority between floating charges*

Where two or more floating charges have been given over the same class of assets then provided they are both registered the rule is that the first in time will have priority even if the earlier floating charge did not contain a 'negative pledge' clause (*Re Benjamin Cope & Sons Ltd* (1914)). But if two registered floating charges compete with each other, then if the later floating charge crystallizes before crystallization occurs on the first registered floating charge the later charge will have priority (*Griffiths v Yorkshire Bank plc* (1994)). If a registered floating charge covers a specific class of assets, such as book debts, then it will have priority in respect to those assets before an earlier floating charge over the general assets (*Re Automatic Bottle Makers* (1926)).

Remedies of a debenture holder

1 *Appointment of a receiver*
  Normally the debenture will contain an express term to allow the holder to appoint a receiver. If this power is not present then the holder can apply to the court for one to be appointed. If a court does make the appointment then the receiver becomes an officer (agent) of the court. The receiver's function is to recover the sums due by realizing charged assets.
2 *Sue the company*
  The debenture holder may sue to obtain repayment of the loan and interest by enforcing his security through sale.
3 *Petition for winding up the company*
  The debenture holder, as a creditor, may petition for the amount of his principal sum and interest, that the company be wound up for insolvency.
4 *Apply for an order of sale*
  If the debenture gives the trustees a power of sale then he may ask that they exercise this power. Alternatively, he may apply to the court for the appointment of a receiver who will be able to sell the asset charged.

Chapter summary

- Common law and statute allow companies to borrow for legitimate business purposes. Creditors acting in good faith are able to enforce the debt transaction against the company if it acted ultra vires the memorandum (lack of capacity) or intra vires the memorandum but ultra vires the purpose (lack of directors' authority).
- Large medium or long-term borrowing is commonly by means of a *debenture* issue.
- Debenture types are: unsecured (rare); secured (by charges); irredeemable; perpetual; redeemable; bearer (a negotiable instrument); and registered.
- The debenture contract is in the formula of a *trust deed* containing protective terms that the trustee, acting for the beneficiary (debenture holder), may use on default by the company.
- Debenture holders demanding security for their loan will receive a charge on

company assets: *fixed charge* is over specific (identifiable) assets most notably land, buildings, machinery; whereas a *floating charge* is over unidentifiable assets in general. While parties may apply their own label to the security the definite description will be given, if need be, by the court.

- Without the debenture holder's written permission a company cannot deal in fixed charged assets whereas with a floating charge assets, present or future, can be dealt with in the normal course of business. The authoritative case for definition of charges is *Re Yorkshire Woolcombers Association Ltd* (1902).
- The floating charge is preferred by companies as it allows dealing in charged assets.
- However, to debenture holders there are disadvantages: charged assets may be disposed of without their knowledge; or a fixed charge created after the floating charge was taken will again gain priority over his security, even if a 'negative pledge' clause is used.
- 'Hidden defects' in a charge may be:
- *– reservation of title clause* – (e.g. Romalpa) whereby the asset charged is not owned by the company but by a supplier: simple Romalpa type clauses do not require registration (*Clough Mills Ltd v Martin* (1985)), but complex ones need to be and if not then they are void (*Re Weldtech Ltd* (1991));
- *– statutory preferential creditors and creditors* – holding an execution order, these rank before a creditor secured by a floating charge.
- *Crystallization* is the term used to describe the transformation of a floating charge into a fixed one. Circumstances that cause this to occur are: breach of the debenture trust deed; start of winding up; a creditor appointing a receiver or taking possession of assets covered by the floating charge; and cessation of business.
- Floating charges may be invalid under the Insolvency Act 1986 for giving one creditor *an unfair advantage* over other creditors, the time period being 2 years for connected persons or 1 year for others or any time between making the presentation of a petition for administration and the making of the order (s. 245); or the floating charge amounts to an *invalid preference* for one creditor at the expense of others with the time period being 2 years for connected persons and 6 months for others (s. 239); or the floating charge was a *transaction at an undervalue* in that it was given for no consideration (a gift) or nominal consideration but there is a defence available in that the charges were given in good faith with reasonable grounds for believing they would benefit the company (the time period is 2 years ending with the making of an administrative order or the start of winding up (s. 238)); or that the floating charge equalled an *extortionate transaction* in that credit terms were, or are, grossly exorbitant or otherwise contravened fair dealing principles (s. 244).
- To be legally enforceable a charge must be registered with the Registrar of Companies within 21 days of its creation (s. 398) and then entered into a Register of charges which is open to public inspection (s. 401). Failure to register in time means that the charge becomes void against a claim from an administrator, liquidator or creditor (s. 395). Late registration, granted by the court, is possible but only where it is found to be equitable and without prejudice to earlier creditors.

- Priority of charges is important in that it determines on insolvency who will be paid before others:
- *– priority between registered fixed legal charges –* generally they will rank in their order of creation but a registered fixed charge will rank before an earlier unregistered fixed charge;
- *– priority between registered fixed and registered floating charges –* a later fixed charge will have priority over an earlier floating charge; a 'negative pledge' clause is commonly used but mere registration is not itself sufficient for constructive notice of this to apply;
- *– priority between registered floating charges –* the rule is that first in time prevails; where two compete then a later charge that has crystallized before crystallization occurs in the first will gain priority; a floating charge on a class of assets will have priority on these assets before an earlier floating charge over general assets.

Discussion questions

1 How good is a floating charge as security for a loan?
2 Read Chapter 9, Shares, and then discuss the similarities and differences between shares and debentures.

Case study exercise

The Cumbrian Bank plc are considering giving a sizeable loan to Soundwell Ltd taking from them a debenture containing a floating charge over the assets of Soundwell Ltd. The Cumbrian Bank plc are concerned over a rumour they have heard that while Soundwell Ltd are now seemingly financially sound they were a few months ago in some financial difficulties.

Explain, in respect to the Cumbrian Bank plc:

a) what preliminary steps you feel it would be advisable for them to take before accepting the debenture;
b) what defects may exist in respect to the floating charge that may subsequently harm their position if the charge is in fact taken;
c) if the debenture is taken what steps they ought to take to ensure its validity;
d) what will be their position if four months after the debenture is taken Warmsley Ltd took a fixed charge on Soundwell Ltd's premises.

Further reading

Registration of Company Charges – The New Regime, E. Ferran (1991), JBL, 152.
Floating Charges – The Nature of the Security, E. Ferran (1988), CLJ, 213.

Registration of Company Charges: The New Law, G. McCormack (1990), LMCLQ, 520.
The Judicial Basis of the Floating Charge, K.J. Naser (1994), Co. Law, 11.
Lightweight Floating Charges, F. Oditch (1991), JBL, 49.
Floating Charges – An Alternative Theory, S. Worthington (1994), CLJ, 81.

COMPANY
MANAGEMENT

11 Directors

Introduction

Put simply, under a company's constitution the shareholders own the company but the directors run it. They are the principals or governors of a company who individually and collectively act as the senior management. They are the decision takers but are ultimately responsible to the shareholders for their efficient stewardship, past and present, as well as the future development of the company. While shareholders, as owners, may feel they have a right to share in the company's success through a dividend payment, they only do so when the directors see fit to declare one. The enormous power wielded by the directors is checked by shareholder rights, most notably that the appointment of directors must be with their agreement, and figuratively like a Sword of Damocles (though infrequently used), they can, by an ordinary resolution, dismiss single directors or the entire board.

Objectives

The purpose of this chapter is, firstly, to ensure that students appreciate the position that directors occupy in respect to both day-to-day management and the longer term interests of their company. Secondly, students must realize that most directors, while accountable to the board and shareholders, work without any form of direct supervision and to guard against abuses of position common law, statute and self-regulation all attempt to 'police' the work and conduct of directors.

Key concepts

- Division of ownership and control between shareholders and directors
- Director is a portmanteau expression covering several types
- The rule in Turquand's case
- The statutory disqualification of directors, especially in relation to unfitness
- The fiduciary duties owed by directors to their company
- Ratification of directors' unauthorized transaction by the shareholders
- The directors' duty of reasonable care that is owed to the company.

In small private companies the distinction between owner and controller is often blurred in that directors will frequently have sizeable shareholdings in the company.

Ownership and control

From the introductory comments it can be seen that the relationship between the shareholders and directors is one of ownership and control in that the shareholders through the articles and company meetings delegate the running of the company to a board of directors. Once delegation has taken place then the shareholders cannot interfere in matters that have been placed under the control of the directors:

Scott v Scott (1943)

Shareholders resolved at a general meeting to pay dividends and to appoint accountants to investigate the company's financial affairs.

Held: These resolutions were invalid since they usurped powers that the articles had given to the directors.

The business of the company shall be managed by the directors, who may exercise all the powers of the company (Table A, article 70). Should shareholders disapprove of how the directors are exercising their powers then appropriate alteration of the articles will curb such actions in the future but will not retrospectively invalidate earlier acts.

The directors are therefore the only persons who can discharge the matters assigned to them and their decision cannot be overruled even by a general meeting of the company, unless the articles are altered by a special resolution (*Automatic Self-Cleansing Filter Syndicate Co. Ltd v Cuninghame* (1906) and *BreckLand Group Holdings Ltd v London & Suffolk Properties Ltd* (1989)) or unless the directors are acting in their own interests against the interest of the company in which case a body of shareholders, majority or minority, may seek a court order to have the directors' decisions set aside (*Howard Smith Ltd v Ampol Petroleum* (1974) – considered later).

Review question

In a limited company explain how power is divided between shareholders and the board of directors.

Who are directors?

It is difficult to identify with any precision who directors are. The Companies Act says that a director is any person occupying the position of director irrespective of what he is called (s. 741). This is recognition through doing whatever directors usually do, including management of the business, making contracts for the company, looking after the property of the company, etc. Other titles for them may be governor, managing partners (both dated), trustees or agents, all of which focus on what the office holder does:

> It does not matter much what you call them, so long as you understand what their true position is, which is that they are merely commercial men, managing a trading concern for the benefit of themselves, and all other shareholders in it. (Jessel MR, *Re Arthur Average Association for British Foreign and Colonial Ships* (1875).)

It is also possible for a person to be declared a director even if he was never so appointed. This may occur where:

An early statutory definition of directors was 'the persons having the direction, and management or superintendence of (a company's) affairs' (Joint Stock Companies Act 1844, s. 3).

... He is held out as a director by the company, claims and purports to be a director, although never actually or validly appointed as such. To establish that a person was a *de facto* director of a company it is necessary to plead and prove that he undertook functions in relation to the company which could probably be discharged only by a director. (Millett J, Re Hydrodam (Corby) Ltd (1994))

An illustration case is:

Re Moorgate Metals Ltd (1995)
MM were buyers and resellers of scrap metal with the company being run by H, who admitted that he was a director, and R, an undischarged bankrupt, who denied being one. Evidence was taken that R was a metal trading expert and he admitted to controlling the company's entire trading operations but only by reason, he argued, of his professional expertise. The question at issue was, was R a *de facto* director?

Held: Warner J found that R had set the company up and had invited H to join him in managing it. R was in sole charge of trading and worked without any limit being placed on him. Both R and H received the same remuneration. Further, H always asked R's advice on important company matters including the appointment of bankers, solicitors, accountants, etc. R's close involvement with the company's affairs were such as to lead outsiders to believe that he acted as if he was a director; indeed on some business documentation R was named before H. All this led Warner J to find that R and H were business equals and not that R was subordinate to H. Therefore, R was a de facto director.

Types of director

Executive

Executive directors are characterized by their close full-time involvement with company affairs. They are normally given a specific and recognizable area of responsibility, e.g. Finance Director, Personnel Director, Sales Director, which indicates that as a director they have overall responsibility for the activities of that particular part of the business. However, they are still expected to have reasonable knowledge about other aspects of the business.

Non-executive

Non-executive directors take no active part in the running of the company but are required to attend board meetings. With no executive responsibility they are in a good position to take a wider long-term view urging caution when they believe it necessary. They have full responsibility as a director notwithstanding their role as an outsider brought into the company, as opposed to being an integral part of it. Non-executive directors have always been a feature of boardrooms with well-known public figures or minor aristocrats acting as an endorsement to the company and so inspiring public confidence. This has been termed window dressing (Romer J, *Re City Equitable Fire Insurance Co. Ltd* (1925)). Now non-executive directors are increasingly valued for their experience of business, their impartiality and for possible resulting contracts with government or business. Their role has been widened further by the Cadbury, Greenbury and Hampel reports (see Chapter 16, Corporate Governance).

Shadow

A shadow director is a person 'in accordance with whose directions or instructions the directors of a company are accustomed to act' (s. 741). It is still uncertain the degree to which the directors must act – whether a governing majority or the whole board. But 'accustomed' seemingly requires a course of established conduct. Where the board regularly acts on the advice of an outsider, in his professional capacity, such as a management consultant, then he will not be deemed to be a shadow director just because the board follows his recommendations.

For guidance on the identification of a shadow director a four-part test was formulated by Millett J in *Re Hydrodam (Corby) Ltd* (1994):

1 Who are the company directors?
2 Did the person concerned direct those directors as to how to act?
3 Did those directors act in accordance with his directions?
4 Were they accustomed to doing so?

From both *Re Hydrodam (Corby) Ltd* (1994) and *Re PFTZM Ltd* (1995) it appears that for a person to become a shadow director he must have total medium or long-term control of the board. Therefore, unless the board is automatized with no trace of independent judgement then a shadow director cannot be affixed to a person however influential he may be.

Nominee

Strictly speaking a nominee director is not legally recognized in law as he is treated as being just an ordinary director even though he would have been appointed, or nominated to be appointed, by a major shareholder or a group of shareholders. However, this practice of placing a person (more than one is possible) onto a board is long established with the benefit of getting either a person of your choice in a benign manner, or of having someone at the very heart of corporate decision making with the intention that he will move the company in the direction his sponsors wish.

While a nominee director may personally feel obligated to his nominator or patron, once appointed he has a duty: to act only for the company as a whole (as opposed to a sectional interest); to avoid any conflicts of interest (such as seeking to strengthen his patron's position); and to avoid acting covertly for others (such as doing his patron's bidding). To avoid accusations of disloyalty the nominee director must be:

> free to exercise his best judgement in the interests of the company which he serves. But if he is put upon terms that he is bound to act in the affairs of the company in accordance with the directions of his patron it is beyond doubt unlawful. (Lord Denning, Boulting v ACTTAT (1963))

What normally happens is that where a substantial shareholding is held, by an individual or group, the company will agree that those shareholders may appoint a stipulated number of directors.

Alternative

Here, the articles will allow two people to share a directorship. A director knowing that he will be unable to attend sufficient board meetings to discharge his duty of attendance may have another person attend on his behalf provided that the appointee is willing to serve. The alternative can be an existing board member or someone else but the board must sanction the appointment (Table A, article 65). Once appointed the appointor and appointee will be like Siamese twins in that should the appointor lose office then so will the appointee and if the appointor loses office but regains it, for instance by re-election, then the appointee will also resume office (Table A, article 67). An alternative director is not an agent of his appointee but a director in his own right with responsibility for his own acts and default (Table A, article 69).

Managing director

Company articles that follow Table A will say that directors are able to appoint one of their number as managing director (Table A, article 84). Where the articles contain this provision then the shareholders are unable to make this appointment (*Thomas Logan Ltd v Davis* (1911)). If, however, shareholders are displeased with the board's appointment then, as a managing director can only hold his appointment while he remains a director, they can pass an ordinary resolution at a general meeting to remove him from his directorship (s. 303) and in so doing end his managing directorship. Equally those appointed by a board resolution can also be dismissed by another board resolution but as it would probably be destructive to have a dismissed managing director still exercising his director's power the practice is that shortly after a dismissal resolution from the board a general meeting will take place where an ordinary resolution will be used to take his directorship away. But unless a just cause exists a managing director dismissed during the subsistence of his service contract may sue for wrongful dismissal (*Nelson v James Nelson & Sons Ltd* (1914)).

Formerly the position occupied by a managing director was felt by the courts to be modest: 'A managing director is only an ordinary director entrusted with some special powers' (Cozens-Hardy J, *Re Newspaper Proprietary Syndicate Ltd* (1900)). Now courts are more willing to acknowledge that a managing director is a company's second in command and it is for the shareholders and board to say how important his position is to be. Indeed the board may delegate to him additional powers, with whatever conditions they feel appropriate, that go beyond powers he would normally have as a director (Table A, article 72).

> While a managing director ought to be formally appointed it is possible for an appointment to be implied. This is ostensible authority (see the section on agency that follows).

> A managing director is the senior executive director of a company subordinate only to the chairman. His role is to implement the decisions made by the board of which he is a member.

Connected persons

Directors have imposed upon them a number of duties which on occasions may prove onerous, for example those relating to substantial property transactions. Therefore, it would be relatively easy for a director to avoid breaking a duty by using a third party as a front behind which he can hide so as to be able to plead innocence of any personal involvement. To avoid this possibility (or temptation) the Companies Act extends certain statutory prohibitions to members of a director's immediate family and to companies that a director may control. The terms used for this extension are *connected persons* and *associated companies* (s. 346).

A person is connected to a director if they are:

a) that director's: spouse, child or step-child. Illegitimate children are included but any child over 18 years is excluded; or
b) a body corporate with which the director is associated; or
c) someone acting in his capacity as the trustee of any trust under which the beneficiaries include the director or anyone coming into (a) or (b) above; or
d) someone acting in his capacity as a partner of that director or of anyone coming into (a), (b) or (c) above.

An associated company is one in which the director and the person(s) connected with him together are:

a) interested in at least 20 per cent in nominal value of its equity share capital; or
b) entitled to exercise or control the exercise of more than 20 per cent of the voting power at any general meeting.

Number of directors

There is a minimum of two directors for a public limited company but one for a private limited company. A sole director cannot also be the company secretary (s. 283).

Age of directors

The object of s. 293 (2) was to reduce the average age of boards of public limited companies. Younger boards would, it was believed, be more dynamic and innovative. Whether true or not any benefit has largely been diminished by the exemption granted (s. 293 (7)).

In relation to public companies (or their private company subsidiaries) a person who is aged seventy years or over cannot be appointed a director. Also a director must retire at the first annual general meeting following his seventieth birthday (s. 293). However, these provisions will not apply if the articles provide for the appointment of directors over seventy years of age or, alternatively, the appointment is made or approved by a special resolution of a general meeting of the company (s. 293).

Appointment of directors

Under Table A all the first directors must retire at the first AGM and at every subsequent AGM one-third of the directors must retire (Table A, article 73). This provision is frequently deleted in the articles of a private company.

Accompanying an application to register the company must be a statement of prospective directors (s. 10) and on incorporation these will become the first directors (s. 13). However, each nominated director must in the registration statement give his signed consent that he agrees to become a director. Should the articles name someone to be a director then it will be void unless it also appears in the registration statement.

Subsequent appointments of directors are made by following the procedure specified in the articles, e.g. by means of an ordinary resolution passed in a general meeting or by the existing directors (Table A, article 79), but again the person nominated to serve must agree. If no provision is made or if the directors fail to appoint then the company in a general meeting has the power to appoint new directors (*Barron v Potter* (1914)). This residual power of shareholders in a general meeting to appoint directors is not taken away by the usual provisions in the articles enabling the directors to fill vacancies or appoint additional directors (*Worcester Corsetry Ltd v Witting* (1936)).

A retiring director is eligible for re-election and if Table A, article 75 is followed then a retiring director standing for re-election will be automatically elected unless an ordinary resolution not to appoint him, or not to fill the vacancy, is passed.

Should a vacancy occur between annual general meetings (AGM) then the board has authority both to fill casual vacancies and to appoint additional directors (Table A, article 79) but they will only hold office until the next AGM when they will be able to stand, if they wish, for election.

A company must keep a register of its directors (s. 288) containing their: names (and any former names), usual residential addresses, their nationality, business occupation (if any), particulars of any other directorships held current or previously and their date of birth (s. 289). The Registrar must within 14 days be notified of any changes amongst directors or changes to their details (s. 288).

Review question

Explain the legal requirements in relation to the appointment and re-appointment of directors.

Defects in a director's appointment

The validity of a director's acts (individual, board of directors or committee of directors) will depend on the type of defect that is involved. If the defect in his appointment is of a technical nature then the director's acts will remain valid (s. 285). Indeed the articles generally contain a clause that if it is afterwards discovered that a director was disqualified, or improperly appointed, any acts done by him shall be valid in spite of the lack of qualification (Table A, article 92). This applies both to dealings with outsiders and to dealings with shareholders of the company (*British Asbestos Co. v Boyd* (1903)).

However, if the defect is substantial then his acts will be invalid:

> ## Morris v Kanssen (1946)
> Two shareholders, C and S, concocted a scheme to get rid of X, a third shareholder. C and S falsified board minutes to show that S had been appointed a director in the company.
>
> Held: The House of Lords said that this was not a defect in S's appointment, but a total non-appointment which the section (now s. 285) could not validate.

A third party will therefore find section 285 extremely helpful in that they may claim, unless they have notice to the contrary, entitlement to rely on the person they did business with as holding a directorship. However, if the alleged director held himself out as having the authority of a director when he did not, then unless the company was compromised to such an extent that they are responsible for his actions, section 285 cannot be used to attach liability to the company (*British Bank of the Middle East v Sun Life Assurance Company of Canada (UK) Ltd* (1983)).

Where s. 285 or article 92 do not apply then a third party will have to rely on either agency principles or s. 35A to make the company liable.

Qualification shares

Unless required by the articles a director need not own shares in the company. Where the articles demand a share holding then the shares must be obtained within two months of the appointment or the director will forfeit his office (s. 291). A share qualification must subsist

Share warrants cannot be treated as qualification shares (s. 291).

167

for the length of the appointment or again the directorship will be forfeited.

If the articles provide that qualification shares must be held 'in his own right' then they have to be held in such a way that the company may deal with him as the owner of the shares:

Sutton v English & Colonial Co. (1902)

The qualification of a director was the holding of 100 shares 'in his own right'. S, a director, held 100 shares. S later became bankrupt. His trustee in bankruptcy notified the company that he claimed the shares but did not wish to be registered for a few days. On this notification the directors excluded S from his directorship alleging that he was disqualified.

Held: While technically a shareholder, S's loss of control over the shares meant that he was disqualified for lack of qualification shares.

Qualification shares may be held jointly with any other person unless the articles state otherwise (*Grundy v Briggs* (1910)).

Board meetings

While the Companies Act 1985 closely regulates the calling and conduct of general meetings, board meetings are, apart from requiring minutes to be kept (s. 382), largely left unregulated. However, a board decision not minuted will still stand (*Re North Hallenbeagle Mining Co., Knights Case* (1867)). In the absence of statutory guidance on board meetings it is necessary to look to the articles or to common law principles.

Obligations imposed by Table A

Where a company incorporates Table A into its constitution, then article 88 leaves the directors to regulate their proceedings as they think fit. Any director is able to call a meeting and issues dealt with are decided by a majority with all directors having an equal vote. Also all directors, apart from those absent from the United Kingdom, must be given oral or written notice of meetings. As in practice most boards meet on a regularized basis notice is not strictly required, but would be needed where the board meets irregularly. Table A, article 88 is silent on what constitutes proper notice. Presumably, it is dependent on circumstances but with the proviso that reasonable notice has to be given for a director to be able to attend:

Bentley-Steven v Jones (1974)

A letter was left at a director's home on Sunday announcing that a board meeting was convened for the next day. The director in question was away for a long weekend and only became aware of the notice on his return, Monday evening, after the meeting had taken place.

Held: The notice given was unreasonably short.

To avoid the necessity of having to have all the directors meet face-to-face, Table A, article 93 says that a written resolution signed by all the directors entitled to receive notice of a directors' meeting (or a committee of directors) will be as valid and effective as if it had been passed at a meeting of directors (or committee of directors) duly convened and held.

In respect to a quorum, article 89 sets this for business to be transacted by directors at two with an alternative director being counted, in the absence of his appointor, in the quorum. Directors may continue to act notwithstanding any vacancies in their number but if their number becomes less than the number fixed as a quorum then the continuing directors may act only for the purpose of filling vacancies or calling a general meeting (Table A, article 89: *Re Bank of Syria* (1901))

Any directors making up a quorum must be qualified to act. If any are unqualified then their presence is to be ignored:

The resolutions signed in place of holding a formal board meeting are akin to the informal resolutions used in place of a general meeting of a private company.

Re Greymouth Point Elizabeth Railway Co Ltd (1904)

The articles provided that a director could not vote on any issue in which he was interested and that two directors were to be a quorum. Two of the three directors lent £2,000 to the company and the three-director board agreed to give them a debenture as security.

Held: As two of the three directors were not qualified to vote on the issue in hand it meant that the granting of security was void for lack of a quorum.

Obligations imposed under the common law

In respect to common law obligations each director is to receive notice of board meetings, have the right of attendance and be allowed to speak (*Harben v Phillips* (1883)). These rights are particularly important for as a decision of the board is binding on all directors it would otherwise mean that an excluded director could be held liable for wrongful trading (Insolvency Act 1986, s. 214) or other wrongful acts. Also shareholders would not receive the benefit of advice from the whole board. The triple rights of notice, attendance and participation are really an expression of natural justice:

Under Table A, article 94 a director is prohibited from voting on any matter in which there is a material conflict of interest, actual or potential, between the company and himself.

> He (a director) has a perfect right to know what is going on at these meetings. It may affect his individual interest as a shareholder as well as his liability as a director, because it has been sometimes held that even a director who does not attend board meetings is bound to know what is done in his absence. (Jessel MR, *Pulbrook* v *Richmond Consolidated Mining Co.* (1878))

Therefore, a meeting called at short notice, when it was known that certain directors would be unable to attend, was held invalid so that the business transacted was set aside (*Re Horner District Consolidated Gold Mines* (1883)).

Informal meetings

Most board meetings tend to be formal but an informal one is permitted provided that *all* qualified directors receive notice and agree to the informality (*Smith v Paringa Mines Ltd*

(1906)), so that where one director disagrees with having an informal meeting then it cannot validly take place:

> ### Barron v Potter (1914)
> The parties to the action were both directors of the same company. As a result of animosity between them they refused to meet at formally called board meetings. However, by chance they met at a railway station where Potter insisted on holding a board meeting there and then, subsequently claiming that he had proposed a motion and had carried it with his chairman's casting vote.
>
> Held: Barran had not consented to the meeting. Mere physical presence without consent did not constitute a valid meeting.

Informality may also be unanimously agreeing on a decision through correspondence (*Runciman v Walter Runciman plc* (1992)). An example of where informal meetings are not feasible is when some directors have to disclose a personal interest in a transaction to which the company is also a party (s. 317). Here a formal meeting will be needed (*Guinness plc v Saunders* (1990)).

The distribution of power between the board of directors and the general meeting of the company

This important relationship is dealt with in Chapter 13, Meetings.

Directors and agency principles

For over one hundred years the undisputed principle is that on incorporation a company becomes an artificial person independent of those who promoted and created it (*Salmon v Salmon & Co.* (1897)). But as an artificial creation it needs others to act for it:

> The company itself cannot act in its own person, for it has no person; it can only act through its directors and the case is, as regards those directors, merely, the ordinary case of principal and agent. (Cairns LC, *Ferguson v Wilson* (1866))

Ostensible authority is also known as apparent authority or agency by estoppel. It is essentially based on a concept of holding out a director as having a certain authority.

When acting on behalf of a company a director may have an actual express authority, in that he will have the specific authority of the board to enter into stipulated contracts with third parties, and in doing so legally bind the company through an implied authority based upon ostensible authority. This is where the company (principal) is deemed to have held the director (agent) out to a third party as having the necessary authority to enter into the contract in hand. The required conditions are:

a) a representation is made by the company to the third party; and
b) the third party relies on this representation; and

c) the third party as a consequence of that reliance alters his position.

If the above conditions are satisfied then the company will be estopped, that is prevented, from denying that the director had the necessary authority.

Ostensible authority may arise in one of two ways. Firstly, a third party may reasonably expect that a person occupying the position of a director is able to contract with him; or, secondly, as a result of previous dealings the third party is led to believe that the director continues to have the necessary authority:

> In the commonly encountered case, the ostensible authority is general in character, arising when the principal has placed the agent in a position which in the outside world is generally regarded as carrying authority to enter into transactions of the kind in question. Ostensible general authority may also arise where the agent has had a course of dealing with a particular contractor and the principal has acquiesced in this course of dealing and honoured transactions arising out of it. (Lord Keith, *Armages Ltd v Mundogas SA The Ocean Frost* (1986))

What is particularly important to appreciate is that ostensible authority may apply where the company has restricted a director's power such as by limiting his authority or by prohibiting him from entering into certain transactions. Here a third party, who is unaware of such limitation or prohibition, may claim that apparently to him the agent had the necessary authority to enter into the transaction. The most authoritative case on ostensible authority is *Freeman & Lockyer v Buckhurst Park Properties (Mangol) Ltd* (1964):

Freeman & Lockyer v Buckhurst Park Properties (Mangol) Ltd (1964)

BP was formed for the purpose of making a quick profit by buying and reselling Buckhurst Park Estate. The property was purchased but although the quick resell did not take place BPP were still anxious to dispose of it for the best deal they could make. In their articles BPP had the power to appoint a managing director but never formally did so.

However, the board of directors allowed one director, Kapoor (K), to act as if he was the managing director both when trying initially to get a quick resell and later in trying to dispose of it. While carrying out the company's business, K instructed FL (a firm of architects and surveyors) to obtain planning permission for the property as well as undertaking a survey and preparing plans on it. FL claimed unpaid professional fees. The question to be decided was who were liable for these fees – BPP or K?

Held: Liability would attach to BPP for they had held out K as being their managing director (agent). K had acted within the scope of the authority normally conferred on a managing director in engaging professional services such as those provided by FL. The fact that FL had not read the articles or asked whether K was properly appointed was immaterial.

In his Court of Appeal judgement in *Freeman Lockyer etc.*, Diplock LJ gave what has become the definitive explanation of ostensible authority:

Should the company wish to do so it may ratify a director's unauthorized act (but not an illegal one) by means of passing an ordinary resolution (Bamford v Bamford (1970)).

Here Kapoor is an example of a de facto director in that he is given the appearance of being one and is therefore to be treated as a director. A director who has been validly appointed to his position is a de jure director.

The word contractor is used as an alternative to third party.

An apparent' or 'ostensible' authority, on the one hand, is a legal relationship between the principal and the contractor created by a representation, made by the principal to the contractor, intended to be and in fact acted on by the contractor, that the agent had authority to enter on behalf of the principal into a contract of the kind within the scope of the 'apparent' authority, so as to render the principal liable to perform any obligation imposed on him by such contract. To the relationship so created the agent is a stranger. He need not be (although he generally is) aware of the existence of the representation. The representation, when acted upon by the contractor by entering into a contract with the agent, operates as an estoppel, preventing the principal from asserting that he is not bound by the contract. It is irrelevant whether the agent had actual authority to enter into the contract.

Subsequently, Lord Keith in *Armages Ltd v Mundogas SA, The Ocean Frost* (1986), restated in a shorter form Diplock LJ's general principle as:

Ostensible authority comes about where the principal, by words or conduct, has represented that the agent has the requisite actual authority, and the third party deals with him in reliance on that representation. The principal in these circumstances is estopped from denying that actual authority existed.

It must be stressed that ostensible authority can never arise where the third party knows that the agent's authority is limited to such an extent that the agent does not in fact have the necessary authority to act for the company. Here the third party will be unable to say that when entering into a transaction he relied upon the principal's representation. A third party attempting to do so acts in bad faith.

The rule in Royal British Bank v Turquand (1856)

In addition to agency principles, if the company disclaimed liability on a contract by saying that the director who entered into it on their behalf had not been validly appointed then a third party could make use of the rule in *Royal British Bank v Turquand* (1856):

If the issue relates not to regularity of constitutional procedures being followed but to the conduct of a director then the rule has no application and in order to make the company liable agency principles or s. 35A must be looked to.

> ### Royal British Bank v Turquand (1856)
> Directors of RBB issued a bond to T. They had authority to issue bonds if authorized by a general resolution of the company. It was claimed that no resolution had been passed.
>
> Held: T could sue on the bond. He was entitled to assume that a resolution had been passed even if in fact it had not.

The rule in *Turquand*'s case also says that where a third party deals with the company in a transaction which is not contrary to the company's constitution then he is not bound to enquire whether all the necessary steps have been taken. He is entitled to assume that the directors have been properly appointed and have acted correctly:

Persons dealing with the company are bound to read the registered documents, and to see that the proposed dealing is not inconsistent therewith. But they are not bound to do more; they need not inquire into the regularity of the internal proceedings. (Jervis CJ, *Royal British Bank v Turquand* (1856))

Therefore, if there was a defect in the director's appointment, for example because proper procedures at the appointment meeting were not followed, it can be ignored provided that the third party did not deliberately close his eyes to the circumstances. Hence the rule will not apply where the third party knows of the irregularity (*Re Patent Ivory Manufacturing Co.* (1888)), or where the circumstances ought to have put the third party on guard to ask necessary questions (*Underwood (AL) v Bank of Liverpool and Martins* (1924)).

As an alternative to using *Turquand*'s case a third party may rely on s. 35A. This states that for a person dealing with the company in good faith, the power of the board of directors to bind the company, or to authorize others to do so, shall be deemed to be free of any limitation under the company's constitution. Good faith, under s. 35A, is still retained even though the third party had knowledge of the limitations in the company constitution.

Review question

Discuss how a third party may try to enforce a transaction against a company entered into by a board of directors exceeding its powers.

A director's contract of employment

Long service contracts are frowned upon for if a director, on losing his appointment unfairly, sued the company for the unexpired period of his contract then he may expect to obtain substantial damages. Therefore, it is not possible to have an unbreakable service contract exceeding five years unless the shareholders are given details of it and agree to it (s. 319). Any contract breaking s. 319 will be void.

Ideally the service contract will state the formal position of the individual as company officer and employee and the position if either are dismissed (it is best if dismissal in one capacity automatically terminates the other). The articles should contain a power that the board may use to vote a director out of office if he is absent without good reason from board meetings for six months (see Table A, article 81).

For recommendations concerning the length of directors' service contracts see also Chapter 16, Corporate Governance.

Directors' remuneration

Directors themselves are unable to vote their own payment. Their remuneration is a matter for the company in a general meeting to fix by ordinary resolution (Table A, article 82) often on the recommendation of a remuneration committee of non-executive directors (see under the Greenbury report in Chapter 16, Corporate Governance). If the remuneration is provided for in the articles then it cannot be changed or increased without a special resolution (*Kerr v Marine Products* (1928)). Also directors are not entitled to any remuneration apart from that expressly provided for – so travelling or other expenses are not reimbursable unless expressly covered (*Young v Naval, Military etc. Ltd* (1905)). Once payment is voted, or if the

Table A, article 83 provides for reimbursement of subsistence expenses incurred by directors attending authorized company meetings.

articles provide for remuneration, then it becomes a debt due from the company to the directors and may be sued for and it may be paid out of capital if there are insufficient profits (Table A, article 82; *Re Lundy Granite Co.* (1972)).

If a director's remuneration is stated to be 'at the rate of £X a year' but he acts for only part of a year then he is entitled to a proportionate rate of remuneration. But if the remuneration is to be 'a yearly sum of £X', or '£X per annum', then he is unlikely to get anything unless he acts for the whole year (*Inman v Ackroyd and Best Ltd* (1901)).

Those who may not be appointed a director

The Company Directors' Disqualification Act 1986 prohibits certain categories of persons from being directors. These are:

The sections in this part are from the CD DA 1986.

a) *Undischarged bankrupts (s. 11)*
   unless the court agrees it is a criminal offence for an undischarged bankrupt to serve as a director. If this provision is broken then a director on an indictable conviction may be imprisoned for up to two years or a fine or both; on a summary conviction imprisonment for up to 6 months or a fine or both.
b) *Those disqualified by the courts (ss. 2–4)*
   There are several grounds for disqualification:
   i)   conviction for an indictable offence relating to a company (s. 2) (e.g. promotion, formation, management, liquidation or relating to receivership or management of a company's property).
        Management is given a wide definition:

R v Georgiou (1988)
G carried on an insurance business without authorization and was duly convicted.

Held (Court of Appeal): The use of limited liability status for an illegal purpose came within the management of a company and in consequence he should be disqualified from being a company director.

In R v Georgiou there was no accusation that G was badly managing the company.

   If the offence is dealt with by magistrates the maximum period of disqualification is 5 years, otherwise it is a 15 year maximum period.
   ii) persistent failure to file documents with the Registrar (s. 3)
        There is a presumption of 'persistent default' if the director in question is found guilty of three or more 'defaults' in any 5-year period. However, a court may choose to ignore this guideline and to use its own discretion:

Re Arctic Engineering Ltd (1986)
Although the director concerned had not previously been convicted for failure to file it was found that his failure to send in 35 obligatory returns was sufficient to disqualify – this easily satisfied the court's finding that 'persistently' required some degree of continuance or repetition.

On conviction under this section there is a maximum period of 5 years' disqualification.

iii) fraud discovered during winding up (s. 4)

This applies where it appears that the director has been guilty of an offence for which he is liable under s. 458 CA 1988 whether convicted or not. This is fraudulent trading where directors keep trading even though they know that the company is insolvent. Alternatively the fraud may relate to matters other than fraudulent trading.

Trading whilst insolvent, which can lead to disqualification, is dealt with in Chapter 18, Winding Up.

The maximum period of disqualification under this section is 15 years.

iv) where a director is found guilty of a breach of duty towards his company (s. 5)

This provision is similar to s. 3 in that a disqualification order can be made following a conviction, or failing to file obligatory returns, or accounts etc., and has been found guilty of at least three such offences in the previous 5 years.

Disqualification can be for up to a maximum of 5 years.

v) by reason of unfitness in respect to insolvent companies (s. 6)

Unfitness to be concerned in the management of a company is by far the commonest ground under the Act for disqualification.

The director's conduct can be examined not only in relation to the directorship of the company in question but to any other directorship that he either has or had, and on examining the circumstances of the company's failure a court is to take account of a litany of possible corporate ills and wrongs: misfeasance; breach of a fiduciary or other duty; misapplication of company money or other property; entering into a transaction at an undervalue that defrauds creditors; involvement with a failure to keep proper accounts etc. (Schedule 1). On completion of the examination of the circumstances the overriding question then posed is how responsible was the director for the causes of the company becoming insolvent:

> Ordinary commercial misjudgement is in itself not sufficient to justify disqualification in the normal case, the conduct complained of must display a lack of commercial probity, although I have no doubt that in an extreme case of gross negligence or total incompetence disqualification could be appropriate. (Brown-Wilkinson V-C, Re *Lo-Line Electric Motors Ltd* (1988))

Unfitness under ss. 6 & 8 concerns general unfitness as opposed to unfitness related to a particular company. Therefore, disqualification from managing a public company will also mean disqualification from managing a private company (Re Polly Peck International plc No 2. (1994)).

Re Continental Assurance Co. of London plc (1977)

CAL was taken over in 1985 by Y Ltd with money provided by S Bank. Y Ltd's only source of income was from commission it received from managing CAL's affairs and dividends again from CAL. In the period 1985–92 CAL 'lent' large sums to Y Ltd and was at the time of its liquidation owed £2+ million by Y Ltd (CAL's overall indebtedness at this time was £8 million). No interest was paid on these unsecured loans with much of the money being used to discharge Y Ltd's indebtedness to S Bank (this was a breach of s. 151 prohibition of financial assistance for the purchase of its own shares). X was a senior employee of S Bank until he left in 1991 but he did continue to advise S Bank on certain of their clients including CAL. In 1988 he had become a non-executive director of CAL and Y Ltd and was aware of the s. 151 prohibition.

Held: Any competent director would have realized what was going on. His failure to know displayed serious incompetence or neglect. He also failed to appreciate what responsibilities he had in relation to the understanding of a company's financial affairs. He was disqualified for 3 years.

How culpable will a director become in acquiescence to a hopeless position?

Secretary of State for Trade and Industry v Taylor etc (1997)

T was a director and minority shareholder. The company was in a perilous financial position but T's suggestions for improvement were ignored. The company later collapsed.

Held: A prudent director finding that his company is trading at the risk of creditors and who cannot persuade fellow directors to alter their conduct nor cure their actions should resign. However, failure to resign does not in itself make a director unfit to be concerned in the management of a company. Here T, whose salary was modest, had not yet reached the stage where he should have recognized that to resign was the only acceptable cause of conduct.

This case was decided under section 300 of CA 1985, now superseded by section 6 of CDDA. This part of Browne-Wilkinson's V C judgement has often been approved by the Court of Appeal.

The object of the CDDA 1986 was the protection of the public.

What is problematic is being able to discern judicial consensus as to what constitutes unfairness. In *Re Contintental Assurance Co. of London plc* (1997) incompetence by itself was felt not to be enough while in other cases incompetence, if gross, was enough to disqualify. In *Re Lo-Line Electric Motors Ltd* (1988), Browne-Wilkinson V-C said that the primary purpose of disqualification was not to punish the individual but to protect the public against future misconduct:

The approach adopted in all the cases to which I have been referred is broadly the same. The primary purpose of the section is not to punish the individual but to protect the public against the future conduct of companies by persons whose past records as directors of insolvent companies have shown them to be a danger to creditors and others. Therefore, the power is not fundamentally penal.

However, this public policy stance was seemingly ignored by the Court of Appeal decision in *Re Gray Building Services Ltd etc* (1995) where it was said that only the alleged misconduct of the defendant could be considered not possible future misbehaviour. While in *Secretary of State for Trade and Industry v Tjolle and Others* (1998) the High Court said that the purpose of disqualification was to protect the public from the activities of those unfit to be concerned in company management!

In relation to the length of the disqualification period, again it is hard to detect unanimity although it has to be conceded that slight variations between what may, in board terms, appear identical cases may make for differences of a few years. In *Sevenoaks Stationers (Retail) Ltd* (1990), Dillon LJ put forward guideline recommendations for a disqualification tariff so that errant directors could be kept 'off the road':

I would for my part endorse the division of the potential 15-year disqualification period into three brackets ... viz: (i) the top bracket of disqualification for periods over ten years should be reserved for particularly serious cases – these may include cases where a director who has already had one period of disqualification imposed on him falls to be disqualified yet again; (ii) the minimum bracket of two to five years' disqualification should be applied where, though disqualification is mandatory, the case is relatively not very serious; and (iii) the middle bracket of disqualification for from six to ten years should apply for serious cases which do not merit the top bracket.

For comment on the evidence relevant to influencing the length of a director's disqualification see Lord Woolf MR, in Secretary of State for Trade and Industry v Griffiths and Others *(1997).*

When considering the length of disqualification a court should not countenance plea bargaining between the Secretary of State and the defendant but negotiations on an admission of fact may be sensible (*Secretary of State for Trade and Industry v Griffiths and Others* (1997), *Re Carecraft Construction Ltd* (1994) and *Re Blackspur Group plc etc.* (1997); also see the proposed new legislation referred to later).

vi) disqualification after investigation (s. 8)

The Secretary of State may make an application to the court for a disqualification order if it appears to him from a report or other documents that it is in the public interest that a disqualification order be made against a director or former director. If the court is satisfied that the conduct of the director concerned makes him unfit to be involved in the management of a company then it will make the order.

This provision gives wide discretion to the Secretary of State but unfitness alone is insufficient ground to make an application – it needs to be allied with public interest. The maximum disqualification period is 15 years.

Number of directors disqualified

Figures are provided in Appendix 2 for the number of directors disqualified in 1996 and 1997 under the CDDA 1986 together with the length of their disqualification period.

Register of disqualified directors

The Secretary of State keeps a register of disqualified directors and this is open for public inspection.

Proposed 'fast-track' bans for directors

Under an initiative announced in February 1998 from the Department of Trade and Industry, legislation is to be passed to introduce a fast-track procedure for the quick and easy disqualification of company directors.

Directors seen as unfit will be told that they can avoid going to court by voluntarily agreeing not to serve as directors for a specified period. Such an agreement would 'have the same legal effects as a disqualification order made by a court' according to Nigel Griffiths, Competition and Consumer Affairs minister. He added, in a parliamentary written answer, that the proposed procedure would be available to any director who 'under the present law is or could be' brought before the courts. To encourage take-up of this fast-track procedure the trade-off is that those taking it up would be offered a shorter disqualification period, perhaps three years, than one that is likely to be imposed by a court.

The motivation for the initiative is to squeeze out 'cowboy' directors. At present many directors identified as being unfit never get to court. Also in addition to speeding up disqualification by saving court time, the measure will cut legal and administration costs. No date has been set for the enabling legislation but it may form part of an Insolvency Bill, dependent on parliamentary time being made available.

Termination of a director's period of office

a) *Death or resignation of the director*
A director may resign his office in the manner provided by the articles. If the articles contain no provision for resignation then he can resign on reasonable notice but his resignation need not be accepted by the board. Once a director's resignation has been accepted then he cannot withdraw it (*Glossop v Glossop* (1907)).

b) *Retirement*
At each annual general meeting (AGM) a third of the directors (those longest in office) must retire (Table A, articles 73 and 74), although they may offer themselves for re-election. Also for public limited companies a director must retire at the first AGM after reaching 70 years of age (s. 293) but this provision can be circumvented by its exclusion in the articles, or in having an 'over-age' director appointed by the company by passing a special resolution.

c) *Dissolution of the company*
On liquidation the directors are automatically dismissed (*Measures Bros Ltd v Measures* (1910)).

d) *Dismissal*
The shareholders may by means of an ordinary resolution remove a director from office (s. 303) provided that 28 days notice, or in some circumstances 21 days notice, of the dismissal resolution is given (s. 379). However, if the dismissed director has a service contract then he may possibly claim damages for breach of contract (*Southern Foundries v Shirlaw* (1940)).

e) *Loss of share qualification*
See the section on share qualification.

It is not uncommon that articles of private companies will contain a clause giving shareholder-directors increased voting rights if they face a dismissal resolution (Bushell v Faith (1970)). Such a clause may well make a director irremovable.

Compensation for loss of office

If a company wishes to make a non-contractual *ex gratia* payment to a director for loss of office then details of the intended payment must be disclosed to the members who will have to approve it (s. 312). If compensation is not disclosed and approved then those directors responsible for the payment will be personally liable for its repayment (*Re Duomatic* (1969)). Where a business is being transferred, such as with a merger or takeover, then any compensation to a director for loss of office is unlawful unless it is again disclosed to and approved by the members (s. 313). A director receiving such a payment is taken to hold it in trust for the company and needs to return it on demand.

Review question

Discuss the dismissal of a company director, including the dismissal before the expiry of a service contract.

Substantial property transactions

Because of their paramount position within companies there is a fear that an unscrupulous director will sell his own property to the company at an overvaluation or, alternatively, buy company property at an undervaluation. To guard against these eventualities a company cannot transfer to or acquire from a director any property the value of which exceeds the lesser of £50,000 or 10 per cent of the company's net assets without the prior approval of the shareholders in a general meeting (s. 320). Section 320 also applies where property is transferred through a third party but with the same objective of benefiting a director. A director in breach of s. 320 will forfeit any gain made and will be required to indemnify the company for any loss incurred. Possible defences are for the director to plead that he took all reasonable steps for the company to comply with s. 320 or, alternatively, the company were not aware of any contravention.

There are a number of exceptions to s. 320, most notably transfers of less than £20,000 in value.

Loans to directors

The capital of a company is for use in its business not for the personal use of directors, especially if a loan was granted at a low rate of interest. Therefore, there is a general prohibition whereby companies cannot make a loan to a director nor give a guarantee or provide security in connection with a loan (s. 330 (2)). However, there are a number of exceptions to this general position, the most important being:

a) a loan etc. that does not exceed £5,000 (s. 330 (3));
b) a loan etc. given to a director to enable him to cover expenses incurred in the performance of his duty (s. 337).

In respect to (b) the loan, guarantee, or security must have been previously approved by the company at a general meeting or, alternatively, when the loan etc. was provided it was stated that if not approved at the next general meeting the loan etc. would be repaid within the following 6 months. If it is a public limited company (or its subsidiary) then the value of the loan etc. must not exceed £20,000.

A transaction that breaches s. 330 is voidable by the company unless: restitution is impossible or the company has been indemnified for any loss or damage suffered; or avoidance of the transaction would prejudice the position of a third party who acquired rights in good faith and for value without notice that s. 330 had been broken (s. 341 (1)). A person receiving benefit of the prohibited transaction has to account to the company for it and any director who authorized it must account for any gain derived from it or give indemnity to the company for any loss it has suffered (s. 341 (2)).

In addition to the above civil consequences of breaching s. 330 there are possible criminal penalties as well. A director of a public company (or a company that is part of a group containing a public company) who authorizes or permits the company to enter into a transaction or arrangement knowing or having reasonable cause to believe that s. 330 will be broken is guilty of an offence under the Companies Act (s. 342). The penalty that may be imposed is imprisonment or fine or both.

The fiduciary duties of directors

Directors of a company are fiduciaries and therefore must use their powers in good faith in the interests of the company. The fiduciary duty of a director is similar in broad terms to that of a trustee. The governing principle is that the company has placed trust in the director who is expected to reciprocate by acting with the utmost good faith towards his company when dealing with it or acting on its behalf. For example in relation to company assets a director, as a trustee, is taken to be a steward of the company so that they must act without any additional purpose, such as self interest, which would affect the main and overriding interest of the company. Similarly, directors are trustees for the company when exercising their powers of approving share transfers, issuing and allotting shares and making calls:

> Alexander v Automatic Telephone Co. (1900)
> The directors of AT paid nothing on their own shares but made all other shareholders pay 3s 6d (17p) on each share, partly on allotment and partly by a call. The directors did not tell the other shareholders of this difference.
>
> Held: The directors had broken their duty of trust and must pay to the company 3s 6d on each of their shares.

In his Court of Appeal judgement in *Alexander v Automatic Telephone Co.* (1900), Lindley MR said:

> The Court of Chancery has always exacted from directors the observance of good faith towards shareholders ... and directors who so use their powers as to obtain benefits for themselves at the expense of the shareholders, without informing them of the fact, cannot retain those benefits, and must account for them to the company.

While it is exceptionally possible for a director to be a fiduciary of a shareholder (*Briess v Wooley* (1954), generally fiduciary duties are owed only to the company:

> Percival v Wright (1902)
> Directors bought shares from a shareholder while they were negotiating for the sale of the business of the company at a very high price, but did not tell him of this fact.
>
> Held: The purchase of the shares was valid. The directors were not trustees of shareholders.

Neither are directors trustees for third parties who have made contracts with the company. However, the trustee analogy, in a pure form, must not be overstated in that directors do not have to account so strictly as, for example, trustees of a marriage settlement or will. But the most striking difference is that legal title in the company's property lies in the company's and not the directors' hands as would apply if they were in fact true trustees:

A trustee is a man who is the owner of property and deals with it as principal, as owner, and as master, subject only to an equitable obligation to account to some persons to whom he stands in the relation of trustee ... The office of a director is that of a paid servant of the company. A director never enters into a contract for himself, but for his principal ... he cannot sue on such contracts, nor be sued on them (unless he exceeds his authority). (James LJ, *Smith v Anderson* (1880))

When examining directors' actions the test to be used is did they act ' ... bona fide in what they consider – not what a court may consider – in the interests of the company, and not for any collateral purpose' (Lord Greene MR in *Re Smith & Fawcett Ltd* (1942)). This test was subsequently refined by Lord Wilberforce in *Howard Smith Ltd v Ampol Petroleum Ltd* (1974) where he said that subjective and objective elements were present:

a) firstly, a court must find that the directors believed that they were acting bona fide (that is in good faith) in the interests of the company;

b) secondly, the court must next find whether the purpose for which the directors acted was proper or improper.

This follows the judgement of Buckley J in Hogg v Crampton Ltd (1967).

If directors fail any part of this two-part test then they have breached their fiduciary duties. The duties owed are:

1 Directors have a duty to act in good faith for the benefit of the company as a whole. Here regard is to be had to the present as well as future interest of the company. In *Rolled Steel Products v British Steel Corp.* (1986) the tests previously formulated by Eve J in *Re Lee Behrens & Co. Ltd* (1932) were said to be still valid for determining whether a transaction was in the interest of the company. These were:
a) Is the transaction reasonably incidental to the carrying on of the company's business?
b) Is it a *bona fide* transaction?
c) Is it done for the benefit and to promote the prosperity of the company?

Evans v Brunner Mond (1921)
Directors of a chemical company made on behalf of the company charitable donations to a number of universities researching into chemicals. E, a shareholder, protested.

Held: The directors had not broken their duty. The company was financially sound and long term the donations could be expected to benefit the industry and through it the company.
But in:

Re Roith (1967)
A controlling shareholder who was also a director wished to provide for his widow without leaving his shares to her. He entered into a service contract with the company under which on his death his widow would get a life pension.

Held: As the purpose was to benefit his widow, as opposed to the company, the agreement was not binding on the company.

2   Directors must use their powers only for the purpose for which they were conferred
    This is known as the *proper purpose* doctrine. It was well put by Turner LJ in *Re Cameron's Coalbrook Steam Coal, & Swansea & Lougher Railway Co., Bennett's Case (1854)*:

> ... in the exercise of the powers given to them ... (directors) must, as I conceive, keep within the proper limits. Power given to them for one purpose cannot, in my opinion, be used by them for another and different purpose. To permit such proceeding on the part of directors of companies would be to sanction not the use but the abuse of their powers. It would be to give effect and validity to an illegal exercise of a legal power..

Where directors act improperly but believe that they are still acting in the interests of the company they may still be liable if they have not used their powers for the purpose conferred. The difficulty here is in drawing a line beyond which a director is not allowed to go. The dilemma was recognized by Lord Wilberforce in *Howard Smith v Ampol Petroleum* (1974):

> To define in advance exact limits beyond which directors must not pass is, in their Lordships' view impossible. This clearly cannot be done by emanation, since the variety of situations facing directors of different types of company in different situations cannot be anticipated.

This seems to be an echo of an earlier call to tread warily when examining directors' conduct:

> I am quite clear about this case. One must be very careful in administering the law of joint stock companies not to press so hardly on honest directors as to make them liable for these constructive defaults, the only effect of which would be to deter all men of any property, and perhaps all men who have any character to lose, from becoming directors of companies at all. On the one hand, I think the Court should do its utmost to bring fraudulent directors to account, and, on the other hand, should also do its best to allow honest men to act reasonably as directors. (Jessel MR, *Re Forest of Dean Coal Mining Co.* (1878))

However, in *Howard Smith v Ampol Petroleum* (1974) Lord Wilberforce was scathing in the issue of self-interest:

> ... it is correct to say that where the self-interest of the directors is involved, they will not be permitted to assert that their action was bona fide thought to be, or was, in the interests of the company.

And he continued:

> ... But it does not follow from this, as the appellants assert, that the absence of any element of self-interest is enough to make an issue valid. Self-interest is only one, though no doubt the commonest, instance of improper motive: and, before one can say that a fiduciary power has been exercised for the purpose for which it was conferred, a wider investigation may have to be made.

In respect to identifying motive, Lord Wilberforce felt that a wider investigation was often necessary to determine why directors acted in the manner they did, citing with approval from the dictum of Viscount Finlay in *Hindle v John Cotton Ltd* (1919):

> Where the question is one of abuse of powers, the state of mind of those who acted, and the motive on which they acted, are all important, and you may go into the question of what their intention was, collecting from the surrounding circumstances all the materials which genuinely throw light upon the question of the state of mind of the directors so as to show whether they were honestly acting in discharge of their powers in the interest of the company or were acting from some bye-motive, possibly of personal advantage, or for any other reason.

An illustration of a bad motive, but one that was not too difficult to locate, was found in:

Hogg v Crampham (1967)

Wishing to defeat a takeover bid, directors issued shares carrying 10 votes each to trustees of an employee pension fund. The company also gave an interest-free loan to enable the trustees to pay for the shares.

Held: As the proper purpose of issuing shares is normally to obtain capital, here there was a mis-use of the authority given to the directors, i.e. their motive was for them to retain control of the company.

---

3 Directors must avoid a conflict between duty to the company and self-interest.
A director must not place himself in a position where his personal financial interest conflicts with his duty to the company. This is the *no conflict* rule:

> The true principle is that if a director places himself in a position in which his duty to the company conflicts with his personal interest or his duty to another, the court will intervene to set aside the transaction without inquiring whether there was any breach of the director's duty to the company. That is an over-riding principle of equity. (*Vinelott J, Movitex Ltd v Bulfield* (1988))

The rule follows the established position that a court of equity will not allow a person in a fiduciary position, unless expressly so entitled, to make a personal profit or to put himself in a position where his duty and his interest conflict. Professor Gower has

In Movitex Ltd v Bulfield (1988), Vinelott J used the term *self-dealing rule* as substitute for the usual term no conflict rule. This alternative had been coined by Sir Robert Megarry V-C, in Tito v Waddell (No. 2) (1977).

divided this obligation into three parts. They are:

a) Where a director makes a contract with the company
   i)   in his own business capacity:

Aberdeen Railway Co. v Blaikie Bros (1854)

A company entered into a contract with a partnership to buy office furniture. It was later discovered that a director of the company was a partner in the firm.

Held: The company was able to set aside the transaction

---

   ii)   in his own personal capacity:

Parker v McKenna (1874)

S agreed to take 9,000 shares on certain terms by which he was to pay £30 now, and the balance by instalments. Subsequently, the directors took over part of the shares and released him from further liability.

Held: The contract was one where they were duty bound to watch the interests of the company. They had not done so, preferring to put their own interest before that of the company. They must therefore refund the profit made on the shares.

In Gower's Principles of Modern Company Law. Sixth edition (1997) by B.L. Davies.

In respect to the degree of the conflicting interest, courts seemingly are willing to ignore insignificant matters as not warranting the full application of the rule. In *Movitex Ltd v Bulfield* (1988), Vinelott found a self-interest to be 'so small that it can as a practical matter be disregarded'.

b) Where a director makes use of corporate property, information or opportunity
Collectively these may be termed the *corporate opportunity* doctrine or the *no profit* rule. They require a director to account to the company for any profit made and to become a constructive trustee for any property acquired (*Carlton v Halestrap* (1988)). Whether the company can itself make a profit is of no importance. What is focused upon is the matter of the profit or advantage:

Did the director's profit arise by reason and in virtue of the director's position and by reason of the opportunity and the knowledge resulting from it? (Lord Wright, *Regal (Hastings) Ltd v Gulliver* (1942))

The strictness of the duty is illustrated by:

Regal (Hastings) Ltd v Gulliver (1942)

A company with one cinema decided to buy two more then sell all three as a group. A subsidiary company was formed to buy the lease of the two cinemas but the owner of

---

the freehold land insisted that the paid up capital be at least £5,000. The subsidiary company couldn't provide this so the directors personally subscribed 3,000 £1 shares. Later the shares in both companies were sold with the directors making a profit of nearly £3 per share in the subsidiary. The new owners of the group later brought an action to recover the former director's profits.

Held: Firstly, what the directors did was so related to the affairs of the company that it could be said to have been done in the course of their management and by the use of an opportunity presented to them as directors. Secondly, their action had made them a personal profit.

In *Regal (Hastings) Ltd v Gulliver* (1942), the court accepted that throughout the directors had acted in good faith but their actions clearly fell within Lord Wright's dictum. The effect was that the new owner acquired the group at a 75 per cent reduction in the price they had agreed to pay for the shares. In the same case Lord Russell assiduously drew attention to the principle that a profit totally untainted with any impropriety would still breach the fiduciary duty:

> ... The rule of equity which insists on those who by use of a fiduciary position make a profit, being liable to account for that profit, in no way depends on fraud, or absence of bona fides; or upon such questions or considerations as whether the profit would or should otherwise have gone to the plaintiff, or whether the profiteer was under a duty to obtain the source of the profit for the plaintiff, or whether he took a risk or acted as he did for the benefit of the plaintiff, or whether the plaintiff has in fact been damaged or benefited by his action. The liability arises from the mere fact of a profit having, in the stated circumstance, been made. The profiteer, however honest and well-intentioned, cannot escape the risk of being called upon to account ...

Should a director resign a directorship and then pursue an advantage, this still will not be enough to escape the duty:

Industrial Development Consultants v Cooley (1972)

C was the managing director of IDC. While negotiating for IDC with the Eastern Gas Board he realized that IDC would probably not get the contract but believed that if he left IDC then he might be able to obtain it himself. C then told IDC that he was ill and they allowed him to end his service contract early. C got the contract with the Eastern Gas Board but IDC later claimed entitlement to the profit he had made.

Held: IDC's claim would succeed:

> Therefore, I feel impelled to the conclusion that when the defendant embarked on this course of conduct ... he was guilty of putting himself into the position in which his duty to his employers, the plaintiffs, and his own private interests conflicted and conflicted grievously. There being the fiduciary relationship I have described, it seems

> to me plain that it was his duty once he got this information to pass it on to his employers and not to guard it for his own personal purposes and profit. He put himself into the position when his duty and his interest conflicted ... (Roskill J)

But what if the company rejects an opportunity – can a director then take it up himself? Provided that the rejection by the board had been genuine then it appears that a director may take the opportunity over:

Peso Silver Mines Ltd v Cropper (1966)

C was managing director of PSM which was an exploration and mineral development company. In 1960 PSM, experiencing financial difficulties in working its large number of claims, declined to purchase others it was offered. In 1962 the board of PSM after consideration again declined to buy more highly speculative claims it was offered. Afterwards C was persuaded by others to join them in forming a company to buy claims that PSM had rejected. C did so and informed PSM of this. The board of PSM demanded that C's interest in the newly formed company be turned over to PSM and on his refusal he was dismissed and sued for an account of profit on the ground that he had breached his fiduciary duty to PSM.

Held: While C had been in a fiduciary relationship to PSM when they were first offered the claims in 1962, he was not in a fiduciary relationship when he joined others to acquire claims that PSM had previously rejected. Consequently, he had not obtained the claims by reason of the fact that he was a director of PSM. Also the offer to PSM had not contained any confidential information to which C, as managing director, had access and the later offer was made to him as a member of the public. For those reasons there had been no breach of C's fiduciary duty to PSM.

Peso Silver Mines Ltd v Cropper (1966), was decided by the Supreme Court of Canada. As such it is not binding in English law. However, the occasions when it has been cited with approval in English courts are such that it is extremely influential.

When a director is disqualified under the articles for 'making a secret profit', the disqualification will not prevent him from subsequently being re-elected after the transaction that led to the disqualification is completed (*Re Bodega* (1904)).

c) Where a director competes against his company

A director has a duty to the company and must therefore ignore outside interest:

Scottish CWS v Meyer (1959)

M and another were minority shareholders in a subsidiary company formed by the SCWS. They held 3,900 shares and the SCWS 4,000. The subsidiary had five directors – three were nominees of the SCWS with M and another making up the five. The three nominees were also directors of SCWS. Both the SCWS and the subsidiary were engaged in the same business, but the subsidiary was dependent on the SCWS for its supplies. The SCWS and M fell out and the CSWS adopted a policy of deliberately running the subsidiary down by cutting off its supplies. The three nominee directors followed SCWS instructions to ruin the subsidiary. At one time the subsidiary shares had been worth £6 each but at the end they were worth almost nothing.

> Held: The three nominee directors had not discharged their duties. The subsidiary was to be liquidated and SCWS were to buy out the minority shareholders at a fair price.

The unhappy saga of the three nominee directors in *Scottish CWS v Meyer* (1959) is not unique in that an appointor of nominees most probably believe that they are his people who will look after his interests first. However, once appointed a nominee has a duty to faithfully serve the company to which he was appointed even if doing so injures the interests of the appointor. In his judgement in *Scottish CWS v Meyer* (1959) Lord Denning set out the conflicting interest that operated:

> These three were therefore at one and the same time directors of the co-operative society – being three out of twelve of that company – and also directors of the textile company – three out of five there. So long as the interest of all concerned were in harmony, there was no difficulty. The nominee directors could do their duty by both companies without embarrassment. But, as soon as the interests of the two companies were in conflict, the nominee directors were placed in an impossible position. Thus, when the realignment of shareholding was under discussion, the duty of the three directors to the textile company was to get the best possible price for any new issue of its shares ... whereas their duty to the co-operative society was to obtain the new shares at the lowest possible price – at par, if they could. Again, when the co-operative society determined to set up its own company, the duty of the three directors to the textile company was to do their best to promote its business and to act with complete good faith towards it; and in consequence not to disclose their knowledge of its affairs to a competitor, and not even to work for a competitor, when to do so might operate to the disadvantage of the textile company ... whereas they were under the self-same duties to the co-operative society. It is plain that, in the circumstances, these three gentlemen could not do their duty by both companies, and they did not do so. They put their duty to the co-operative society above their duty to the textile company in this sense, at least that they did nothing to defend the interest of the textile company against the conduct of the co-operative society. They probably thought that as 'nominees' of the co-operative society their first duty was to the co-operative society. In this they were wrong. By subordinating the interest of the textile company to those of the co-operative society, they conducted the affairs of the textile company in a manner oppressive to the other shareholders.

Ratification

Contracts relating to a director's fiduciary duties are voidable so that ratification is possible. The company can therefore at a general meeting pass an ordinary resolution to ratify an unauthorized transaction (*Hogg v Cramphorn* (1967)). The members must be given full details before they vote. Ratification cannot be by the board of directors (not even if interested directors abstain) as the court takes the view that a board is only really effective when it acts as an *entire* board. However, a director owning shares is allowed to vote on the same

A company cannot relieve a director from liability if his breach is fundamental and unforgivable (Attorney General's Reference No. 2, 1982). This probably must equal a fraud on the company.

basis as other shareholders even though he may have a personal interest in what is being voted on (*North-West Transportation & Co. Ltd v Beatty* (1887)). But if ratification amounts to being a fraud on the minority then it will be ineffective (*Ngurli v McCann* (1953)). It must be appreciated that ratification will not make good a director's improper acts but it will prevent the company taking legal action against offending directors.

In *Bamford v Bamford* (1970), Harman LJ felt that ratification was a routine procedure:

> It is trite law, I had thought, that if directors do acts, as they do every day, especially in private companies, which, perhaps because there is no quorum, or because their appointment was defective, or because sometimes there are no directors properly appointed at all, or because they are actuated by improper motives, they go on doing for years, carrying on the business of the company in the way in which, if properly constituted, they should be carrying it on, and then they find that everything has been so to speak wrongly done because it was not done by a proper board, such directors can, by making a full and frank disclosure and calling together the general body of the shareholders, obtain absolution and forgiveness of their sins; and provided the acts are not ultra vires the company as a whole everything will go on as if it had been done all right from the beginning. I cannot believe that that is not a commonplace of company law. It is done every day. Of course, if the majority of the general meeting will not forgive and approve, the directors must pay for it ...

The statutory duty for a director to disclose

A director has a statutory duty to disclose any interest he may have at the first board meeting that discusses the matter or, alternatively, to disclose at the first board meeting after his interest arose if the matter had been previously discussed (s. 317). Breach of the statutory duty can result in an unlimited fine and the company will be able to rescind the contract unless it is too late do so. The weakness of s. 317 is that disclosure is to the board and not to the members. The board may consist of friends. Section 317 applies even to a sole director. Here the director has to observe s. 317 by holding a meeting on his own, make the declaration to himself (a silent 'declaration' will suffice), pause for thought about what has been declared, and then record the declaration in the minutes of the meeting (*Neptune (Vehicle Washing Equipment) Ltd v Fitzgerald* (1995)).

Power of the court to grant a director relief from liability

Section 727 offers relief to company officers and to the company auditor whether an officer or not.

The absolutist nature of fiduciary duties may lead to injustice. Therefore, there is a facility within the Companies Act for a director facing a breach of trust action (or one of negligence or other default) to seek the protection of the court. Relief can be granted if it appears to the court that liability exists or may exist but that the director had acted honestly and reasonably. Therefore, having regard to all the circumstances the court feels that it is fair that it may relieve him either wholly or partly from his liability on such terms as it thinks fit (s. 727):

Re Duomatic Ltd (1969)

While DL was in financial difficulties E, a director, paid £4,000 compensation for loss of office to get another director, who was frequently intoxicated, indiscreet with company secrets and had no tenure of office, to give up his directorship.

Held: E had not acted reasonably so s. 448 (now s. 727) was unavailable.

The offending director in *Re Duomatic Ltd* (1969) had, in the opinion of Buckley J acted unreasonably by adopting a go it alone policy when circumstances showed he ought to have obtained independent legal advice:

> ... In my judgement a director of a company dealing with a matter of this kind who does not seek any legal advice at all but elects to deal with the matters himself without a proper exploration of the considerations which contribute, or ought to contribute, to a decision as to what should be done on the company's behalf, cannot be said to act reasonably ... I do not think he was acting in the way in which a man of affairs dealing with his own affairs with reasonable care and circumspection could reasonably be expected to act in such a case, for I think that any such imaginary character would take pains to find out all the relevant circumstances, many of which in this case depend on some knowledge of the law and ought to have encouraged ... the assistance of a legal adviser.

A more recent case on s. 727 is:

Re D'Jan of London Ltd (1994)

D, a director of a property company, signed without reading it an insurance proposal form. The form had been filled in by D's broker. An answer given to one question stated that no director had been involved with an insolvent company. In fact D had previously been involved with three such companies and on making a claim, because of the false declaration, the insurer refused to pay. As a result the company became insolvent and the liquidator sued D for the loss suffered by the company (under the Insolvency Act 1986, s. 212).

Held: D's oversight was not grossly negligent in that it was the kind of thing that could happen to a busy man although this was not enough to completely excuse it. He would have to contribute £20,000 towards the losses suffered.

In *D'Jan*, Hoffman LJ found that D owned 99 per cent of the shares and when the form had been signed the company was solvent, so that the only persons whose interests had been put at risk by failing to read the form were D and his wife. The court was satisfied that D had acted honestly and reasonably (Hoffman LJ felt that it was unreasonable to expect a busy director to read everything presented to him for signature) so his liability had been limited. Judicial relief under s. 727 may be given in respect to any penalty imposed by the Companies Act and any civil action brought by the company against a director of theirs but it has no application in respect to a civil action brought by a third party, such as a shareholder of the company against a director:

Wide and general though the words in s. 727 are, read in their context they do not allow an officer or auditor to escape relief in 'any' legal proceedings which may be brought against him in his capacity as an officer or auditor of the company by the rest of the world. (Stephen LJ, *Commissioners of Customs and Excise Commissioners v Hendon Alpha Ltd* (1981))

The director's duty of care and skill

When directors first began to be appointed custodians of companies very few of them had any business related skills or experience and seldom gave their time exclusively to one company. It was the era of the gentleman director. The courts took the view that shareholders chose their own directors and that the court was not equipped to assess necessary director attributes. Indeed when pressed for judicial guidance on the standard of care a director owed his company the courts consistently pitched it relatively low anticipating that if it was set too high then not enough people of good character would put themselves forward to be directors.

This duty of care and skill is derived from common law negligence.

As examples, in the *Marquis of Bute's Case* (1892), the Marquis inherited from his father the position of President of the Cardiff Savings Bank. He was aged six and in a thirty-eight year period he attended only one board meeting. It was held that he could not be liable for the Bank's improper lending as he knew nothing, nor could he reasonably be expected to know, of what was going on. And in *Re Denham & Co. Ltd* (1883), the chairman and board of directors fixed the accounts to show a fictitious profit. A director was cleared of liability for not detecting this fraud as he was found to be a country gentleman and not a skilled accountant.

Despite its age the leading case on the duty of care and skill of a director remains *Re City Equitable Fire Insurance* (1925) where Romer J stated a subjective proposition:

... a director need not exhibit in the performance of his duties a greater degree of skill than may reasonably be expected from a person with his knowledge and experience.

Re City Equitable Fire Insurance Ltd (1925)

Directors delegated the complete responsibility of uninvested funds to B, the managing director, who was also senior partner in the firm of brokers the company used. Large sums were left with the brokers to invest and these sums were lost. The directors were themselves honest and had placed considerable confidence in B who at the time enjoyed a high reputation as a financier.

Held: The directors were liable in negligence. They had a duty of care to ascertain how the funds appearing in the balance sheet were actually invested.

While the directors were found to be in breach of their duty of care towards the company they were actually excused liability because a clause in the articles said that liability would only apply to directors in wilful default and their actions had not gone that far.

Therefore, when examining an alleged lack of care a court ought not to take as a comparator an over-careful, prudent director but should firstly locate the level of skill and experience held by the director in question and, secondly, then ask how a reasonable director with this same level of skill and experience would have acted. If this notional reasonable man would have acted in a similar way to the director in question then negligence is not found.

However, if the reasonable director would have acted in a more careful manner then the actual director thus far is negligent. Romer J's proposition is derived from an earlier judgement that he referred to:

> If directors act within their powers, if they act with such care as is reasonably to be expected from them, having regard to their knowledge and experience, and if they act honestly for the benefit of the company they represent, they discharge their equitable as well as their legal duty to the company. (Lindley MR, *Langunas Nitrate Co. v Langunas Syndicate* (1899))

No minimum standard of skill is therefore imposed and the less knowledge and experience a director has the less will be expected of him. It has led some directors, who were said to be allegedly negligent, to use what is cynically known as the *ignorance is bliss* defence:

Should someone wish to allege breach of duty then that person will have the burden of proof in establishing it (Re New Mashonaland Co. (1892)).

Re Brazilian Rubber Plantations & Estates (1911)

Four directors who knew absolutely nothing about rubber and another aged 75 and deaf were persuaded to be appointed to the board of a rubber company. They had been told that it would give them a little pleasant employment without their incurring any liability.

Held: The directors had not breached their duty of care. Neville J said:

... a director is not bound to bring any special qualities to his office. He may undertake the management of a rubber plantation in complete ignorance of everything connected with rubber without incurring liabilities for his mistakes.

While the proposition given by Romer J in *Re City Equitable Fire Insurance* (1925) remains valid the courts may be slowly introducing public policy considerations, such as that directors ought to be 'encouraged' to be more professional, through the courts becoming more critical of their failings. In *Re D'Jan of London Ltd* (1993), Hoffman LJ said that it was unrealistic to expect a busy director to read everything presented to him for signature but he had to *exercise some judgement where the unread document consisted only of a few sentences*. Perhaps what is emerging is a minimum standard of care.

While Romer's proposition remains at common law correct the modern standard of care is now felt to be found in the test used for establishing wrongful trading under s. 214(4) Insolvency Act 1986.

Also it must be appreciated that while the test of the duty of care is the same for executive and non-executive directors (*Dorchester Finance Co. Ltd v Stebbing* (1989)) there is a higher expectation for an executive director employed under a service contract. In the absence of an express term, an implied term will be read into his contract requiring him to exercise reasonable skill in the performance of his duties. As a senior executive he will have specific knowledge of fairly large parts of the business, if not its whole, as well as having access to the company secretary and the auditor. Hence the *ignorance is bliss* defence is really a non-starter.

Delegation

Table A, article
72 allows
directors to
delegate to a
committee
consisting of
one or more of
the directors; or
delegate to a
managing
director.

Generally it is permitted for a director to delegate some or all of his duties to others provided that they do not delegate their discretion, i.e. their freedom of action:

> In the absence of grounds of suspicion then subject to the articles and normal business practice a director may leave his duties to some other official and trust that official to perform such duties honestly. (Romer J, *Re City Equitable Fire Insurance Co. Ltd* (1925))

The willingness of the court to recognize delegation as being a valid business practice – indeed it is the only way that business can function efficiently and effectively – caused Romer J in his judgement in *Re City Equitable Fire Insurance Co. Ltd* (1925) to invoke a previous authority:

> Business cannot be carried out upon principles of distrust. Men in responsible positions must be trusted by those above them, as well as by those below them, until there is reason to distrust them. We agree that care and prudence do not involve distrust; but for a director acting honestly himself to be held legally liable for negligence, in trusting the officers under him not to conceal from him what they ought to report to him, appears to us to be laying too heavily a burden on honest business men. (Lindley MR, *Re National Bank of Wales Ltd* (1899))

The *Re National Bank of Wales* (1899) was a Court Appeal case. On appeal to the House of Lords, under the name of *Dovey v Cory* (1901) it was dealt with thus:

Dovey v Cory (1901)

A director was found not liable for relying on assertions received from the company chairman and a general manager in respect to dividends and capital advances improperly made. The Earl of Halsbury said:

... I cannot think that it can be expected of a director that he should be watching either the inferior officers of the company or verifying the calculations of the auditors himself. The business of life could not go on if people could not trust those who are put into a position of trust for the express purpose of attending to details of management.

However, it has to be stressed that much depends on the context and circumstances of delegation. A director, for example, cannot blindly accept as correct all documents placed before him that have been prepared by another (see *Re D'Jan of London Ltd* (1994) discussed earlier).

Diligence

Diligence relates to the degree of attention that a director is expected to devote to the business. Early case law indicates that not too much was expected: a director is not bound to attend all board meetings (*Marquis of Bute* (1892)); a director is not obliged to take an active part in the conduct of the company (*Re Brazilian Rubber Plantations & Estates* (1911)); a director is not bound to give his continuous attention to the affairs of the company (*Re City Equitable Fire Insurance* (1925)). From these and similar judgements it may be said that it was formerly in a director's interest not to attend board meetings for then he would be able to avoid liability for poor decisions taken at those meetings:

Re Denham & Co. (1883)

All powers of management were placed in D. C, one of the directors, as a rule did not attend board meetings. Dividends were paid for four years out of capital. On one occasion C himself moved a resolution for a dividend but he had no reason to suspect any misconduct.

Held: C was not liable for any breach of duty.

In more recent years the judiciary has taken a different view: it is unreasonable for a director not to attend board meetings or take an active part in the company's affairs, and those who do not do so may be liable in negligence (*Dorcester Finance v Stebbing Ltd* (1989)); the House of Lords had little sympathy for directors who plead ignorance of their duties and fail to discover or exercise their powers (*Winkworth v Edward Baron Development Co. Ltd* (1986). Therefore, a director should now attend sufficient meetings to know what is going on. Once again executive directors working under a service contract will have contractual terms which will require them to attend a stipulated number of board meetings. In addition public limited companies now require even non-executive directors to attend most board meetings.

Under statute s. 214, Insolvency Act 1986, a director, or former director, may be liable for wrongful trading. A defence is available where the director took every step to minimize the potential loss to company creditors that he ought to have taken in the circumstances. The reference to 'every step' is imprecise but it is difficult to see how a director who has not been diligent can claim to have taken 'every step' and without benefit of the defence the director will be required to contribute to company assets in order to fully satisfy creditors. Where a contribution is made then that person may be disqualified from holding a directorship (CDDA 1986, s. 10).

A report of a study carried out by Warwick University Business School stated that many directors of leading British companies undergo little or no suitable training and are ill-equipped to carry out their full range of corporate responsibilities (Report published November 1996).

Should the standard of care of directors be raised?

It has been argued that directors ought to be placed on a par with other professionals and that by applying an objective standard to their conduct it is hoped to make them more liable. In consequence, the argument continues, it will provide an incentive for them to be more careful, skilful and diligent. The problem is that there is no distinct profession of being a director. Indeed the term is a portmanteau one in that it covers a considerable range of varying experience spread over small, medium and large companies which may be private or public.

Institute of Directors – chartered directors' code

The Institute of Directors (IoD) announced in October 1997 that in order to establish a professional standard for United Kingdom directors they intended to create a new class of *chartered directors*. All directors, whether of small, medium or large companies, will be eligible to gain the award provided that they:

- are proposed by a fellow of the IoD;
- have sufficient experience;
- pass a three-hour examination (this will be set on finance, strategic business directions, marketing and employee issues);
- pass an interview conducted by a panel of senior directors.

The motivating factors for the introduction of the charter are to reduce the number of corporate failures and improve the reputation of company directors.

The long-term intention of the IoD is that eventually companies will be reluctant to appoint directors to senior positions unless they are chartered and this status would be forfeited on a director breaching the code. No date has been set for the start of the charter programme but it is hoped that it will be introduced sometime in 1999.

Chapter summary

- Companies are owned by shareholders but management is delegated under the articles to directors who have full control over day-to-day matters. If shareholders are displeased with the directors' stewardship then the articles, through a special resolution, may be amended or the directors by means of an ordinary resolution may be dismissed.
- Directors come in different types: *executive* are full-time professional managers usually responsible for a specific operational area; *non-executive* are part-time managers taking a long-term consultative role; a *shadow* is someone who controls a board of directors without himself sitting on it; a *nominee* is someone who is appointed or nominated by a major shareholder(s) but once in office they owe duties not to their patron but to the company; *alternative* refers to a shared directorship; a *managing* director is a company's chief executive officer responsible for implementing board decisions. And *connected persons* are those close to a director by family tie or association, so that duties and obligations to which a director is subject will spill over and include them as well.
- There must be at least two directors for a public company but there need only be one for a private company. No one aged 70 years or over can be appointed, or re-

elected, to a public company directorship unless the articles allow it or unless approval was given by a special resolution of a general meeting. Qualification shares, if required, must be obtained within two months of the appointment.

- A statement of prospective directors is sent with the registration application and those listed will become the first directors. Subsequent directors are then appointed in accordance with the articles or by general meetings. However, the articles normally allow directors to fill casual vacancies who will hold office to the next AGM. A register of directors must be kept, with certain information given, and be available for public inspection.

- A technical defect in a director's appointment will not invalidate his acts (s. 285; *British Asbestos Co. v Boyd* (1903)), but if the defect is substantial then it will (*Morris v Kanssen* (1946)).

- A director, as an agent, can bind the company either through actual express authority of the board or through the operation of ostensible authority (*Freeman Lockyer v Buckhurst Properties (Mangol) Ltd* (1964)). The rule in Turquand's case (the indoor management rule) states that outsiders, in dealing with the company in a transaction that is not ultra vires, may reasonably assume that all internal procedures have been satisfied and so they need not themselves make enquiries to ascertain that all is in order.

- Long employment contracts for directors are discouraged: by the Cadbury Code (not to exceed three years unless the shareholders agree; nor an unbreakable contract exceeding five years, again unless the shareholders agree) (s. 319).

- Shareholders set the directors' remuneration, not the directors themselves. The Greenbury Code recommended the use of remuneration committees, made up of non-executive directors, to advise shareholders what executive directors should receive but the code said that the remuneration ought not to be 'excessive'.

- The CDDA 1986 prohibits certain categories of persons from being directors: undischarged bankrupts – unless the court agrees; those convicted of an indictable offence – commonly this will relate to fraud; those persistently failing to file returns; those involved in fraud discovered during winding-up proceedings; those in breach of duty towards the company; those felt to be unfit – this is the commonest ground and relates to general company management (*Re Continental Assurance Co. of London plc* (1997)), with despite some dicta to the contrary, the future protection of the public being an important consideration; and disqualification after an investigation.

- A director's appointment can be terminated by: death, resignation, retirement, dissolution of the company, dismissal (but if wrongful then damages may be sought), or loss of a share qualification.

- A director involved with a substantial property transaction (s. 320), or a loan etc. (s. 330) must have it approved by shareholders, who have full details, in a general meeting.

- A director's fiduciary duties are owed to the company only exceptionally to shareholders. These duties may be broken down into:
  i) to act in good faith for the benefit of the company as a whole;

ii) to use their powers for the purpose for which they were conferred – here motive of action is important; and

iii) to avoid a conflict of duty between the company's interest and the director's self-interest. A conflict of interest occurs when a director: makes a contract with the company; makes use of corporate information or opportunity; or if he competes against his company. A director has a duty to disclose to the company any personal interest (s. 317).

- A company may ratify a director's unauthorized acts but not illegal ones. A court can also relieve a director from liability if he has been found to have acted honestly and reasonably (s. 727).

- A director owes duty of care and skill to the company based upon a comparison between the level of skill and experience held by the director in question and a reasonable director having the same level of skill and experience. One standard is applied to all directors.

- A director at common law is permitted to delegate duties to appropriate others but he can never delegate his discretion. Delegation is also allowed under Table A, article 72.

- Formerly a director could be lax in the attention he gave to his company. Now a higher degree of diligence is expected both by the courts and companies. Arguments have been put forward that a director's professional performance ought to be increased (e.g. the Institute of Directors Chartered Directors' Code).

Discussion questions

1 What powers are usually given to the directors?
2 Is a company legally bound by the actions of its directors, if the directors exceed the authority given to them?
3 a) Are directors liable for:
    i) acts of negligence; and
    ii) acts of misjudgement?
  b) What relief may be available to directors found liable in (a) above?

Case study exercise

Hallamfield Football Club Limited (HFCL) is the controlling company of Hallamfield Football Club which plays in the Football League Division Two. HFCL has four shareholder-directors: East, West, North and South. The company do not own the club ground (Endcliffe Park) but lease it from the local authority. North and South are both busy business people who are often abroad for 2–3 months at a time. Therefore, East and West have to do more than their share to keep things running. East, a local funeral director, often finds this a problem but occasionally the team manager, Sidney Parrot, helps out. Indeed the board is apt to listen to and act on what Parrot says as they all respect his 30 years' experience of professional football.

Over the last year the following occurred:

a) The local authority (Hallamfield City Council), anxious to cover a cash short-fall, offer HFCL the freehold of Endcliffe Park at a discounted price. North is away yet again on private business but the remaining three directors agree, in the club members' lounge, that they themselves will acquire the freehold and then lease the ground to HFCL on similar terms to those currently in force with Hallamfield City Council.

b) All clubs in Division Two are invited by Digital Television Limited (DTL), a division of Global Communications plc, to become founder members of their digital television subscription service. Founder members will be able to acquire 10,000 ordinary shares in DTL at the price of £1 per share fully paid. East agrees to investigate whether HFCL ought to get involved in this development. He later persuades the board that DTL are 'time wasters' and 'a subscription channel for Division Two is a non-runner'. HFCL do not take up the DTL offer. However, within a year DTL's subscription channel proves to be a huge financial success – so much so that Global Communications plc sells it to Burdock plc for £50 per share.

c) At a properly constituted board meeting it is agreed to pay East and West a £7,000 supplement to their normal directors' fees in recognition of their additional efforts.

d) Sidney Parrot entered into a contract with UpperCrust, a catering company that HFCL occasionally use, for the supply of food and drink to the executive box holders for the England Under-21 fixture with Mongolia. Unfortunately, at short notice the Football Association switched the venue from Endcliffe Park to Hillsborough, Sheffield. UpperCrust refuse to accept the cancellation that HFCL try to make.

e) North makes a seven-month visit to the United States. This absence is not sanctioned by HFCL who are also put out when he refuses to allow HFCL to recover his company car saying that his girl friend has 'gotten used to the Mercedes'. This last remark is particularly hurtful to South for North's 'girl friend' was formerly Mrs South. Also HFCL receive an anonymous tip-off that North has a small financial interest in Kingsley Football Club Limited, a Football League Division One football club.

f) Sidney Parrot has bought and sold a number of players. The result of this transfer activity is that HFCL are currently in debt. This position is expected to worsen in that contractual bonuses will soon become payable to most players. However, East, West and South are positive about the future and take no immediate action. Subsequently, creditors press for repayment of debts and HFCL is then discovered to be insolvent.

Comment on the legal position of the above.

Further reading

Personal Liability and Disqualification of Company Directors, S. Griffin (1998), Wiley.
Corporate Governance and Corporate Opportunities, G.M.D. Bean (1994), Co. Law, 266.
The Director's Fiduciary Duty Not To Compete, M. Christie (1992), MLR, 506.

Nominee Directors: The Law and Commercial Reality, P. Crutchfield (1991), Co. Law, 136.
Disqualification of Directors, J. Dine (1991), Co. Law, 6.
Directors' Authority: The Companies Act 1989, S. Griffin (1991), Co. Law, 98.
Personal Liability and Disqualification of Company Directors: Something Old, Something New, D. Millman (1992), NILQ, 1.

12 Company secretary

Introduction

Every company must have a secretary, but a sole director is unable to also be the secretary (s. 283). Normally the appointment of a secretary is left to the directors who will decide on the length, payment and other terms of the appointment as well as having the power of dismissal (Table A, article 99). Except for single-director companies a board may delegate to a director tasks which would normally be performed by the secretary but clearly tasks that specifically require the presence of both secretary and director would be impossible (s. 284).

Objectives

The purpose of this chapter is to draw attention to the role of the company secretary. It is often overlooked that he is a company officer and as such may legally bind the company by his actions.

Key concepts

- Qualification requirements (only for a public company)
- Agency principles
- Duties to be performed.

Qualifications of a secretary of a public company

While private companies may appoint whoever they choose, the directors of a public company when deciding on an appointee must, firstly, take all reasonable care to ensure that the appointee is a person who appears to them to have the requisite knowledge and experience in order to discharge the functions of secretary (s. 286 (1)). Secondly, more specifically, the appointee must satisfy one of the following (s. 286 (1)):

a) already holds the office of secretary, assistant or deputy secretary of the company; or
b) for at least 3 of the 5 years immediately proceeding his appointment as secretary, held the office of secretary of a public company; or

Table A, article 99 states that the secretary may be appointed by the directors for such term, remuneration and conditions as they may think fit; and any secretary so appointed may be removed by them.

c) is a member of one of these professional bodies:
   i)   the Institute of Chartered Accountants;
   ii)   the Chartered Association of Certified Accounts;
   iii) the Institute of Chartered Secretaries and Administrators;
   iv)   the Institute of Cost and Management Accounts;
   v)   the Chartered Institute of Public Finance and Accountants;
d) is a lawyer qualified in the United Kingdom; or finally,
e) is a member who, by holding or having previously held any other position, or by being a member of any other body, appears to the directors to be capable of discharging the functions required.

Notification of appointment to the Registrar

If the company is newly formed then the appointment has to be notified to the Registrar (s. 10 (2)) with any subsequent change being notified to the Registrar within 14 days of it being made (s. 288 (2)).

The company secretary as an agent of the company

Under agency principles a company secretary will be able to legally bind his company (the principal) in respect to acts that he carried out or, on occasions, the company will be responsible when the company secretary failed to act. Liability may attach to the company in two ways. The first one of these (both are dealt with below) needs particular attention for as no direct authorization from the company is required the company will not know until much later that it has legally been bound to a third party possibly for quite some time.

Ostensible authority of the company secretary

This method of creating agency is based upon the impression given to the third party when he was negotiating with the company secretary and subsequently contracting through him with the company. Therefore, should the company attempt to avoid a contract entered into by the company secretary through alleging that the company secretary was not authorized to transact on its behalf, then agency by ostensible authority may come into force. This is where the third part, who acted in good faith, will argue that he was induced to enter into the contract by the company secretary being held out by the company as having the usual authority to enter into that particular transaction, i.e. the authority bestowed on the company secretary is based on the status or professional position that he occupies. Therefore, ostensible authority (also known as apparent authority or agency by estoppel) arises where a principal, such as a company, holds out to an innocent third party that a person, in this context their company secretary, has, through the position he occupies in the company, the necessary authority to act for them. As a consequence of this 'holding out' it appeared to the third party that the agent (company secretary) held the necessary authority and this representation was relied upon – the evidence for this being the contract entered into.

Ostensible authority must relate to transactions of an administrative nature in that one can objectively expect a company secretary to be involved in them. Examples include: hiring and

For a fuller explanation of ostensible authority see the section on directors and agency principles in Chapter 11, Directors.

dismissing office staff; contracts for the purchase of office equipment, stationery and computer software; and, it seems, hiring limousines:

Panorama Developments (Guildford) Ltd v Fidelis Furnishing Fabrics Ltd (1971)

The company secretary of FFF hired from PD Rolls-Royce and Jaguar cars saying that they were required for meeting important customers at airports etc. On each occasion the secretary always signed the hire forms as 'company secretary' and told PD that they should send their account to FFF. The cars were in fact used by the secretary for his own purpose – what he told PD being all lies. On discovering the fraud PD sued FFF for the unpaid hire amounts. FFF defence was that their secretary had no authority to hire such cars and so no liability could attach to the company.

Held (Court of Appeal): It was within the ostensible and usual scope of the company secretary's authority to hire cars. FFF were therefore liable.

In *Panorama Developments* reference was made to an earlier authority, *Barnett, Hoares & Co. v South London Tramways Co.* (1887), where Lord Esher had said:

A secretary is a mere servant; his position is that he is to do what he is told, and no person can assume that he has any authority to represent anything at all ...

But in the later case Lord Denning went on to explain:

But times have changed. A company secretary is a much more important person nowadays than he was in 1887. Here is an officer of the company with extensive duties and responsibilities ... He is no longer a mere clerk. He regularly makes representations on behalf of the company and enters into contracts on its behalf which come within the day-to-day running of the company's business. He is clearly entitled to sign contracts connected with the administrative side of a company's affairs, such as employing staff, ordering cars, and so forth. All such matters now come within the ostensible authority of a company secretary.

However, case law has established that ostensible authority will not extend to: borrowing money for the company (*Re Cleadon Trust Ltd* (1939); commencing litigation on the company's behalf (*Daimler Co. Ltd v Continental Tyre and Rubber Co. Ltd* (1916); or personally calling a general meeting of the company (*Re Haycroft Gold Reduction and Mining Co.* (1900)). For such acts to be valid actual authority needs to have been expressly delegated to the company secretary.

In agency law, where an agent acts outside his appointment then the principal may, provided the usual rules of ratification are satisfied, ratify the agent's unauthorized act. For example in *Alexander Ward & Co. Ltd v Samyang Navigation Co. Ltd* (1975) all the directors had resigned office but in order to keep the company functioning two individuals, without direct authority, acted on its behalf. Later when the company was in liquidation the House of Lords held that the company could, through the liquidator, ratify the actions taken

At common law an illegal or unlawful act cannot be ratified. However, a company may now ratify an ultra vires act by means of passing a special resolution (s. 35 (3)).

earlier by the two individuals. By analogy, therefore, a company may ratify the unauthorized acts of their company secretary.

Actual authority of a company secretary

As an alternative to implied ostensible authority a company secretary may have an actual express authority. Indeed with the increased importance of a company secretary their having a wider role in company business is now becoming more common. In public companies, to meet the qualification requirement, it is routine to have a lawyer or accountant or a member of the Institute of Chartered Secretaries and Administrators as the company secretary and such professionalization is often now found in private companies as well. Therefore, a company may be more willing to directly authorize their company secretary to carry out responsibilities which would formerly be considered outside the traditionally narrow functional role outlined in the Companies Act 1985.

Duties of a company secretary

These may be divided into three broad areas. They are:

i) *Compliance*

   The company secretary must ensure that their company complies with an ever-growing range of legislation and regulatory control, for example: returns and notification to the Registrar; the maintenance of company registers; giving due notice to shareholders (and possibly creditors) of resolutions and meetings; certifying the validity of meetings; and verifying the genuineness of directors' signatures.

ii) *Assisting the board*

   The secretary must help the board of directors to operate effectively and efficiently, for example: being responsible for full and accurate minutes of meetings; drawing the board's attention to appropriate matters of administrative concern etc.

iii) *Taking responsibility for certain security matters*

   The secretary, as senior administrative officer, tends in many organizations to take responsibility for certain security matters, e.g. drafting codes of conduct that the directors may wish to adopt, maintaining the security of the company's computerized records (and seeing that the obligations of the Data Protection Act 1998 and the Computer Misuse Act 1990 are met), and ensuring that confidentiality undertakings are signed by appropriate employees.

Under s. 450 there is a general requirement to retain documents affecting or relating to a company's property or affairs. This will include all of the various books, registers and records of the company, especially those that have to be made available for inspection by members or creditors (or, exceptionally, by others).

Chapter summary

- While private companies may appoint whoever they choose, directors of public companies must only appoint a person they believe possesses the necessary knowledge and experience. To support the directors' judgement an appointee needs to satisfy one of several conditions. All appointments and changes must be notified to the Registrar.
- A company secretary may become an agent of his company through either operation of ostensible (implied) authority based upon the company holding the secretary out as having authority (*Panorama Developments Ltd v Fidelis Furnishing Fabrics*); or, alternatively, actual express authority where the secretary is appointed to carry out specified tasks.
- A company secretary's duties are to ensure: that all the legal administrative requirements are *complied* with; that full *assistance* is given to the board of directors; and that *responsibility* is taken for certain security matters.

Discussion questions

1 The company secretary of Umbrellas Unlimited Limited will shortly retire. The company chairman has let it be known that he wishes to appoint his nephew as the new company secretary on the grounds that 'Simon Simple is a splendid lad who has just got a degree in Anglo-Saxon studies and will be a big asset next year when we become a public company.'
Discuss
2 A company secretary is little more than a glorified office worker.
Discuss.

Case study exercise

Oscar Bronte is the company secretary of Kiddy Write Limited (KWL), a publishing company specializing in children's books. Over the past several years KWL has enjoyed considerable financial success due to the huge sales of its most coveted author Dudley Cuddles.

Oscar has learnt that the four directors of KWL have been informally discussing amongst themselves the terms of a new five-book deal that needs to be offered pretty quickly to Cuddles or else another publisher may step in and sign him up. However, before the directors formally act events take over in that the four directors go on a management team-building weekend to the Scottish Highlands where unexpected appallingly bad weather maroons them for what is likely to be at least a week (no communications are working, including mobile phones).

In their absence Oscar learns through the 'grapevine' that Cuddles is about to be poached by Mega Publishing plc so on his own initiative he sends out a standard extension of contract for Cuddles to sign in respect to a three-book deal at £100,000 per book. On receipt

Cuddles signs and immediately returns this contract, with Oscar in turn writing back to thank Cuddles for staying loyal to KWL.

The storms in Scotland are now over and the directors have returned to KWL where they are found pondering the day's leading news item – Official: Dudley Cuddles, the famous children's author, is a child molester.

Advise Kiddy Write Limited whether they are legally bound by the actions of Oscar Bronte.

13 Company meetings

Introduction

In response to the question *who controls a company's affairs* the answer is largely determined by the business laid before and carried out at the respective company meetings. *General meetings* of shareholders provide an opportunity for members collectively to approve or reject matters placed before them so that they may ultimately control the direction the company is to take. Unfortunately, the tendency is for shareholders to adopt a fairly passive role in the control of companies. Only, it seems, in exceptional circumstances, when their investment is threatened, will shareholder action groups emerge to take a positive role in steering an ailing company in a certain direction.

Board meetings may be said to be much more helpful in identifying those who in practice control a company in that virtually all important commercial and financial policy matters are formulated and adopted by the full board or a committee of it. Policy is then promoted and implemented by the managing director (or chief executive officer) who acts under authority delegated by the board.

To the extent that a **company meeting** may supervise, check, regulate and restrain the **board**, shareholders may be said to be the controllers of a company. However, when examining what actually happens a **board**, as a proactive decision making body, de facto controls the company especially where the board is headed by a forceful chairman or where there is an entrenched managing director or chief executive officer.

Objectives

The purpose of this chapter is to enable students to understand the relationship between the board of directors and shareholders. Also full awareness is expected that for a company meeting to function legally and efficiently several important technicalities need to be satisfied, e.g. there must be a quorum, the chairman's conduct has to be exemplary and voting rights must be adhered to. Finally, students have to be aware that business put before a general meeting will be in the form of resolutions of which there are several types.

Key concepts

- The division of power within a company
- The Annual General Meeting
- The Extraordinary General Meeting
- Provision of notice for meetings
- Conducting the meeting – essential requirements
- Resolutions.

The division of power: board of directors and general meetings

For many years the board of directors were subservient to a general meeting. Should a board embark on a course of action disliked by shareholders then they were able to call a company meeting and if the protest was sufficiently strong pass a resolution that would instruct the directors to change their direction:

> ... if you want to alter the management of the affairs of the company go to a general meeting, and if they agree with you they will pass a resolution obliging the directors to alter their course of proceedings. (Cotton LJ, *Isle of Wight Railway Co. v Tahourdin* (1883))

This ability of a general meeting to override the decision of the directors was derived from the view that directors were merely agents of the company and as such could be subjected to whatever degree of control that shareholders as a body decided to exert. However, this model, while relevant to the nineteenth century, increasingly became redundant in respect to the evolution of the large-scale modern company. This recognition was exemplified, a generation after Cotton LJ's judgement (given above), by Buckley LJ:

> ... even a resolution of a numerical majority at a general meeting of the company cannot impose its will upon the directors when the articles have confided to them control of the company's affairs.

And more pertinently:

> The directors are not servants to obey directions given by the shareholders as individuals; they are not agents appointed by and bound to serve the shareholders as their principals, they are persons who may by the regulations be entrusted with the control of the business, and if so entrusted they can be dispossessed from the control only by the statutory majority which can alter the articles. (*Gramophone and Typewriter Ltd v Stanley* (1908))

Such expression records the movement from shareholders commonly wanting to be closely involved in monitoring and controlling the board to passive shareholder-investors exemplified by institutional investors. If the board takes a direction you disapprove of then switch your investment to another company. This reorientation can be traced to *Automatic Self-Cleansing Filter Syndicate Ltd v Cunninghame* (1906), in which the Court of Appeal was invited to support the established position that shareholders in a general meeting can interfere in the day-to-day management of the company as carried out by the directors even though they may be acting within their authority. This invitation was declined in that the Court of Appeal held that a shareholder majority could not block the directors in their lawful exercise of their powers. For the company in a meeting to interfere with the directors' decision then a majority will have to pass an extraordinary resolution to alter the articles and by so doing to limit the directors' authority:

> ... the directors have absolute power to do all things other than those that are expressly

required to be done by the company; and then comes the limitation of their general authority; 'subject to such regulations as may from time to time be made by extraordinary resolution'. Therefore, if it is desired to alter the powers of the directors that must be done, not by a resolution carried by a majority at an ordinary meeting of the company, but by an extraordinary resolution. In these circumstances it seems to me that it is not competent for the majority of the shareholders at an ordinary meeting to affect or alter the mandate originally given to the directors, by the articles of association. (Collins, MR)

There has been a line of judicial decisions that support *Automatic Self-Cleaning Filter Syndicate Ltd v Cunninghame* (1906), the latest being *Breckland Group Holdings Ltd v London & Suffolk Properties Ltd* (1989). The earlier decision in *Marshall's Valve Gear Co. Ltd v Manning Wardle & Co. Ltd* (1909), that held that under the then Companies Act 1862 specimen articles (which remained substantially unchanged through a number of subsequent company acts) that an ordinary resolution, carried by a majority of shareholders, could override the board is now accepted as being a decision out on a limb.

It is now firmly established, as outlined above, that a general meeting had no right to interfere with the managerial function delegated to the directors and exercised by them through properly constituted board meetings. Should the company, in a general meeting, wish to have more control of the board then it may do so through alteration of the articles. Until alteration of the articles takes place directors retain their managerial discretion. However, there are a limited number of circumstances where a general meeting of shareholders can take over powers that are normally only the prerogative of directors or, alternatively, where they have retained powers exclusively to themselves. These are:

1 *Where the board fails to act*
   An obvious example will be a deadlock in management between two directors who jointly form the board (*Alexander Ward & Co. Ltd v Samyang Navigation Co. Ltd* (1975)).
2 *Where statute law demands that only a meeting may act*
   Examples where the Companies Act 1985 will only permit certain matters to be dealt with by a general meeting are: alteration to the company's constitution through a special resolution – memorandum (s. 4) and articles (s. 9); alteration to its capital clause (if allowed to do so by the articles) through an ordinary resolution (s. 12); removal of a director from office through an ordinary resolution (s. 303) etc.
3 *Ratification by a meeting of a director's irregular acts*
   Irregular acts are those where a director breaches his duty or exceeds his authority. If the company in a general meeting so wishes it may, by means of an ordinary resolution, ratify a director's act in excess of the powers delegated (*Bamford v Bamford* (1970)), or resolve not to sue a director who has breached a duty owed to the company (*Pavlides v Jensen* (1956)). Where a director has usurped a power that only the company in a general meeting can exercise then a company meeting may agree to validate this irregularity. However, where a director's act not only exceeded his own authority but also exceeded the company's capacity then ratification will have to be by means of a special resolution.
   A potential problem with ratification, more likely to occur in a private company, is that the voting majority in a general meeting to ratify a director's irregular act may be

The resolution remains an ordinary one even where the power usurped by a director would have required a special resolution (Grant v United Kingdom Switchback Railway Co. (1888)). But if an ordinary resolution to ratify an irregular act would result in a breach of the articles then that resolution will be void (Boschoek Proprietary Co. Ltd Fuke (1906)).

made up of shareholder-directors who will control the meeting. In this situation what has to be avoided is the majority using their voting strength to prejudice the position of minority shareholders to such an extent that a claim of fraud on the minority can be substantiated. Also if creditors would be harmed then a resolution to ratify passed by a general meeting may, on a creditor's application, be set aside on grounds that the meeting acted inequitably (*Re Horsley Weight Ltd* (1982)).

For more detail on minority protection see Chapter 14.

Types of meeting

Annual General Meeting (AGM)

Breach of s. 366 may lead to the company and officers being fined.

Every company must hold an AGM every calendar year (s. 366 (1)), with not more than 15 months between them (s. 366 (3)). With newly created companies the first AGM may be held within the opening 18 months and it need not, therefore, hold it in the year of incorporation or in the following year (s. 366 (2)). If a company fails to hold an AGM then a member can complain to the Secretary of State who may order that one be held as well as, if need requires, fixing the quorum of members who must be present (s. 367 (1)).

Election by a private company to dispense with AGMs

A private company may elect to dispense with the holding of AGMs (s. 366A (1)). If an election is made then it has effect for the year in which it was made and subsequent years (s. 366A (2)), but any shareholder may give notice to the company, not later than three months before the end of the year in which an AGM was due to take place, requiring the holding of an AGM in that year (s. 366A (3)).

Business to be transacted

Under Table A, article 38 the notice of the meeting will also indicate the general nature of the business to be transacted.

While s. 366 demands that an AGM be held the Act does not say what business has to be conducted. In practice AGMs are used to satisfy s. 241 which requires directors to lay before a general meeting copies of the company's annual accounts, together with the director's and auditor's reports on these accounts. For convenience the AGM is also used for the appointment or re-appointment of directors and auditors (including their remuneration) although these matters are now increasingly being dealt with separately.

Extraordinary General Meeting (EGM)

Table A provisions

Automatically any company meeting which is not an AGM is an EGM (Table A, article 36). The directors may call an EGM (Table A, article 37) and must do so to consider the position when the company's net assets have fallen to 50 per cent or less of its called up capital (s. 142 (1)). However, directors are under a fiduciary duty only to call an EGM when they believe it is in the best interests of the company to do so. They must not call one for an ulterior motive (*Pergamon Press Ltd v Maxwell* (1970)).

On a member's requisition

Shareholders holding 10 per cent or more of the paid up capital that carries the right to vote may demand that the directors call an EGM (s. 368 (2)). When making this demand the requisitionists must say what the objectives of the meeting are and sign the written demand for the meeting, leaving it at the company's registered office (s. 368 (3)). The articles can never take away this shareholder right to demand an EGM. However, where the articles allow for shareholders holding less than 10 per cent of the paid-up voting capital to have the right to demand an EGM, then it is expected that a court will ignore s. 368 and enforce whatever percentage the articles provide. On receipt of a shareholder demand for an EGM the directors have 21 days to convene it giving all shareholders notice that it is to take place (*Re Windward Islands (Enterprises) Ltd* (1983)). If the directors call, without good cause, a meeting more than 28 days after notice was sent out then they will be in breach of s. 368 (8) and their tardiness may amount to conduct unfairly prejudicial so that a court will order an earlier date (*McGuiness v Bremner plc* (1988)).

If the directors refuse to acquiesce to a shareholder demand for a meeting then the requisitionists, or any of them representing more than 50 per cent of the total voting right of all of them, may call the meeting themselves. If so called it must be held within three months (s. 368 (4)), with the company reimbursing the requisitionists for all reasonable expenses that they incurred (s. 368 (6)).

In addition to the right of shareholders to demand that directors call an EGM or, on their refusal to do so, call one themselves, there is another provision for shareholders to obtain an EGM. This is where two or more shareholders, holding not less than 10 per cent of the issued share capital (or if there is no share capital, then 5 per cent in number of members) may call an EGM (s. 370 (3)). However, it must be noted that section 370 only operates where the articles do not make any provision for shareholders to request an EGM.

If the directors are of the opinion that a meeting they have been requested to convene is for a purpose that cannot lawfully be achieved then they are justified in refusing to call it (*Isle of Wight Railway Co. v Tahourdin* (1883)). However, if the suspected illegality relates to only some of the purposes for the meeting then these can be omitted.

Class meetings

Meetings of a class of shareholder are normally called to consider variations in class rights. Holders of other classes of shares have no right to attend (*Carruth v ICI* (1937)). The articles should contain terms governing the calling of class meetings and in general they have to be conducted in the same manner as general company meetings (s. 125 (6)). Usually the quorum will be two class shareholders holding, or representing by proxy, at least $33\frac{1}{3}$ per cent in nominal value of the issued share capital of the class concerned (s. 125 (6)).

A final point on convening company meetings. Once they have been duly called they can only be postponed or cancelled if the articles permit (*Smith v Paringa Mines Ltd* (1906)).

Notice of meetings

Length of notice

Minimum notice periods are required in order to prevent abuses occurring, e.g. a meeting being called deliberately with very little notice knowing that most shareholders would be unable to attend.

The minimum periods for a limited company are:

For unlimited companies the notice period is 7 days for both AGM and EGM (s. 369).

AGM
- 21 days written notice; however, a shorter period is possible if all shareholders entitled to attend and vote agree (s. 369 and Table A, article 38);

EGM

> These are the statutory minimum notice periods. The articles may require longer ones.

- 14 days written notice unless a special resolution is to be tabled when 21 days notice is required. Again a shorter period is allowed if agreed by a simple majority in number of shareholders holding at least 95 per cent in nominal value of shares that carry the right to attend and vote (s. 369 and Table A, article 38). A private company can decide by elective resolution to reduce the 95 per cent requirement for a shorter notice period but it cannot be reduced below 90 per cent (ss. 369, 379A). Also the interpretation of days is clear days in that the day the notice was given on and the day of the meeting itself are both ignored.

Those entitled to notice

On the convening of a general meeting, unless the articles say otherwise, all shareholders must be given notice (s. 370 and Table A, article 38). The company auditor must also be notified of all general meetings and be given the right to attend (s. 387 (1)).

To avoid the consequences of the common law, where failure to give notice to one shareholder would invalidate the business transacted at the meeting (*Musselwhite v C.H. Musselwhite & Sons Ltd* (1962)), companies virtually always incorporate into their articles Table A, article 39. This says that the accidental failure to give notice of a meeting to, or the non-receipt by, any person entitled to receive notice shall not invalidate the proceedings at that meeting. However, if it is found that a shareholder was *deliberately* denied notice of a meeting then this would invalidate that meeting (*Royal Mutual Benefit Building Society v Sharman* (1963)).

> Where a person does not receive proper notice they may waive their right to have received it and still attend the meeting (Re Oxted Motors Co. Ltd (1921)).

Contents of the notice

As expected the date, place and time of the start of the meeting must be specified. The notice must also point out that the recipient is entitled to attend and vote or is allowed to appoint a proxy to attend and vote for them. Ordinary business that is to be transacted need not be given but any other business must be mentioned. However, notice may be interpreted fairly robustly. In *Betts & Co. Ltd v Macnaughton* (1910) a notice that a certain resolution would be passed 'with such amendments as shall be determined on at the meeting' was held to be valid.

If a special or extraordinary resolution is to be tabled then the full text of it must be provided with the notice. If subsequently at the meeting an amendment to the special or extraordinary resolution is proposed then all shareholders (including those not in attendance) must agree to waive their right to notice of it (*Re Moorgate Mercantile Holdings Ltd* (1980)):

Re Moorgate Mercantile Holdings Ltd (1980)

Wishing to cancel its share premium account the company sent shareholders a notice on 2 April informing them of a special resolution which was proposed to be put at an EGM on 26 April that '... the share premium account of the company amounting to £1,356,900.84 be cancelled'. At the meeting on 26 April it was belatedly found that a sum of £321.17 had not been credited to the share premium account. The resolution was then altered to read 'That the share premium account of £1,356,900.84 be reduced to £321.17'. This altered resolution was passed unanimously. The company then asked the court to confirm the reduction in the share premium account.

Held: Notwithstanding the complete lack of opposition to the reduction it would not be confirmed as the notice distributed to shareholders on 2 April was inaccurate:

The notices of 2 April specified the intention to propose one resolution; the resolution passed at the meeting on 26 April was another, different resolution. Furthermore, the difference was not one merely of form but also of substance, albeit of slight substance, in as much as one provided for the entire cancellation of the company's share premium account, while the other provided merely for its reduction, albeit by almost the entirety thereof. (Slade J)

For a similar outcome see Normandy v Ind.Coope & Co. Ltd (1908).

In his judgement in *Re Moorgate Mercantile Holdings Ltd* (1980) Slade J went on *orbiter* to make a number of recommendations in respect to provision of notice of resolutions. These were:

1 If a notice of the intention to propose a special resolution is to be valid for the purpose of s. 141 (2) it must identify the intended resolution by specifying either the text or the entire substance of the resolution which it is intended to propose.
2 If a special resolution is to be validly passed in accordance with s. 141 (2) the resolution as passed must be the same resolution as that identified in the preceding notice.
3 A resolution as passed can properly be regarded as the resolution identified in the preceding notice even though (i) it departs in some respects from the text of a resolution set out in such notice (for example by correcting grammatical or clerical errors which can be corrected as a matter of construction, or by reducing the words to more formal language) or (ii) it is reduced into the form of a new text, which was not included in the notice, provided only in either case there is no departure whatever from the substance.
4 However, in deciding whether there is complete identity between the substance of a resolution as passed and the substance of an intended resolution as notified there is no room for the court to apply the *de minimis* principle ... The substance must be identical ...

Company circulars

The practice is for a company to issue with notice of a general meeting a circular informing shareholders of the views taken by the board who will also usually ask that shareholders who are unable to attend give the chairman of the board a proxy to vote in the board's favour. The circular ought to convey sufficient information to enable shareholders to decide whether to attend the meeting or not (*Tiessen v Henderson* (1899)).

Providing the information given in the circular is for the benefit of the company as a whole, and not designed to either benefit the board personally or to mislead shareholders over the company's true position, then the cost of the circular may be charged to the company. Indeed if it is subsequently discovered that a circular (or notice of a meeting) contained misleading information to such a degree that it misrepresented the position of the company then any resolution passed at the meeting which favoured those responsible for the misrepresentation may be set aside (*Baille v Oriental Telephone & Electric Co. Ltd* (1915).

Under the listing rules The London Stock Exchange requires that a circular is sent by a listed company with notice of meetings other than a routine AGM. The listing rules also require that the circular provides a clear and adequate explanation of its subject matter as well as containing sufficient information to enable a properly informed decision to be taken.

Should the inaccuracy in a circular be spotted early enough then a shareholder may obtain an injunction to prevent the tabled resolution being passed until a corrective circular has been distributed. Where directors are unable to avoid a conflict of interest (actual or potential) then this should be clearly stated in the circular (*Pacific Coast Coal Mines Ltd v Arbuthnot* (1917)).

Provision of special notice

Special notice – which must not be confused with notice of a special resolution – is required for three types of ordinary resolution. They are:

a) to remove a director from office, or to appoint someone in his place (s. 303);
b) to appoint a director aged 70 years or over to a public company or to a subsidiary of a public company (s. 293);
c) to remove an auditor from his position, or to appoint any auditor other than the retiring one (s388).

Where special notice is demanded the proposer must give the company 28 days notice of their intention to table a resolution. The company then gives shareholders notice of the resolution when it notifies them of the meeting. If it is too late to include the resolution in the notice of the meeting then it may be communicated separately to shareholders (or advertised) at least 21 days in advance of the meeting.

Notice of shareholder resolutions at AGM

Shareholders of at least 5 per cent of the share voting capital, or at least 100 shareholders (with or without votes) who have paid up an average of at least £100, can compel the company (s. 376):

a) by six weeks' notice (s377) to notify shareholders of any *resolution* that they intend to table at an AGM;
b) by one week's notice to circulate to shareholders a *statement* of up to 1,000 words in respect with any proposed resolution to be dealt with at that AGM.

Notice to the company concerning the shareholder resolution or statement must be deposited at the company's registered office.

The above is called a *requisitioned circular* and the requisitionist may be asked to deposit a reasonable sum with the company to cover the costs of distributing the circular and/or statement.

Where the board, or an aggrieved party, believe that the requisitionist's resolution or statement are libellous then the directors can refuse to distribute it.

Management of company meetings

A growing practice is for tele-conferencing, where people may be linked up by audio-visual

The quorum

The quorum is the minimum number of shareholders who have to be present at a meeting for it to commence and for the decisions subsequently made to be valid. Unless the articles state otherwise the quorum for all company meetings is two shareholders (or their proxies) entitled to vote personally present (s 370 (4) and Table A, article 40). With single-shareholder companies the presence in person, or by proxy, of that shareholder is sufficient (s. 370A).

However, if the articles so permit one shareholder may constitute a valid quorum (*Re Fireproof Doors Ltd* (1916)) or if all the shares of a particular class are held by one person (*East v Bennett Brothers Ltd* (1911)).

If within 30 minutes a quorum is not present, the meeting will stand adjourned to the same day, time and place in the following week, or some day, time and place that the directors shall decide on (Table A, article 41). However, case law is uncertain of the position where a meeting commences with the necessary quorum but subsequently the quorum is lost. There is authority for business transacted after the quorum is lost to still be valid (*Re Hartley Baird Ltd* (1955)).

If it is not possible to satisfy the requirements for calling or conducting a meeting then a director or shareholder entitled to vote at the meeting may apply to the court for assistance in allowing the meeting to take place under any direction the court thinks fit to give (s. 371):

Re El Sombrero (1958)

X and Y were directors each owning 5 per cent of the shares with the remaining 90 per cent held by Z who was not a director. Under the articles the quorum for a meeting was two shareholders. Wishing to remove X and Y from their directorships Z called a meeting (under what is now s. 368) but X and Y refused to attend so that no quorum was possible. Subsequently Z applied to the court for assistance, which was granted (under what is now s. 371) whereby a meeting had to take place and that the quorum need only be one shareholder. X and Y were both removed from office.

---

equipment. This has been judicially accepted subject to it being possible to engage in debate and subsequently vote. Consequently, it is not strictly necessary that all shareholders physically attend a meeting (*Byng v London Life Association Ltd* (1990)).

In relation to general meetings the discretion of the court is paramount and may overrule the articles (or a unanimous shareholder agreement) that intentionally gives a shareholder a right to prevent the holding of a general meeting (*Re British Union for the Abolition of Vivisection* (1995)). But such overruling will apparently only be exercised in exceptional circumstances which do not include making an order under section 371 where the purpose of the meeting is to disregard a shareholder's class rights (*Harman v BML Group Ltd* (1994)).

The chairman

The chairman of general meetings is normally appointed under the articles – '... the chairman, if any, of the board of directors or in his absence some other director nominated by the directors shall preside as chairman of the meeting ...' (Table A, article 42). If no director is willing to act as chairman, or if no director is present within fifteen minutes after the proposed start of the meeting, then the shareholders present and entitled to vote shall choose one of their number to be chairman (Table A, article 43).

Duties

A chairman has the following duties:

1 To act honestly and fairly in the interests of the company as a whole (*Blaire v Consolidated Enfield Corporation* (1955)). A chairman, as a director or shareholder (or both), will have a personal interest in most issues to be dealt with at company meetings, but he must curb any tendency to over-promote an interest lest he be accused of acting in bad faith. Therefore, objectivity and impartiality are essential attributes.

2 To ensure that business is conducted in an orderly manner and in the order set out in the agenda. What he must avoid is allowing anyone (or group) to 'hi-jack' the meeting.

Therefore, at all times he must remain in firm but courteous control. What is important is to permit, within reason, all relevant opinions to be expressed. To do otherwise may raise the suspicion of bias. Once an issue has had sufficient time devoted to it he must allow a resolution to be put:

Wall v London and Northern Assets Corporation (1898)

After a long discussion, several shareholders still wanted to speak. The chairman moved that 'the question now be put to the meeting' and the resolution was passed.

Held: The chairman had acted in a proper manner so that the resolution would stand.

On completion of voting a chairman must formally declare the result.

3 To use his discretion as to whether an amendment to a resolution is admissible. If a proposed amendment falls outside the business, as given in the notice of the meeting, then it should be rejected.

4 To adjourn any meeting that is unable to complete its business with the proviso that a quorum must be present and the meeting either directs the chairman to adjourn or consents to it (Table A, article 45). If the meeting cannot be reconvened in under 14 days then at least 7 days clear notice of the reconvention is required (Table A, article 45). Generally, an adjourned meeting on its resumption is treated as a continuation of the original meeting (*Spencer v Kennedy* (1926)). However, any resolution passed at a reconvened meeting must be treated as having been passed on the date on which it was actually passed and not retrospectively. Shareholders attending an adjourned meeting may not be the same as those who attended the original meeting.

When adjourning a meeting the chairman must act in good faith (*Byng v London Life Assurance Ltd* (1990)). In *John v Rees* (1970) the chairman of a company meeting was held to have acted responsibly on adjourning the meeting when disorder made it impossible to conduct business or to arrange through the meeting an agreed adjournment.

Should a chairman, without just cause, prematurely close a meeting then another chairman may be elected so that the meeting may continue:

National Dwellings Society v Sykes (1894)

At a general meeting the chairman proposed 'that the accounts be passed'. A shareholder moved an amendment that a committee of inquiry be appointed to investigate the accounts. The chairman refused to take the amendment. He again put the unamended resolution and on it being lost immediately closed the meeting. The shareholders present then appointed a new chairman and a committee of inquiry.

Held: The appointments were valid.

---

5 To sign the minutes of the meeting as constituting a true record of all that took place.

Minutes

Every company must keep minutes of both general company and board meetings (s. 382 (1)). These must be kept in bound books, the pages of which cannot be removed. Therefore, a loose-leaf book is not a proper minute book (*Hearts of Oak Assurance Co. v Flower & Sons* (1936). When signed by the chairman the minutes become evidence of the proceedings (s. 382 (2)). Indeed unless a poll is demanded the signed minutes are conclusive evidence that a resolution has been carried or been lost (Table A, article 47).

Minute books of general meetings must be kept at the company's registered office and be available for inspection by any shareholder without charge (s. 383 (1)). A shareholder is entitled to request a copy of minutes and these must be provided within 7 days on payment of a small charge.

'Available for inspection' means available for at least two hours each business day.

Where a private company makes a *written resolution* under section 381A in place of passing a resolution at a general meeting then it must be recorded as if it was a minute of a general meeting (ss. 381A (4), 382). A shareholder has the right to inspection of written resolutions and on payment of a small fee to be provided with copies.

Failure to maintain minutes or written resolutions or to make them available to shareholders or to refuse to supply copies will mean that every company officer in default will be liable in respect to each failure to a fine (s. 383 (4)). To overcome any such refusal a court may order the company to make an immediate inspection available as well as to provide any copies that may be required (s. 383 (5)).

Voting

Usually the articles will say how the voting rights are allocated. Where Table A is followed then subject to any rights or restrictions attached to a share issue, each shareholder when present at a company meeting on a show of hands is to have one vote irrespective of how many shares are held, and on a poll one vote for each share held (Table A, article 54).

A poll, which in practice is fairly rare, may be demanded either in place of a hand vote or after one has been taken. The right to a poll cannot be totally excluded by the articles except where the vote is for the election of a chairman or an adjournment motion. To prevent abuse the articles cannot make it too demanding for a poll to be obtained in that the minimum support for a poll may not be set above either 5 shareholders entitled to vote at that meeting or any numbers of members holding at least 10 per cent of the voting shares (s. 373 (1)). Table A, article 46 confers a similar right but reduces the number of shareholders required for a poll from 5 to 2. The chairman is also able to demand a poll as may shareholders representing at least 10 per cent of the total voting rights of all shareholders having the right to attend and vote at that meeting, or shareholders holding voting shares on which 10 per cent of the total sum paid up on all voting shares has been paid up.

As private companies normally have relatively few shareholders the article will usually allow any one shareholder (in person or by proxy) to demand a poll.

Where monies are owing on shares they will be void in respect to conferring voting rights (Table A, article 57) and if shares are jointly held the voting entitlement is given to the first name that appears in the registers of members (Table A, article 55).

Shareholders are free to vote as they wish but if they enter into voting agreements, with other shareholders they will be enforceable by injunction (*Greenwell v Porter* (1902)).

Proxies

Table A, article 60 states that a proxy must be appointed in writing and provides a stipulated form that should be followed.

A proxy is a person authorized by a shareholder to attend and vote at a meeting on his behalf. A proxy is appointed under a written authority and becomes the special agent of the appointing shareholder.

Every shareholder has the right to appoint a proxy who himself need not be a shareholder (s. 372 (1)). Therefore, where Company A is a shareholder in Company B it will be able to appoint a proxy to attend and vote at meetings called by Company B. Also a corporate shareholder, as a legal person, is given increased representational authority in that it may appoint by resolution of its directors (or other governing body) any person it thinks fit to act as its representative at any company or class meeting. Such a representative (a human person) is to have the same powers as those of the appointing company shareholder (s. 375).

In addition, for private companies a proxy also has not only the right to attend and vote but may also *speak* at a meeting (s. 372 (1)). With public companies a proxy only has the right to speak if the articles permit.

A proxy may be general in that a discretional authority is given to the proxy to vote any way they feel inclined to do so; or it may be limited to voting on a particular resolution strictly as instructed. If a proxy votes against his instructions the vote taken will normally stand unless it is shown that the vote of the proxy was crucial to the outcome of the vote (*Oliver v Dalgleish* (1963)). A shareholder is able to revoke his proxy appointment (provided that his proxy has not voted) but if Table A, article 63 is followed, then revocation to be effective must be notified to the company before the meeting commences. A shareholder who personally attends and votes will automatically revoke the proxy's appointment (*Cousins v International Brick Co.* (1931)).

To facilitate the use of proxies, companies having a share capital must in every notice calling a meeting of the company state with reasonable prominence that a shareholder entitled to attend and vote may appoint a proxy to do so on their behalf (s. 373 (3)). The common practice is for public companies to issue proxy forms or cards inviting shareholders to appoint as a proxy a specified person (usually the board chairman), or other alternatives. If this practice is used then the invitation must be made to the whole membership, not part of it. Every officer who knowingly and wilfully authorized or permitted such a partial invitation to be made will be liable to a fine (s. 372 (6)). This provision guards against directors only issuing proxy forms or cards to those they believe will be responsive to recommendations to vote in the manner the board wishes.

The London Stock Exchange requires listed companies to issue 'two way' proxy forms so as to allow proxies to vote either for or against resolutions. Also the form must say that a proxy can be chosen and provide a space for one to be written in.

Where a proxy is to be used then the form or card has to be deposited with the company any time up to 48 hours before the meeting commences. The articles may specify a shorter period but a longer one is not allowed (s. 372 (5)).

In respect to *shareholder democracy*, proxies are overwhelmingly used as a means of enabling the shareholders to record their view on an issue in a cost-effective way. If actual attendance was required then those with modest share holdings would find it rather expensive to do so. However, what tends to occur is that a board in advance of a meeting will obtain sufficient proxies from large institutional shareholders so that the meeting itself will cease to be a real decision-making body.

Review question

In relation to a general meeting explain:

a) what is meant by ordinary and special business;

b) when a poll vote must be taken;

c) when a chairman may refuse to take a shareholder vote.

Resolutions

A resolution is a decision made at a company meeting. The antecedent of a resolution is a motion tabled at a general meeting which when carried becomes a resolution. They may be of the following types.

Ordinary

For the motion to become a resolution a simple majority in favour of shareholders, personally present or represented by proxy, of those entitled to vote and actually voting is needed (*Bushell v Faith* (1970)). Where an ordinary resolution is required it will be determined by legislation or the articles. Examples are: the removal of a director (s. 303); the removal of an auditor (s. 391); and the alteration of capital (s. 121).

Generally copies or details of ordinary resolutions do not have to be sent to the Registrar but there are exceptions, e.g. the appointment or removal of a director (s. 288); the removal of an auditor (s. 391 (2)); change of registered office (s. 287 (3)); alteration of the authorized share capital (s. 121); authorization of the directors to allot shares – where the articles do not allow them to do so (s. 80 (8)); revocation of an elective resolution (s. 379A (3)); and voluntarily wind-up due to the period fixed for its duration having expired or due to an event occurring as a result of which the article states the company is to be dissolved (Insolvency Act 1986, s. 84 (1)).

There are no particular requirements as to notice for ordinary resolutions. For this reason amendments may be validly taken at the meeting itself provided of course that they come within the scope of the notice of the original resolution.

Special

For a motion to become a special resolution a three-quarters majority in favour of shareholders, personally present or represented by proxy, of those entitled to vote and actually voting is needed (s. 378 (2)).

Special resolutions are required in respect of fundamental changes to the company. This may be appreciated from the following examples:

i) to alter the company's memorandum or articles (ss. 4, 9);

ii) to re-register a company (ss. 43, 51, 53);

iii) to reduce, with the leave of the court, its capital (s. 135);

iv) to cancel or alter statutory pre-emption rights (s. 95);

v) to change, with the leave of the Secretary of State, the company name (s. 28);

vi) to ratify an ultra vires act (s. 35 (3));

vii) to authorize a private company to purchase or redeem its own shares out of capital (s. 173);

viii) to authorize a private company to give financial assistance for the purchase of its own shares (s. 155);

ix) to authorize the terms of a proposed contract so that an off-market purchase of a company's own shares may be made (s. 164);

x) to commence a winding up – voluntary or compulsory (Insolvency Act 1986, ss. 84, 122).

The notice period for a special resolution is normally 21 days but if a simple majority in number holding 95 per cent in value of the voting shares agree then a shorter period may be substituted. A copy of every special resolution must be sent for filing to the Registrar within 15 days of it being passed.

A private company may by elective resolution (under s. 379A) reduce the 95 per cent requirement but it cannot be set lower than 90 per cent (s. 378 (3)). If a company does not have share capital then members holding at least 95 per cent of the voting rights must agree to the proposed shorter period (s.378 (3)).

Extraordinary

An ordinary resolution is similar to a special resolution in relation to the necessary three-quarter voting majority (s378(1)). The difference between them is that only 14 days notice is required for an extraordinary resolution but, as with a special resolution, a shorter period is possible. Similarly the notice period means that amendments to an extraordinary resolution cannot be made at the meeting.

An extraordinary resolution is required in order to:

i) sanction a variation of class rights at a separate meeting of the class concerned (s. 125 (2));
ii) voluntarily wind up the company on grounds of insolvency (Insolvency Act 1986, s. 84);
iii) sanction, in a voluntary winding up, certain actions of the liquidator, e.g. to make a compromise arrangement with creditors, or to pay in full a class of creditors (Insolvency Act 1986, s. 165).

As with special resolutions a copy of all extraordinary resolutions must, within 15 days of being passed, be sent to the Registrar for filing.

Elective (private companies only)

An elective resolution will enable *private companies*, either by means of a resolution in a general meeting or through the use of a written resolution, to dispense with the need for certain internal procedures and requirements.

As originally introduced, to use the 'elective regime' a minimum of 21 days notice was required with the notice giving full details of the resolution that was proposed and the fact that it was an elective one. The resolution, to be successful, had to be agreed to at the meeting, in person or by proxy, by *all* the shareholders entitled to attend and vote at the meeting (s. 379A). However, the 21 day notice period was acknowledged to be a disadvantage so now, subject to *all* shareholders entitled to vote agreeing, a shorter period may be substituted (SI 1996/1471).

A private company may pass an elective resolution on the following matters:

i) to disengage s. 80 (4) (5) whereby directors will base the authority to allot shares for a period in excess of 5 years. Where s. 80 (4) (5) cease to operate the allotment of shares will be governed by s. 80A and the new authority will need to say the maximum amount of relevant securities that can be allotted and whether the authority is for a fixed or infinite period (s. 80A);
ii) to dispense with having to tender accounts and reports at general meetings unless shareholders request that this is done (s. 252 (1));
iii) to dispense with the requirement to hold AGMs. With many small private companies it is overwhelmingly common that directors will also be shareholders so

it is superfluous to have them call AGMs. Should a shareholder require an AGM to take place then he may, at least 3 months before the end of the year, notify the company of his wish for an AGM and the company will have to hold one in that year (s. 366A);

iv) to reduce the majority required to authorize short notice of a general meeting from shareholders holding at least 95 per cent in nominal value to 90 per cent of those entitled to attend and vote (ss. 369 (4), 378 (3));

v) to dispense with the appointment of auditors annually. This will mean that the existing auditors will hold a permanent appointment (s. 386 (1)).

Elective resolutions may be revoked at any time by passing an ordinary resolution (s. 379A (3)). Should a private company re-register as a public company then all elective resolutions will automatically be revoked (s. 379A (4)). After being passed, a copy of an elective resolution must be sent to the Registrar (s. 380 (4)). Failure to do so will not invalidate it but will leave those in default liable to a fine (s. 380 (5)). Similarly, where an elective resolution is revoked then the Registrar needs to be notified.

Informal resolutions – unanimous consent

As an alternative to a formally put resolution before a general meeting, a resolution may be approved by all those who are entitled to attend and vote had a general meeting been called. This is the *Duomatic* principle (*Re Duomatic Ltd* (1969)). The unanimous resolution originated in the common law (*Parker & Cooper Ltd v Reading* (1926)), although it is now usually incorporated into company articles (Table A, article 53). The assent of *all* relevant shareholders is not required simultaneously but may be given at different times (*Parker & Cooper Ltd v Reading* (1926)). However, it is uncertain whether the same requirement as to provision of notice to all shareholders, as required for formal resolutions, is needed.

For informal resolutions see also alterations through assent in Chapter 6, Articles of Association.

Where an informal resolution is passed then by its unanimous nature such a resolution is as valid as if it had been passed in a general meeting (*Cane v Jones* (1980)). Informal resolutions need not be in writing (*Re Duomatic* (1969)) unless the articles say that they must be (Table A, article 53). Where legislation insists that a resolution be passed at a general meeting, such as for the removal of a director, then an informal resolution would normally be ignored by the court. However, the court may exceptionally uphold the validity of an informal resolution even though technically the resolution ought to have only been passed at a general meeting, such as in *Re Home Treat Ltd* (1991) where an informal resolution to alter the company's object clause in the articles was allowed to stand even though section 5 lays down a statutory procedure that has to be followed.

The provision contained in section 381A while similar to Table A, article 53 is broader in that it may be used even where a legislative prohibition prevents a company from passing a resolution other than in a general meeting.

Informal resolutions – written procedure

Where a *private company* may pass a resolution at a general meeting (or at a class meeting), be it ordinary, extraordinary or elective, then the need to do so may be replaced by a written resolution (s. 381A (1)). For a written resolution, which does not require previous notice, to be introduced all shareholders entitled to vote must show their agreement by signing, in person or by proxy, the resolution. It is not necessary that they sign the same document provided that each document used accurately states the terms of the resolution (s. 381A (2)). The resolution will be effective from the date the last shareholder signed (s. 381A (3)).

While the written procedure under section 381A is *prima facie* attractive, subject to unanimous consent being forthcoming, there are two specific resolutions that the written proce-dure cannot replace (given in Schedule 15A). They are the removal of a director (s 303) or auditor (s. 391). However, it is conceded that where there are only a few shareholders the effort of organizing a resolution and having it passed at a company meeting will most likely be approximately the same as the effort involved in obtaining a written resolution.

Review question

Discuss how shareholders in a private company ought to proceed in order to achieve the fol-lowing:

a) the early removal of a director;

Chapter summary

- Generally shareholders in a general meeting cannot interfere with how the board of directors manages the company. If shareholders are unhappy with the directors' stewardship then 'control' can be exercised through alteration of the articles. Exceptions (where interference is possible) are: where the board fails to act; where the Companies Act protects the position of shareholders; and where shareholders decide to ratify a director's irregular act.
- All companies must hold an AGM every calendar year at which ordinary business is to be conducted. However, a dispensation from having an AGM is available to private companies that pass an elective resolution.
- An EGM is any meeting that is not an AGM. Special business will be conducted. Directors are statutorily required to call an EGM when there has been a serious deterioration in the company's net assets (a fall to 50 per cent or less of its called up capital). Shareholders (10 per cent or more of the paid up capital) can request an EGM. If they do so the directors have 21 days to convene it. Failure on their part to do so will allow the shareholders to call it themselves.
- Notice of all general meetings must be given to all shareholders. This is usually: 21 clear days for an AGM; 14 clear days for an EGM (21 days if a special resolution is to be moved). The notice must contain relevant information (date, time and place of the meeting). Special, but not ordinary, business must be mentioned. A full text of all special or extraordinary resolutions must be given with the notice.
- Circulars may be included with notice of meetings. These frequently are used to solicit shareholders to appoint company officers as their proxies. Shareholders may also request that a circular and statement of their own be distributed.
- For a general meeting to transact business validly there must be a quorum of two unless a single shareholder company where it is one. However, a court may itself convene a meeting where it thinks fit even though a quorum may not be present.
- The chairman of meetings must be independent and allow as many shareholders as possible to speak provided that they do not deviate from the business in hand. Adjournments are only possible if the meeting consents or instructs but in exceptional circumstances a chairman may use his discretion and adjourn.

- Voting is usually covered by the articles – if on a show of hands then one vote per shareholder attending and voting. A poll vote, based on the number of shares held, can be demanded by five or more shareholders entitled to vote or those holding at least 10 per cent of the voting shares.
- Proxies can be appointed by any shareholder – natural or artificial. The appointment may be limited in that stipulated instructions have to be followed, or discretional in that they are free to vote as they wish. Proxies of private companies have a right to speak whereas with public companies this right is governed by the articles.
- Resolutions may be: ordinary, based on a simple majority; special and extraordinary, requiring a 75 per cent majority or better; elective and written procedure which require 100 per cent agreement.

b) the re-registration of the company to a public one.

Discussion questions

1 To what extent may a general meeting engage in the management of the company? If it does adopt a managerial role what procedures must it follow?
2 Outline how the Companies Act allows shareholders to control the board of directors. In reality is the control substantive or meaningless?

Case study exercise

Compass Limited has a fully paid up share capital of £100,000 divided into £1 shares. Four directors, East, West, North and South, each hold 10,000 shares with the remainder being divided between ten other shareholders. For some time the ten non-director shareholders believe that the four directors have proved to be appallingly bad as managers of the company and wish to get rid of them.

Offer legal advice to the non-director shareholders on how they ought to proceed.

Further reading

Contractual Obligations of the Company in General Meetings, P. Jaffey (1996), LS, 27.
Power of the Court to Convene a Meeting of Shareholders, A. Mays (1991), Co. Law, 23.
See also the Xueres articles under Further Reading in Chapter 14, Minority Protection.

SHAREHOLDER AND CREDITOR PROTECTION

14 Minority protection

Introduction

Members of a company limited by shares are part of a shareholder body with each ordinary shareholder (and possibly other shareholders as well) entitled to vote with the usual basis being one vote for each share held. This is shareholder democracy with members being able to participate in the 'management' of the company by their ability to signify their wishes through attendance and voting at general meetings. In most instances shareholder democracy works well. Even when dissenting shareholders have been, for example, unsuccessful in attempting to dismiss directors, they may not feel resentful but accept that in a democracy the majority view has to prevail. However, when there is an entrenched majority shareholding, commonly held by a few, then there is a real danger of a tyranny by the majority at the expense of the minority. To guard against possible abuse by the majority the principle of minority protection has developed.

Objectives

The purpose of this chapter is to show how the courts, while anxious wherever possible to uphold majority rule, are willing to use equitable principles to provide remedies for oppressed minority shareholders. In addition students are expected to become familiar with the statutory protection available to shareholders against unfairly prejudicial conduct. Students are also required to become aware of the remedies an aggrieved minority shareholder may obtain. Finally the role of the Department of Trade and Industry in relation to company inspections must be understood.

Key concepts

- Majority rule – Foss v Harbottle
- Minority protection and exceptions to Foss v Harbottle
- Statutory unfairly prejudicial conduct
- Judicial orders that may be granted
- The appointment and role of company inspectors.

Position of majority shareholders

The majority will have sufficient votes to be able to pass or block resolutions. Therefore, in respect to management by resolution in general meetings a majority will have control of the company. As shareholders, when voting, do not owe fiduciary duties to the company it means that the majority shareholders are free to use their voting rights as they please. They may vote in their own self-interest even if it proves detrimental to the company. Should a director be included in the shareholder majority, which is common in private companies, then normally they are able as directors to disregard both their fiduciary duties and their duty of care and skill. This is subject to their making appropriate disclosure of any conflict of interest and receiving approval of a resolution allowing their action. This may not be too demanding in that advance approval can be received by means of disclosure at the first possible board meeting (s. 317) even though the board could consist of cronies. Alternatively, retrospective 'approval' may be obtained in the form of ratification by a general meeting of an unauthorized act whereby the company will waive taking legal action against the errant director (*Bamford v Bamford* (1970)). Here the 'compromised' director is allowed, notwithstanding his personal interest in the matter, to vote in his capacity as a shareholder (*North-West Transportation & Co. Ltd v Beatty* (1887)). As the potential, in such an inequitable relationship, for serious harm to be caused to minority shareholders is a real one, equity and statute law have intervened to redress the power deficiency of the weaker party.

Majority rule

The normal position in law is that a company is to operate on the basis of majority rule. This requires an examination of the rule in *Foss v Harbottle*:

> ## Foss v Harbottle (1843)
> Minority shareholders brought an action against directors alleging irregularities in the management of the company. They tried to get them to make good the loss suffered by the company when those directors sold their own land to the company at an artificially high value.
>
> Held: The minority shareholders could not bring this action. It was for the company to take the action itself. Alternatively, the company could exonerate the directors from blame.

This seminal case must now be read with Daniels v Daniels (1978) given in the exceptions to the rule which follows shortly. Also while the facts related to the wrong being done by directors the same rule also applies where it is done by others such as a liquidator (Leon v York-O-Matic Ltd (1966)).

This rule is one of procedure, not one of law. It means that if a wrong is done against a company, whether externally or internally, and the question of enforcing the legal rights of the company arises, then it is for the company to decide what action to take. Should legal action in fact be taken then the company itself will be the proper plaintiff – hence the rule is also known as the *proper plaintiff rule*.

As a direct consequence of enforcing *Foss v Harbottle* another rule has emerged whereby if an irregularity is capable of being condoned or ratified by a majority of shareholders then minority shareholders cannot take legal action themselves (*Edwards v Halliwell* (1950)). Thus majority rule is strengthened still further despite the fact that those in breach of their duty will be likely to vote in their own favour for ratification!

Therefore, if minority shareholders believe that their interests have been prejudiced by someone injuring the company then they are not normally allowed to take legal action themselves against the person responsible but must leave it to the company to do so. When making that decision the company, as a separate legal person, can only act through the rule of its majority shareholders. If the majority are against an action then the minority, under shareholder democracy, must abide by that decision. The problem that minority shareholders face is that the majority are able to block resolutions at company meetings favouring taking legal action so that conduct prejudicial to minority shareholders is left undefended.

Justification for the Foss v Harbottle rule

Foss v Harbottle is such an entrenched rule that justification for it is rather superfluous. However, the following are regularly put forward:

1 The rule is an inevitable consequence of a company being a separate legal entity. Therefore, if harm is caused to a company then only the company itself can take legal action. No one else, irrespective of their losses, will have the necessary *locus standi* to take legal proceedings.
2 Directors of a company owe their duties only to their company and not to its shareholders. Therefore, if they breach their duties, commit misfeasance, or misappropriate their company's property then only the company that was owed the duty may take action against them.
3 The rule maintains the principle of majority control. If, for example, a director commits wrongful acts then members of the company may in a general meeting vote to remove him or to ratify his acts (for these resolutions a simple majority will be needed). Alternatively, the shareholders may vote to sue the director for damages! This is shareholder democracy – the will of the majority making itself known. A shareholder accepts by implication majority control when he buys his shares.
4 The rule prevents multiple actions. It would prove intolerable if each shareholder was allowed an individual right of action.
5 The rule stops pointless actions. If the company can deal with the matter in a general meeting then it is absurd to engage in litigation without the approval of a general meeting.

The validity of points 4 and 5 was recognized quite early in MacDougall v Gardiner (1875).

The Law Commission – observations on the Foss Harbottle rule

The Law Commission on looking at the rule in *Foss Harbottle* and its exceptions put forward six guiding principles. These were:

1 The *proper plaintiff* rule should be retained. A shareholder should be able to take proceedings about wrongs done to the company only in exceptional circumstances.
2 *Majority control* should be retained.
3 The directors' *commercial discretion* should continue. This is provided that a commercial decision by a director was made in good faith, on proper information, and in the light of the relevant considerations, and appears to be a reasonable decision for

The Law
Commission
Report on
Shareholder
Remedies
reported in
October 1997
(Law Com. No.
246); the prior
Consultation
Paper was No.
142.

that director to have taken. If this is the finding then a court ought not to substitute its own judgement for that of the director.

4 The *integrity* of the company's memorandum and articles is to be supported. Therefore, a shareholder on acquiring shares is contractually bound by the company's constitution and the sanctity of contract should apply. Failure to do so will, in the Law Commission's opinion, create unacceptable commercial uncertainty.

5 Companies must be protected from *unnecessary shareholder interference*. If not then a company may be 'killed by kindness' or waste money and managerial time in dealing with unwarranted proceedings.

6 All shareholders' remedies should be made as *efficient* and *cost effective* as possible.

Position of minority protection

Provision of minority protection equals exceptions to the rule in *Foss v Harbottle*. This is where, individually or in groups, minority shareholders may sue the wrongdoers. The exceptions are designed to prevent fraud by the majority at the expense of the minority but as fraud is notoriously difficult to establish it may not be specifically pleaded. Therefore, it has to be appreciated that there is no requirement for the majority to have had a dishonest intent. Rather the exceptions to *Foss v Harbottle* are needed because the majority shareholders are in a position of considerable strength which on occasions needs to be curbed.

The willingness of the courts to permit minority shareholders to bring an action is a judicial recognition that those in majority control may abuse their position by refusing to let the board or general meetings take action against those who have committed a wrong against the company. Here the wrongdoer would be a controller of the company who uses his voting strength to gain immunity from legal proceedings. If the court is sufficiently offended by the majority's conduct then an action will be allowed as an exception to *Foss v Harbottle*.

Preliminary matters

To bring a successful action the plaintiff will have to establish the following:

For defendant
control see also
the section on
derivative
actions that
follows shortly.

1 *That the defendants are in control of the company*
Controlling shareholders are those with at least 50 per cent of the votes, i.e. sufficient to block an ordinary resolution, such as that for the removal of a director. This will include votes derived from shareholders who normally vote with the controlling majority, either out of being influenced to do so or by apathy – voting with the herd (*Barratt v Ducket* (1995)). While it is usual to have a minority protection action after a general meeting has exposed the often cynical voting method of the majority, this is not strictly necessary if the plaintiff can show that the controllers would have blocked any 'unfavourable' resolutions should they have been tabled (*Russell v Wakefield Waterworks* (1875)).

2 *That the harm committed against the company was perpetrated by those in control of the company*
The problem a plaintiff faces here is that while it may be suspected that those in control are responsible for the harm the company suffered, actually proving they were

the true cause is in all but a few cases extremely demanding. Commonly those bringing an action can be cast as outsiders in that they are seldom privy to internal management decisions, whereas those in control of the company (the insiders) may be expected to be uncooperative, if not outright hostile, to any demand for an inquiry into how certain decisions were arrived at.

3 *That the action is brought in good faith for the benefit of the company as a whole*
This requirement may be assisted by showing that if the action is successful then the company will be the main beneficiary with the plaintiff only indirectly benefiting.

4 *That no other remedy is available for the alleged wrongs to be put right*
Clearly if an alternative remedy is available then it is not realistic to expect that the court will allow the claim to proceed as exceptions to Foss v Harbottle are reserved as a 'last ditch' remedy.

5 *That in the circumstances it would be inequitable to allow a general meeting to ratify the wrongful act complained of.*

As equitable maxims apply any impugnation that the plaintiff had an ulterior motive in seeking to bring the action will most likely result in the court refusing to hear the claim (Barret v Duckett (1995)).

Exceptions to the rule in Foss v Harbottle

Case law has recognized the following categories though new ones are capable of being created.

1 *Where the company does an illegal act*
An illegal act in this context includes an *ultra vires* one. The common law position is that even if the company wishes to ratify, ratification of an illegal act is not possible (*Simpson v Westminster Palace Hotel Co.* (1860)). However, shareholders have a legitimate expectation that the company will act legally:

Parke v Daily News Ltd (1962)
The company wanted to make an *ultra vires* payment to employees who were to be made redundant. P, a minority shareholder, wanted to prevent this payment being made.

Held: An injunction would be granted preventing the company from implementing their decision.

Such a payment would now be allowed by s. 719, CA 1985 and s. 187, Insolvency Act 1986.

It is now necessary, where a company acts on an improperly passed resolution, to refer to s. 35A which may, in respect of a third party, validate the company's acts.

Statute law now curbs the right of shareholders to obtain restraining injunctions by allowing companies to ratify ultra vires acts by passing a special resolution (s. 35 (3)). But shareholders may sue directors or others responsible for the illegal act unless another special resolution is passed to relieve them of liability.

2 *Where the company acts on an improperly passed special resolution*
This category safeguards the integrity of the articles or memorandum in that without it the company could substitute ordinary resolutions instead of special resolutions as demanded by its constitution (*Edwards v Halliwell* (1950)). Similarly a company may

be prevented from acting on a special resolution where insufficient notice of it had been given (*Baille v Oriental Telephone Co.* (1915)).

3 *Where the company infringes the individual rights of a shareholder*
This category is a common cause for actions to be taken. In *Wood v Odessa Waterworks Co.* (1889)) the company attempted to avoid its liability to make cash dividend payments by issuing in their place debentures. This was held to infringe on the personal rights of shareholders.

4 *Where fraud is committed on the minority*
The courts have never stated exactly what conduct constitutes fraud. For this reason they have retained considerable discretion:

> ... the essence of the matter seems to be an abuse or misuse of power. 'Fraud' in the phrase 'fraud on the minority' seems to be being used as comprising not only fraud at common law but also fraud in the wider equitable sense of that term, as in the equitable concept of a fraud on a power. (Megarry VC, *Estmanco (Kilner House) Ltd v G L C* (1982) when analysing Templeman J's judgement in *Daniels v Daniels* (1978)

For the facts of Menier v Hooper's Telegraph Works (1874) see Chapter 6, Articles of Association; and for Alexander v Automatic Telephone Co. Ltd (1900) see Chapter 11, Directors.

At its crudest extreme it is where the majority will be clearly seen to 'put something into their pockets at the expense of the minority' (per James LJ in *Menier v Hooper's Telegraph Works* (1874)). However, there need not be any criminal element present so that dishonesty on the part of the majority is not required. Therefore, conduct far less malevolent may still be adjudged as amounting to a fraud on the minority. Indeed the minority when seeking a remedy may not raise the allegation of fraud, thus saving themselves the onerous burden of having to substantiate it. If subsequently the court finds in their favour then it will be the court that will affix an appropriate label when giving equitable relief as in *Alexander v Automatic Telephone Co.* (1900) where the minority had second thoughts about alleging fraud but the court still found in their favour on the ground that the directors had broken their duty of trust owed to the company.

The following are commonly cited examples of fraud on the minority:

a) *Double dealing of directors towards the company*
Here double dealing will equal disreputable or discreditable conduct carried out by those in a position of trust for personal advantage:
   i) *expropriation of company property:*

Cook v Deeks (1916)

Directors whilst negotiating a contract on behalf of the company took it over into their own names. They then used their majority voting strength to have passed at a general meeting a resolution declaring that the company had no interest in the expropriated contract.

Held: The resolution was ineffective as it amounted to a fraud on the minority.

For the facts to Regal Hastings Ltd v Gulliver (1942) see Chapter 11, Directors.

The blatant profiteering in *Cook v Deeks* (1916) was such that ratification of the directors' act was not possible. This may be compared with *Regal (Hastings) Ltd v Gulliver* (1942) where the profit made by the directors was held to be incidental so that ratification of their act was possible.

ii) *Selling undervalued assets to the company:*

Atwool v Merryweather (1864)

On incorporation M, a promoter, took £39,940 in cash and 600 shares as part payment for various mines allegedly worth £7,000 that he sold to the company. Subsequently, it was discovered that the mines were valueless. A, a minority shareholder, started legal proceedings to recover the monies paid to M but M, together with an associate, holding between them a majority of votes, attempted to have the action struck out.

Held: The contract for purchase of the mine was a complete fraud:

> If I were to hold that no bill could be filed by shareholders to get rid of the transaction on the ground of the doctrine of Foss v Harbottle, it would be simply impossible to set aside a fraud committed by a director under such circumstances, as the director obtaining so many shares by fraud would always be able to outvote everyone else. (Sir W. Page Wood VC)

---

b) *Improper manipulation of the company's constitution*

This is where controlling shareholders will attempt to use the articles to achieve a permitted outcome but as it will be done with an ulterior motive, as opposed to benefiting the company as a whole, minority shareholders may have a right of action.

i) *expelling a shareholder without just reason*

Dafen Tinplate v Llanelly Steel (1920): The articles contained an unrestricted power to buy out any shareholder. This was too wide and instead of being used legitimately it could, as here, be misused.

If a power is limited then it may be legally valid. In *Sidebottom v Kershaw* (1920) a power of expulsion was limited to where a shareholder was found to be competing against the company. As the exercise of this power would be in the interests of the company as a whole its use was legitimate.

For the facts to Dafen Tinplate v Llanelly Steel (1920) and Sidebottom v Kershaw (1920) see Chapter 6, Articles of Association.

ii) *an issue of shares designed to alter voting power*

Where the articles authorize directors to issue new shares they must be issued in good faith for the benefit of the company as a whole. The courts have consistently held that the primary purpose of a share issue must be to obtain additional share capital (*Bamford v Bamford* (1970)). Illegitimate reasons for a share issue are to defeat a takeover bid (*Hogg v Cramphorn* (1967)), to help achieve a takeover (*Howard Smith Ltd v Ampoll Ltd* (1974)) and to secure the passing or blocking of a resolution:

For Hogg v Cramphorn (1967) and Howard Smith Ltd v Ampoll Ltd (1974) see Chapter 11, Directors.

Clemens v Clemens Bros Ltd (1976)

A niece (the plaintiff) and her aunt (the defendant who was also a director) held 45 per cent and 55 per cent of the issued shares. The aunt used her quarter voting strength to have new shares issued in such a manner that it resulted in the watering down of her

Where directors have incorrectly issued shares the courts generally will allow a general meeting to ratify their act but holders of the newly issued shares will not be permitted to vote (Hogg v Cramphorn Ltd (1967)).

niece's shareholding to 24.5%. The niece was therefore unable to block special or extraordinary resoutions.

Held: The resolution to issue new shares had not been exercised in good faith. It had in fact been designed to stop the plaintiff from having any element of control in the company, i.e. the niece's negative control had been removed.

c) *A negligent act that benefits the majority*
   For the minority to take action both parts, *a negligent act from which the majority accrues a benefit*, must be established. Negligence by itself is insufficient:

Daniels v Daniels (1978)

Mr and Mrs D were the only directors and controlling shareholders. They authorized the sale of land belonging to the company to Mrs D for £4,250. A few years later Mrs D resold it for £12,000. Minority shareholders contended that the sale was at an undervalue. Mr and Mrs D argued that as fraud had not been alleged the minority could not come within an exception to *Foss v Harbottle*.

Held: The minority could bring an action in the name of the company. The essential element was that the two directors had used their powers in a manner which benefited them at the expense of the minority. It mattered not whether they had acted intentionally, unintentionally, fraudulently or negligently.

The distinction between negligence *per se* and negligence allied to a personal benefit gained by the majority was drawn by Templeman J in *Daniels v Daniels* (1978) who followed an earlier case where directors negligently sold an asset at an undervalue but did not themselves benefit from the sale (*Pavlides v Jensen* (1956)).

Review question

Discuss what is meant by the term *wrong doer control*

From the above survey of exceptions to the *Foss v Harbottle* rule it is difficult to detect cast-iron principles as to when the rule may be relaxed. Clearly any set of circumstances that fall squarely within an established exception will present no problem – precedent dictates that the minority are to be protected. However, with novel circumstances (or significant variations of established ones) it is not easy to second guess the courts' likely response as to whether, using a pragmatic approach, they will agree that the rule ought to be set aside. These difficulties were recognized by Megarry VC in *Estmanco (Kilner House) Ltd v GLC* (1982):

> ... If the rule in *Foss v Harbottle* had remained unqualified, the way would have been open to the majority to stultify any proceedings which were for the benefit of the minority and to the disadvantage of the majority. Accordingly, a number of exceptions from the rule have been established; and it is here that the difficulties begin ... I do not think that it can simply be said that there is an exception from the rule whenever the justice of the case requires it ... If the test were simply justice or injustice, this would mean different things to different men ...

Megarry VC then went on to put forward a possible solution to the problem:

> ... no doubt one day the courts will distil from the exceptions some guiding principle that is wide enough to comprehend them all and yet narrow enough to be practicable and workable. It may be that the test may come to be whether an ordinary resolution of the shareholders could validly carry out or ratify the act in question ...

Yet if the determining characteristic of exceptions to *Foss v Harbottle* is whether or not a directors' act could be ratified then you may not be providing a satisfactory solution but merely moving the problem to a different locality, i.e. exactly what directors' unauthorized acts cannot be ratified by a company meeting; and, who exactly are permitted to vote on the resolution?

Types of actions available to minority shareholders

For exposition these are dealt with separately but it is common to use a combination of them when taking action. However, no 'double recovery' of damages will be possible.

Personal

There are two possible remedies that may be pursued:

a) *An action to have a resolution set aside*
   This is for a minority shareholder who has been deprived of an individual right such as in *Wood v Odessa Waterworks Co.* (1889) referred to earlier. Where minority shareholders sue, as the action is personal, the rule in *Foss v Harbottle* has no application.

b) *An application to restrain the company from doing an* ultra vires *act*
   A shareholder is able to apply for an injunction to prevent the company from doing an *ultra vires* act (s. 35 (2)). However, this statutory right is qualified to the extent that if the alleged *ultra vires* act is being done in fulfilment of a legal obligation that arises from a previous act of the company then an injunction will not be granted. While there is a common law right to restrain a company from taking an *ultra vires* act (*Smith v Croft* (No. 2) (1988)) it will most probably not override the statutory provision given in section 35 (2).

Derivative

Here a shareholder's right to sue is derived from the company which is the injured party with the injury being caused through the actions of the majority. In the resulting dispute the company may be ordered to allow the minority to appear as the plaintiff on its behalf. This is a departure from the *proper plaintiff* principle and is used where the alleged wrongdoers have voting control which they use to stop the company itself from pursuing a remedy.

While a derivative action may be attractive in practice they are comparatively rare. Firstly, a minority shareholder may not come within an exception to *Foss v Harbottle*. It must be remembered that the minority are complaining of oppression by the majority. However, this in itself may not be enough. In *Smith v Croft (No. 2) Ltd* (1988) wrongdoers had voting

The procedure adopted is for the minority shareholders to make out a prima facie case that the company is entitled to the relief sought and that the action comes within a recognized exception to Foss v Harbottle (Prudential Assurance Co. Ltd v Newman Industries Ltd (No. 2) (1982) and Order 15, rule 12 A, Rules of the Supreme Court).

control in company meetings but of the remaining independent votes the plaintiffs had only a minority. Knox J said that of the minority right to a derivative action:

> Is the plaintiff being improperly prevented from bringing these proceedings on behalf of the company? If it is an expression of the corporate will of the company by an appropriate independent organ that is preventing the plaintiff from prosecuting the action he is not improperly but properly prevented and so the answer to the question is no. The appropriate independent organ will vary according to the company concerned and the identity of the defendants who will in most cases be disqualified from participating by voting in expressing the corporate will.

This requirement of Knox J, that the majority within the minority has to be considered, is an addition to the normal evidential burden that minority shareholders must discharge.

Knox J then continued to say that the independent shareholders did constitute an *independent organ* and as a majority of them did not wish to take action the minority of the independent organ could not mount it themselves.

Secondly, a derivative action is a discretional procedure subject to the maxims of equity. For example a plaintiff must have been at all times untainted with any misconduct – having, as it is termed, clean hands (*Towers v African Tug Co.* (1904)).

Thirdly, a minority shareholder while suffering a personal loss still has to take action not for himself but for the benefit of the company as a whole. Any award that is made must go not to the minority but to the company. Therefore, a minority shareholder will only obtain, on a successful action, an indirect benefit.

Fourthly, a derivative action is not possible if a better alternative remedy is available such as ordering the winding up of the company. But if a shareholder properly brings an action then he may expect to be indemnified for legal costs and other associated expenses. To obtain these costs and expenses a Wallersteiner order may be requested (*Wallersteiner v Moir (No. 2)* (1975)) and may be granted provided that the action does not appear unlikely to be successful (*Smith & Croft (No. 2)* (1986)).

Also it should be noted that in a derivative action a plaintiff cannot have a larger right to relief than the company would have if it was taking the action itself (*Burland v Earle* (1902)). Should the company go into liquidation then a derivative action will no longer be possible as any action felt necessary will be for the liquidator to investigate (*Fargo Ltd v Godfroy* (1986)).

Representative

Where a minority shareholder has suffered a personal loss in addition to a loss suffered by the company itself, the shareholder may take action on behalf of both himself and other shareholders. Should the action succeed then the plaintiff will ask for a declaration that improper conduct was established. This will enable each shareholder injured to be able to claim without their having to again prove improper conduct.

Access to Justice, the Final Report to the Lord Chancellor on the Civil Justice System in England and Wales (July, 1996).

The Law Commission – shareholder actions

The Law Commission in its report on Shareholder Remedies (published in 1997) said that remedies should be made as efficient and effective as possible. They put considerable faith in the proposals contained in the Woolf Report (1996). The Law Commission also felt that any enlargement of shareholder derivative actions be treated with caution. However, while an entirely new derivative action was not supported the Law Commission recommended 'that there should be new derivative procedure with more modern, flexible and accessible criteria for determining whether a shareholder can pursue the action.' The area of this *derivative procedure* would be:

> ... that the new procedure should only be available if the cause of action arises as a result of an actual or threatened act or omission involving (a) negligence, default, breach of duty or breach of trust by a director of the company, or (b) a director putting himself in a position where his personal interests conflict with his duties to the company. The cause of action may be against the director or another person (or both). We also recommend that, for these purposes, director should include a shadow director.

The Law Commission went on further to recommend that this derivative action be available only to shareholders of the company.

Unfairly prejudicial conduct under s. 459

As an alternative to the common law, a shareholder may petition that the affairs of the company:

a) are being or have been conducted in a manner which is unfairly prejudicial to the interest of the shareholders generally or some shareholders in particular, including at least himself; or,

b) that any actual, or proposed, act or omission of the company (including an act or omission on its behalf) is or would be prejudicial (s. 459 (1)).

Only a petitioner's interests as a shareholder are protected – not interests in another capacity. In *Elder v Elder & Watson Ltd* (1952) the petitioners had been dismissed from their directorships as well as from their positions of employment (company secretary and manager respectively). Their claims failed because the injury caused to them had been done in their capacity as company officers and employees, not as shareholders.

However, interests may not be restricted to just rights given by the company's constitution. Indeed the term *unfairly* conjures up the use of equitable discretion (*Re A Company* (1986)) in a similar manner when dealing with a winding-up petition under the just and equitable ground. But strictly the provisions ought to be construed on their own merit and not be influenced by 'just and equitable' considerations that are a throw-back to the predecessor provision (CA 1948, s. 210) although all cases successful under section 210 would still be successful under section 459.

No statutory definition is given as to what unfairly prejudicial conduct equals. But the test to be applied is an objective one:

> ... (would) a reasonable bystander observing the consequences of their conduct regard it as having unfairly prejudiced the petitioner's interest. (*Slade J, Re Bovey Hotel Ventures Ltd* (1981))

To illustrate the use of s. 459 the following relatively modern examples are provided:

The original wording of s. 459 (1), CA 1985 was 'unfairly prejudicial to the interests of some part of the members'. This has been amended to 'unfairly prejudicial to the interests of the members generally or of some part of its members' (Schedule 9, paragraph 11 (a), CA 1989).

1 *Unfairly prejudicial in company affairs*

Re A Company (No 00789 of 1987) (1990)

A petitioner alleged a number of irregularities including holding EGMs without giving proper notice. At these meetings new shares had purportedly been created. The petitioner had himself subscribed for some of these shares and had bought more from other shareholders.

Held: The shares had been improperly created in a manner that was unfairly prejudicial to the interests of the petitioner, i.e. he had paid money for shares that did not exist.

---

2 *Unfairly prejudicial to legitimate expectations*

Re Sam Weller & Sons Ltd (1990)

The petitioners, holding 42.5 per cent of the shares in a family business, complained that the company despite making large profits had consistently for 37 years paid low dividends (e.g. in 1985 its net profits had been £36,000 but only £2,520 was paid in dividends). The company was controlled by the petitioner's uncle, Sam Weller, who, with his sons, received generous directors' fees and an increase in the capital value of their shareholding.

Held: Unfair conduct was held to exist. While the controlling shareholder incurred a greater prejudice than the minority (he had a greater proportion of shares) shareholders may have different interests even if their shareholder rights are the same:

> As their (minority shareholders) only income from the company is by way of dividend, their interests may be not only prejudiced by the policy of low dividend payments, but unfairly prejudiced. (Gibson J)

Also:

Re Blue Arrow plc (1987)

The petitioner over a 26-year period built a business up and then transferred it to the company for 45 per cent of the shares. She became an executive director and president. Subsequently she withdrew from active management and spent long periods abroad. The company was later floated, adopting articles more appropriate to a public company. While the petitioner continued as a director and president her holding was reduced to 2.1 per cent of the shares. On announcing, after she had given up her directorship, that she wanted active involvement in the company the directors sought to remove her from the position of president. They proposed that the articles should be altered so that the board by a majority could remove the president from office. The petitioner alleged that under s. 459 the affairs of the company were being conducted in a manner unfairly prejudicial to her, in that she had a legitimate expectation to participate in the affairs of the company and contrary to this expectation the proposed alteration to the articles would result in her exclusion. She therefore asked for a restraining order preventing the company from voting on a special resolution at an AGM to alter the articles.

Held: The petition must fail. Her right to be president was a personal right and could therefore be altered by special resolution. As investors in the company were entitled to assume that the company was contained in the articles and the Companies Acts there was no basis for finding that the petitioner had a legitimate expectation that the articles would not be altered to allow for a different method of terminating her presidency.

With public companies the court is generally very unwilling to place reliance in agreements or understanding that are not put into a document available to other shareholders. However, they may be more willing to do so with a small or modest size private company (*Re Carrington Viyella plc* (1983)). In *Re Harrison, Saul D & Sons plc* (1994), Hoffman LJ said that in relation to identifying legitimate expectations the starting point was the contractual terms which govern the relationships of shareholders with the company and each other. These terms are contained in the articles. He then went on to say that even if the articles were adhered to, unfairly prejudicial conduct could still arise:

> ... the personal relationship between a shareholder and those who control the company may entitle him to say that it would in certain circumstances be unfair for them to exercise a power conferred by the articles upon the board or the company in general meeting. I have in the past ventured to borrow from public law the term 'legitimate expectations' to describe the correlative 'right' in the shareholder to which such a relationship may give rise. It often arises out of a fundamental understanding between the shareholders which formed the basis of their association but was not put into contractual form, such as an assumption that each of the parties who have ventured his capital will also participate in the management of the company and receive the return on his investment in the form of salary rather than dividend.

3 *Unfairly prejudicial in company management*

Re Macro (Ipswich) Ltd (1994)

T was sole director and majority shareholder of two property leasing companies. Petitioners claimed mismanagement by T caused by: being abroad during winter periods; in the period 1930s–1987 he wasted money on building repairs and let property at poor rents; in the period 1970–1988 he received commissions from builders that he did not account for; also he left management in the hands of an inexperienced person.

Held: The mismanagement was serious and amounted to unfairly prejudicial conduct. T was ordered to purchase the petitioner's shares.

In practice it may be exceedingly difficult to distinguish between cases where a court was willing to find mismanagement present and cases where it refused to do so. In *Re Macro (Ipswich) Ltd* (1994). Arden J made the following comments:

> With respect to alleged mismanagement, the court does not interfere in questions of commercial judgement, such as would arise here if (for example) it were alleged that the companies should invest in commercial properties rather than residential properties. However, in cases where what is shown is mismanagement, rather than a difference of opinion on the desirability of particular commercial decisions, and the mismanagement is sufficiently serious to justify the intervention by the court, a remedy is available under s. 459.

An inference of unfairly prejudicial mismanagement may be based on Slade J's observation in *Re Noble R.A. & Son (Clothing) Ltd* (1983):

> ... a member of a company will be able to bring himself within the section if he can show that the value of his shareholding in the company has been seriously diminished or at least seriously jeopardized by reason of a course of conduct on the part of those persons who do have de facto control of the company, which was unfair to the member concerned.

However, the courts tend to work on the premise that shareholders on acquiring shares must accept the risk that poor management may occur and that this is very likely to be reflected in the share price. The courts do not want to set themselves up as being the arbitrator of what is and what is not good management practice. Therefore, a plea of bad management must be backed up by evidence of specific breaches of duty by directors (*Re Elgindata* (1991)).

When operating section 459 a court must be wary of the provision being misused by a petitioner. In *Re BSB Holdings Ltd* (1993) Arben J noted that unless carefully controlled section 459 could be used as a vehicle for oppression caused by unwarranted threats.

Review question

Discuss the meaning of the concept *unfair prejudice* within s. 459.

Judicial orders

In a successful action under s. 459 a court may not bother with s. 461 but grant an immediate winding up order (Re Full Cup International Trading Ltd (1995)).

On finding that a minority has been subjected to unfairly prejudicial conduct by the majority, the court has absolute discretion to make any order it thinks fit (s. 461 (1)). The idemized remedies provided in section 461 (2) do not take away the court's power to award any other remedy that it thinks appropriate.

While overwhelmingly orders are made against controlling shareholders, in exceptional circumstances an order may be made against someone who is not a shareholder or who was not involved in the unfairly prejudicial conduct that took place:

Supreme Travels Ltd v Little Olympian Each-Ways Ltd and Others (1994)

ST was a preference shareholder in LOEW and presented a petition alleging that LOEW directors had sold the company's business and goodwill to Owners Abroad Group plc, a company that they (the directors) controlled, for a gross undervaluation. The result was that LOEW was now a non-trading shell company. Therefore, the petitioners sought to include OAG as additional respondent even though it had never been a shareholder or director in LOEW; nor had it been accused of any wrong doing.

Held: Relief could be granted against a non-shareholder of the company. However, a non-shareholder could not be included as a respondent when it was likely that the relief sought against the non-shareholder was so remote as to equal an abuse of process. This was such a case and in consequence OAG would not be included as an additional respondent

The idemized judicial orders are (s. 461 (2)):

a) *Regulate the conduct of the company's affairs in the future*:

Re H R Harmer Ltd (1959)

H had voting control and acted as chairman with his two sons as directors. H's sons, as minority shareholders, petitioned alleging oppression in that H regularly ignored the board and made the business decisions himself.

Held (Court of Appeal): The minority shareholders deserved relief. The Court approved Roxborough J's order that H be removed from the board and appointed life president without any rights, duties or powers. He was also ordered not be involved with the company's affairs in the future unless asked to do so by the board.

This case was decided under s. 210, CA 1948 which required a course of oppressive conduct and circumstances that would enable a winding up order to be made on just and equitable grounds. However, a court using s. 461 may be similarly innovative in respect to the order it wishes to make.

b) *A restraining order to stop the Company from doing, or repeating, an act complained of by the repetitioner*
A typical injunction would be to stop a company from altering its constitution in such a manner that would be unfairly prejudicial to minority shareholders.
c) *Authorize civil proceedings to be brought in the name and on behalf of the company by such persons as the court recognizes and on such terms as it may direct*
This remedy, on which there is no case law, is akin to a statutory derivative action. It will, for example, enable a minority shareholder to take action, in the company name, against a director. This will be particularly useful if the shareholder cannot petition in one of the existing exceptions to the rule in *Foss v Harbottle*.
d) *Order the purchase of shares of any shareholder of the company by other shareholders or by the company itself*
This is the commonest order that the court makes. It is often the most satisfactory outcome as the minority shareholder will be able to unlock his capital from the

An order for share purchase

is most commonly made against a majority shareholder whereby he must buy out the shareholding of the minority. Uncommonly, a court, to dispense justice, can make an order whereby a majority shareholder must sell his shares to minority shareholders (Re Brenfield Squash Racquets Club Ltd (1996)).

business and, if he wishes, make a clean start elsewhere. However, what he will be acutely interested in is how much he will get for his shares. This will be dependent on the following considerations:

i) *the date of the share valuation*

There are contrasting dicta for when shares have to be valued. In *Re D.R. Chemicals Ltd* (1989) valuation at the date the order was made was put forward; whereas in *Scottish Co-operative Wholesale Society Ltd v Meyer* (1959) the valuation was to be taken on the date of the petition. However, *Re Cumana Ltd* (1986) provides the better view in that the valuation date is left to the discretion of the trial judge (where admittedly it has always resided!).

Should evidence show that the majority deliberately depressed the value of the shares then the valuation when made ought to take this into account (*Scottish Co-operative Wholesale Society Ltd v Meyer* (1959), especially if the deliberate driving down of the share price was in contemplation of a possible share purchase order being made by the court (*Re Cumana Ltd* (1986)).

ii) *the basis of the valuation*

There are two alternatives here. Firstly, the valuation can be *pro rata*, or, secondly, a discount can be imposed in acknowledgement that with non-voting shares the market may value them less highly than controlling shares. Again there is no firm position. In *Re Bird Precision Bellows* (1986) it was held that the valuation of minority shares in a small quasi-partnership should be on a *pro-rata* basis. But here the petitioner had been the sufferer of considerable unfairly prejudicial conduct. Usually, a discounted purchase is felt to be fair especially if the petitioner was not a founder shareholder but had himself acquired his shares at a discount on the basis that they were minority shares. Also any culpable conduct on the petitioner's part may make a court more inclined to order a discounted purchase.

iii) *where a method for valuation is given in the articles*

If a method of valuation is given in the articles then, unless the petitioner can show that it is unfair or is being manipulated in an unfair manner, a court can be expected to order that it be followed (*Re Castleburn* (1990)).

The Law Commission – sections 459–461

The Law Commission in their 1997 report on Shareholder Remedies said that the cost effectiveness of the personal remedy for unsatisfactory conduct of a company's business could be seriously questioned. They found that 97 per cent of s. 459 petitions filed at the High Court in London in 1997 related to private companies with 93 per cent of then being made in respect to companies with ten or fewer shareholders. Here it was felt that proceedings under s. 459 were 'costly and cumbersome' with trials 'often lasting weeksrather than days'.

With the above finding in mind and with a finding that petitioners of companies with five or fewer shareholders most commonly allege that they have been excluded from management, the Law Commission proposed in their Consultation Paper that an exist article be used so that if a shareholder–company relationship breaks from them a quick and cheap alternative to a s. 459 action would be available. This would be a 'divorce settlement' inserted in the articles. However, it was subsequently rejected in the report in preference to new statutory presumptions that would be incorporated into sections 459–461. The recommendation is:

... that there should be legislative provision for presumptions in proceedings under section 459–461 that, in certain circumstances, (a) where a shareholder has been excluded from participation in the management of the company, the conduct will be presumed to be unfairly prejudicial by reason of the exclusion; and (b) if the presumption is not rebutted and the court is satisfied that it ought to order a buyout of the petitioner's shares, it should do so on a pro rata basis.

Department of Trade and Industry investigations

The Department of Trade and Industry (DTI) have been given sweeping powers to investigate companies. On occasions the decision may be entirely a legal or commercial one but on other occasions it can be the result of political sensitivity in regard to high profile disclosure of alleged corporate wrong doing.

Appointment of inspectors

1 *By application of shareholders or the company* (s. 431)

The DTI *may* appoint inspectors to investigate the affairs of a company on the application of not less than 200 shareholders or of shareholders holding not less than 10 per cent of the issued shares. If there is no share capital then applications must be made by 20 per cent of the members. In addition the company itself may apply to the DTI following the passing of an ordinary resolution.

With all applications under this section the Secretary of State has to receive supporting evidence showing that the applicant(s) have good reason for requiring the investigation. Also before making an appointment the Secretary of State may require the applicant(s) to provide security not exceeding £5,000 (this sum may be increased by statutory instrument). Any security taken will be used for part payment of the costs of the investigation.

The Secretary of State has discretion as to whether to make an appointment or not but provided that the decision is made in good faith then it cannot be challenged (*Norwest Holst Ltd v Department of Trade* (1978)).

2 *By order of the court (s. 432 (1))*

The Secretary of State *must* appoint inspectors if the court declares that the company's affairs should be investigated.

Circumstances motivating an appointment (s. 432 (2))

The Secretary of State is authorized to appoint inspectors on the application of any person if there appears to be conduct unfairly prejudicial to some shareholders of the company, or fraud, misfeasance or misconduct, or if shareholders are not receiving all reasonable information. Additionally, an appointment may be made where there is evidence that the company has been run to defraud creditors or to prejudice a minority, or if the company has a fraudulent or unlawful purpose.

Where inspectors are appointed, it tends to be under section 432 (2). The practice is that if there is good reason for the DTI to believe that wrongdoing is taking place then it will use the powers contained in section 447 to obtain production of company documents and to

If it is felt necessary, inspectors are authorized to investigate the affairs of other companies related to the company which is the subject of the investigation (s. 433).

apply to a Justice of the Peace for a search warrant if there are reasonable grounds to believe that there are documents on the premises which have been requested but not produced (s. 448). The power conferred in section 447 includes a right to take copies of any document produced and to require present or past company officers or employees to provide an explanation on any company document that comes into the possession of the DTI (s. 447 (5)). Also the Secretary of State may authorize 'any other competent person', e.g. a solicitor or accountant, to exercise on his behalf his power to require production of documents. A person so appointed will report directly to the Secretary of State (s. 447 (3)).

Should documents be requested but not be produced, or if persons refuse, on being asked, to provide explanations then a criminal offence will have been committed (s. 447 (6)).

The notice given for production of documents must not be 'unreasonable'.

However, those accused of failing to produce documents may plead benefit of a statutory defence if it is established that they were not in possession or control of the documents in question and that it was therefore not reasonably practicable to comply with the requirement that documents be produced (s. 447 (7)).

From an examination of the documents provided and any explanations concerning them the DTI can make an informed decision whether or not to proceed to a full investigation. If the decision is not to have an investigation then as no publicity should have been given to the call for documents the company's reputation would not have been harmed.

Power to investigate company ownership (s. 442)

Where it appears that there is good reason to do so the DTI has the power to appoint an inspector to investigate the ownership of a company and to try to find out who is or has been interested financially in its shares (s. 442 (1)). Where the DTI is requested by at least 200 shareholders or shareholders holding 10 per cent or more of the issued share capital (or if there is no share capital by at least 20 per cent of the members) that an investigation into ownership is made then the DTI *must* appoint inspectors to carry this out (ss. 442 (3), 431 (2)).

If the inspector experiences difficulty in finding out relevant information on any shares then the Secretary of State may place restrictions on them such as the suspension of voting rights and any agreement to transfer them will be void unless a court or the Secretary of State agree to it (ss. 445, 454).

Prohibition on directors dealing in share options (s. 323)

A director is prohibited from dealing in options on the shares or debentures of his company, or those of its holding company, or its subsidiary company if the shares or debentures are listed on any stock exchange anywhere (s. 323). Directors of *all* companies are also requested to notify the company of their interest, and that of any persons connected with him, e.g. spouses and children, in shares or debentures of the company (ss. 324, 328). If it is suspected that undisclosed dealings in company securities have taken place that contravene these provisions then the DTI *may* appoint an inspector to investigate the matter with a view to civil or criminal proceedings being instigated (s. 446).

As they are not meant to act in a legal capacity it can be said that the inspectors act in an administrative one.

Status of the examination and report

While inspectors are not adopting a judicial or quasi-judicial role they must act *fairly* (*Re Pergamon Press Ltd* (1971)). However, to make the process under Section 459 effective certain aspects of natural justice have been dispensed with. The procedure used is a secret one in that there is no right of public attendance or for witnesses to know what others have said about them in evidence. Also there is no right to present your side of the case to the inspector. You need to be called to give evidence and then only answer the questions asked.

Responses to questions put under oath by inspectors may be used in evidence against that person (s. 434 (5)) (*London & County Securities Ltd v Nicholson* (1980)). It is no excuse to refuse to answer questions for fear of self-incrimination (*Re London United Investments plc* (1992)). The obstruction of an inspector's investigation, such as by refusal to cooperate, may be treated as a contempt of court (s. 436).

An inspector's report is not, apart from the Company Director Disqualification Act 1986, admissible as fact (*Savings and Investment Bank Ltd v Gasco Investments (Netherlands) BV* (1984)), but it may be used in court to convey the inspector's opinion (s. 441). There is no right of appeal against an inspector's findings (*Re Pergamon Press Ltd* (1971)).

Response of the DTI to an inspector's report

An inspector may submit interim reports either when he feels that he ought to do so or if called upon to do so. If from an interim report it appears that a criminal offence has been committed then an investigation may be suspended or ended with the matter being passed to the relevant prosecuting body (s. 437). Where a final report is presented the DTI may make, assuming that it does decide to act, the following responses:

1 Apply for an order under section 459 on the grounds that the company's affairs are or have been conducted in a manner which is unfairly prejudicial to the interest of all or some of its shareholders.
2 If it is believed that it is in the public interest then a winding-up petition under the just and equitable ground may be presented (s. 124A, Insolvency Act 1986). A shareholder may use an inspector's report to support his own petition for winding up again using the just and equitable ground (s. 122 (1) (g); *Re St Piran* (1981)).

> Responses 1 and 2 may be taken jointly.

3 Bring civil proceedings in the name of the company. Action will only be taken if it appears that the public interest considerations warrant it (s. 438 (1)). Legal costs that arise from the proceedings will be paid by the DTI (s. 438 (2)).
4 Apply for an order for the disqualification of a director (Company Director Disqualification Act 1986, s. 8).
5 If it is felt necessary a copy of the report may be sent to the company's registered office. Copies may also be provided to any shareholder who requests one as well as to those referred to in the report. Auditors may have their own copies (s. 437 (3)). If the inspector was appointed under section 432 then the court is to receive a copy (s. 437 (2)).
6 The report may be placed in the public arena through it being published (s. 437 (3)).
7 As with interim reports the DTI can arrange for criminal proceedings to be taken against anyone believed guilty of a criminal offence.

Inspectors and confidentiality – a postscript

In *Thomas and Another v Maxwell etc* (1999), Sir Robert Scott VC said that inspectors owed to those from whom they had obtained information or documents no duty that might inhibit them in their use. Also a person under examination could not be forced to sign a wide-ranging confidentiality undertaking not to disclose information put to him in the course of questioning. More worryingly for inspectors was a finding that excessive questioning of an unrepresented person could be unfair and oppressive.

> This decision, together with the implementation of the Human Rights Act, may well seriously affect inspectors' compulsive inquisitorial powers.

Chapter summary

- Companies operate on a majority rule basis whereby majority shareholders are able to pass their resolutions and block those of minority shareholders. In consequence when a wrong is done against the company then it is for the company not a shareholder to take legal action against the wrong doer – this is known as the principle in *Foss v Harbottle*.
- In most instances the wrong doers are directors who are also controlling shareholders. However, unauthorized acts (but not at common law illegal ones – but note intervention of statute) can be ratified. While a director as a fiduciary is not able to vote on an issue in which he is personally interested, he is able to do so in his personal capacity as a shareholder.
- There are several grounds to justify the rule in *Foss v Harbottle*: an inevitable consequence of the company being a separate legal entity; maintenance of majority control; prevention of multiple and frivolous legal actions.
- Because of the abuse by the majority of their dominant position, minority protection at common law was developed whereby in certain circumstances exceptions to *Foss v Harbottle* will be judicially recognized. Exceptions are where the company: commits an illegal act; acts on an improperly passed resolution; infringes the individual rights of a shareholder, also where fraud is perpetrated on the minority.
- Fraud on the minority has a special non-criminal meaning. Examples are: discreditable conduct carried out by those in control for their own advantage; selling assets at an over value to the company or having the company sell assets at an under value; an unfair alteration of the company's constitution; a negligent act that enriches the majority.
- Minority shareholders have a few legal actions that they may take: personal; derivative; representative; and a combination of them.
- Because of dissatisfaction with the common law exceptions to *Foss v Harbottle*, statute law has intervened to offer additional protection to minority shareholders. Section 459 is based upon a concept of unfairly prejudicial conduct. Examples of successful actions are: the internal operation of the company; injury to a legitimate expectation; mismanagement.
- The court has considerable powers when attempting to rectify unfairly prejudicial conduct. These are under s. 461: regulation of the company's future affairs; a restraining order; authorization of civil proceedings in the name of the company; and an order that minority shares be acquired (or that the majority sell their shares to the minority).
- The DTI may appoint inspectors to investigate a company but where a court orders the appointment then inspectors must be appointed. Unfairly prejudicial conduct, fraud, misfeasance, misconduct or shareholders not receiving information all justify an investigation (s. 432).
- Inspectors may also look into company ownership (s. 442) and directors dealing in share options (s. 323).
- Inspectors are given extensive powers to request documents, question company officers and employees etc. Witnesses cannot plead fear of self-incrimination when questioned.

- On receipt of a final report the DTI have a number of responses: apply for a court order under s. 459; petition for winding-up order on just and equitable grounds; take civil proceedings; seek a directors' disqualification order; send copies of the report to interested parties; and publish the report.

Discussion questions

1 Discuss how common law and statute allow a minority shareholder to bring a legal action to rectify a perceived wrong.
2 Discuss, in relation to minority protection, what is meant by the requirement in the interests of the company as a whole.

Case study exercise

Homer owns 10 per cent of the issued shares in Odyssey Holidays Limited (OHL). The two directors of the company, who have a somewhat eccentric style of management, are Hector Paris and his partner Helen Troy who each own 45 per cent of the issued shares. Homer understands that Paris and Troy intend to merge OHL with a more profitable and growing company that the two directors wholly own. If this plan goes ahead Homer's shareholding will be reduced to 3 per cent of the merged business. Homer is financially dependent on the dividends he gets from OHL but is concerned that future dividends may be much less.

Advise Homer of his legal position.

Further reading

The True Spirit of Foss v Harbottle, C. Baxter (1987), NILQ, 5.
The Relative Nature of a Shareholder's Right to Enforce the Company Contract, R.R. Drury (1986), CLJ, 219.
Statutory Protection of Minority Shareholders: Section 459 of the Companies Act 1985, S. Griffin (1992), Co. Law, 83.
Minority Shareholders Remedies: A Comparative View, L. Griggs and J.P. Lowry (1994), JBL, 463.
Section 459 of the Companies Act 1985 – A Code of Conduct for the Quasi-partnership? B. Hannigan (1988), LMCQ, 60.
The Theory of the Firm: Minority Shareholder Oppression: Sections 459–461 of the Companies Act 1985, D.D. Prentice (1988), OJLS, 55.
Contracting Out of Company Law: Sections 459 of the Companies Act 1985 and the Role of the Court, C.A. Riley (1992), MLR, 782.
Minority Shareholders: Another Nail in the Coffin, M. Stamp (1988), Co. Law, 34.
The Theory and Policy of Shareholders' Actions In Tort, M.J. Sterling (1987), MLR, 468.
Restating the Scope of The Derivative Action, G.R. Sullivan (1985), CLJ, 236.
Derivative Actions and Foss v Harbottle, Lord Wedderburn (1981), MLR, 202.

Voting Nights: A Comparative Review, P.G. Xuereb (1987), Co. Law, 16.
Remedies for Abuse of Majority Power, P.G. Xuereb (1986), Co. Law, 53.
The Limitation on the Exercise of Majority Power, P.G. Xuereb (1985), Co. Law, 199.
See also the Chesterman and Prentice articles under Further Reading in Chapter 18, Winding Up.

15 Auditors

Introduction

At each general meeting all companies must appoint one or more auditors. Failure to do so will result in the appointment being made by the Department of Trade and Industry. The auditor, who must be a member of a recognized body of accountants, has to examine the accounts in order to find and report the true financial position of the company. To help accomplish this task an auditor has the right of free access to the company's books as well as the right to ask the company's officers for any information or explanation he believes necessary. While for some purposes an auditor is a company officer he is not on the same level as a director or the company secretary. Therefore he is not a member of the company's management team so that his independence is not compromised.

The purpose of an audit is primarily to enable shareholders to monitor the directors' stewardship of the company as well as to give creditors an opportunity to check that the company's position has not deteriorated. Also it is common for anyone considering becoming a shareholder to refer to the latest audited accounts and audit report.

The word audit derives from the Latin to hear. Historically, a mediaeval Lord would entrust his estate to a steward with an auditor giving his lordship regular, oral accounts of the state of his estate and the performance of his steward.

Objectives

The purpose of this chapter is to acquaint students with the appointment requirements of auditors and more importantly to make them appreciate the duties expected of auditors and the requisite level of skill demanded of them.

Key concepts

- Appointment criteria
- Significance of the auditor's report
- Provision of care and skill
- Professional negligence under Hedley Byrne v Heller & Partners Ltd (1963).

Small companies: audit exemptions

The Department of Trade and Industry has accepted that the full rigour of the auditing obligations under the Companies Act would be in many instances prohibitively expensive to moderately sized companies. Therefore, partial or full exemption is available.

Abbreviated accounts

Abbreviated accounts do not apply to: a public company; one connected to banking or insurance; or to an authorized person under the Financial Service Act 1986.

This partial exemption is available to small or medium sized companies (Sch 8). Classification is based on satisfying two from the following three factors:

Factor	Small	Medium
Turnover not in excess of	£2.8m	£11.2m
Balance sheet not in excess of	£1.4m	£ 5.6m
Average number of employees not in excess of	50	250

Total exemption from audit

To be eligible for not having to appoint auditors the company must not exceed: a turnover of £350,000; a balance sheet total of £1.4 million; and shareholders holding at least 10 per cent in nominal value of the issued share capital must not have deposited written notice at the company's registered office requesting an audit (s. 249A).

Dormant companies

A dormant company need not appoint auditors provided that it is classed as a small private company not engaged in banking, insurance or financial services (s. 220).

Appointment

First auditors may be appointed by the directors at any time before the first annual general meeting (AGM). They will hold office until the close of a general meeting at which accounts are laid. Should the directors not make an appointment then the company in a general meeting may do so (s. 385).

If no appointment or reappointment is made at a general meeting where accounts were laid then the company must notify the Secretary of State within 1 week who will then make an appointment (s. 387).

Subsequent auditors are appointed by ordinary resolution at each AGM where accounts are laid. They will hold office from the end of the meeting to the end of the next meeting where accounts are laid but of course they may be reappointed (s. 385).

Casual vacancies may be filled by either the directors or the company by an ordinary resolution in a general meeting making an appointment. They will hold office until the end of the next meeting where accounts are laid (s. 388).

Where a private company has passed an elective resolution to dispense with laying accounts then the following will apply: first auditors may be appointed within 28 days after the first annual accounts are sent to members (s. 385A); and if the company has not elected to dispense with the annual appointment of auditors then it must still hold an AGM to reappoint the auditor(s) (again such a meeting must be held within 28 days of sending accounts to members) (s. 386).

Qualification

An individual or a partnership may be appointed as a company auditor.

An auditor must be a member of a recognized supervisory body and be eligible for appointment under the rules of that body (CA 1989, s. 25). As a consequence of the Eighth EC Company Law Directive (1984), Chartered Accounting bodies for England and Wales, Scotland or Ireland have assumed a supervisory role in respect to any of their members who wishes to undertake auditing work thus making them 'registered auditors'. Supervision includes maintaining appropriate professional standards, investigating complaints against members and taking action if a complaint is upheld.

To increase and maintain standards the Department of Trade and Industry (DTI) can scrutinize examinations that have to be taken and will not allow the designation 'registered auditor' to be used until at least three years' practical training has been completed with a substantial part being specifically spent on company audit work. Should an audit be carried out by an ineligible person then the DTI may ask for a second audit or, alternatively, commission a report by a qualified auditor on whether a second audit is needed.

Those who are ineligible for appointment

Even if they are theoretically qualified for appointment the following are ineligible on the grounds that they lack independence (CA 1989, s. 27):

a) an officer or employee of the company;
b) a partner or employee of such a person, or a partnership of which such a person is a partner;
c) a person who is 'connected' either personally or by association to the company or any associated undertaking.

Any ineligibility under (a) or (b) also relates to any associated undertaking of the company.

Connection would include where a company to be audited was owned or controlled by the auditor's family, or where an auditor has a financial stake in the audited company. *Association* is based on close relationship, e.g. an auditor's spouse or young children; *associated undertaking* is a parent or subsidiary of the company to be audited.

Remuneration (s. 390A)

Whoever makes the appointment will fix the level of payment but normally this is delegated to the directors. However, if the Secretary of State made the appointment then he will fix payment (s. 390A).

Removal from office

A company may by ordinary resolution at any time remove an auditor from office, notwithstanding anything in any agreement between it and him. The registrar must be notified within 14 days of the resolution being passed with the company and every officer being liable if such notice is not given (s. 391). An auditor who has been removed may attend a meeting where his term of office would have expired, or a meeting which will fill his vacancy, and shall be allowed to speak as a former auditor. In addition he is to receive the same information relating to his removal as is given to shareholders and may make written representations to the company requesting that copies of that information to be sent to members (s. 391, s. 91A).

For a resolution removing an auditor, either before his term of office expires or appointing as auditor a person other than a retiring auditor, special notice is required (s. 391A).

Resignation of an auditor

An auditor may resign his appointment by sending written notice to the company's registered office (s. 392). Resignation is invalid unless it is accompanied by a statutory statement confirming that there are no circumstances connected with his resignation which he feels ought to be drawn to the attention of shareholders or creditors of the company (s. 394). If such circumstances exist then the statement must disclose them and the company has 14 days to send a copy of the statutory statement to all those entitled to a copy of the accounts or, alternatively, apply to the court for permission not to circulate the statement on grounds that it is, for example, defamatory.

If the auditor's notice of resignation is accompanied by a statement containing circumstances which he considers ought to be brought to the attention of members or creditors of the company then the auditor has the following rights:

a) to require the directors to call an extraordinary general meeting to receive and consider his explanation of those resignation circumstances; and
b) to request the company to circulate before the EGM a statement of the resignation circumstances, or before any general meeting at which his term of office would otherwise have expired or at which it is intended to fill the vacancy caused by his resignation (s. 392A).

Review question

a) Can the directors remove an auditor from his appointment or must they wait until his term of office expires?
b) What rights on vacating office does an auditor have?

Auditor's report

With exempted small companies an auditor will only have to say whether in his opinion the annual accounts have been properly prepared in accordance with the small company provisions (s. 235).

An auditor, during his term of office, is under a statutory duty to report to members on accounts presented to the company (s. 235). The report has to be presented at the general meeting where accounts are to be laid (s. 241) as well as being sent to every member, debenture holder and anyone else entitled to receive notice of the general meeting (s. 238). In practice an auditor will deliver his report to the company secretary who will ensure that it is distributed.

The importance of the report is that the auditor must state whether in his opinion the accounts were properly prepared and give a true and fair view of: the balance sheet, the profit and loss account and (if relevant) group accounts (s. 235). If the accounts are qualified then the report must say whether they cast doubt on the legality of any dividend proposed in the directors' report. Also an auditor must consider consistency between their report and any statement or opinions made in the directors' report. If inconsistency is detected then they must state this in the audit report (s. 235). Finally, should the accounts not disclose certain matters relating to directors (fees, loans, pension provisions, compensation for loss of office and any sum paid to third parties in respect to directors' services) then these matters must be given in the auditor's report (s. 232 and Sch 6).

Wider duties

An auditor has a duty to carry out investigations so that he will be in a position to say:

a) whether the company is keeping proper accounting records; and
b) whether the accounts for the financial year in question agree with the accounting records.
A positive outcome from his investigations will enable the auditor to have confidence in the financial information given to him. Should the investigations reveal any reservations on these matters then their subsequent report needs to disclose it. However, wider duties do not entail giving business advice to the company on how to conduct its affairs (*Re London General Bank (No. 2) (1895)*).

Auditor's rights

To enable an auditor to perform his duties the following rights are given:

a) to have access at all times to the books, accounts and other relevant documents of the company (s. 389A);
b) to require from any company officer such information and explanation they believe is necessary (s. 389A). It is a criminal offence for any company officer to knowingly or recklessly make a statement which is misleading, false or deceptive to a material degree (s. 389A);
c) to receive notice of general meetings and to be able to attend them with the right to address it on any matter of company business which is relevant to them (s. 390);
d) to receive, in respect to private companies, copies of written resolutions and:
   i) if the company is professionally affected, to require the company to call a general (or class) meeting in order to consider them; or
   ii) alternatively to say that a resolution does not affect them or that while it does, a general (or class) meeting is unnecessary.

If the company is in dispute with the auditor and it is not established that the auditor's appointment will continue whatever the outcome of the dispute then a court may not order the company to produce its financial records to the auditor (Cuff v London & County Land Co. (1912)).

While the judicial comments in the Kingston Cotton Mill Co. are informative the circumstances are no longer correct – see Westminster Road Construction and Engineering Co. Ltd.

Standard of care skill

General

Periodically the courts have commented on the standards expected:

Re Kingston Cotton Mill Co. (No. 2) (1896)

As a result of stock in trade being overvalued for several years, directors were able to pay dividends out of capital. It had been the practice of the auditors to rely on the certificate of the company manager regarding the valuation of stock and not to require the production of stock records.

Held: (Court of Appeal): The auditors would be excused liability.

In his judgement in *Re Kingston Cotton Mill Co. (No. 2) (1896)* Lopes LJ said:

It is the duty of an auditor to bring to bear on the work he has to perform that skill, care, and caution which a reasonably competent, careful, and cautious auditor would use. What is reasonable skill, care, and caution must depend on the particular circumstances of each case. An auditor is not bound to be a detective, or to approach his work with suspicion, or with a foregone conclusion that something is wrong. He is a watchdog not a bloodhound. He is justified in believing hired servants of the company in whom the company places confidence. He is entitled to assume that they are honest.

Where circumstances are suspicious an auditor ought to investigate and it would be unwise merely to confine himself with checking the arithmetical accuracy of accounts presented to him but should, where he deems it necessary, check them against the actual books:

Leeds Estate Co. v Shepherd (1887)
The articles stated that directors were to receive their fees only if dividends exceeded 5 per cent. A manager prepared a deceptive balance sheet which enabled the directors to declare a dividend of over 5 per cent so that they could obtain their fees. The auditor ignored both the articles and the company books but accepted the manager's balance sheet certifying the accounts 'to be a true copy of those shown in the books of the company'. The dividends, it was later discovered, had been paid out of capital.

Held: The auditor was liable.

A later authoritative case on auditor's care and skill was:

Re City Equitable Fire Insurance Co. (1925)
Stockbrokers owed a company £250,000. Just before the end of the financial year they bought £200,000 Treasury Bills for £200,000 and credited them to the company so that the balance could be prepared showing not a debt owed of £250,000 but one of £50,000. Shortly after the balance sheet was published the stockbrokers sold the Treasury Bills and again the true debt owed to the company became £250,000. This fraudulent practice was arranged by the company chairman who was also the senior partner in the stockbroking firm. The ploy was carried out three years in a row and on each occasion the auditors had not made any query.

Held: The auditors were not liable for failing to detect the fraudulent arrangement. It was one item in a very large audit.

However, the standards owed by auditors have progressively increased in line generally with professional standards. In broad terms an auditor must exercise the degree of reasonable care and skill that his particular investigation merits. Above all he must be honest and only certify what he believes to be true after exercising reasonable care and skill (per Lindley LJ in *Re London General Bank* (No. 2) (1895)).

A much later case was:

> **Re Thomas Gerrard & Son (1968)**
> The managing director inflated company profits by including non-existent stock into the accounts resulting in over-generous dividends being declared and too much tax being paid. The auditors, noticing that invoices had been altered, had their suspicions but accepted the managing director's explanations and did not pursue the matter further.
>
> Held: The circumstances merited a fuller investigation. Therefore, the auditors were liable to the company for the cost of recovering from shareholders the excess dividends paid and for dividends and tax not recovered.

The most recent authoritative call for improvements in audit standards was made by the Cadbury Committee. In its Code published in December 1992 it called for the financial audit of companies to be tightened up but did not provide any detailed recommendations on how this was to be achieved.

Specific examples

1 When ascertaining the true financial position of the company an auditor needs to do more than verify the numerical accuracy of the accounts:

> He (the auditor) is not to be written off as a professional 'adder-upper and subtractor'. His task is to take care to see that errors are not made, be they errors of computation, or errors of omission or commission, or downright untruths. To perform this task properly he must come to it with an inquiring mind ... but suspecting that someone may have made a mistake somewhere and that a check must be made to ensure that there has been none. (Lord Denning in *Formento (Sterling Area) Ltd v Selsdon Fountain Pen Co. Ltd* (1958))

2 The company's bank balance and cash in hand need to be checked.
3 The company's securities need to be located and the auditor must ensure that they are placed in safety. It may not be good enough to rely on the company's stockbroker that they hold certain securities on behalf of the company – the auditor would be advised to see them for himself (*Re City Equitable Fire Insurance Co.* (1925)).
4 The auditor does not himself have to take stock but he does need to verify that the stock-take was done on a sound basis and ought for safety to stock-check the occasional item.

What would undoubtedly now be considered by a court is whether the auditor adhered to the Statements of Standard Accounting Practice and the Financial Reporting Standards. They set out what the profession regards as being the correct standard so that an auditor who keeps within these standards may escape censure whereas one who departs, without justification, from them may be found liable (see *Lloyd Cheyham & Co Ltd v Littlejohn Co* (1987)).

The Association of Chartered Certified Accountants have in their *Rules of Professional Conduct* the following guidance:

... members should carry out their professional work with *due skill, diligence* and *expe-*

In a *Financial Times* interview Lord Weinstock, a long-time managing director of GEC, sagely said of auditors: 'The idea that current auditors produce a "true and fair view" is either excessively bold or meaningless. Auditors can never know enough to give a true and fair view, but they can comment on a lack of financial controls, exaggerated profits or other possible abuses. They should make more limited and specific claims, and then take legal responsibility for their accuracy.' (*Financial Times*, 4.1.1997).

dition and with proper regard for the technical and professional standards expected of them as members.

Review question

A newly appointed non-executive director is disturbed at finding several things amiss with the financial record keeping of the company. Explain how the company auditor may be able to help.

To whom are the auditor's duties owed?

a) *The company*
   When companies commission financial reports there is clearly a contractual relationship between the auditor of the report and the company so that if the auditor provides misleading information or draws defective inferences from the figures etc. they can expect to be sued by the company for breach of contract.
b) *Third parties*
   The situation envisaged here is that a third party will not personally commission a financial report on a company but will examine a report commissioned by another and will rely upon it. If the third party suffers a financial loss because of the auditor's negligence can they sue the auditor for compensation? In *Hedley Byrne & Co. Ltd v Heller & Partners* (1963) the House of Lords departed from earlier precedents by holding that provided it could be found that a special relationship existed between the parties it was possible for a person to sue for having suffered a financial loss even though there is no contracted relationship between the parties.

For a plaintiff to succeed in a *Hedley Byrne* type action it must be shown that there was a *special relationship* between the parties. This will be achieved by establishing the following:

1 The defendant claimed to have a special skill and judgement.
2 The defendant knew that the plaintiff would be relying on them or, alternatively, the information or advice was given in circumstances such that a reasonable person if asked would acknowledge that they knew they were being relied upon.
3 The defendant, not under a contractual or fiduciary obligation to give the information or advice, chose to give it and did so without a disclaimer or clear qualification to show that they did not accept responsibility for the accuracy of it.
4 The plaintiff did in fact rely on the defendant's skill and judgement and in the circumstances it was reasonable for them to do so.
5 The information or advice was negligent and caused the identifiable plaintiff economic loss.

The minority judgement (Lords Reid and Morris) said that a duty of care in such a situation would only arise where the plaintiff had made it clear that they were seeking advice and indicated that they intended to act on it in a certain way, e.g. by investing in the company if the defendant considered the advice was positive. It is this influential minority view that paved the way for the development in later cases of the *Hedley Byrne* principle.

However, in order to limit the operation of the *special relationship* to manageable proportions a court may take into account wider commercial consideration as in:

Caparo Industries plc v Dickman (1990)

Dickman audited the accounts of company X. Caparo Industries had shares in company X and in reliance on Dickman's audit they acquired more shares and made a successful takeover of that company. Subsequently Caparo Industries said the accounts prepared by Dickman were inaccurate and that Dickman's negligence had caused them a financial loss. The first evidential hurdle was in establishing that Dickman owed them a duty of care.

The House of Lords held that auditors owe a very limited duty of care. The duty is owed solely to the company that employed them. Therefore, any third party relying on audited accounts cannot claim against the auditor if the accounts are negligently prepared as no duty will be owed to them.

In Caparo the House of Lords were anxious to limit the class of persons who were owed a duty otherwise, in the event of a negligent audit on a major company where many investors would be involved, the consequences could easily mean that auditing firms would be forced out of business through having to meet an avalanche of claims (with such potential liability insurers would either refuse to provide professional indemnity cover or only do so at prohibitive premium). In addition the House was influenced by the statutory purpose of audited accounts on companies. Lord Jauncey said:

> ... the purpose of annual accounts, so far as members (shareholders) are concerned, is to enable them to question the past management of the company, to exercise their voting rights ... and to influence future policy and management. Advice to individual members in relation to present or future investment in the company is not part of the statutory purpose of the preparation and distribution of the account.

When examining the conduct of people claiming to have relied upon the advisor's statement (e.g. auditors) an objective standard is to be used. In the circumstances it must have been reasonable for those persons to have relied on the statement and equally it must have been reasonable to expect the advisor to appreciate that their advice was likely to be relied on. From judgement in both *Hedley Byrne* and *Caparo* this appears to be the position, but if the plaintiff's reliance was unreasonable, such as where they follow the advice of a very junior audit clerk working in a firm of auditors, then it may mean that there is in fact no causation between the alleged reliance and the loss suffered – unreasonable reliance is no reliance.

However, if all other requirements are present then it may mean that a defendant can still be held liable under the *Hedley Byrne* principle even though their reliance was unreasonable but here a court could be expected to reduce the plaintiff's damage claim on the basis that unreasonable reliance equals contributory negligence.

The Caparo decision means that a company making a takeover bid with the price to be paid being largely determined by audited accounts does so at their own risk, because, if the audit was negligently carried out, causing the bidder to pay excessively, then no action will lie against the auditor. Bidders, therefore, are best advised to make their own financial enquiries about target companies and not rely exclusively on audited accounts made for other purposes:

James McNaughton Paper Group Ltd v Hicks Anderson & Co. (1991)

James McNaughton were negotiating over the takeover of a group of companies. The chairman of the target group instructed, at short notice, Hicks Anderson to prepare audited accounts on the group. These accounts were headed 'final drafts' and showed a net loss for the year. Responding to questioning from James McNaughton, Hicks Anderson said that the group were 'breaking even or doing marginally worse'. James McNaughton took over the group but later discovered that the accounts were erroneous in a number of respects and alleged negligence against Hicks Anderson.

The Court of Appeal held that, as the accounts had been prepared for the benefit of the chairman and not for James McNaughton, there was no special relationship or proximity between the parties so that Hicks Anderson did not owe James McNaughton a duty of care. In the court's opinion, as the accounts were draft accounts and not final ones, Hicks Anderson could not have been expected to foresee reliance on them by James McNaughton. It would, therefore, not be fair, just and reasonable to impose a duty.

In his judgement in *James McNaughton Paper Group Ltd v Hicks Anderson & Co.*, Neil LJ identified a number of factors which may be relevant. These are:

1 The purpose for which the statement is made. In Caparo the purpose of an audit report was to enable the shareholders to question the managers of the company, not to assist a third party to make an investment decision: hence the stricture in Caparo of the statement having to be made for the specific purpose of being communicated to the recipient.
2 The purpose for which the statement was communicated, for instance who had requested the statement and what they intended to do with it.
3 The relationship between the adviser, the advice, and any relevant third party.
4 The size of any class to which the adviser belonged. So that if there was a single adviser or the adviser came from a small class then it may be easier to infer a duty than if the adviser is one of a large, possibly indeterminate, class.
5 The state of knowledge of the adviser. Did the adviser know of the purpose for which the statement was made? It must be noted that knowledge includes both actual knowledge, and the knowledge that is attributable to the adviser by inference.
6 The degree of reliance by the adviser on the adviser's statement.

The importance of the reliance factor can be seen in the following:

Morgan Crucible plc v Hill Samuel Bank Ltd (1991)

During takeover negotiations the directors and financial advisers of a target company made statements supporting the accuracy of financial statements and profit forecasts intending that a bidder should rely on them. The bidder did so rely and alleged that he suffered loss as a result of the statements being prepared negligently.

The Court of Appeal held that, where the statements were made after an indefinable bidder had emerged, intending that the bidder rely on them, a duty of care might be owed.

What must not be forgotten is that a negligent audit must be the cause of the financial loss suffered by the party relying on it:

JEB Fasteners Ltd v Marks, Bloom & Co. (1983)

MB, a firm of auditors, overvalued stock resulting in profits being shown instead of a loss. At the time they knew the company (BG Fasteners) had liquidity problems and was seeking financial assistance from a third party. JEB were shown MB's figures (without MB's knowledge) and while thinking the stock value was high did agree to take over BG Fasteners for a nominal price primarily to obtain the service of two key directors. The takeover was not a success. JEB took legal action alleging that the takeover would not have occurred if the true value of the stock had been given.

Held: As MB knew that outside financial help was needed they ought to have foreseen that a takeover was a real possibility and that the party making the takeover bid would rely on the accounts. Therefore, MB did owe a duty of care to JEB and that it had been broken. However, JEB knew BG Fasteners were in financial difficulties and the main reason for the takeover was to obtain the service of the two directors. Hence the negligence of MB was not the cause of the loss suffered by JEB. Accordingly the action was dismissed.

Relief from liability

Judicial relief from civil liability

A court has the authority to grant relief from legal liability where in any proceedings from negligence, default, breach of duty or breach of trust against an officer of a company or a person by a company auditor (whether he is himself an officer of the company or not) if it appears that he acted honestly and reasonably, and that having regard to all the circumstances of the case he ought fairly to be wholly or partly excused from liability. If need be the court may impose whatever terms of discharge it thinks fit (s. 727).

Company relief

Formerly it was possible either in the articles or in a separate contract of employment to exempt a company officer (including an auditor) from any liability caused by breach of contract or negligence (*Re City Equitable Fire Insurance Co. Ltd* (1925)). A company's ability

The Court of Appeal has interpreted s. 727 as being limited to claims made by, or on behalf of, the company or its liquidator against an officer or auditor in respect to their personal failings. The court went on to say that the section is invalid in relation to any third party claims that may be made against an officer or auditor (see Commissioners of Custom & Excise v Hedon Alpha Ltd and Others (1981)).

to grant such blanket relief from liability is now prohibited but a company may, nevertheless, take out liability insurance cover or in certain circumstances agree to indemnify a company officer who becomes liable (s. 310).

Limited liability partnership

As a response to auditors' fear of *Doomsday Claims* (this is where claims brought for professional negligence will exceed a firm's indemnity insurance cover, resulting not only in that partnership being declared bankrupt but all the parties' personal assets also being seized to meet claims), the Government announced in September 1998 the intention to introduce legislation for Limited Liability Partnerships (LLP). These would restrict liability for professional negligence to the partnership and the personal assets of the negligent partner so that the personal assets of other partners would be unaffected. A partnership opting for benefit of the LLP status would in return have to follow the same external obligations as limited liability companies, most notably in having to publish financial information.

Auditor's liability: a response from the profession

As a direct consequence of increased vulnerability to claims over negligent mis-statements a number of British accounting firms have indicated that they are considering placing their audit work into a limited company based off-shore in the Channel Islands. The intention is to protect individual partners from the threat of punitive legal action over accusations of professional negligence. If this proposal becomes reality then it would mean that parties would become audit directors and while they will no longer be personally liable, the company which is to be created will of course be fully liable for the negligence of their personnel.

More generally the auditing profession has for some time voiced its concern over the substantial increase in recent years in company auditors' liability claims. The problem is that when a company fails, largely through the fraud or negligence of its directors, all those deemed legally responsible will bear joint and several (that is individual and shared) liability. However, shareholders who have lost their investment will be advised that it is usually pointless to sue those directly responsible, the directors, as they would either have too few assets to pay compensation or, alternatively, they would have placed their assets beyond the reach of any creditor. As a consequence auditors, who by law must carry liability insurance, are an attractive target for a compensation claim.

If the Limited Liability Partnerships are introduced (see the section above) then the move to incorporated status based off-shore may well be checked.

In a March 1996 discussion paper, *Finding a Fair Solution*, the Institute of Chartered Accountants in England and Wales put forward a proposal that a system of proportionate liability ought to be introduced where blame and liability for company failure are apportioned among those responsible for a company failure. Such systems are already in existence in the USA and Australia. Whether the Department of Trade and Industry will be minded to sponsor enabling legislation for the introduction of proportionate liability is perhaps doubtful. A recently published Law Commission (England & Wales) Report on joint and several liability concluded that no alteration to the current position should be made.

Chapter summary

- As a form of de-regulation small and medium sized companies are excused fully or partly from having to have their accounts audited.
- *First* auditors will usually be appointed by the directors and will hold office until the AGM. *Subsequent* auditors will be appointed at each AGM with any *casual* vacancy being filled by the directors or company in a general meeting. But a private company passing an elective resolution may dispense with having to have an annual appointment.
- Auditors must be members of a recognized supervisory body in order that they may become a *registered auditor*. Those prohibited from being an auditor are anyone directly or indirectly associated with the company.
- An auditor may by ordinary resolution be dismissed from office irrespective of whatever a service contract says. A dismissed auditor has certain statutory rights: to receive the same information as shareholders; to attend and speak at meetings where he normally would have been professionally present.
- An auditor by provision of written notice and a statutory statement saying that financially all is in order may resign his appointment. But if resignation is connected with circumstances that need to be notified to shareholders or creditors then he must disclose them for subsequent distribution. Additionally, he may request directors to call an EGM (if need be after first circulating details of the circumstances that are connected with the auditor's resignation) at which the auditor will explain why he resigned.
- An auditor has a statutory duty to report on the financial health of the company, e.g. in his opinion the accounts were properly prepared and that they give a true and fair view of the accounts actually being presented. If accounts need qualification then this must be done. Consistency between the auditor's and the directors' statement needs to be considered – if inconsistency is detected then this must be commented upon. When not disclosed in the accounts then the auditor's report ought to refer to directors: fees, loans, pensions etc.
- Auditors have a range of rights: full access to company books, accounts and other documents; to require information and explanations from any company officer; to receive notice of general meetings, as well as being able to attend and speak at them. If a private company then there is the right to receive copies of written resolutions and to say whether a general or class meeting needs to be called or not.
- An auditor must demonstrate the 'skill, care and caution which a reasonably competent, careful and cautious auditor would have used' (Lopes LJ, *Re Kingston Cotton Mill Co.*). Therefore, an actual auditor will be compared with a hypothetical auditor who, while not perfect, has a very high professional standard of performance.
- An auditor's duty of care is owed contractually and in negligence to the company. A duty of care in negligence is only owed to a third party if they come within the *special relationship* required in *Hedley Byrne v Heller & Partners*, i.e. the auditor: claimed a special skill; knew that his statement, given without a disclaimer, would be relied upon by the third party; that such reliance was reasonable and that the statement was negligent. However, public policy considerations have limited the

operation of the special relationship whereby an auditor owes a duty of care solely to the company (*Caparo Industries plc v Dickman* – explained in *James McNaughton Paper Group Ltd v Hickman Anderson & Co.*).
- An auditor may be relieved from liability caused by negligence, default, breach of duty or breach of trust where the court believes that he acted honestly and reasonably.

Discussion questions

1 Discuss what has to be established in order to successfully sue an auditor for professional negligence.
2. 'An auditor is not bound to be a detective, or to approach his work with suspicion, or with a foregone conclusion that something is wrong. He is a watchdog not a bloodhound' (Lopes LJ, Re Kingston Cotton Mill Co. (1896)).
This often quoted judgement was delivered over 100 years ago. Discuss whether it is still relevant.

Case study exercise

Tinsel Productions plc is a high profile entertainment company making programmes for television companies. Its chairman and chief executive is Owen Moore, a flamboyant, charismatic personality. For each of its seven-year existence Black, White & Grey have audited Tinsel Production's accounts and passed them without qualification. Now *A Word In Your Ear*, a television investigative programme, has made allegations that since its incorporation Tinsel Productions has been used to launder drug trafficking money. The programme further states that this illegal activity was easy for the investigative team to confirm and follow up once a whistle-blower had alerted them to what was going on. Black, White & Grey recall that on a few occasions when asking Moore specific questions he had always pleaded pressure of work and passed them on to an associate.

The broadcasting of the investigative programme had a devastating effect on Tinsel Productions' share price (a fall from 357p to 172p) as well as leading to a number of contracts for programmes being cancelled with proposals for others not being taken up. It is accepted, even at this early stage, that the end of year results will be disastrous.

Advise Tinsel productions plc and individual shareholders as to whether or not it is likely Black, White & Grey may, if the allegations are substantiated, be held liable.

Further reading

The Regulation of the Company Auditor under the Companies Act 1989, A. Arora (1991), JBL, 272.
True and Fair Revisited, H. Evans (1990), LMCLQ, 255.
Auditors and Lawyers, K.P.E. Lasok and E. Grace (1993), Co. Law, 130.

The True and Fair View, K.P.E. Lasok and E. Grace (1989), Co. Law, 13.
The 'True and Fair View' Debate: A Study in the Legal Regulation of Accounting, A. McGee (1991), MLR, 874.
Auditor's Liability – Reforms and Risksharing, P. Ormrod (1994), Co. Law, 273.

16 Corporate governance

Introduction

The expression corporate governance has, in the last decade, come into vogue. What has apparently motivated the examination of how companies are managed is firstly a general call that long established institutions need to examine themselves asking the question, 'Can our current role be justified or do we need to reinvent ourselves?' This general reappraisal applies not only to companies but also legal, financial, parliamentary and government institutions as well.

Corporate governance is defined in Modern Company Law (a DTI consultative paper) as 'the system by which companies are directed and controlled'.

Secondly, there is a public perception that companies, as closed institutions, in that *de facto* management is concentrated into a small number of individuals (directors) who while not breaking company legislation, run things for their own advantage. The spur for this belief, whether justified or not, was the post-privatization scenario that occurred when statutory bodies were taken out of the public sector and became newly minted public limited companies. The former managers (now directors) were seen to award themselves greatly inflated salaries, generous share options and long-term bonus schemes, all based upon undemanding performance indicators, as well as enviable pension rights. The justification that they had to have the rate for the job was felt to be a lame excuse in that they invariably ran monopolistic businesses (gas, water, electricity) so that their job was not comparable with directors of similarly sized companies in genuinely competitive industries. Privatization caught the public imagination so that the newly created companies enjoyed high visibility with the press initiating and maintaining a prolonged campaign with the message that self-rewarding directors amounted to little more than corporate corruption.

Other companies, including 'blue chip' ones, were also seen to have directors enjoying the bounty of high office even when the company they steered hit turbulent waters. Indeed poor performance as a director or chief executive officer too often resulted in their receiving a golden parachute in the form of a sizeable pay-off to leave early. The pay-off would be bloated through the use of rolling contracts so that a director would always be in a position to press for the maximum compensation for loss of office.

The argument was that if shareholders were upset with greedy or poor management then they could organize and table resolutions at company meetings either to curb boardroom excesses or to dismiss them from office. While this sounds appealing, the reality is that with shareholdings largely held by institutions such shareholder power rarely occurs. Rather than take a stand, institutional investors, unable to reach an understanding with a recalcitrant company, will sell their holdings and not take the longer route of publicly showing disquiet at company meetings.

Objectives

The purpose of this chapter is for students to embrace the issue of whether those who have had senior managerial responsibilities delegated to them run the company for the benefit of shareholders or for themselves. Following on from this is the expectation that students will become familiar with the various self regulatory codes of good practice that attempt to put shareholder interests before those of directors.

Key concepts

- Cadbury Code of Best Practice
- Greenbury Code
- Hampel supercode.

The Cadbury Code (The Code of Best Practice)

In response to criticism over lax corporate governance that allowed in the late 1980s the fraudster Robert Maxwell to milk employee pension funds of enormous sums to prop up his ailing business empire and the Bank of Credit and Commerce International catastrophe, a Committee on the Financial Aspects of Corporate Governance was set up by the Stock Exchange, the Financial Reporting Council and the chartered accounting bodies. Published in December 1992 the Code covers all United Kingdom public listed companies who are required under 'Yellow Book' rules to state in their annual report how and to what extent they have complied with the Code giving reasons for any part not complied with.

The Committee's guiding principle was that companies are managed best where openness, accountability and integrity prevail. The Code consists of a number of guidelines for the improvement of company boards. These guidelines are given under the following heads.

The Committee was chaired by Sir Adrian Cadbury and it was hoped that all commercial undertakings, not just listed companies, would adopt the Code or a derivative of it. The City Group for Smaller Companies (CISCO) subsequently looked at how smaller companies (those with a market capitalization of up to £150 million) could comply with the Code.

The board of directors

a) Regular board meetings should be held so that the executives can be monitored and controlled.

b) Responsibility at the top should be clearly defined and divided so that misuse of power does not occur and also to avoid collusions taking place.

c) Good quality non-executive directors ought to be recruited – enough to see that a strong and independent part of the board exists so as to be able to influence decisions.

d) Directors should be able to take independent professional advice at the company's expense.

e) Matters that require board clearance ought to be drawn up into a schedule.

Executive directors

a) Their service contracts should not exceed three years unless the shareholders agree to a longer period.

b) Their pay should be set by a remuneration committee consisting mainly or wholly of non-executive directors.

c) There should be full disclosure of the emoluments total as well as disclosure of what the chairman and highest paid director received. The breakdown between salary and any performance-related payment, such as a bonus, is to be given for these officers. If any performance-related benefit applies then the criteria set for it have to be stated.

Non-executive directors

a) They should be selected by a formal process such as the use of a nomination committee controlled by existing non-executive directors. However, selection ought to be by the whole board.

b) They should be appointed for a specified term with re-appointment not being a mere formality.

c) Ideally they should be independent of management or any other interest that could affect an impartial outlook.

Reporting and control

a) The board should present a balanced and comprehensive assessment of the position of the company in its report and accounts. Comprehensive words and terms are to be used as well as figures.

b) The board is to maintain objective and professional relationships with the auditors.

c) An audit committee, consisting of at least three non-executive directors and internal and external auditors, with clear and relevant terms of reference should meet as and when required. However, there should be a meeting with the auditor at least once a year at which executive directors are not present.

d) There should be an explanation of the directors' responsibilities for the accounts next to a statement by the auditors on reporting responsibilities.

e) The directors should report annually upon the effectiveness or otherwise of their systems of internal financial controls.

f) The directors should state in their annual report that the business is a going concern (assuming that it is), together with any supporting comments or qualifications.

Company failure as well as successes are to be disclosed.

For most meetings executive directors are to have right of attendance but they should never actually become committee members.

Review question

There is no point in constructing complex systems to improve corporate governance if the wrong people are on the board in the first place.
Discuss.

The Greenbury Report

The Greenbury Committee was a response to public and investor concern regarding inflated pay increases awarded to themselves by directors of privatized utilities. At the same time these companies were in colloquial terms 'downsizing' with the loss of thousands of unskilled and semi-skilled employees. The public perception was not just of corporate greed but of inequality as well.

Sponsored by the Confederation of British Industry the Committee was chaired by Sir Richard Greenbury. The resulting report goes further in some significant aspects than the earlier Cadbury Committee were willing to do.

The remit of the Committee was to review the process for paying directors and to make recommendations for improvements. The Stock Exchange has made compliance with the Greenbury Report a listing requirement. The Report published in July 1995 is somewhat rambling in its presentation but the essential points are given below.

Remuneration committee

Membership is to be restricted to non-executive directors but only if they have 'no personal financial interest other than as shareholders in the matters to be decided'. The committee chairman should account directly to shareholders attending AGMs and take any questions on the remuneration of executive directors. In addition the chairman may meet principal investors separately to obtain their views and allay any concerns.

The board itself is to decide the remuneration of non-executive directors.

The committee is to deal with all aspects of executive directors' pay including compensation (golden parachutes) that may be paid on their early withdrawal from a service contract with a strong stance being taken when performance has been poor. The period of service contracts should ideally be for one year or less, occasionally for two years but seldom for longer. If longer than two years then they need to be disclosed, explained and justified to shareholders. Any severance compensation ought to be paid in stages rather than in a single sum, and payments should cease if the former director obtains another appointment. Consultation with the chief executive officer is encouraged and when necessary professional advice can be sought.

With respect to the actual level of remuneration the committee should pay 'not too much, not too little, but just right with sensitivity being shown to pay elsewhere in the company as well as in the community at large'. This somewhat idealistic exhortation not to be too generous is to be achieved through the company matching their pay levels against those of comparable companies. In the three-year period after the report was published, company directors' pay increased by more than twice the rate of inflation.

This fits into the vogue for demonstration of shareholder value i.e. increased dividends and a higher share price.

Where pay is performance related (as it invariably is for executive directors) then performance incentives should lean towards shareholder interests – hence demanding targets need to be set, with bonuses not being extravagant. If share options are exercised then the shares should not be sold immediately but be held for a reasonable period. Also share options really should operate over a period rather than on a once-only basis.

Finally, any longer term policy of remuneration needs to have shareholder approval.

According to a survey on executive pay published in July 1998 (William M. Mercer Executive Pay survey), the average bonus for chief executives of the UK's 20 largest public companies exceeds 50 per cent of their basic pay. Therefore, remuneration is now even more closely linked to company performance. Of these 20 companies the survey reported that the average basic salary for chief executives was £549,000 (23 per cent higher than in 1995) with an average bonus of £311,000. Taking an overview of directors' remuneration trends over the last survey, it was said that the Greenbury Report had:

> ... achieved its key objectives of promoting greater transparency of directors' earnings, greater corporate governance and a stronger link between directors' pay and corporate performance.

Cross directorships

Where cross directorships are present there should be no conflict of interest. Such conflict could occur where, for example, an executive director of ABC plc is also a non-executive director of XYZ plc and an executive director of XYZ plc is in turn a non-executive director of ABC plc. The suspicion is that if in their non-executive directorship capacity they sat on remuneration committees then they could urge higher pay for directors as the basis of, 'I'll scratch your back if you scratch mine.'

Annual reports

The remuneration committee is to report to members in the annual report on their policy on remuneration as well as fully detailing each part of individual directors' remuneration – salary, pension, share options etc.

Where corporate governance under the Greenbury Code has been largely successful is in newly floated companies. A study by Arthur Anderson (the consultancy firm) published in September 1997 found that 68 per cent of chief executives and 85 per cent of finance directors of newly formed public companies have 12-month contracts as recommended by the Greenbury Code of Best Practice. This compared with fewer than 25 per cent of directors in the FTSE 250 list of public companies. However, the study felt that while new public companies wanted to get corporate governance 'right first time' they were merely ticking off the Code's recommendations without providing any real remuneration strategy. Also less than 10 per cent of the FTSE100 list of public companies had, two years after Greenbury, reduced their directors' service contracts to one year or less. Moreover, three-quarters of them still had some executive directors on contracts longer than one year (a finding of Pirc – a consultancy on corporate governance).

Review question

'The Greenbury Committee's recommendations are more exacting than Cadbury's recommendations.' Say, with reasons, whether you agree or disagree with this statement.

The Hampel Committee

The Hampel Committee on Corporate Governance was established in November 1995 to review the recommendations made by the Cadbury and Greenbury Committees and whether on implication they had proved helpful. Its final report was published in January 1998 and it suggested, rather than recommended, ways in which companies may, in the light of the two earlier reports, be managed more effectively.

The committee took the opportunity of looking at the position of companies from both a macro and micro standpoint. For example the traditional unitary board structure was contrasted with the two-tier structure which is the norm on the continent, especially in Germany. Advocates of this alternative model argue that having a supervisory board to monitor the performance of the managerial board would act as a brake on managerial excesses in that the supervisors sitting on a separate board can be more effective than the supervisors (non-executive directors) on the unitary board model who sit cheek-by-jowl with those they seek to control. It would be expected that a clear division between supervisors and managers would lend credibility to the claim for independence of non-executive directors.

While not opting for two-tier boards Hampel suggested that companies identify a senior non-executive director to provide a link between the board and shareholders, giving early warning of poor management. However, company directors and the Institute of Chartered

Although under Cadbury disclosure of the directors' remuneration in total had to be given, Greenbury requires full *openness* in that there has to be disclosure of each individual director's remuneration. The Companies Accounts (Disclosure of Directors Emoluments) Regulations 1997 requires public companies to provide in their annual accounts and report full details of director emoluments, including pension contributions and other non-monetary benefits, made on their behalf.

The Hampel Committee was sponsored by the Stock Exchange, the Confederation of British Industry, the Institute of Directors and accountancy, pension and insurance bodies.

Secretaries and Administrators warned that such an appointment would be likely in practice to prove divisive.

Hampel also considered the role of institutional shareholders in corporate governance. They were aware that in the United States institutional shareholders are required to vote at general meetings. In Britain, such a public stance is generally considered 'poor form' in that it is felt that the way to influence corporate behaviour is through informal contact and not a public display of openly voting against board-inspired resolutions. In the Report again Hampel fell short of making a firm recommendation that institutional shareholders be obligated to vote, preferring instead to speak of their responsibility to do so.

Shareholder voting was a contentious issue of the National Association of Pension Funds (NAPF) who had urged the committee to recommend a direct vote for shareholders on remuneration committee reports at annual meetings. The NAPF also supported shareholder activism in saying that there ought to be an 'absentee' box on voting forms for shareholders to tick in order that their discontent could be registered. Such a box would show that failure to vote yes or no was not down to apathy but disgust at managerial misperformance. Greenbury had suggested that shareholders be given a separate vote in the remuneration committee's report but Hampel side-stepped this issue.

Another criticism of Hampel was made by the Corporate Governance Forum (a body representing leading fund managers) who expressed disappointment over the failure of the committee to define what an independent non-executive director is meant to be, or, conversely, to give guidance on how to identify non-executives who are not independent.

The Corporate Governance Forum (CGF) were also critical in that Hampel did not come out and say that the combined role of company chairman and chief executive officer was no longer tenable. The Committee's silence, the CGF fear, could encourage a strongly entrenched individual to continue to defy the growing trend to separate these roles.

While Hampel investigated a number of avenues for corporate governance improvement, the report produced takes a non-interventionist position in that the Committee was reluctant to move the debate of corporate governance too far. Preference was given to a flexible approach that shareholders and other interested parties could use. For example the Committee felt that the 'tick box' procedure where a board is judged by its adherence to a compliance menu ought to be dropped in favour of taking due account of the diversity of 'circumstances and experience among companies'.

At present shareholders are unable to vote directly on executive pay, being able to vote only on the company's annual report and accounts and the re-election of executive directors.

Review question

Hampel, and earlier corporate governance committees, considered the interests of the company and its shareholders, but to fully embrace corporate governance who else needs to be taken into account?

The Stock Exchange response to Hampel

At the time of writing the Stock Exchange has yet to officially announce their response to the Hampel 'supercode' but it is widely expected that they will append it to their listing rules (but, perhaps, significantly not incorporate it into them), so that when public companies publish their 1999 annual reports they will have to say whether or not they have complied with it and to justify any divergence.

Enforcement of the Hampel code, as with the earlier ones, remains with the shareholders. Whether they are willing to police it will surely largely depend on the circumstances, with a prosperous company probably getting away with breaches that a company in financial difficulties would be unable to. A better method of compliance would be to make strict adherence to the listing requirement, and in turn the code, mandatory. Failure to do so would lead to de-listing until remedial action was taken, including the removal without compensation of recalcitrant directors.

The Government's position post-Hampel

A commentator on the working of the Hampel committee likened it to a *reductio ad tedium* outcome in that after taking lengthy deliberations (two and a half years) the final conclusion was that there was nothing radically new to say. Cynically, this observer went on to say that the object of all three corporate governance committees was not to significantly alter how business conducts itself but to persuade government that something is being done. With an incoming Labour administration, the first for 18 years, being an unknown factor but potentially sceptical towards, if not hostile to, self-regulation there is a ring of truth that the Hampel committee was partly looking over their shoulders at what the Department of Trade and Industry (DTI) would be prepared to buy.

The stance taken by Margaret Beckett, Secretary of State for Trade and Industry, is to adopt a wait-and-see policy in that the Hampel regime has been placed under review. In particular the DTI are keen to see whether the institutional investors are willing to make Hampel work by engaging in shareholder activism or retain their traditional passive position. Indeed Hampel noted that institutional inertia resulted in a majority of them failing to cast any votes at all. Such indolent behaviour led Margaret Beckett to retort:

> The best governance standards require a change in attitudes more than a change in the law. They require, for example, a change of attitude by shareholders – above all by institutions. Of course there needs to be regular, informed contact between companies and institutions on strategy and performance. But institutions hold their shares largely on behalf of individuals, and this gives both managers and trustees a particular duty to ensure there is transparent stewardship of their investments. Transparent stewardship means making positive use of voting rights, as both Cadbury and Hampel recommend, and a readiness to show clients what those voting records are.

Such apathy has been termed the 'empty box syndrome' in that institutional investors are not even willing to complete the boxes printed on voting forms.

The eagerness of the DTI to have a positive institutional response to Hampel is due to the fact that shareholder activism is seen as a major way to make British business more competitive. At present too often, it is argued, the remedy for poor management is a takeover which is disruptive, costly and time consuming. Shareholders taking poor management to task by means of attendance at annual general meetings where searching questions can be put and notes cast ought, it is felt, to keep management on their toes.

The Hampel Committee took the opposite view saying that there was no evidence to support the contention that shareholder activism was linked to business success. In fact Hampel was against compulsory voting.

Another reason why the DTI wants to monitor the performance of the Hampel supercode

Research in the USA lends credence to the DTI view.

is that it is a long-standing objective of Labour to get away from a perceived short-termism of British business:

> We want forms of governance and company law that encourage companies to invest and grow – to take the long-term strategic view, and a broad view of their obligations. (Margaret Beckett, in a speech to the CBI, 11.11.1997)

In this speech the Cadbury principle of openness, transparency and accountability between management and shareholders was affirmed. Currently, the better view seems to be a reluctance of the Government to pass major legislation reforming corporate governance, preferring instead to exhort directors and institutional shareholders to fully embrace the triple codes with the fear that if they do not do so then penal legislation may finally follow. What is certain is that the Government is not going to lose interest in corporate governance.

This was the tenor of the consultation paper on the reform of company law issued on 4 March 1998. See Appendix 1 for possible areas that may be 'legally underpinned'.

The proposed OECD code also stresses the importance of society at large which seemingly is an acknowledgement of the stakeholder-based view popular on the continent and in Japan.

Corporate governance – an international dimension

A group of six 'wise men' including Sir Allen Cadbury, appointed by the Organization for Economic Cooperation and Development recommended (Spring 1998) the creation of minimum international standards in corporate governance of companies. If agreed, the 29 member countries, including the leading industrialized nations, would introduce a set of internationally recognized corporate governance guidelines. The report produced by the group of experts calls on the OECD to draw up standards to promote 'fairness, transparency, accountability and responsibility'. This will be achieved through the adoption of a voluntary code of best practice aimed at improving boardroom responsibility and independence. It is hoped that greater disclosure by international companies will be made.

The OECD code, if the recommendations are accepted, will reject the 'one-size-fits-all' approach in that differences between member countries will be recognized. However, the importance of shareholder value in the code fits in well with the Anglo-Saxon (UK and USA) corporate governance models. Failure to follow the OECD code, or similar national code, may eventually mean that a company's access to the capital markets is restricted in that either loans will be unavailable or available but on more demanding terms.

Chapter summary

- Corporate governance is a response of business to public and political criticism resulting from over-generous remuneration packages awarded to company directors.
- The Cadbury code recommended:
  Company boards
  - regular meetings
  - monitoring
  - the recruitment of independent non-executive directors
  Executive directors
  - service contracts of three years or less

- pay set by a remuneration committee
- full disclosure of chairman's and highest paid director's pay

Non-executive directors
- nominated and selected by a formal process•
- no automatic reappointment
- fully independent

Reporting and control
- reporting to shareholders to be full and balanced
- directors to disclose the overall position of their company, e.g. a going concern or technically insolvent
- the board to maintain professional detachment from the auditors
- creation of audit committee
- directors to explain their role in relation to the accounts and whether internal financial systems are effective.[slr]
- The Greenbury code recommended:

Remuneration committees
- to be comprised of independent non-executive directors with a chairman who reports to shareholders at AGMs
- director service contracts ideally one year or less
- tough criteria to be set for directors' performance-related pay
- compensation for loss of directorship to be restrictive

Cross directorships
- these ought never to lead to conflicts of interest

Annual reports
- to contain a report from the remuneration committee.
- The Hampel Committee:
- Considered but did not support a two-tier board structure; suggested the appointment of a senior non-executive director to liaise between board and shareholders at AGMs; wanted to see institutional shareholders vote more frequently but was against compulsory voting.
- The Hampel report was subject to considerable criticism:
  - from ICSA over the possibility that the appointment of a senior director could be divisive
  - from NAPE over failure to provide shareholders with a separate direct note on the remuneration committee's report
  - from CGF on a failure of the committee to provide definitions, guidance and a ban on combined chairmen and CEO roles.

Post-Hampel responses:

Stock Exchange
- appendage of Hampel to its listing rules

DTI
- waiting to see if Hampel works judged by: the degree of increased institutional voting; assisting with competitiveness of business; and the taking of a long-term view.
- The OECD has an international code of corporate governance which it may introduce.

Discussion questions

1 What principles underpin the Cadbury code and to what extent are they satisfied?
2 Hampel, through its unwillingness to be too radical, missed an opportunity to take corporate governance a major step forward.
Discuss.
3 Sed quis custodiet ispos custodes?
(But what about the vigilantes? Who is going to watch after them?) (Juvenal, Satires)
Discuss.

Case study exercise

Penny Sterling is the executive chairman of Brocco Bank plc (BB), a medium size merchant bank. Currently the company has a board of seven executive directors. The company plans to expand and Sterling feels a few outsiders on the board will 'make it look right'. She therefore approaches Donald McDonald, a well respected owner of a construction business (and a member of Sterling's Rotary Club), asking him if he would like to become non-executive deputy chairman of BB. McDonald agrees and is appointed. Another 'outsider' appointed to the board is Ivan Overdraft, a financier who BB regularly advance credit to.

Of the seven established directors, three are on rolling contracts of five years but these will be reduced to three years in return for what Sterling feels is appropriate compensation. The chief executive officer works out what directors are to be paid basing his recommendations on directors' pay scales produced by the Institute of Directors. The corporate client director is paid a bonus based on the fees he brings in. All directors are eligible to acquire shares in BB at any time over the next two years at a price of 300p per share (the market price when this scheme was introduced was 275p per share).

In relation to corporate governance offer comment on the above.

Further reading

Report of the Committee on the Financial Aspects of Corporate Governance, Cadbury Report (1992), Gee.
Committee on Corporate Governance, Final Report, Hampel Report (1998), Gee.
Corporate Governance and Corporate Opportunities, G.M.D. Bean (1994), Co. Law, 266.
A Principled Approach to Self-regulations? The Report of the Hampel Committee on Corporate Governance, A. Dignam (1998), Co. Law, 140.
The Governance of Governance, J. Dine (1994), Co. Law, 73.
Board Performance and Cadbury Corporate Governance, V. Finch (1992), JBL, 581.
Shareholders vs Stakeholders: The Bogus Argument, P. Goldenberg (1998), Co. Law, 34.
Directors' Remuneration: Constraining the Power of the Board, A. Griffiths (1995), LMCQ, 392.
UK Company Shareholder Protection: A Call for Reform, L. Miles (1994), Co. Law, 202.

17 Insider dealing

Introduction

Successful investment in quoted companies is widely accepted to be largely based on information and timing. Observers have for many years felt that those who are professionally close to a company have a considerable advantage in that they may use for personal benefit privileged (i.e. non-public) information that they acquired through being connected with the company in whose shares they deal. They, therefore, are able to make investment decisions with the advantage of foresight. Indeed some financial journalists regularly base their share recommendations on directors' share movements. If one or more director discloses that they have bought a significant number of shares in their company then this is taken to be the most positive statement they could make about the financial health and prospects of the company. Conversely, if it is disclosed that director(s) have sold their shares without just reason (such as funding a divorce settlement, or to lessen taxation liability) then this is perceived as a pessimistic statement about the company so that other investors may ask why they should retain their shares.

Some commentators take a stricter position in holding that unprivileged information is still to be included under insider dealing or trading.

The suspicion is that what causes these connected persons to buy or sell at precisely the moment they do so is information that if widely known would cause many unconnected persons to also buy or sell so that the shares in question would be subject to sharp upward or downward movement. Information that could be expected to dramatically move a share price would, for example, be early knowledge of a takeover bid or advance knowledge of a profit collapse. An insider with such knowledge could, unless prevented, astutely move into or out of the company's shares and in modern parlance make a financial killing with modest exposure to risk.

In R v Reardon-Smith (1985), a director of a company in acute financial difficulties sold shares in it just before it was wound up. He pleaded guilty to insider dealing and was fined £3,000.

Although for many years personal use of inside financial information was accepted as being perfectly valid, in the last 20 years since this activity was first criminalized it has come to be widely regarded as morally unjustifiable in that it rewards those who are favourably placed (senior employees, or advisors and their relations and friends), at the expense of those who are not. As insider dealing can lead to loss of confidence in the market it can be said that the control over insider dealing is to safeguard the financial markets for company securities as opposed to protection of individual investors.

Objectives

The purpose of this chapter is to highlight the controversial issue that market information may be used by insiders for personal gain at the expense of those who lack this competitive advantage. In consequence, and what students must fully appreciate, is that a regulatory regime has been created to curb this abuse.

Key concepts

- The offence of insider dealing
- The use of non-public information that is known to be inside information
- The Stock Exchange model code on how directors should behave when dealing in securities.

The offence of insider dealing

Part V implemented the EC Directive on Inside Dealing 89/52/ECC the preamble to which emphasized that the overriding concern was to secure the confidence of investors in the working of the securities market.

This is derived from Part V of the Criminal Justice Act 1993 where an individual who has information as an insider is guilty of insider trading if:

i) he acquires or disposes on a regulated market (or by using a professional intermediary to do so) securities covered by the Act that are price-affected in relation to the information held; or

ii) he encourages another person to deal in such securities knowing, or having, reasonable cause to believe, that the dealing would take place; or

iii) he discloses the information to another person other than when doing so in the proper performance of his employment or professional duties (CJA 1993, s. 52).

Review question

What justifications are there for making inside dealing a criminal offence?

Securities covered by the Act

The others are: depository receipts, options, futures and contracts for differences.

These are set out in schedule 2 and are subject to Treasury orders. The three commonest securities are:

a) shares in the share capital of the company;
b) debt securities, e.g. debentures, loan stock, bonds and certificates of deposit; and
c) warrants that confer a right to subscribe for shares or debt securities (CJA 1993, s. 54).

In relation to the jurisdiction of the Act, the offence (whether committed by an individual or professional intermediary) has to have been carried out within the UK. The market being regulated must also be in the UK (CJA 1993, s. 62).

As the Act is derived from an EC Directive there is an international dimension in that it extends to securities which are officially listed on or, alternatively, are submitted to dealing under the rules of any investment exchange established within any member state of the European Economic Area (Insider Dealing (Securities and Regulated Markets) Order 1994).

The meaning of dealing in securities

A person deals if he acquires or disposes of securities whether for himself or an agent of another, or, alternatively, if he procures directly or indirectly another person to acquire or dispose of the securities (CJA 1993, s. 55).

The meaning of inside information

This means information that relates to particular securities or their issues which is specific or precise and has not been made public, but if it were then it would be likely to have a significant effect on the price of any security (CJA 1993, s. 56).

Normally, inside information will be internal to the company but information may come under s. 56 if it relates to a company issuing securities 'where it may affect the company's business prospectus' (CJA 1993, s. 60). For example if a company, trying to gain approval for a takeover, learned privately that the EC Commission had blocked it on anti-competition grounds this would be external inside information.

Insiders under the Act

To be an 'insider' a person must have information that he knows is inside information and that was obtained from one of the following inside sources:

i) through being a director, employee, or shareholder of an issuer of securities; or
ii) by having access to the information through his employment, office or profession; or
iii) obtaining the information directly or indirectly from a person coming within (i) or (ii) above (CAP 1993, s. 57).

Those falling into categories (i) and (ii) are classed as primary insiders; those in (iii) are secondary insiders.

The second category will of course catch a professional advisor, such as someone working for a merchant bank or for the company's stockbroker. However, it will also cover others as well, such as a financial journalist given a briefing by the company or an employee of the printers that produces the company's document for distribution to shareholders and so gains advance knowledge of price-sensitive information. The crucial feature is that it is immaterial whether the insider actively sought the information, or had it gratuitously given to him, or even accidentally came across it.

What is information made public?

Information is in the public domain if:

a) it has been published in accordance with the rules of a regulated market (such as those of the Stock Exchange) for the purpose of informing investors and their professional advisors; or
b) it is contained in records that by law are open to public inspection; or
c) it can be readily obtained by those likely to deal in any securities or issues to which the information relates; or

Information may be treated as made public even though diligence, observation or expertise is required to locate it; or where it is communicated to only part of the public; or it is communicated only on payment of a fee; or it is published only outside the UK.

d) the information is derived from information which has been made public (CJA 1993, s. 58).

Review question

The Directive, to promote investor confidence, refers to the need for all those dealing in security markets to be 'placed on an equal footing'. Does this therefore mean that all investors must be equal in respect to information?

Penalties on conviction

An individual guilty of insider dealing shall be liable on summary conviction to a fine not exceeding £5,000 or up to 6 months imprisonment, or both. On indictable conviction there is an unlimited fine and up to 7 years imprisonment or both (CJA 1993, s. 61).

The decision to prosecute rests with either the Secretary of State (who may delegate his power to the Stock Exchange) or the Director of Public Prosecutions.

The Act does not contain any civil remedy. However, if a director is convicted then his company may seek to recover any profit he made. Also if the prosecution was on indictment then the scope of an unlimited fine could be used to prevent any profit being made. A conviction for insider dealing may give grounds for a person to be barred from participating in the management of a company (Company Directors Disqualification Act 1986, ss. 2 & 8).

Defences available under the Act

An individual is not guilty of either *inside dealing* or *encouraging another person to deal* if he can show:

a) that he did not at the time expect the dealing to result in a profit derived from use of price-sensitive information; or
b) that at the time he believed on reasonable grounds that the information had been disclosed widely enough to ensure that none of those taking part in the dealing would be prejudiced by not themselves having the information; or
c) that he would have done what he did even if he had not had the information.

To satisfy the defences the defendant has the burden of showing, on a balance of probabilities, that he comes within the defence pleaded (CJA 1993, s. 53; and R v Cross (1991)).

In respect to the disclosure of information an individual is not guilty if he can show:

a) that he did not at the time expect any person, because of the disclosure, to deal in the securities; or
b) if he did have such an expectation at the time, he did not expect the dealing to result in a profit that was attributable to the fact that the information was price-sensitive in relation to the securities.

The Stock Exchange's Model Code

Because of their unique relationship to their companies, directors in particular are almost always insiders. The Stock Exchange Council has recognized this and have for listed companies a model code of conduct for directors in respect to their dealing in shares. While listed companies can produce their own code, which must meet the broad tenor of the model one, most companies simply use the model one. Whilst a director is not directly bound by the code a breach of it will be a breach of conduct imposed on the director by his company and it will be to the company that he will have to account. The code requires listed companies to take 'all proper and reasonable steps' to see that the code is followed by all directors and employees who have price-sensitive information. The duty extends to subsidiary companies.

> In Chase Manhattan Equities Ltd v Goodman (1991), a director who sold shares in breach of his company's code was held by the High Court not to be liable to the third party who purchased them.

The code attempts to ensure that dealings by those covered by it take place within stipulated periods, namely no dealings within a two-month period from when preliminary results of the companies are announced (whether annual or interim). When dealings do occur then advance notice of them must be given to the chairman or a committee of directors appointed for this purpose. For compliance the main sanction used by the Stock Exchange Council is that they can declare a person in breach of the code to be unfit to be a director of a listed company.

The Financial Services Authority's Code of Conduct

The Financial Services Authority (FSA) announced in a draft code of conduct published in June 1998 that it intends to widen the offence of market manipulation or insider trading. The code, which will apply to individuals and companies, will give the right to the FSA to impose unlimited fines on offenders as well as ordering them to surrender their profits and compensate victims. While the code is not actually incorporated into the law an infringement of it will be evidence of wrongdoing.

> The FSA is the regulatory body for banking and investment. The draft code is intended to become enforceable in 2000 after enabling legislation has been passed.

With a lower burden of proof for its civil fines than the current criminal standard of guilt for insider trading under the Criminal Justice Act 1993 the code shows the FSA determination to stamp out market abuses. The code is supported by widespread powers of investigation similar to those of Department of Trade and Industry inspectors. The FSA will order anyone to answer questions and to produce documents. Failure to cooperate may lead to prosecution but statements made to FSA investigators will only be used in civil or regulatory proceedings and not in any later criminal prosecution.

While the Criminal Justice Act 1993 deals with the criminal aspects of insider dealing the FSA code of conduct is designed to be a civil deterrent. And while the Act primarily focuses on individuals possessing price-sensitive information which they mis-use to their financial advantage, the code is aimed at those giving improper investment advice to third parties; the outcome ought to be a general tightening up of mis-use of market information and related dealing. A common factor between them is that insider dealing of whatever aspect is essentially about misappropriation of information and abuse of trust.

Chapter summary

- Insider dealing is increasingly looked upon as the promotion of illegitimate self-interest over the interests of others. Unless controlled it could lead to a serious loss of confidence in financial markets.
- An individual commits the offence where in price-sensitive prescribed securities in a regulated market he: deals personally; or uses a professional intermediary to deal for him; or encourages another person to deal foreseeing that this will occur; or he discloses the information to another other than in the proper performance of his professional or employment duties.
- The commonest *securities* covered by the Act are shares, debentures or warrants that give a right to acquire them.
- *Dealing* simply means acquiring or disposing of prescribed securities whether done personally, or through another person, or by procuring someone else to do so.
- *Inside information* relating to securities has to be non-published specific or precise information that if publicly known would be likely to have a significant effect on securities.
- *Insiders* are those obtaining price-sensitive information through: being a director or employee of whoever issued the security; or by gaining the information through his employment or profession; or by obtaining it from a person who is himself an insider.
- Information becomes *public* when under the rules of a regulated market it is published to inform investors or their professional advisors; or it is contained in documents of public record; or it is derived from public information
- The Act imposes only criminal liability with *penalties* of fine or imprisonment. No civil remedies are given.
- *Defences* are general and special. General ones relating to *dealing* or *encouraging another to deal* are: that there was no expectation of profit from use of the price-sensitive information; or there was a sufficiently wide publication of information that no harm would be caused to those lacking the information; or the defendant would have acted the same irrespective of having the information. The general defences for *disclosure of information* are: that he did not expect the disclosure to lead to anyone dealing; or if he did so expect he did not foresee a profit being made.
- The Stock Exchange *model code* restricts directors of listed companies from dealing within the period of two months prior to the announcement of preliminary or interim results. When made all dealings should be notified to the company chairman or committee.
- The Financial Services Authority's Code of Conduct, if introduced without being watered down, ought to open up a civil dimension to insider dealing. The effectiveness of the code will be increased by the FSA investigators having sweeping powers in pursuance of their enquiries.

Discussion questions

1 Why has the Act omitted to give a civil remedy and why did it exclude incorporated bodies from criminal liability?

2 Identify and discuss exactly what an 'insider' is prohibited by the Act from doing.

Case study exercise

Broomsgrove plc is a medium sized company specializing in fitting out newly built offices. Consider each of the following and say whether or not Part V, Criminal Justice Act 1993 has been broken:

a) John Walker, the finance director of Broomsgrove plc, is trying to fight a drinking problem. During a coffee break at an alcoholics anonymous meeting he casually mentions to another member, Stella Artois, that his company had earlier in the day been notified that it had won a very large contract the announcement of which is being delayed until next week's AGM. The next day Stella Artois buys £5,000 worth of shares in Broomsgrove plc.

b) Six days later John Walker, having to meet a divorce settlement, tells his stockbroker to sell all his (Walker's) shares in Broomsgrove plc saying that he is looking for a very good price as he knows the announcement of the contract is now imminent.

Further reading

The European Communities Directive on Insider Dealing: From Company Law to Securities Markets Regulation?, P.L. Davies, Oxford J. Legal Studies, 92.
Company Securities – Misinformation and Litigation, A. Hofler (1995), Co. Law, 67.
Publication of Price-sensitive Information, A. Hofler (1995), Co. Law, 247.
Release of Price-sensitive Information: Stock Exchange Guidance, P. Smith (1994), Co. Law, 89.
Insider Dealing: Law and Regulation, G. Brazier, Cavendish Publishing Ltd (1996).

COMPANIES IN TROUBLE

18 Winding up

Introduction

A company has perpetual succession until it is dissolved. Winding up, also known as liquidation, is the legal process which leads to the existence of the company ceasing with its assets being administered for the benefit of creditors and shareholders. Dissolution of a company is the actual removal by the Registrar of a company's name from his list of companies and when this occurs the company legally ceases to exist with the winding-up order being akin to a death certificate. Winding up may take place when the company is insolvent (the commonest situation) or when it is solvent. Whether for reasons of insolvency or because the shareholders wish the company, for other reasons, to be wound up a liquidator is appointed to administer the assets of the company so as to, firstly, pay creditors in their proper order, and then, secondly, to distribute any surplus among the shareholders according to their class rights.

In this section unless otherwise stated all references are to the Insolvency Act 1986. The Act is operated in conjunction with the Insolvency Rules 1986. Together they provide a formidable set of regulations so that what is given here is only a broad overview.

Objectives

The purpose of this chapter is to give an overview of the procedures that apply when a company's existence as a separate legal entity is to end. The concern that has to be appreciated is to avoid commercial disorder by having available, under the Insolvency Act 1986, legal methods for dissolution. Also it must be understood that the interests of creditors are of primary importance but creditors very seldom will get back their debt in full.

Key concepts

- Insolvency practitioners
- Methods of company winding up
- Petitioners and the grounds they may use
- Consequences of winding up
- The liquidator as a fiduciary of the company
- Contributors
- Fraudulent and wrongful trading
- Priority of payment

Insolvency practitioners

Before the Insolvency Act 1986 anyone was able to set themselves up either as a company liquidator or receiver and whilst the majority were competent a minority were not. Also on occasions creditors and shareholders believing the assets were being disposed of for far less than their true worth suspected that the person dealing with the insolvency was not as honest as he should be. For these reasons the Insolvency Act 1986 introduced a requirement that an insolvency practitioner has a minimum qualification.

Meaning of insolvency practitioner

An insolvency practitioner is an individual who in relation to a company acts (s. 388):

a) as its liquidator or provisional liquidator; or
b) administrator; or
c) administrative receiver; or
d) as the supervisor of a voluntary arrangement approved under the Insolvency Act 1986.

Qualification of insolvency practitioner

An individual to lawfully act as an insolvency practitioner must be authorized to do so by (s. 390):

a) a recognized professional body; or
b) a competent authority set up by the Secretary of State.

The official receiver may act as a company insolvency practitioner without necessarily meeting these requirements.

Also the individual, when acting, must carry appropriate security (s. 390). An individual acting as an insolvency practitioner without being qualified to do so is liable on conviction to imprisonment or a fine, or both (s. 389).

Those not eligible to be insolvency practitioners

In addition to those not gaining an authorization the following are also disqualified (s. 390):

a) an undischarged bankrupt;
b) an individual subject to a disqualification order made under the Company Directors Disqualification Act 1986; or
c) a patient within the meaning of the Mental Health Act 1983.

Recognized professional bodies

To be recognized by the Secretary of State for Trade and Industry a professional body must have enforceable rules to secure that those of its members who act as insolvency practitioners (s. 391):

a) are fit and proper persons to do so; and
b) meet acceptable requirements as to education, practical training and experience.

The Secretary of State may revoke recognition if it appears to him that the professional body has failed to maintain or enforce correct standards on its insolvency practitioner members (s. 391)

Authorization by competent authority

An individual who is not a member of a recognized professional body may apply to a competent authority for authorization to act as a company insolvency practitioner (s. 392). The authority may grant authorization if it is satisfied that the applicant is a fit and proper person having the appropriate education, training and experience.(s. 393). Authorization can be subsequently revoked if the competent authority believes that the individual is no longer a fit and proper person to act as an insolvency practitioner, or the applicant supplied false, inaccurate or misleading information or that there was a failure in relation to other specified matters (s. 393).

Insolvency statistics

Figures are provided in Appendix 3 for the number of companies wound up on insolvency grounds in the period 1993–97. As may be expected, more insolvencies occur during and immediately after an economic recession and this is supported by the figures showing markedly higher company failures in 1993–94 than in the mid 1990s. For the 1993–97 period in England and Wales company failures caused by insolvency averaged 1.76 per cent of the number of companies in active registration.

Voluntary winding up

The object of a voluntary winding up is that the company and its creditors are left to settle their affairs themselves and so avoid having to apply to the court for assistance.

Procedure and grounds for a voluntary winding up

To start the winding up process a resolution at a company meeting needs to be tabled and passed. With a members' voluntary winding up it is a *special resolution*, with or without a reason for it being given, whereas with a creditors' voluntary winding up it is an *extraordinary resolution* that by reason of its liabilities the company cannot continue in business and wishes to be wound up (s. 84). Where the company is wound up by an extraordinary resolution then the notice calling the meeting must state that insolvency is the cause (*Re Silkstone Fall Colliery Co.* (1875)).

Both resolutions to succeed need a vote of 75 per cent or more in favour with the difference between them being that an extraordinary resolution, because time is of the essence, normally requires only a 14-day notice period, whereas with a special resolution it is normally 21 days. Section 84 also provides a third possibility that where the articles of association state that on the occurrence of a stipulated event, or at a future date, then the company is to be wound up, then on the occurrence of that event or date an *ordinary resolution* (simple majority) for winding up can be passed at a general meeting. Extreme care should be taken before passing a voluntary winding-up resolution for once passed the liquidation has to proceed as the resolution cannot, for example, be revoked by a later resolution to stop the process.

A copy of a winding up resolution must within 15 days be sent to the Registrar with notice of the resolution being published within 14 days in the London Gazette (s. 85).

An ordinary resolution is very uncommon and such provisions in the articles in practice only relate to an investment trust company.

The type of voluntary winding up

The procedure for a voluntary winding up is divided into two: a members' or creditors' (s. 90).

A members' voluntary winding up

This is where a majority of directors of a company make a *statutory declaration* of solvency that in their opinion after a full enquiry into the company's financial affairs they are satisfied that it will be able to pay all its debts in full, together with any interest on them, within a 12-month period from the commencement of the winding up (s. 89).

Accompanying the declaration must be a financial statement, as at the latest practicable date, on the company's assets and liabilities (s. 89). For it to be valid the declaration has to be made within a period of five weeks prior to the special resolution for winding up being passed. To ensure that directors act in a responsible manner, if the declaration is not met, that is the company's debts and interest on them are not paid in full within the 12 month period, then unless they can show that they had reasonable grounds for making the declaration, the directors will be liable to a fine or six months imprisonment or both. If the debts and interest are not paid within the 12-month period then it is presumed that there were no reasonable grounds for such a belief (s. 89 (5)).

The attraction of the members' voluntary winding up is that with the company being solvent all creditors will be paid in full so that the liquidation process is fully controlled by the members who get to appoint a liquidator of their choice. Also no meetings of creditors are held and no liquidation committee is appointed. With an extraordinary resolution a liquidator is permitted to pay any class of creditor and to make such compromises as he or she deems prudent.

In this context a compromise is where the liquidator will negotiate the most advantageous settlement with creditors.

If the winding up continues for more than one year the liquidator must call a general meeting of the company at the end of the first year, and each successive year, and lay before it an account of the progress he has made to liquidate the company (s. 93). When the company is finally wound up the liquidator must call a final general meeting which must, with at least a month's notice, be advertised in the *London Gazette*. At this final meeting the liquidator has to account for all that he has done and state how the company's assets have been disposed of. A week after this meeting the liquidator has to send the Registrar a copy of the winding-up accounts and make a return of the holding of the final meeting (s. 94). The Registrar registers the accounts and returns and has published in the *London Gazette* a notice of the receipt of the return (CA 1985, s. 711). At the end of three months from the date of registration of the return the company is dissolved.

The company's affairs may not be fully wound up but so long as the liquidator believes that they have been then he is allowed to make his return to the Registrar (Re Cornish Manures Ltd (1967)).

A creditors' voluntary winding up

This starts with an extraordinary resolution that by reason of its debts the company should be wound up. If the resolution is passed then within 14 days a meeting of creditors must take place to consider the position. At least seven days' notice of the creditors meeting has to be given with identifiable creditors being notified by post and attempts to contact others being made through advertisements in the *London Gazette* as well as in two newspapers local to the company's principal place of business during the previous six months. Initially an insolvency practitioner will be appointed between the calling of the creditors' meeting and it taking place for the purpose of answering, if it is possible to do so, creditors' questions. The notice of the creditors' meeting ought either to give the name and address of the insolvency practitioner or, alternatively, state a local place where on two business days before the meeting takes place a list of known creditors' names and addresses will be available free of charge (s. 98).

At the creditors' meeting the directors must be in attendance with one of them, nominated by the others, acting as the chairman (s. 99). The directors are required to disclose to the meeting details of the company's assets and liabilities as well as a list of known creditors with details of any security they hold and the date when it was given as well as any other information required by the insolvency rules (s. 99). Both the company meeting that passed the winding-up resolution and the creditors' meeting will consider who should be appointed the liquidator. If one is appointed by the shareholders then he will have limited powers until his appointment is confirmed by a creditors' meeting. If there is a disagreement between the shareholders and creditors over the choice of liquidator then the creditors' nominee will succeed (s. 100).

If the creditors wish, at any creditors' meeting, they may appoint a liquidation committee of not more than five persons (s. 101 (1)). There is also a reciprocal right that if a liquidation committee is appointed then the company may at a general meeting itself appoint up to five persons to serve on the committee (s. 101 (2)). However, the creditors may object to anyone appointed by the company and unless the court otherwise directs they will not be allowed to serve (s. 101 (3)). The court has the authority, on an objection application, to appoint other persons to serve on the committee in place of those selected by the company (s. 101 (3)).

The liquidation committee or the creditors may set the liquidator's fees. On the appointment of the liquidator all the powers of the directors cease except in so far as the liquidation committee or, if there is not a committee, the creditors sanction their continuance (s. 103). Should the liquidator decide to dispose of assets to a person connected with the company then he must, if there is a liquidation committee in existence, give it advance notice of his intention (s. 167 (2)).

As with a members' voluntary winding up, if the winding up continues for more than a year the liquidator must call both a general meeting of the company and a meeting of creditors at the end of the first year and in successive years and present an account to them (s. 105). When the company is fully wound up, the liquidator prepares accounts and calls final meetings of the company and creditors at which the accounts are tendered (s. 106). These final meetings must be advertised in the *London Gazette* giving time, place and object of the meeting with at least one month's advance notice (s. 106). Within one week after the final meetings the liquidator must send to the Registrar a copy of the accounts and a return or, alternatively, inform the Registrar that there was not a quorum for the meetings. The documentation sent to the Registrar will be registered and three months later the company will be dissolved. The Registrar will publish a notice in the *London Gazette* concerning the return by the liquidator in respect to the final meeting of the company on a winding up and the order for the dissolution of the company (CA 1985, s. 711).

The consequence of a voluntary winding up

Insolvency winding up commences with the passing of the appropriate resolution (s. 86) notice of which must be published in the *London Gazette* within 14 days of it being passed (s. 85). The following consequences then apply:

i) the company, apart from acts necessary to complete the winding up, should immediately cease trading;

A connected person is one falling within s. 249, e.g. a director or shadow director of the company being wound up or an associate of theirs. The concern is that connected persons may get assets knocked down to them for much less than their true worth. Advance notification to the committee is a valuable safeguard against this possible occurrence.

ii) the company's status and powers continue;

iii) the directors' ostensible authority to bind the company will cease as soon as publication of the resolution takes place, although they are still able to act during liquidation proceedings providing the liquidator, in a creditors' voluntary winding up, sanctions their actions or, in a members' voluntary winding up, the company does so in a general meeting,

A transfer of debenture is not prohibited.

iv) transfers of shares are void except with the approval of the liquidator (*Taylors' Case* (1897));

v) alterations to the status of shareholders are void (*Castello's Case* (1869)).

Review question

Discuss the main difference between a members' and a creditors' voluntary winding up.

Compulsory winding up

Compulsory winding up occurs where a petition is made to the court and after a hearing a winding-up order is granted.

The petitioners

The following may, either separately or jointly, make a winding-up petition (s. 124):

a) *The company*
While this is possible it is rare. A special resolution is needed but of course if the company, at a general meeting, wish to vote for winding up then a members' voluntary winding is eminently preferable.

b) *The company directors*
If the articles permit it the directors may petition but to be valid their decision must be unanimous (*Re Instrumentation Electrical Services Ltd* (1988)).

While the specimen Table A, article 70 gives managerial powers to directors, it does not itself empower them to present a petition for winding up as this amounts to a stoppage of the company and not its management (Re Emmadart Ltd (1979)).

c) *A contributory*
Contributories are present and past shareholders of the company (s. 70) who are liable to contribute to the assets of the company on its winding up (s. 124 (1)). In reality the right of a contributory to present a petition is restricted to:

i) where the number of shareholders is reduced to less than two;

ii) where some, or all, of his shares were originally allotted to him, or have been held by him, and are registered in his name for at least six months in the 18-months period before winding up commenced or the shares dissolved on him through the death of a former holder (s. 124).

d) *A shareholder*
A court will not normally allow a petition to be presented if the number of shareholders seeking to do so is small (per *Re Professional Building Society* (1871)). However, Lord Buckley has said that a fully paid up shareholder may successfully petition but:

... he must show either that there will be a surplus available for distribution amongst the shareholders or that the affairs of the company require investigation in respects which are likely to produce such a surplus. (*Re Othery Construction Ltd* (1966))

Generally the court will allow a petition to be presented by a shareholder where there is anything which seems to require investigation:

Re Varieties Ltd (1893)

The company was formed to build a music hall on land leased to it by S who was to build the hall. S and his nominees held 3,700 shares. On the county council refusing planning permission holders of 3,900 shares voted for a voluntary winding up and appointed the company secretary as liquidator. 847 independent shareholders wanted a compulsory winding up so that the court could inquire into the conduct of S.

Held: The conduct of S merited investigation, therefore, the company would be compulsorily wound up.

---

e) *A creditor*

Creditors, individually or in a group, are the commonest petitioners. However, a court may refuse to hear a creditor's petition if the majority of creditors oppose it (*Re Ilfracombe Building Society* (1901)). Indeed the wishes of creditors and contributories are most important determining factors as to whether a hearing will take place and a court can direct that appropriate meetings are held so as to gauge their wishes (s. 195). But if the company is insolvent then only the wishes of the creditors will prevail. In the case of creditors due regard is paid to the value of each creditor's debt (s. 195) and if there are different classes of creditors then the views of a class particularly affected will carry more weight than those of less affected classes. Where a petition is made by a creditor for non-payment of a debt, should the company make a counter-claim against him then it is up to the court whether or not to accept the petition (*Re A Company (No. 006273 of 1992)* (1992)).

It is not uncommon for a creditor attempting to bring a petition to face a defence by the company that there is either no debt owed or that the validity of the debt is disputed. In *Mann v Goldstein (1968)*, Ungoed-Thomas J dealt with the possibilities thus:

What then is the course for this court to take (i) when the creditor's debt is clearly established; (ii) when it is clearly established that there is no debt; and (iii) when the debt is disputed on substantial grounds?

i)   When the creditor's debt is clearly established it seems to me to follow that this court would not, in general at any rate, interfere even though the company would appear to be solvent, for the creditor would, as such, be entitled to present a petition and the debtor would have its own remedy in paying the undisputed debt which it should pay.

ii) When it is clearly established that there is no debt, it seems to me similarly to follow that there is no creditor, that the person claiming to be such has no locus standi and that his petition is bound to fail. Once that becomes clear, pursuit on the petition would be an abuse of process, and this court would restrain its presentation or advertisement.

iii) When the debt is disputed by the company on some substantial ground (and not just on some ground which is frivolous or without substance and which the court should, therefore, ignore) and the company is solvent, the court will restrain the prosecution of a petition to wind up the company. As Jessel MR said in (*Niger Merchants Co. v Capper* (1877): 'When a company is solvent, the right course is to bring an action for the debt'. So, to pursue a winding up petition in such circumstances is an abuse of the process of the court:

> ... For my part, I would prefer to rest the jurisdiction directly on the comparatively simple propositions that a creditor's petition can only be presented by a creditor, that the winding-up jurisdiction is not for the purpose of deciding a disputed debt (that is, disputed on substantial and not insubstantial grounds) since, until a creditor is established as a creditor he is not entitled to present the petition and has no *locus standi* in the Companies Court; and that, therefore, to invoke the winding-up jurisdiction when the debt is disputed (that is, on substantial grounds) or after it has become clear that it is so disputed is an abuse of the process of the court...

Therefore, a creditor whose debt is disputed in some substantial way cannot generally obtain a winding-up order. The court may prefer to stay the petition until the validity of the debt is settled. But if the court is of the opinion that the dispute is not substantial then it may decide the validity itself:

Re Imperial Silver Quarries Co. (1868)

J sold a silver mine to the company for shares and debentures. The principal loan secured by the debentures was repayable out of profits. J sold six debentures to A. One and a half years' interest became due, but there had been no profits. A petitioned to wind up the company. The company disputed A's claim on the ground that the interest was payable out of profits only.

Held: This was not a very substantial dispute, and depended only on the construction of the debentures; the court decided that A's claim was good and made the order to wind up.

It is not unknown for creditors to present a petition, or threaten to petition, as a ploy to put pressure on a company. While such commercial conduct may be repugnant it is not unlawful:

> It seems to me that to pursue a substantial claim in accordance with the procedure provided and in the normal manner, though with personal hostility or even venom and from some ulterior motive, such as the hope of compromise or some indirect advantage, is not an abuse of the process of the court or acting mala fide but acting *bona fide* in accordance with the process. (Ungoed-Thomas, *Mann v Goldstein* (1968))

However, if it is adjudged that the petitioner has an improper underlying motive for having the company wound up then a court may decide to cut short the petition hearing:

> (if a court) ... sees a petition to wind up presented, not for a *bona fide* purpose of winding up the company, but for some collateral and sinister object, on that ground it will be dismissed with costs. (Malins VC, *Cadiz Waterworks Co. v Barnett* (1874))

Re Metropolitan Saloon Omnibus Co. (1859)

A creditor had brought an unsuccessful winding-up petition against the company which had been dismissed with costs. They then persuaded a shareholder to present a petition for the purpose of annoying the company.

Held: The petition had been brought in bad faith and would be dismissed.

Indeed a petition presented knowing that there is no just case for winding up (or publishing a notice advertising such a petition) may amount to a malicious falsehood justifying an action by the company without it having to show actual damage (*Quartz Hill Gold Mining Co. v Eyre* (1883)).

In respect to a debenture holder they are allowed to petition if the principal sum is payable directly to them but if it is payable to the trustees of a debenture trust deed then they cannot themselves petition (*Re Uruguay Central Rail Co.* (1879)). Also, if the debenture contains a power to appoint a receiver and the debenture holder has not done so then his petition may be refused (*Re Exmouth Docks Co.* (1873)).

Where assets have been charged against liabilities that are in excess of the assets, a court cannot refuse to hear a petition (or refuse to grant a winding-up order) just because of this fact (s. 125 (1)), although it will seem unlikely that in such a situation an unsecured creditor will find it worthwhile bringing a petition. Also if debenture holders have mortgaged all the assets, and they are against an unsecured creditor petitioning, they have to show that there is not a reasonable prospect of the unsecured creditor benefiting from the winding up or else the petition will be heard (*Re Crigglestone Coal Co. Ltd* (1906)).

If a debt is assigned (i.e. transferred) then the person taking it either complete or in part may petition for winding up (*Re Steel Wing Co.* (1921)). Also a creditor who has petitioned may assign his debt and ask the court to substitute the assignee for himself on the petition (*Perak Pioneer Ltd v Petroleum National Bhd* (1986)). A creditor whose claim is contingent or prospective can petition but an undertaking on costs may have to be given as well as making out an arguable case for winding up (*Re British Equitable Bond Ltd* (1910)).

Finally, what is perhaps an obvious point. A court will not take kindly to a petitioner trying to wind up a company for non-payment of a debt if that debt has never been demanded or no opportunity was given for it to be repaid (*Re A Company (No. 001573 of 1983)* (1983)).

f) *The Secretary of State*

Where the Secretary of State for Trade and Industry is of the opinion that it is in the public interest, after publication of a company inspector's report, or on obtaining information from the company, to have it wound up then he may present a petition subject to the court agreeing that it is just and equitable for it to be wound up (s. 124A).

A company anticipating a damning DTI inspector's report may try to avoid a compulsory winding up, which would entail considerable external scrutiny of the company's conduct, by passing a voluntary winding-up resolution. Such a blatant strategy may not succeed:

Re Lubin, Rosen and Associates Ltd (1975)

The company was formed in 1974 with capital of £5,000 £1 fully paid shares. Its business was the development of land in Spain. The company got into difficulties and a DTI investigation revealed that at no time had the company a sufficient share capital base to finance its activities. Also while the company was insolvent the directors, knowing this, had allowed the company to continue trading. For these reasons the DTI felt that a further investigation by a liquidator was needed. The company later passed a resolution for its voluntary winding up and appointed a liquidator. A creditors' meeting confirmed the liquidator's appointment. However, the Secretary of State decided that it was in the public interest to wind up the company compulsorily and to achieve this he presented a petition alleging that it was insolvent and in the circumstances it was just and equitable that it should be wound up. Against the petition were 198 creditors with claims of over £540,000.

Held: That a petition for compulsory winding up which was opposed by many creditors with claims of large value, and was not supported by any creditor, had a formidable obstacle in its way, but that where such a petition was presented by the Secretary of State after he had reached the conclusion, as a result of investigations, that it was expedient in the public interest to wind up the company compulsory, the Secretary of State's conclusion, without being decisive, ought to be given appropriate weight by the court; that where there were circumstances of suspicion it was highly desirable that the winding up should be by the court, with all the safeguards that provided; that the passing of a resolution for a voluntary winding up shortly before the petition was presented, and its subsequent confirmation, ought not to be allowed to put the voluntary winding up into an entrenched position which could be demolished only if the Secretary of State could demonstrate that the process of voluntary winding up would be markedly inferior to a compulsory winding up; and that, accordingly, the order for compulsory winding up should be made.

The Official Receiver is an office holder appointed by the DTI. He is attached to insolvency courts and acts as an interim liquidator in winding up proceedings (5136).

g) *The Official Receiver*

Where a company is already in voluntary liquidation the Official Receiver can, in England, petition for compulsory winding up. If the court is satisfied that the interests of creditors and contributories are not best served by allowing the voluntary winding up to continue then the Official Receiver's petition for compulsory winding up will be granted (s. 124 (5)).

h) *The Bank of England*

The Bank of England may petition for a bank deposit taker to be wound up where it is in the public interest to do so (Banking Act 1979, s. 18).

i) *The Attorney General*

This normally relates to companies that are registered charities (Charities Act 1960, s. 30). However, the Attorney General can bring a petition when he believes public policy considerations demand it:

Ultra bondage ultra vires by Alan Rusbridger

Much to her disappointment Miss Lindi St Claire, the undisputed queen of the torture chamber, was told by two High Court judges that she could no longer continue to offer her wide-ranging services as a limited company.

Lord Justice Ackner ruled that it had been wrong of the Registrar of Companies to allow Miss St Claire to set up in business as Lindi St Claire (Personal Services) Ltd, when she had admitted that the sole purpose of the company was prostitution. The company had operated from an Earls Court basement for the past year with two shareholders and £20,000 worth of equipment designed to 'cater for every taste'. (*The Guardian*, 18 December 1980)

Review question

Compare the rights of a contributory to petition the court for winding up with those of a reditor.

The grounds for a petition

The grounds for bringing a winding-up petition are (s. 122):

1 If the company passes a special resolution to be wound up. This is extremely rare for it would be more advantageous to use voluntary winding up.
2 If a company, first registered as a public one, has not been issued with its trading certificate and more than a year has expired.
3 If the company fails to commence business within one year of its incorporation, or it suspends business for one year. The power of the court to make a winding-up order in this instance is discretionary. It will not be exercised unless there is evidence that the company has no intention of neither starting or recommencing its business (*Re Capital Fire Insurance* (1882)).

    A quicker way to dissolve a company for not carrying on business is to use the procedure under section 652. Here the Registrar will write to the company asking if it is still in business and if no reply is received within one month, send, two weeks after the end of the month reply period, a second letter. If a reply is still not received then a notice may be placed in the *London Gazette* (with a third letter going to the company)

The debt must not be one the company is legally disputing as the court will not allow winding up proceedings to be used as a substitute for debt collection (Re A Company ex parte Fin Soft Holding SA (1991)).

While for insolvency grounds (6) to (8) no minimum debt is stipulated, in practice courts in England and Wales are reluctant to make a winding up order unless the debt claimed is £750 or more. But if a company refuses to pay a debt believing that it is so small a sum that the court will find it insufficient to support a petition, the court may decide to do so (Re World Industrial Bank (1909)). However, courts in Scotland will allow a creditor, whatever amount he is owed, to bring a winding up petition unless special circumstances exist whereby it may be refused (the author acknowledges Charlesworth & Morse, Company Law, fifteenth edition, for the observations contained in this note).

advising that at the expiry of a three-month period the company, unless cause is shown to the contrary, will be struck off the register and it will be dissolved. However, the liability of every director or shareholder of the company will continue as if the company had not been dissolved (CA 1985, s. 652 (6)).

4 If the shareholders of the company fall below two (apart from the exception for private limited companies under the Companies (Single Member Private Limited Companies) Regulations 1992). A creditor who is owed at least £750 and after making a written request, in the proper form, for payment and leaves it at the company's registered office, is not paid within 21 days or been given security for their debt.

5 If a creditor can prove that he has an undisputed debt of £750 or more and the debt had been duly served then the court has to make a winding-up order. Clearly to avoid later difficulties it would be advisable for a creditor to have the company acknowledge in writing the value of the debt and that it had been served on them. The £750 statutory minimum (which may be increased) can be made up by a number of creditors aggregating their debts. The 21 days are clear days so that the day of serving and the day of petition are both excluded (Re Lympne Investment Ltd (1972)). If security is given by the company then it must be marketable, e.g. liquid (*Commercial Bank of Scotland Ltd v Lanark Oil Co. Ltd* (1986)).

6 If the court believes that the company cannot pay its debts as they fall due for payment. What is looked at here is the liquidity of the company assets (*Re Capital Annuities Ltd* (1978)). Also a court may take into account contingent liabilities as well as any reasonable indication that a company is unable to pay its debts on time:

Re Globe Steel Co. (1875)
The company took a bill of exchange in part payment for goods it had bought. The company later dishonoured the bill by not paying it.

Held: The failure to pay was sufficient evidence of insolvency.

The business practice of delaying paying debts until a final demand is made, or until the debtor company is actually taken to court, is not uncommon especially in a recessionary period. However, where a company persistently refuses to pay its debts on time until forced to do so a company may be declared insolvent, even though it has funds available to meet the debt in question (*Re A Company* (1986)).

7 If the court believes that the company's present and future liabilities are such that the value of its assets is less than the amount of its liabilities. Again overall liquidity is looked at so that a company may be wound up even though it has substantial assets if they are not readily disposable and the company is being carried on at a loss. However, where a company makes a loss but its available assets exceed its liabilities then it is not to be regarded as being insolvent merely because of the unprofitability (*Re Joint Stock Coal Co.* (1869)). Proof that the company is unable to make a profit is called for so that where, for example, a change of management is likely to lead ultimately to a profit being made then a winding-up order will be refused (*Re Suburban Hotel Co.* (1867)).

8 Where a court execution judgement in favour of the petitioner has not been fully satisfied. This ground is straightforward. However, if the execution debt, which bears

interest, is not met then it may not be worth seeking a winding-up order unless the creditor is sure that assets do exceed liabilities.

9 If the court is of the opinion that it is just and equitable to wind the company up. This ground, infrequently used, gives considerable discretion to the court:

> ... the foundation of (the law) lies in the words 'just and equitable' ... The words are a recognition of the fact that a limited company is more than a mere judicial entity, with a personality in law of its own: that there is room in company law for recognition of the fact that behind it, or amongst it, there are individuals, with rights, expectations and obligations, *inter se* which are not necessarily submerged in the company structure ... The 'just and equitable' provision does not ... entitle one party to disregard the obligation he assumes by entering a company, nor the court to dispense him from it. It does, as equity always does, enable the court to subject the exercise of legal rights to equitable considerations; considerations, that is, of a personal character arising between one individual and another, which may make it unjust, or inequitable, to insist on legal rights, or to exercise them in a particular way. (Lord Wilberforce, *Ebrahimi v Westbourne Galleries Ltd and Others* (1973))

Therefore, a shareholder petitioning for a winding-up order may plead circumstances where his petition as a shareholder has deteriorated, or been affected in some other way, by the conduct of the company or other shareholders. However, a court will expect a specific allegation of misconduct so that for example a general complaint of fraud is usually insufficient:

Re Medical Battery Co. (1894)

Serious charges of defrauding the public were made against the company. The company went into voluntary liquidation but some creditors wanted to have the company wound up by the court.

Held: Fraud to the outside world is not a ground justifying compulsory winding up.

But if the whole object of the company is fraudulent, such as where the company is a *bubble* with the promoters or directors never intending trading, then it may be wound up:

Re Brinsmead (TE) & Sons Ltd (1897)

J.B. Brinsmead & Sons was an established firm. Three employees (T.E. Brinsmead and his two sons) left and started a similar business called T.E. Brinsmead & Sons Ltd. The company obtained share capital from the public under a fraudulent prospectus with most of it going not to the stated promoters but to undisclosed ones. The company had been formed to confuse the public and 'poach' as much business as possible from J.B. Brinsmead & Sons. Shareholders brought actions alleging fraud in the prospectus.

Held: The company had been formed to carry out a fraud. Therefore, it was just and equitable that it should be wound up.

Other examples of just and equitable under s. 122 (1) (g):

This was
categorized as a
deadlock in the
management of
a private
company.

> ## Re Yenidjie Tobacco Co. Ltd (1916)
> Two shareholder-directors repeatedly failed to agree on important managerial matters. They refused to speak directly to each other but resorted to passing notes via the company secretary.
>
> Held: Petition granted.

also:

See also
Ebrahimi v
Westbourne
Galleries Ltd
and Others
(1973); and
Loch v John
Blackwood Ltd
(1924) where
similar failures in
personal
relationships
supported just
and equitable
winding up.

> ## Re Zinotty Properties Ltd (1984)
> ZP had been formed by two individuals to acquire and develop a certain site. The petitioner held 25 per cent of the shares whilst the respondent had 75 per cent. The development was completed but instead of making an expected distribution from the fund now available the minority shareholder alleged that the majority shareholder had used the money from the development for his own business purposes.
>
> Held: Petition granted.

The powers of the court on hearing a petition

The court on hearing a winding-up petition may (s. 125):

i) dismiss the petition;
ii) adjourn the hearing with or without condition;
iii) make an interim order, or any other order it thinks fit.

Generally, the court will be guided by the wishes of the creditors and contributors. If they are not in agreement then a majority view will be canvassed, such as by calling meetings. If the petition is successful, the petitioner's costs will become a first charge on the assets of the company available (assuming that there are assets available) to the unsecured creditors.

The consequences of compulsory winding up

The main consequences are:

1 *Before the grant of a winding-up order*
   a) The winding up is taken to have commenced on the date the petition was presented. If initially the winding up had been voluntary then the commencement

date will be when the resolution for voluntary winding up was passed (s. 129).

b) Between the presentation of the petition and the winding-up order the court may appoint a provisional liquidator (s. 135). Whoever asks for this appointment is responsible for the costs which means that they must deposit money or security with the court. The provisional liquidator, who is normally the official receiver, acts as custodian of the company's property (s. 144). See also (c) below.

c) When a winding-up order has been made, or a provisional liquidator appointed, any action or legal proceeding brought against the company will be stayed unless the court agrees to it continuing (s. 130 (2)).

d) Any disposal of assets, transfer of shares or alterations of a member's status will be void unless the court agrees to it (s. 127).

The overriding concern of the court was stated by Buckley LJ in *Re Gray's Inn Construction Co. Ltd* (1980):

Any seizure by a creditor of company assets to satisfy a debt will be void (s. 128).

> In considering whether to make a validating order the court must always, in my opinion, do its best to ensure that the interests of the unsecured creditors will not be prejudiced. Where the application relates to a specific transaction this may be susceptible of positive proof. In a case of completion of a contract or project the proof may perhaps be less positive but nevertheless be cogent enough to satisfy the court that in the interests of the creditors the company should be enabled to proceed, or at any rate that proceeding in the manner proposed would not prejudice them in any respect. The desirability of the company being enabled to carry on its business generally is likely to be more speculative and will be likely to depend on whether a sale of the business as a going concern will probably be more beneficial than a break-up realization of the company's assets ... Each case must depend on its own particular facts. Since the policy of the law is to procure so far as practicable rateable payments of the unsecured creditors' claims, it is, in my opinion, clear that the court should not validate any transaction or series of transactions which might result in one or more pre-liquidation creditors being paid in full at the expense of other creditors, who will only receive a dividend, in the absence of special circumstances making such a course desirable in the interests of the unsecured creditors as a body.

Where a company is trading with no imminent threat of serious insolvency then transactions within the ordinary course of business may be approved as well as the normal operation of the company's bank account (*Re A Company (No 007532 of 1986)* (1987)).

e) The directors' powers cease and employees are made redundant. If the provincial liquidator wishes to keep the company operating as a going concern then he may re-engage employees and payment of their wages will not fall foul of s. 128 (see (d) above and *Re Park, Ward & Co. Ltd* (1926)).

f) Any floating charges crystallize (see the section on charges in Chapter 10, Debentures).

2 *On the granting of a winding-up order*

a) Until a permanent liquidator is appointed the Official Receiver becomes an interim liquidator (ss. 136–137):

i) He may ask the directors, or others, for a statement of affairs which must be produced within 21 days (s. 131 (1)). The statement, verified by affidavit, has to contain (s. 131 (2)):
- details of the company's assets, debts and other liabilities;
- the names and addresses of the company's creditors and details of any securities they hold together with the date when the security was given.

ii) He is also required to carry out an investigation as to why the company failed and (if need be) to look into all the affairs of the company.

Where the Official Receiver feels it necessary he may apply to the court for permission to hold a public examination of any present or past company officer (directors, secretary, auditors, salaried solicitor); any promoter or manager of the company; any liquidator, administrator or receiver. Should either 50 per cent of the creditors or 75 per cent of the contributories request it then the Official Receiver must apply for a public examination. A person being examined under oath must answer questions relating to hearsay and even questions that may incriminate himself (*Bishopsgate Investment Management Ltd v Maxwell* (1992)).

iii) In addition the Official Receiver must, within 12 weeks of the winding-up order, decide whether to call separate meetings of creditors and contributories. Should 25 per cent in value of the creditors demand it then meetings have to be called (s. 136). The main purpose of these meetings is to appoint a liquidator. If each meeting nominates a separate liquidator then the creditors' nominee is successful. However, a creditor or contributory unwilling to accept this appointment may apply to the court for the contributories' choice (or someone else) to be appointed (s. 139). Should the meetings be unable to choose a liquidator then the Official Receiver may ask the Secretary of State to intervene and appoint (s. 137 (2)).

Indeed there is available to the Official Receiver a quicker method of having a liquidator appointed. This is to apply directly, without bothering to call creditors' and contributories' meetings, to the Secretary of State asking that he appoint a liquidator (s. 137 (1)). If the Secretary of State does make an appointment then the liquidator has to inform the creditors of this, or alternatively, advertise (s. 137(4)).

b) Once appointed the liquidator, if he is of the opinion that the business can be sold at a higher price as a going concern, is allowed to keep the company in business until it is sold and he can re-engage dismissed staff to help achieve this objective.

c) The assets of the company remain the legal property of the company until such time as the court vests them in the liquidator who may then dispose of them to satisfy creditors.

The liquidator

By way of a thumbnail sketch the following comments may be made:
a) *Functions*

The functions of a liquidator of a company which is being wound up by the court are to ensure that the assets of the company are got in, realized and distributed to the company's creditors and if there is a surplus, to the persons entitled to it (s. 143 (1)).

b) *Powers*

All powers enjoyed by the board of directors will pass to the liquidator. Therefore, he may: bring and defend actions in the company's name; carry on the business of the company so far as necessary to achieve a satisfactory winding up; sell and transfer company assets; engage staff or agents to assist him; call meetings of creditors and contributories; etc.

c) *Liability*

As a liquidator owes fiduciary duties to the company it means that he must act with the utmost probity so that no personal advantage is obtained (*Silkstone and Haigh Moore Coal Co. v Edey* (1900)). As he has taken over the directors' powers he is an agent of the company so that provided he acts within his powers he will not be personally liable on contracts that he makes while winding it up (*Stead, Hazel & Co. v Cooper* (1933)).

However, what a liquidator is potentially vulnerable to is an application to the court from a creditor or contributory alleging that in the course of the winding up that he (as liquidator) misapplied or retained money or other property or was guilty of a misfeasance or breach of duty (s. 212 (1)). If the accusation is substantiated the court may compel him to repay or restore what has been taken or to contribute such sums to the company's assets as will be appropriate compensation for any misfeasance or breach of duty (s. 212 (3)).

Where a liquidator is unsure as to the proper course to take, especially if large sums are involved, then he may apply to the court, or call creditors' and contributories' meetings, seeking instructions (*Re Windsor Steam Coal Co.* (1929)).

> Misfeasance is the improper performance of a lawful act. In this context the commonest example would be where the liquidator carried out his duties in a negligent manner (Pulsford v Devenish (1903)).

Review question

What are the duties of a liquidator?

The winding-up process

Creditors

As previously mentioned the liquidator has to get in all the company's assets then dispose of them in order to, as far as it is possible, satisfy the creditors. Therefore, *proof of debts* by creditors will be required. Should they wish a secured creditor may give up his security and prove for the whole amount (*Re Ligonel Spinning Co.* (1900)). This may seem strange in that security is normally much prized. However, if the security is not as valuable as it was believed, such as obsolete machinery, or if it is anticipated that the liquidator will success-fully challenge the validity of the security, it may be advisable to disclaim it so as to avoid an investigation of the circumstances of it being taken. Also a secured creditor may value his security and prove in the winding up for any balance.

Contributories

A contributory
means every
person liable to
contribute to
the assets of the
company in the
event of it being
wound up (s.
79).

The liquidator can look to both present and past shareholders for a contribution towards payment of the company's debts and winding-up expenses. Therefore, he will prepare a list of contributories. They are those placed on:

- the 'A' list consisting of present shareholders at start of winding up; and
- the 'B' list of those who were past shareholders within a year of start of winding up.

If the company is limited by shares then no contributory can be called upon where his shares are fully paid. Therefore, the liquidator is looking for unpaid shares with present shareholders (the 'A' list) being called upon first to contribute the amount, in full or in part, that is still outstanding on their shares. If such contributions are insufficient to meet the company's liabilities then the liquidator will move onto past shareholders who had held partly paid shares that the existing shareholder has not paid (the 'B' list). Again a call will be made that they contribute the amount unpaid on the shares. However, a past shareholder does not have to contribute where (s. 74(2)):

a) he was not a shareholder of the company for over a year before winding up commenced; or

b) the company's debts to which he is expected to contribute were contracted after he ceased to be a shareholder; or

c) it appears to the court that present shareholders of the company are able to satisfy the contribution required of them.

Where shares have, in the year preceding winding up, been held by a number of shareholders all of them will be placed on the 'B' list but the principal obligation to pay will fall on the last transferor (Humby's Case (1872)).

The authority of the liquidator to make a call on contributories in a compulsory winding up derives from the committee of inspection or an order of the court; while in a voluntary winding up the liquidator can make a call on his own choosing. A contributory refusing to meet a call can have action taken against him for failure to pay a debt. And where a contributory is also a creditor of the company he is unable to set off his debt against his liability for calls even if a written agreement purports to allow him to do so (*Re Law Car and General Corporation* (1912)). On death a contributory's assets may be looked to (s. 81), and if a contributory is made bankrupt then any call will be provable in his bankruptcy (s. 82).

While calls are primarily made to pay creditors a shareholder of unpaid shares, present or past, may also be called upon to make a contribution so as to be able to distribute assets fairly among shareholders (*Welton v Saffery* (1897) unless the articles provide for a different arrangement (*Re Kinatan (Borneo) Rubber Ltd* (1923)).

Earlier transactions of the company that a liquidator may avoid

When going through the affairs of the company a liquidator will look for any transactions previously entered into by the company that he may be able to avoid. If he is able to do so then the value of any transaction avoided will swell the assets avoidable to creditors. Transactions that the liquidator may be able to avoid are:

1 transactions at an undervalue (s. 238);
2 an invalid preference (s. 239);
3 an extortionate credit transaction (s. 244);
4 invalidity of a floating charge (s. 245).

All of these are dealt with in Chapter 10, Debentures. In addition there is the possibility of breach of section 423 given below.

5 Transactions that defraud creditors (Insolvency Act 1986, s. 423)

Section 423 of the Insolvency Act 1986 may be used as an alternative to section 238 in order that a transaction at an undervalue may be invalidated. A transaction will come within this section if:

a) it amounted to being a gift in that no consideration was received for it;

b) the value of the consideration received for it was significantly less than the value of the floating charge (s. 423 (1)).

For a court to be willing to hear an application made by the Official Receiver, liquidator, administrator or debtor (s. 424) to set aside the transaction it has to be satisfied that the charge was given with the aim of:

a) putting assets beyond the reach of a creditor who is making (currently or in future) a claim against him;

b) otherwise prejudicing the interests of creditors in relation to a claim that he is making (or may make) (s. 423 (3)).

If the court is satisfied that the applicant has made out his case then it may order the restoration of the parties to the position they would have been in had the floating charge not been given and also make any protective order it feels necessary to those who suffered under the transaction (s. 423 (2)).

> Section 423 operates as a general provision which allows a court to set aside a transaction and make restoration and restitution orders.

Fraudulent trading

This is where in winding up it appears that an insolvent company continued to trade so as to defraud creditors or for any other fraudulent purpose (s. 213). *Any person* who knowingly allowed this to happen will be liable, on the liquidator's application to the court, to pay compensation to creditors for the harm the fraudulent trading caused:

> If a company continues to carry on business and to incur debts at a time when there is to the knowledge of the directors no reasonable prospects of the creditors ever receiving payment ... it is in general a proper inference that the company is carrying on business with intent to defraud. (Maugham J, *Re Williams C Leitch Bros Ltd* (No. 1) (1932))

> Fraudulent trading is also a criminal offence (CA 1985, s. 458) whether the company is being wound up or not. Those convicted can be fined, imprisoned or both.

A practical difficulty with fraudulent trading is that dishonesty, as opposed to incompetence, is required (*Re L Todd (Swanscombe) Ltd* (1990)):

Re A Company (No 001418 of 1988) (1990)

Having not made a profit for a few years, in which there had always been a negative net current assets to liabilities balance, the company went into a creditors' voluntary winding up with an estimated loss to unsecured creditors of £212,000. Earlier the company had exceeded its bank overdraft limit and fallen behind with PAYE, NICs and VAT payments as well as not paying ordinary trade creditors. However, during this period it had continued to pay significant sums as remuneration to the respondent's chairman, managing director and majority shareholder. The liquidator alleged fraudulent trading under section 630 of CA 1985 (now IA 1986, s. 213).

Held: There had been fraudulent trading.

In his judgement in *Re A Company (No. 001418 of 1988)* (1990), Bromley J drew attention to the two conditions necessary for the accusation of fraudulent trading to be founded:

> A finding that a person was knowingly party to the business of a company having been carried on with intent to defraud creditors may be made if the following two conditions are satisfied:
>
> 1 if that person realized at the time the debts were incurred that there was no reason for thinking that funds would be available to pay the debt in question when it became due or shortly thereafter; and
> 2 there was actual dishonesty involving, according to current notions of fair trading among commercial men, real moral blame.

While fraud may be strongly suspected, actually proving it is hard so that relatively few allegations are sustained. What may be preferable is for a liquidator to try to use the narrower, but rather more easily proven, remedy of wrongful trading.

Wrongful trading

Where, in a winding up, it appears to the liquidator that a *director, former director* or *shadow director* has been responsible for wrongful trading he may apply to the court for a compensation order. Wrongful trading occurs where the company continued trading even though the director knew, or ought to have concluded, that there was no reasonable prospect that the company would avoid insolvent liquidation and the company did subsequently go into liquidation (s. 214 (2)). What makes wrongful trading easier to make out than fraudulent trading is that an element of constructive knowledge applies in that the director is taken to know that the company could not avoid insolvent liquidation if that would have been the conclusion of a reasonably diligent person having:

For wrongful trading there is no criminal liability.

a) the general knowledge, skill and experience that might reasonably be expected of someone carrying out the duties of the director in question; and
b) the general knowledge, skill and experience actually possessed by that director (s. 214(5)).

Re Produce Marketing Consortium Ltd (1989)
The company had traded successfully for several years as agents for the importation of Spanish fruit. However, it later drifted into insolvency evidenced by: exceeding its bank overdraft; assets less than liabilities; cheques returned unpaid; trade creditors unpaid; a warning by the company auditor to the directors of the possibility of fraudulent trading etc. The company finally went into insolvent liquidation owing nearly £318,000. The liquidator applied to the court for a compensation order against the company's two directors.

Held: The directors had allowed the company to trade wrongfully and were ordered to make a contribution of £75,000.

Commenting in *Re Produce Marketing Consortium Ltd* (1989) on the new powers of the courts to find wrongful trading without there having to be an element of fraud Knox J said:

Two steps in particular were taken in the legislative enlargement of the court's jurisdiction. First, the requirement for an intent to defraud and fraudulent purposes was not retained as an essential, and with it goes the need for what Maugham J called 'actual dishonesty involving real moral blame'. The second enlargement is that the test to be applied by the court has become one under which the director in question is to be judged by the standards of what can be expected of a person fulfilling his functions, and showing reasonable diligence in doing so ... It follows that the general knowledge, skill and experience postulated will be much less extensive in a small company in a modest way of business, with simple accounting procedures and equipment, than it will be in a large company with sophisticated procedures.

On liability for wrongful trading being established a director may avoid having to pay compensation by showing that after he first became aware of the wrongful trading, he took every step to minimize the potential loss to the company's creditors as he ought to have taken in the circumstances. This is where the difficulties with wrongful trading are encountered. How do you identify the moment when a director first became aware? Also what is exactly meant by taking every step? Does it mean every reasonable step that such a director could be expected to take or literally every step that it was possible to take?

There is a six-year liability period for wrongful trading running from the commencement of insolvent liquidation (Limitation Act 1980; R v Farmizer (Products) Ltd (1995)).

The priority of payment on winding up

While creditors within a class must be treated equally, between classes of creditors there is inequality as a statutory order of repayment of creditors operates. Each class of creditor must be repaid in full before any payment can be made to the next class. The order of repayment is:

1 *Fixed charge secured creditors*
   Provided that the charge was properly registered then the security can be disposed of and the sum obtained used to pay their debt. If the sum obtained is insufficient to discharge the whole of their debt then they will have to plead as an unsecured creditor for the balance unpaid.

2 *Liquidation expenses*
   All expenses properly incurred in the winding up, including the remuneration of the liquidator, are payable out of the company's assets in priority to all other claims (s. 115). But as mentioned a registered fixed charge secured creditor can claim his security.

3 *Preferential creditors*
   These are listed in sections 175 and 176 and the Insolvency Rules. They are:
   a) wages or salaries, excluding commission and holiday pay, for each employee up to £800 owed within the four-month period prior to winding up;
   b) statutory deductions of income tax (PAYE) that should have been paid but were not paid within the 12-month period prior to winding up;
   c) value added tax (VAT) that should have been paid but was not paid in the six-month period prior to winding up;
   d) social security contributions (National Insurance Contributions) that should have

For exposition these have been listed (a) to (f) but it must be remembered that all preferential creditors rank pari passu, that is equally, among themselves. Also there are other minor preferential creditors.

been paid but were not paid in the 12-month period prior to winding up;

e) employer contributions to an occupational pension or state scheme that should have been paid but were not paid;

f) a loan by a third party to enable employees in (a) to be paid, also where a third party pays into an occupational or state pension scheme under (e).

4 *Floating charge secured creditors*

The main qualification here is that the floating charge should either have been created 12 months or more prior to winding up, or, if given within this 12-month period, that the company was solvent at the date the floating charge was created (s. 245).

However, a floating charge will be valid for new monies lent to the company since the date of its creation (s. 245; *Re Yeovil Glove Co. Lt*d (1964)).

5 *Unsecured creditors*

These include the general trade creditors as well as the unsecured part of a secured or preferential claim. In the majority of instances assets, at this stage, would have been sufficiently exhausted that unsecured creditors will be fortunate to receive more than a modest percentage of their debts.

6 Post-insolvency interest on debts

Interest is payable on all debts proved in winding up and is paid once all the proved debts have been paid. The rate of interest is set either by contract or under section 17 of Judgements Act 1830 (s. 189).

This is also termed deferred interest.

7 Shareholders of the company

It will be doubtful if any funds by this stage will be left. If there are then the company would have been solvent! Technically, shareholders are not creditors but owners of the company and as such the order of their being paid back capital or unpaid dividends will be given in the articles of association.

Dissolution of a company

Once the winding-up process is completed a company must be dissolved.

Dissolution following a voluntary winding up

The liquidator has to tender his accounts to a final general meeting of the company as well as, if the company was insolvent, to a final meeting of creditors. A copy of these accounts, together with a return, must then be sent within seven days to the Registrar who will register them

Dissolution following a compulsory winding up – early dissolution in England and Wales

Where the Official Receiver was appointed liquidator, and it appears to him:

a) that the realizable assets of the company are insufficient to cover the expenses of the winding up, and

b) that the affairs of the company do not require any further investigation.

Early dissolution in Scotland can be achieved by following a similar procedure under s. 204.

then he may at any time apply to the Registrar for the early dissolution of the company (s. 202 (2)). If the Official Receiver is minded to make a dissolution application then he must give at least 28 days notice of his intention to the company's creditors and contributories as well as to the administrative receiver if one has been appointed (s. 202 (3)). On receipt of the Official Receiver's application it will be registered and three months later the company is dissolved (s. 202 (5)).

Should any creditor, contributory or (if appointed) the administrative receiver object to the application for early dissolution then he may in the 28-day notice period apply to the Secretary of State for directions on the grounds that:

a) the assets are sufficient to cover the expenses of the winding up; or
b) the affairs of the company do require further investigation; or
c) for some other reason the early dissolution of the company is inappropriate (s. 203).

If the Secretary of State does give directions, they will be that the winding up is to continue as if no application had been made by the Official Receiver for early dissolution.

Dissolution otherwise under sections 202–204

Where the Registrar receives notice that the final meeting of creditors has taken place, or a notice from the Official Receiver that the winding up is complete, then he will register it and three months later the company will be dissolved (s. 205 (1)).

The Registrar's authority to strike a defunct company from the register by following the procedure s. 652 is dealt with under the grounds for compulsory winding up in this chapter.

Chapter summary

- By statute (Insolvency Act 1986) insolvency practitioners must be fit and qualified persons authorized to practise by a recognized or competent body.
- Voluntary winding up is of two types: a members' or creditors'. For both, a resolution (special for members, extraordinary for creditors) is required with the liquidator being appointed by either the members or creditors.
- A members' voluntary winding up requires the directors to make a statutory declaration of solvency and to provide a financial statement. In a creditors' voluntary winding up a liquidation committee may be appointed (creditor and shareholder membership) to monitor the winding-up process.
- The consequences of winding up are: the company must cease trading (apart from where it assists winding up); directors forfeit their powers; transfer of shares and charges to shareholder liability are banned.
- A petitioner for compulsory winding up must come within recognized categories: company; director; contributory; shareholder; creditor (the commonest petitioner); Secretary of State, Official Receiver, Bank of England and Attorney General.
- The grounds for compulsory winding up are: a company passing a special resolution; non-receipt of a trading certificate; failure to commence business within a year of incorporation as cessation of business for a year (with no intention of starting or restarting); fewer than two shareholders (but not in a single-member private company); insolvency (the commonest ground), e.g. £750 or more not paid within 21 days of a written demand; an unsatisfied execution judgement; judicial opinion that the company cannot pay its debts on time); and judicial opinion that it is just and equitable to wind the company up.

- On a compulsory winding-up order being made the Official Receiver is made a temporary liquidator until a permanent one is appointed. He may ask the directors for a statement of affairs; carry out an investigation as to why the company collapsed; examine under oath anyone connected with the company; and decide within 12 weeks whether to call meetings of creditors and contributories.
- A liquidator has the primary function of getting in company assets and disposing of them to satisfy creditors. All powers held by the directors are transferred to him including those of agency. As a fiduciary he must account, with the utmost good faith, to the company.
- A contributory is a holder or former holder of partly paid shares in the company. Present shareholders are placed on an 'A' list, past shareholders on a 'B' list. If assets are insufficient to discharge all liabilities then those on the 'A' list will be called upon to pay all or part of the balance outstanding on their shares. If those on the 'A' list cannot pay then those on the 'B' list will be called upon to contribute in their stead. Once a share is fully paid then no one can be asked to contribute more. Past shareholder liability as a contributory ceases: if he was not a shareholder for over a year before winding up started; or the company debts were contracted after he ceased to be a shareholder; or the court is satisfied that present shareholders can meet the contributions requested of them.
- Fraudulent trading, a civil and criminal offence, is where an insolvent company continues trading so as to defraud creditors. Anyone knowingly allowing this to occur will be liable to compensate creditors. However, fraud requires dishonesty, which is difficult to prove.
- Wrongful trading is where a director (present, past or shadow) knew, or should have known, that there was no reasonable prospect that the company would avoid insolvent liquidation (and which it did not avoid), but he allowed the company to continue trading. An objective–subjective test of liability is used: the general knowledge, skill and experience of a typical director is compared to the general knowledge, skill and experience of the director being examined. A director found liable (there is no criminal penalty) will have to compensate creditors unless a statutory defence is available, i.e. after first becoming aware of the insolvency situation, the director immediately took all steps to minimize the potential loss to creditors.
- Priority of payment on winding up requires that creditors are paid in full in a strict order: fixed charge creditor to claim his security; then, winding-up expenses; preferential creditors; floating charge creditors; unsecured creditors; post-insolvency interest on debts and finally shareholders.
- Dissolution takes place following a bureaucratic procedure that requires the Registrar to be notified of certain matters which three months after their receipt lead to dissolution.

Discussion questions

1 How may the insolvency of a company be established?
2 To what extent can a shareholder petition for winding up?
3 Is it possible that directors may be held personally liable for the debts of their company?

Case study exercise

Fatima Afzal, Semina Patel and Deepak Kaur are equal shareholder-directors in a private limited company trading as *Asian Delight* – a fashionable city centre restaurant. Fatima, the chef, has gained considerable celebrity status through appearing in her own television series *Fatima Fancies*. While Fatima's success led to increased business for the company it also resulted in her being absent from the company while she pursued her television work and wrote the book that accompanied the series. Therefore, for convenience Semina and Deepak fell into the habit of making company decisions themselves and letting Fatima know afterwards. Subsequently, they do not even bother to inform her of their decisions – most notably to give each other (but not her) increased director fees. Fatima, on learning of these increased fees from a study of the company accounts, falls out with her fellow directors. She wishes to realize her investment in the company but Semina and Deepak are unhelpful – they want her to continue to lend her name to the enterprise!

Advise Fatima as to whether or not she may have the company wound up.

Further reading

Principles of Corporate Insolvency Law, R.M. Goode (1997), Sweet & Maxwell.
Applications to Wind Up Companies, D. French (1993), Blackstone.
Pennington's Corporate Insolvency Law, R. Pennington (1997), Butterworth.
The 'Just and Equitable' Winding Up of Small Private Companies, M.R. Chesterman (1973), MLR, 129.
Judicial Attitudes to Insolvency Law, M. Crystal (1998), Co. Law, 49.
Winding Up on the Just and Equitable Ground: The Partnership Analogy, D.D. Prentice (1973), LQR, 107.

Appendix 1
The modernization of company law

In March 1998 the Department of Trade and Industry (DTI) published a consultation paper, *Modern Company Law for a Competitive Economy*, that introduced the Government's intention to review and modernize company law. In its foreword the then Secretary of State wrote:

> Company law lies at the heart of our economy ... Our current framework ... is essentially constructed on foundations which were put in place by Victorians in the middle of the last century. There have been numerous additions, amendments and consolidations since then, but they have created a patchwork of regulations that is immensely complex and seriously out of date. The resulting costs and problems may not be obvious to all, but they are real and substantial nevertheless ... Modern companies are one of the three key pillars of our approach to competitiveness, and we are determined to ensure that we have a framework of company law which is up-to-date, competitive and designed for the next century, a framework which facilitates enterprise and promotes transparency and fair dealing. (Margaret Beckett)

The above encapsulates the motivation and direction of current government thinking and action.

Starting with a recognition that company law evolved from Victorian times to become a 'patchwork of regulations that is immensely complex and seriously out of date', successive piecemeal reforms have, in the DTI's opinion, made law 'difficult for business people to understand, especially those in small and medium sized enterprises, and its rules are inclined to be too detailed and too regulatory'. The fear is that over-burdensome legislation that is prone to be obscure could seriously hamper Britain's ability to compete in an increasingly global marketplace:

> In a number of areas the present arrangements are holding back rather than facilitating competitiveness, growth and investment.

For these reasons the Government is committed to act.

The overall objective is the streamlining and simplification of company law. While the consultation paper flags up the problem it is sparse in substance. This, presumably, is to be expected in a consultation paper that is basically a declaration of intent. What it has done,

In 1991 the Law Society's Company Law Committee had published a paper (The Reform of Company Law) in which current company law was said: not to be of a high enough standard; not meeting its stated aims; and failing to take a long-term view of company law.

however, is to identify a number of concerns and most probably these will be the areas of existing law that will be the most radically changed. These areas are:

a) *Inappropriateness*

Current legislation is at fault in two broad areas:

i) Over-formal language, which is not user friendly. For example Table A, which is widely used as a specimen set of articles, is written in technical, legalistic language and would be of more practical use if it was rewritten in plain English.

ii) Excessive detail, which makes for complexity. For example the distinction between special and extraordinary resolutions at general meetings.

b) *Over-regulation*

This causes difficulties. The paper refers, as an example, to capital maintenance rules. While it is right for the Companies Act to attempt to reduce the risk of insolvency, the provisions are too detailed, too expensive, and lead to inflexibility in the use of capital. By dispensing with the requirement for shares to have a nominal value (par value) simple statements of share capital in a company's accounts ought to be possible.

c) *Complex structure*

The Companies Act does not in its entirety apply to all companies. Some parts, such as disclosure of who owns shares, apply only to public companies; while other parts, such as dealings by directors, apply differently to public and private companies. Therefore, future legislation ought to differentiate more markedly between public and private as well as between large and small companies. The review that will be carried out will examine the feasibility of having separate regulations for different types of companies. If the premise is correct that the existing law is over-complex then simplification should reduce the costs of compliance and make it easier for small companies and their directors to know their responsibilities.

d) *Efficiency gains*

Those parts of company law that fail to achieve their purpose need to be looked at either to make them more effective, or, if this is unnecessary or impossible, to repeal them. For example, part of the bureaucracy of administering company law is accepted as being inefficient in that Companies House allows material to be filed only in a paper-based format. This ignores the much heralded revolution in information technology. Therefore, it is felt by the DTI that Companies House should allow electronic filing. Also, at AGMs shareholders ought to be able to vote directly electronically without their having to attend or use a proxy.

e) *Corporate governance*

While acknowledging that self-regulation, in the form of codes, was preferable to specific legislation, three possible exceptions were identified where 'legal underpinning' may be needed. These are:

i) Director duties to be broadened. At present, while theoretically a director's fiduciary duties are owed to the company as a whole, in practice this is interpreted narrowly as equating with majority shareholder interests. This sectional view does not sit well with Labour's belief in a stockholder economy where a company must account not just to major shareholders but to other interested parties as well e.g. employers, creditors and the community.

ii) The conduct of AGMs may have to be amended in order to make it easier for

The consultation paper, comparing British company law with other countries, such as Canada, leads the DTI to believe that a framework that is easier to operate with greater general freedoms is possible.

shareholders to table resolutions, and if they do not hold shares in their own name, to attend and to vote.

iii) Shareholders may need to have a legal right to vote separately on directors' pay and not the present system of having to vote en bloc on a whole package that includes directors' pay.

Review timetable

On publication of the Consultative Paper in March 1998 the DTI outlined a broad timetable that it was determined to adhere to. This was:

March 1998	–	Steerage Group and Consultative Committees to be set up and start working followed shortly after by various working groups
June 1999	–	The first Working Group, having consulted widely, to complete its report on the strategic framework for company law reform
December 1999	–	Other Working Groups, under the coordination of the Steerage Group, to consult interested parties on their draft proposals
June 2000	–	All Working Groups, following wide consultation, to complete their reports
Autumn 2000	–	Final report to be drafted
March 2001		
	–	Final report to be published in conjunction with a White Paper. Legislation to follow some time in the next Parliament

The *Steerage Group* is charged with the task of overseeing the management of the Review and 'ensuring that its outcome is clear in concept, internally coherent, well articulated and expressed, and workable'. For reasons of efficiency the Steerage Group will be small, comprising: lawyers, representatives of business (large and small), the Chairs of Working Groups, the Project Director and a Scottish representative.

The *Consultative Committee* will be widely based with the members drawn from the Steerage Group, the professions and business, e.g. the Law Society, CBI, TUC, the accountancy bodies and other Government departments.

The *Working Groups* will do most of the detailed work but to ensure that they do so within a common framework a first Working Group will concentrate on an overall strategic framework. This legal framework will cover the requirements for the birth, existence and death of companies:

> ... it will identify the fundamental rules governing the procedures for incorporation, the basic constitutional structure, and cessation of existence. It will examine the rights and responsibilities of the entity and its participants and identify in which areas there should be mandatory rules to protect the interests of shareholders, creditors, employees and other participants.

As the new Companies Act must be 'user-friendly' the first Working Group will look at the structure and style of the new legislation to see that it is as accessible as possible to non-specialists.

To make shareholders' voting more meaningful it may be necessary for it to be made mandatory, especially for institutional shareholders. This would mean increased voting rights having to be paid for by the imposition of a shareholder obligation!

The procedure to be adopted is that the work of the first Working Group will be published for wide consultation. Other Working Groups, set up by the Steerage Group, will consider detailed aspects identified in the strategic framework as needing in-depth examination. Drawing on a wide range of legal and business expertise the work of each Working Group will be published for full consultation with a final report drawing together the work of all the Working Groups.

Company Law Steerage Group Report

In February 1999 the Steerage Group published its consultation report. Three themes may be identified as follows.

Stakeholders

Actually only a short chapter is devoted to stakeholders. This is a considerable shrinkage from what was expected when the review was originally set up.

Stakeholders (employees, customers, creditors, the local community, as well as shareholders) had to be recognized and included into company thinking. The report provided comments on two stakeholder approaches. Firstly, the *enlightened* approach is where progress may be made subject to current company law being amended so that, for instance, more corporate information will be made available to the public. Secondly, a *pluralist* approach is more pro-active in that directors will be either encouraged or compelled to balance shareholder interests against those of other stakeholders.

Small companies

Currently there are approximately 1.32 million registered companies in the UK, of which only 12,000 are public limited companies, with 2,500 of these being listed on the Stock Exchange (DTI statistics).

Company law grew out of the need to support large commercial concerns, and thus much in the Companies Act is inappropriate to small company ventures. Therefore, the report advocates making the law simpler to understand, e.g. company formation and how car capital needs to be maintained with, possibly, removing the need for court approval for capital reduction.

Information technology

Electronic communication and data storage should, the report urges, be introduced at the first opportunity so as to enable companies to reach their shareholders via the internet as well as being able to file returns and other information with Companies House. Indeed the report believes that the electronic media ought to markedly improve the quality of registration and data registration as well as making more available and transparent company information to outsiders.

Future possibilities

The Steering Group is currently examining whether electronic media may be extended to 'virtual meetings' with, perhaps, electronic voting. Financial reporting is also being looked at with the idea being floated that responsibility for accounting standards be delegated to private sector monitors such as the Accounting Standards Board.

Appendix 2
Statistics of director disqualification

Introductory comment

The Disqualification Unit considers on behalf of the Secretary of State for Trade and Industry whether it is in the public interest for an application to be made to the court for the disqualification of a particular director. If the decision is to make such an application then proceedings are instigated by the Disqualification Unit.

Number and sources of complaint against directors

For England and Wales in 1997 the Disqualification Unit received 5,253 *reports* (1996 = 4,825) identifying aspects of unfit conduct by directors of which 3,174 (1996 = 2,919) were from insolvency practitioners and 2,079 (1996 = 1,906) from the Official Receiver when carrying out compulsory liquidations. A further 8,771 *returns* (1996 = 9,914) were received where no misconduct was alleged. In Scotland the Disqualification Unit received 183 *reports* (1996 = 167) and 397 *returns* (1996 = 461).

Gratitude is expressed to the Disqualification Unit (part of the Insolvency Service of the DTI) for the provision of the statistics reproduced in this appendix.

Results of applications for disqualification orders 1996 and 1997

1996 No. of directors disqualified	No. of years disqualified	1997 No. of directors disqualified
115	2	128
215	3	203
187	4	264
169	5	216
98	6	151
62	7	106
47	8	76
17	9	19
20	10	30
2	11	3
6	12	15
3	13	1
–	14	–
4	15	7
945		1,219
30	Applications dismissed	19
103	Applications withdrawn	155
133		174

Appendix 3
Statistics of company insolvencies

Company insolvencies in England and Wales

Year	Type of liquidation		Total
	Compulsory	Voluntary	
1993	8,244	12,464	20,708
1994	6,597	10,131	16,728
1995	5,519	9,017	14,536
1996	5,080	8,381	13,461
1997	4,735	7,875	12,610

NB: The above numbers are slightly increased by the inclusion of partnership insolvencies.

Company insolvencies in Scotalnd

Year	Type of liquidation		Total
	Compulsory	Voluntary	
1993	286	265	551
1994	242	202	444
1995	252	189	441
1996	266	175	441
1997	254	223	477

These statistics were kindly supplied by the Statistics Directorate, Department of Trade and Industry. In relation to England and Wales they were derived from compulsory liquidation orders recorded by the Lord Chancellor's Department and voluntary liquidations recorded at Companies house.

Index

Tutor Support material is available....

A free lecturer's supplement containing:

♦ *Guidelines*
♦ *Model answers*
♦ *Solutions to activities*
♦ *Ideas for development of case studies*

is also available either as **hard copy** or is **downloadable from the BH website (password protected)** from Autumn 1999.

To order a **Tutor Resource Pack for Company Law**, please contact our Management Marketing Department, quoting **ISBN 0 7506 3702 1,** on:

Tel: 01865 314477
Fax: 01865 314455
E-mail: bhmarketing@repp.co.uk